worrying the line

# worrying the line

Black Women Writers,

Lineage, and Literary Tradition

CHERYL A. WALL

The University of North Carolina Press

Chapel Hill and London

Designed by Rebecca Giménez

Set in Quadraat by Tseng Information Systems, Inc.

The paper in this book meets the guidelines for permanence and durability of the Committee on Production Guidelines for Book Longevity of the Council on Library Resources.

Lucille Clifton, "Study the Masters," from *Blessing the Boats: New and Selected Poems, 1988–2000*, copyright © 2000 by Lucille Clifton; "Album," from *The Terrible Stories*, copyright © 1996 by Lucille Clifton; and "Ca'line's Prayer" and "Light," from *Good Woman: Poems and a Memoir*, *1969–1980*, copyright © 1987 by Lucille Clifton, all reprinted with the permission of BOA Editions, Ltd., <www.BOAEditions.org>; Lucille Clifton, "In Populated Air," first published in *Two-Headed Woman*, copyright © 1980 by the University of Massachusetts Press, published by the University of Massachusetts Press, then in *Good Woman: Poems and a Memoir, 1969–1980*, copyright © 1987 by Lucille Clifton, published by BOA Editions, Ltd., reprinted by permission of Curtis Brown, Ltd.; Ntozake Shange, "Bocas," from *A Daughter's Geography*, copyright © 1983, 1991 by Ntozake Shange, reprinted by permission of St. Martin's Press, LLC; Alice Walker, "Revolutionary Petunias" and "Be Nobody's Darling," from *Revolutionary Petunias and Other Poems*, copyright © 1972 and renewed 2000 by Alice Walker, reprinted by permission of Harcourt, Inc.

Library of Congress Cataloging-in-Publication Data

Wall, Cheryl A.

Worrying the line : black women writers, lineage, and literary tradition / Cheryl A. Wall.

p. cm. — (Gender and American culture)

Includes bibliographical references and index.

ISBN 0-8078-2927-7 (cloth : alk. paper) — ISBN 0-8078-5586-3 (pbk. : alk. paper)

1. American fiction—African American authors—History and criticism. 2. American fiction—Women authors—History and criticism. 3. American fiction—20th century—History and criticism. 4. Domestic fiction, American—History and criticism. 5. American prose literature—History and criticism. 6. African American women—Intellectual life. 7. African American families in literature. 8. Influence (Literary, artistic, etc.) 9. Genealogy in literature. 10. Kinship in literature. 11. Family in literature. I. Title. II. Gender & American culture.

PS374.N4W354 2005

810.9'9287'08996073—dc22      2004018014

cloth   09 08 07 06 05   5 4 3 2 1

paper   09 08 07 06 05   5 4 3 2 1

For my daughter,

*camara rose*

# contents

## illustrations

# acknowledgments

It is my great good fortune to have begun my career in the 1970s, just as the authors discussed in this book began to remake the literary landscape of our time. Writing about their work has been a privilege and a joy. It has been a challenge as well, one that many generous people have helped me meet. I thank first the American Association of University Women; a 1996–97 AAUW American Fellowship supported a crucial phase of my research.

Scholarship is a collaborative enterprise. I have tried to discharge my debt to my colleagues mainly by citing their books and articles, but some I need to thank by name. For reading all or part of the manuscript, I thank Abena Busia, Virginia Fowler, Donald Gibson, Mae Henderson, Nellie McKay, Ashraf Rushdy, Mary Helen Washington, and the anonymous readers at the University of North Carolina Press. Their insights and suggestions have made this a much better book than it would otherwise have been. For helping me understand "recollection," I thank Sibyl Moses; for all our Toni Cade Bambara conversations, I thank Linda Holmes. I thank Gail Jones of the University of Western Australia for showing me how the issues I contemplate here resonate across continents. For sharpening my thinking with their questions and comments, I thank audiences at the Black Atlantic Seminar, the Department of English, and the Institute on Research by Women, all at Rutgers University; the American Studies Association; the 1999 Conference on Religion and Modernity in Bellagio; the Modern Language Association; the Toni Morrison Society; and Howard, Northwestern, and Princeton Universities.

At Rutgers, Richard Foley and Holly Smith, who served consecutively in the Office of the Executive Dean of the Faculty of Arts and Sciences, provided material support. Barry Qualls, Dean of the Humanities, has been both mentor and friend. I thank my colleagues Wesley Brown, Alice Crozier, Marianne DeKoven, Elin Diamond, Brent Edwards, Daphne Lamothe, John McClure, Alicia Ostriker, and Larry Scanlon for hours of conversation and debate. For their good ideas and camaraderie, I thank Deborah Gray White and the Black Women Scholars caucus. I thank Leslie Mitchner for her wise counsel, Russell Clarke for his technical expertise, and Roz McInerney for her calming influence. I thank English Department chair Richard Miller for enabling me to engage the research assistance of Soyica Diggs, who took up where the indefatigable Rick Lee left off. Most of all, I thank my students, whose ideas and enthusiasm make the books I teach new to me each time I teach them.

At the University of North Carolina Press, I found editor Sian Hunter's immediate and engaged response to my manuscript gratifying; it has been my pleasure to work with her and members of the press staff including Grace Carino and Paula Wald. My deep appreciation also goes to Thadious Davis, Linda Kerber, and members of the editorial board for the Gender and American Culture series.

The editors of *Callaloo*, *Contemporary Literature*, and Rutgers University Press gave permission to reprint in revised form material that I previously published. I am grateful to the poets who granted permission to quote from their work; I owe Lucille Clifton special thanks for permitting me to reproduce her family photographs. I thank two visionary artists, Julie Dash and Betye Saar, for allowing their images to grace my book.

Finally, I count among my richest blessings the love of my sister Gatsie, who is my best friend, and of my daughter, Camara Rose Epps, who is my greatest gift. During the years that I worked on this book, Camara grew into a young woman of extraordinary beauty, intelligence, and grace. She extends the line.

*worrying the line*

## prologue

I Looked Down the Line . . .

I remember the day, if not the date, in spring 1974 when I brought *The Black Book* home to my parents. The book fascinated me, with its vividly colored photographs of quilts and baskets, the sheet music that I was eager to try out, the letters and the speeches. I could not forget the pictures of Gordon, the slave with the whip-scarred back who became a Union soldier. The three images could have been a frontispiece for John Hope Franklin's *From Slavery to Freedom*. Having been raised in a family that celebrated Negro History Month, I knew about George Washington Carver's experiments with the peanut and sweet potato; I even knew that Lewis Latimer had worked in the lab alongside Thomas Edison, making crucial but unrecognized contributions to the invention of the light bulb. But I had not known that black men held patents for the clothes dryer, fountain pen, and airship. I had heard of black cowboys, but I'm pretty sure that this was the first time I had seen the handsome faces of Nat Love and Isom Dart. The book was crammed with the stuff of history. Its documents and memorabilia, tools and toys, bills of sale and recipes intrigued me, and I felt certain that they would interest my parents as well.

My parents could not put the book down, or more precisely, they could not *stop* putting it down. They knew more sports figures and inventors than I did. The fact that blacks had once dominated horse racing the way they now dominate the NBA was not news to them. My parents laughed ruefully at the advertisement for Sunlight Soap; they recognized fashions that their relatives had worn; they each claimed to have eaten hoe cake; and, as they often did, they argued about Lena Horne's age. On every other page, they saw something that caused them to look up, either to laugh or to tell a story. To me that was the most amazing thing. My parents traded stories for hours. My father, who never spoke about his childhood, could not stop, and my mother, who was a woman from Meridian who loved her hometown and spoke of it often, embellished stories I had heard before and told new ones.

That day was the first time I learned how my father had come north. He looked up from a page in The Black Book and started telling a story about his cousin Charlie, who was already living in New York. My father was living in Charlotte, North Carolina, having left his home in rural South Carolina at the age of twelve. (This was news to me. I had never thought about how my father got to New York, I had never heard him mention Charlotte or Cousin Charlie, for that matter, and the idea that my father had run away from home had never crossed my mind. I realized how little I knew about my father and how much there might be to find out. But when I tried to interrupt with my questions, he kept on talking.) Cousin Charlie had written my father with instructions to meet him after he got off from work. He told Daddy where to go to wait, and it turned out there was a crap game, and the police came, and my father (who had been a minister all my life) talked his way out of being arrested on his first day in New York City.[1] Later I did learn who Charlie was and how he had helped my father find a job and a place to live in Harlem. Since that day, I have appreciated The Black Book for what is in it, but I treasure it for the gift of the family stories it inspired my parents to tell.

At the time I was so grateful for the stories that I did not think much about the relationship between them and the images on the page. I only knew that somehow looking at pictures, even advertisements for the most mundane products, triggered memories in my parents that had lain dormant for decades. In Worrying the Line: Black Women Writers, Lineage, and Literary Tradition, I try to understand the process that brought those memories to consciousness and elicited the stories that opened up a past I had not imagined. That process is at work in much of the poetry and prose that I study in this book.

Toni Morrison was the in-house editor of The Black Book. In 1987, she published "The Site of Memory," an essay in which she discusses her writing process, a process in which she moves from image to text. Pictures are the key to creating a fictional world. She describes how for Song of Solomon she used images to re-create the world her father inhabited as a young man and how the image of corn on the cob and the associations of the food with her childhood memories led her to create the scene in *Beloved* in which Sethe and Halle make love. Among many other things, *Beloved* is a novel about storytelling. It addresses the overarching question—who can tell the collective story of slavery, that is, its history—by representing a large cast of characters who tell their individual stories to each other. In a pattern that I explore here, those stories are frequently occasioned by an image that evokes a memory and hence a tale.

About her own family Morrison writes, "[T]hese people are my access to me; they are my entrance to my own interior life. Which is why the images that float around them—the remains, so to speak— . . . surface first, and they surface so vividly and so compellingly that I acknowledge them as my route to a reconstruction of a world, to an exploration of an interior life that was not written and to the revelation of a kind of truth." [2] Her statement is borne out in the words and the works of most of the writers in this study. Its truth is confirmed for me in my memory of a spring afternoon. Alas, my memory is incomplete and unreliable. While writing *Worrying the Line*, I have searched *The Black Book* many times in the hope that I would recognize the image that evoked my father's memory. I kick myself for not keeping a journal, for not at least sharing this conversation with my sister, who could perhaps refresh my recollection. But I have resigned myself to cherishing what I do remember. I also acknowledge yet another debt to my parents. This book began with their stories.

# one

## Introduction

> Genealogical trees do not flourish among slaves.
> —Frederick Douglass, *My Bondage and My Freedom*

> My great-grandmama told my grandmama the part she lived
> through that my grandmama didn't live through and my
> grandmama told my mama what they both lived through and
> my mama told me what they all lived through and we were
> suppose to pass it down like that from generation to genera-
> tion so we'd never forget. —Gayl Jones, *Corregidora*

> The problem of the Twentieth Century is the problem of the
> color-line. —W. E. B. Du Bois, *The Souls of Black Folk*

On the cusp of a new century, black women's writing has been preoccupied with the recuperation and representation of the past four hundred
years of black peoples' lives in the United States and throughout the African diaspora. The impulse to represent the past by reconstructing family
genealogies recurs in texts such as Lucille Clifton, *Generations*; Gayl Jones,
*Corregidora*; Audre Lorde, *Zami: A New Spelling of My Name*; Paule Marshall,
*Praisesong for the Widow* and *Daughters*; Toni Morrison, *Song of Solomon* and
*Beloved*; Gloria Naylor, *Mama Day*; and Alice Walker, *In Search of Our Mothers'
Gardens*. Genealogies are woven together out of individual and collective
memory, encoded in stories, songs, recipes, rituals, photographs, and
writing. Black women writers' rereading of the African American and
American literary traditions produces what Adrienne Rich called a quar-

ter century ago "re-vision—the act of looking back, of seeing with fresh eyes, of entering an old text from a new critical direction."[1] While not rejecting Du Bois's baleful prophecy, these writers also explore how gender and class differences within black America complicate the color line.[2]

As critics have frequently noted, black women's writing does not focus on the traumatic encounters of blacks and whites across the color line. The interracial conflicts that are at the heart of narratives by black male writers from Frederick Douglass to Ralph Ellison to Amiri Baraka do not take center stage. Contemporary black women writers focus instead on those intimate relationships in which the most painful consequences of racism are played out.[3] Racism corrodes love between black men and women, fractures families, and destroys mothers' dreams for their children. The best defense against the destructiveness of racism, these writers assert, is the formation of a cultural identity derived from an understanding of history. For example, Marshall expresses indignation at the distorted version of history she was taught as a child, which denigrated black people at every turn. She explains that her preoccupation with history derives from the need "to set the record straight, if only for myself; to get at the whole story."[4] Even if not a successful defense, historical knowledge ensures personal integrity.[5]

The cultural identity that the history of African Americans in the United States informs is necessarily multidimensional. Its complexities mitigate against the formation of a unitary identity. Moreover, a crucial tenet of black feminist theory is the multiple subjectivity of black women, a subjectivity that begins with the inextricability of the terms "black" and "woman." What Mae Henderson calls the awareness of "racial difference within gender identity" and "gender difference within racial identity" negates the possibility of a unitary self. She argues that "black women speak from a multiple and complex social, historical, and cultural positionality which, in effect, constitutes black female subjectivity."[6]

As important as the understanding that race and gender are socially constructed is, Michele Wallace cautions correctly that individual desire is never fully determined or delineated by such constructions.[7] The representation of individual desire worries the line of even the most heuristic fiction. Social positionality in these black women's texts is in large measure the consequence of history, but individuals have room to maneuver. Ironically, those who desire to "free" themselves of the bonds of history are least able to understand the forces that kept them in bondage. Upward social mobility weakens the will to know the past and consequently inhibits the formation of cultural identity; it leaves individuals vulnerable to psychic dislocation and despair.

A confluence of social and historical events enabled the creation of "the community of black women writing" that Hortense Spillers designated a "vivid new fact of national life." Chief among these were the civil rights movement and the women's movement. These movements gave rise both to a group of writers and to an audience for their work that was at first largely made up of African American women.[8] This audience, better educated and more affluent than any that had existed for black writers in the past, also represented the first generation of black people for whom cultural assimilation was a possibility. To a great extent, the urgent preoccupation with history in the writings of black women in the 1970s and 1980s registered alarm at the potential loss of a history that had never been accurately recorded. Morrison asserted in a 1980 interview, titled "Rootedness: The Ancestor as Foundation," that these social and cultural transformations gave the novel an urgent function in African American life: "We don't live in places where we can hear those stories anymore; parents don't sit around and tell their children those classical, mythological archetypal stories that we heard years ago." For Morrison, the novel became the way to preserve the stories and to communicate "new information."[9] For other writers, poetry, the essay, and the memoir served similar ends.

The title *Worrying the Line* is a blues trope, which seems apt in part because, as Wallace attests, "the black female blues singer as a paradigm of commercial, cultural, and historical potency pervades twentieth-century Afro-American literature by women."[10] For many contemporary black women writers, the blueswoman is a symbol of female creativity and autonomy whose art informs and empowers their own. In her volume *Some One Sweet Angel Chile*, Sherley Anne Williams makes Bessie Smith the subject of a cycle of poems. Individual poems reimagine moments from Smith's biography, revise lyrics of her signature tunes, and represent the relationship between the singer and her audience. That relationship is reified in the intimate relation between Bessie and the speaker, a relation captured in the lines

Bessie singing
just behind the beat

that sweet sweet
voice throwing
its light on me.[11]

Not only can this speaker "see" Bessie's face, but she can improvise on her lines. Analogously, in Walker's *The Color Purple*, the protagonist Celie hears in Shug Avery's blues, as she sees in her life, the possibilities of her own renewal. Ursa, a blues singer and protagonist of *Corregidora*, finds in the blues a vocabulary, of emotion as well as of verbal expression, that allows her to confront and work through a family history of slavery, sexual subjugation, and survival that is accessible only through memory and oral lore. Even some fictions that do not depict blueswomen portray women, like Pilate in *Song of Solomon*, who sing the blues.

Stephen Henderson in *Understanding the New Black Poetry* defines "worrying the line" as "the folk expression for the device of altering the pitch of a note in a given passage or for other kinds of ornamentation often associated with melismatic singing in the Black tradition. A verbal parallel exists in which a word or phrase is broken up to allow for affective or didactic comment." In "The Blues Roots of Contemporary Afro-American Poetry," Sherley Anne Williams observes that "repetition in blues is seldom word for word and the definition of worrying the line includes changes in stress and pitch, the addition of exclamatory phrases, changes in word order, repetition of phrases within the line itself, and the wordless blues cries that often punctuate the performance of the songs."[12] As a technique, worrying the line may be used for purposes of emphasis, clarification, or subversion. In appropriating the trope for critical purposes, I hope to show how black women's writing works similar changes on literary traditions.

Of the multiple meanings of "the line," the two that most interest me are the line as a metaphor for lineage and the line as a metaphor for the literary traditions in which these texts participate. *Worrying the Line* focuses on the points of intersection between these two meanings. What happens at those moments in literary texts when the genealogical search is frustrated by gaps in written history and knowledge? For example: What happens when, after friends of his father fill in the details of his life, Milkman Dead is left with a series of unanswered and apparently unanswerable questions about his father's father? How can Miranda Day, the titular protagonist of *Mama Day*, apprehend the history of her great-grandmother Sapphira when she has only legend and a ledger on which water damage has removed "the remainder of that line"? How does Avey Johnson, the widow for whom Paule Marshall writes a praisesong, learn to dance the "Carriacou Tramp, the shuffle designed to stay the course of history," when she does not know her nation?[13] How does "Audre," Lorde's fictive double and the protagonist of Zami: A New Spelling of My Name, bond with Dahomey goddesses?

Worrying the Line argues that it is at those moments when the quest for answers to the genealogical search is thwarted, when the only access to the past comes from what Morrison describes in "Rootedness" as "another way of knowing," that these texts are most likely to subvert the conventions of literary tradition so that the connection to the past can be forged nevertheless. Through memory, music, dreams, and ritual, it is. A frequent catalyst for the recollection of stories of lost kin is an image—sometimes a family photograph as in Generations and sometimes an intangible representation of family as in Beloved—that is inserted into the narrative. These texts require and enact "re-visions," that is, different ways of seeing as well as of writing. For the characters within the texts, the images provoke stories that close the gap between past and present. For the reader, the images and words combine to create a new kind of text that extends both meanings of the line.

Although the impulse to reconstruct family history in the texts in Worrying the Line is particularly urgent, it has antecedents in the African American literary tradition. One of the most eloquent articulations of the line as a genealogical metaphor comes at the resolution of James Baldwin's short story "Sonny's Blues," where the narrator finally comprehends his brother's art:

> And Sonny went all the way back, he really began with the spare, flat statement of the opening phrase of the song. Then he began to make it his. It was very beautiful because it wasn't hurried and it was no longer a lament. I seemed to hear with what burning he had made it his, with what burning we had yet to make it ours, how we could cease lamenting. Freedom lurked around us and I understood, at last, that he could help us to be free if we would listen, that he would never be free until we did. . . . He had made it his: that long line, of which we knew only Mama and Daddy. And he was giving it back, as everything must be given back, so that, passing through death, it can live forever.[14]

In a manner that many of the texts in this study adopt, Baldwin's metaphor of the line fuses music and memory. Music is at once the container and transmitter of memory. In the story's representation of communal performance, Sonny's solo is encouraged by an older jazzman, identified only as "Creole," an epithet that evokes New Orleans and the musical ancestors who constitute Sonny's artistic lineage. Creole on bass "initiates a dialogue with Sonny" and his piano. The pattern of call and response, characteristic of jazz and African American expressive culture more generally, shapes the climax of the story. A spiritual guide, Creole leads Sonny to the depths where he can "sound" his past. Sonny in turn earns his place on the bandstand by letting the long line of memory resound in his playing. Sonny's gesture is then reciprocated in his brother/auditor's recognition of their shared lineage. Although Baldwin does not exclude women from the family genealogy, he is most concerned with healing the fractured bonds between men, whether fathers and sons or sons and brothers. Black women writers focus more on the rifts between men and women, mothers and daughters. As Baldwin's fictions often do, "Sonny's Blues" figures the moment of reconciliation in metaphors borrowed from the Old Testament, a figuration that serves to reinscribe spirituality as a fundamental component of the blues.

Baldwin's Old Testament allusions notwithstanding, lineage for African Americans bears little resemblance to Genesis. As Frederick Douglass articulated with characteristic irony, "genealogical trees do not flourish among slaves." [15] Extending Douglass's observation in her aptly titled "Mama's Baby, Papa's Maybe," Spillers argues that the beginning of the African American symbolic order is a rupture, "a radically different kind of cultural continuation." It is a radically worried line. Under the law children born to slaves followed the condition of the mother, and enslaved men and women were denied the right to marry. As a consequence, to quote Spillers: " 'Family,' as we practice and understand it in the West' — the *vertical* transfer of a bloodline, of a patronymic, of titles and entitlements, of real estate and the prerogatives of 'cold cash,' from *fathers* to *sons* and in the supposedly free exchange of affectional ties between a male and female of *his* choice—becomes the mythically revered privilege of a free and freed community." [16] Bereft of this "privilege," African American families historically assume configurations for which the dominant order has no category. In contrast to most public discourses however, in black women's writing these configurations, like Morrison's three-woman households, do not necessarily become a cause of despair but a site of possibility.[17]

Scholars have set forth competing theories of African American literary tradition, for which the line is a fitting metaphor. Whether one perceives texts as responding to their precursors or as signifying on them, tradition constitutes a theoretical line in which texts produce and are produced by other texts. These intertextual connections may be thematic or mythic, rhetorical or figurative. For example, Robert Stepto asserts that the African American literary tradition is bound "historically and linguistically" to a "pregeneric myth," that is, the quest for freedom and literacy. As this literary line develops, slave narratives as well as texts such as Up from Slavery and The Souls of Black Folk issue a "call" to which twentieth-century texts respond.[18] Rather than their thematic or mythic commonalities, Henry Louis Gates Jr. argues that the formal and rhetorical features of black-authored texts enable us to posit a black literary tradition. In his theory, tradition may be understood as a line in which texts revise, contest, and parody elements in preceding texts. I maintain that nonliterary texts, such as blues, sermons, and recipes for conjure, insert themselves in African American tradition and worry this literary line.[19]

Writing in the 1970s and 1980s, black women confronted an Anglo-American tradition to which they could lay claim—it was the tradition they had studied in school—but one that was not eager to claim them. At the same time, they responded to a black literary tradition with which they were deeply familiar and to which they were explicitly indebted but whose classics ignored or dismissed as insignificant the experiences of black women. Their responses were complicated and various; they compelled the re-visions that are at the heart of this book. Necessarily then, even as I focus on texts by black American women writers, I do not read them in isolation; these texts exist in the web of tradition; they are enmeshed in its intersecting lines.

Despite the effort to shift the emphasis from filiation to common myths, themes, and tropes, the existence of an African American literary tradition inevitably derives from a racial identity that its authors are presumed to share. Too often that common racial classification has veiled differences of gender, class, ethnicity, and sexual preference. In order to highlight those differences, Barbara Smith called for a perspective she named "black feminist criticism" in 1977. In her most influential intervention, she identifies the "politics of sex as well as the politics of race and class [as] crucially interlocking factors in the works of black women." She asserts that "thematically, stylistically, aesthetically, and conceptually Black women writers manifest common approaches," noting in particular "their use of specifically Black female language" and "cultural experience."[20] Deborah McDowell and other subsequent critics build on Smith's theory of the simultaneity of oppressions in black women's lives and writing—notably arguing that the creative responses to these oppressions were equally significant—and they refine her critical observations.[21]

Black feminist critics are particularly skeptical of the concept of tradition, which, as Mary Helen Washington observes, has often been used "to exclude or misrepresent women." In "'The Darkened Eye Restored': Notes toward a Literary History of Black Women," Washington restores *Maud Martha*, the novel by Gwendolyn Brooks, to the line of African American tradition. Noting that the neglected texts critics in the 1970s were recuperating refused to fit into a neat historical narrative, Spillers redefines "'tradition' for black women's writing community [as] a matrix of *discontinuities* that partially articulate various periods of consciousness in the history of an African-American people." In an intervention similarly inflected by the influence of poststructuralist theory, Hazel Carby suggests that rather than being considered the site of a new literary tradition, "black feminist criticism be regarded as a problem, not a solution, as a sign that should be interrogated, a locus of contradictions."[22]

Metaphors of kinship exert an appeal nonetheless, and that appeal goes beyond the titles and themes of poetry and prose. In "In Search of Our Mothers' Gardens" Walker conflates her desire to pay tribute to the legacy of her mother with her quest for a literary and artistic tradition in which to locate her writing. The gardens of the title refer explicitly to the flowers planted by her mother but also to books written by her precursors. She defines an aesthetic that includes both. In response to Walker's essay, numerous critical projects charted a literary matrilineage initiated by Hurston and extending to Walker, Morrison, Naylor, and others.[23] Such projects are vulnerable to charges that a tradition of black women's writing that excludes texts that are not centered on rural southern experience and written in regional vernacular is too narrow.[24] Scholars also take issue with the reliance on family metaphors as critical tools.

Feminist and queer theorists argue that family metaphors are premised on heterosexuality, while postcolonialist theorists consider these metaphors part of a discourse of African American nationalism.[25] I take these warnings to heart. For my purpose however, I am more concerned with looking at family metaphors *within* texts than in adopting familial metaphors to represent relationships between texts. These texts invariably challenge the structures of patriarchy; they mainly reject heterosexism, and they usually oppose nationalist ideologies. For the most part, they invoke metaphors of family to revise the meaning of family.

In using the line as a metaphor for "literary tradition," I do not intend to imply a strictly linear progression. A worried line is not a straight line. Writing in and across diverse genres, contemporary black women writers revise and subvert the conventions of the genres they appropriate, whether the essay, the lyric, the memoir, or the novel. The writers studied here lay claim to Western tradition—from *The Odyssey* to the King James Bible, from Walt Whitman to Mark Twain, and from Flannery O'Connor to Virginia Woolf. But they rewrite canonical texts in order to give voice to stories those texts did not imagine. Their revisions are often signaled by the recurrence of metaphors and structures drawn from African American oral forms, such as folktales, sermons, spirituals, and blues, which worry the line of Anglo-American literary tradition. In the process they extend that line. Of course, these forms themselves partake of Western literary traditions, most notably the Bible but also political rhetoric, classical myths, and popular fiction. The fact is that some texts circulate so widely in a culture that people do not need to have read them to quote them. Even the illiterate may make literary allusions.

Although Morrison is widely acclaimed as an American novelist, all the authors in this book work within the American (U.S.) literary tradition; they extend its line. In interviews and essays, several of them echo Marshall's desire to get at "the whole story." In their writing, they add what has been missing from the national story—narratives of the enslaved and exploited, stories of black workers (cooks, cobblers, factory workers, and maids) and of residents of rural backwaters and inner cities. They insist that the history of the nation cannot be understood without these. Treating their writing as central rather than marginal reshapes the contours of American literary tradition. The inclusion of texts like *Generations* and *Corregidora*, for example, compels us to redefine that tradition to include different concepts of the heroic as well as the poetic, a revised and expanded sense of beauty, and a moral consciousness that extends outward and upward from communities of the oppressed.

These writers ask their readers to consider how important the lives of "invisible" black women are and have been to the definition of the American nation. In her poem "study the masters," Clifton demonstrates their exclusion from the national history and their central position in it.

> study the masters
> like my aunt timmie.
> it was her iron,
> or one like hers,
> that smoothed the sheets
> the master poet slept on.
> home or hotel, what matters is
> he lay himself down on her handiwork
> and dreamed. she dreamed too, words:
> some cherokee, some masai and some
> huge and particular as hope.
> if you had heard her
> chanting as she ironed
> you would understand form and line
> and discipline and order and
> america.[26]

This poem turns on a series of paradoxes. The identity of the master defies our expectations. She is neither the owner of slaves, nor the guardian of wealth, nor the painter of classic works of art. In another paradox, the worker's dreams are as significant as the poet's. The spatial arrangement of the poem gives them equal weight (line 8). Moreover, words are their common medium. Whether the African American woman is the speaker's aunt or someone like her, the woman's identity is tied to Native Americans and African people. At some level of consciousness, she recognizes the multicultural ideal of America, even as she acknowledges that achieving the ideal remains a dream. In another paradox, the woman's song, chanted as she works, provides lessons for poetry. Significantly, the lessons have less to do with what she sings than with how she sings it; poets need to look to masters like Aunt Timmie to understand poetic form. Readers need to study masters of life like black domestics, whose work, whose dreams, and whose songs define America. The poem is in dialogue with Walt Whitman's "I Hear America Singing" and Langston Hughes's "I, too, sing America." But its claims are more particular than Whitman's and bolder than Hughes's. Neither the nation nor its poetry can be understood, it avers, unless the experiences and expressions of poor black women are taken into account.

Even as they insist on a more inclusive mapping of U.S. literary tradition, the writers discussed in *Worrying the Line* draw on histories and traditions from outside the nation. Histories of Grenada and Brazil, for example, are used to amplify and critique narratives of life in the United States. African (as well as Native American) cosmologies inform spiritual understandings and patterns of imagery. Some of the protagonists in these narratives are travelers who retrace the routes of the Middle Passage in search of the past that will give them access to themselves. But in almost every case the traveler returns to the U.S. mainland. The narratives likewise become part of the fabric of an American literary tradition that is increasingly multivoiced.

Black women write with an acute awareness of the African American literary tradition, a tradition that is being analyzed and institutionalized in the present as never before. They interrogate and extend texts in the black tradition from the slave narratives to classic twentieth-century texts by Baldwin, Du Bois, Ellison, and Wright. For the most part, these texts ignored concerns central to the experiences and histories of black women or shifted those concerns to the margins. In their revisions, such as when Morrison revises Du Bois or Lorde revises Baldwin, black women writers pay their respect to the line of African American literary tradition while worrying that line in order to recollect stories that were never written but were passed down orally from generation to generation, as well as to imagine stories that were too painful ever to be told.

Regularly writing as critics as well as novelists and poets, contemporary black women are highly conscious of their female precursors' exclusion from the tradition. Walker's reclamation of Zora Neale Hurston is only the most celebrated example of a wide-ranging impetus. The act of recuperation enables a process of revision as Walker reimagines the plot of *Their Eyes Were Watching God* in *The Color Purple*; a process of critique as Naylor revises the themes and metaphors of Morrison's *Sula* in *Mama Day*; and a process of subversion as Paule Marshall invokes novelist Jessie Fauset alongside the "poets in the kitchen" in *Praisesong for the*

*Widow*. These writers' relation to literary tradition is complicated, as is their relation to the vernacular tradition. In this regard, "worrying the line" is congruent with Houston Baker's theory of blues as "an ancestral matrix . . . where endless antinomies are mediated and understanding and explanation find conditions of possibility."[27] The contradictions to which Baker refers are heightened in black women's writing, and they often remain unresolved. The blues and black vernacular tradition in general both inspire and silence women; they authorize articulations of self yet too often demean the individual woman who finds the courage to speak. Black women who draw on this wellspring write through and beyond the blues.

Like any blues-inflected line, African American literary tradition insinuates itself as the beat, the repetition that James Snead argues is the organizing principle of African and African American music. For singers and soloists the beat, in his words, is "the thing that there is to pick up"; it creates the safe space in which musicians improvise. Within that space singers like Bessie Smith can sing ahead or behind the beat. The "cut" is another salient characteristic of the music. At once a break with the repeated pattern and an assertion of the pattern's central importance, "the cut" accentuates the "repetitive nature of the music, by abruptly skipping it back to another beginning which we have already heard." "Cuts" or "breaks" in the line of literary tradition allow for the "discontinuities and the cross-currents" that, as Spillers asserts, are characteristic of black women's writing.[28]

"Worrying the line" is inevitably a trope for repetition with a difference. It owes much to Gates's "Signifyin(g)" because it is tropological and congruent with his assertion that "black formal repetition always repeats with a difference, a black difference that manifests itself in specific language use." It builds on aspects of Henderson's paradigm in "Speaking in Tongues" as it charts the "dialogic of differences" that locates black women's writing in relation to the multiple literary traditions that inform it and a "dialectic of identity" that defines black women's writing itself as a multivocal tradition. By rewriting or reading the dominant story, and delegitimating or displacing that story, black women inscribe their own.[29]

Black women's stories discussed in *Worrying the Line* explore the historical struggle to sustain family ties when the law did not recognize the existence of black families. Their stories celebrate the will to claim and reclaim kin in the face of officially sanctioned destruction and dispersal. The gaps in the written record are consequences of that history. So, too, is the damage done to the psyches of the slaves and their descendants. To know "my people" in these texts is a cause for celebration. But it is also a source of shame and grief, guilt and anger. For good reason, in Black English vernacular the phrase "my people" registers ambivalence. In Hurston's autobiography, *Dust Tracks on a Road*, for example, it sums up her complicated relation to the African American community. In the texts considered here, the phrase registers black people's complicated relation to one another at home. Charting the line as lineage is to confront its fractures.

In *Worrying the Line*, I identify a series of leitmotifs that signal moments in which protagonists manage to close the gap between the available written knowledge and the connections to the past they seek. The link between music and memory is perhaps the most insistent; every text under consideration explores this link in one way or another. Pilate remembers the song her father sang; passed down to her nephew, it becomes the key that opens the family's history. Audre's mother, Linda, misses the music of Grenada and can find no song to sing in New York. Music is a connection to a place and past, a connection that is at times unshakable. "It seems as if you're not singing the past, you're humming it" is how Ursa puts it. In *Corregidora* blues is the music that represents a past that is there, even if one is not conscious of it. Music is also a metaphor for the unspeakable: what cannot be said both because it is too painful or dangerous to express in words and because no one could hear or understand the words if they could be found. As Paul D reflects on the traumas of his enslavement, "Sang it sometimes but I never told a soul."

Most of the texts in *Worrying the Line* represent images, either as word pictures as in *Beloved* or photographs—figuratively in *The Color Purple* and literally in *Generations*—that conjure memory and produce the storytelling that both recollects and reimagines the past. Even when photographs become elements in the texts, they are never mere illustrations; they are an intrinsic part of the printed text. Indeed, as often as not, they call the written text into being. Meditating on the photograph of her great-grandmother, Clifton is able to summon her ancestor's story, even as she remains painfully conscious of the gaps in her knowledge and the limitations of her imagination.

Scenes of reading and writing are significant, although they are not commensurate with the meanings Stepto assigns to the pregeneric myth of literacy and freedom. In keeping with his theory, these scenes can represent acts of self-definition, as in Lorde's writing her name with her own spelling and in the poems that Avey and her husband, Jay, read and recite to each other in *Praisesong*. On the other hand, scenes of reading and writing in these texts also register the limits of written language. In the author's note that prefaces her novel *Dessa Rose*, Sherley Anne Williams states, "Afro-Americans, having survived by word of mouth and made of that process a high art—remain at the mercy of literature and writing; often these have betrayed us." [30] Through her own act of writing, Williams lays claim to a past ("I now own a summer in the 19th century," she boasts) from which official histories excluded people like her and her characters (5). Although her novel is based on two historical incidents, the characters are invented, and so is their language. The novel begins with a field holler in which a black male character makes music of his lover's name. The field holler, a musical form that precedes the blues, constituted a vocal signature for the singer and thus provided a way for an illiterate person to lay claim to his art. "Hey, hey . . . sweet mama/say hey hey . . . sweet mama/say hey now/Dessa da'ling" (11). Frequently in this novel the lyricism of the characters' speech approaches poetry; here it liquifies into song. Demonstrating her deep knowledge of the African American literary tradition, Williams names her character Kaine, a homonym for *Cane*, Jean Toomer's lyrical masterpiece. Unlike *Cane*, however, in which the proper speech of the northern-born male intellectual protagonists distinguishes and distances them from the southern-born female characters and their communities, all of Williams's black characters speak a blues vernacular of which they make, as she states, a high art.

The achievement is hard won. Some of the novel's most powerful scenes portray Dessa's struggle to escape physical imprisonment and the concurrent threat of being captured in writing by the white would-be amanuensis Adam Nehemiah. Dessa refuses to speak rather than make herself vulnerable to the betrayal of his transcription. The vexed relationship between the spoken and written word resolves itself when at the end of the novel an aged Dessa, having told her story to her children and grandchildren so often that they know it by heart, also writes it down. The politics of reading and writing thus becomes an element of the novel's theme, as it does in *Generations* and *In Search of Our Mothers' Gardens*, among a range of texts considered here. Dessa becomes an analogue for the author, whose task is to write what has not been written and to do so in the language in which her characters would have lived their experiences.

In an essay reflecting on one of the attempts to censor *The Color Purple*, Walker explains her decision to write that novel in the language of the people who lived the experience she fictionalizes: "[W]ho we have been has come down to us as the vibration of souls we can know only through the sound and structure, the idiosyncrasies of speech." Her comment suggests the extent to which the "sound" provides access to the memory. In a similar vein, Morrison expresses her goal "to restore the language that black people spoke to its original power." Explaining that the language "must not sweat," she confessed to an interviewer that "the part of the writing process that I fret is getting the sound without some mechanics that would direct the reader's attention to the sound. . . . That sound is important to me."[31] Although these writers use the singular noun, each has her own particular sound. Not unlike blues singers, they have distinctive vocal signatures.

In "From the Poets in the Kitchen," Marshall extends our sense of the vernacular and reminds readers that black Americans speak in various accents. The speech that inspires and shapes Marshall's art is that of the Barbadian immigrants who sat in "the wordshop" of her mother's kitchen. As she describes it, these women who did domestic work in Brooklyn during the 1930s "had taken the standard English taught in the primary schools of Barbados and transformed it into an idiom, an instrument that more adequately described them—changing around the syntax and imposing their own rhythm and accent so that the sentences were more pleasing to their ears." The characteristics that Marshall observes in their expression bear a strong resemblance to those that Hurston enumerated in her now famous 1934 essay "Characteristics of Negro Expression," particularly the "raft of metaphors, parables, Biblical quotations, sayings and the like."[32] Specific examples suggest cultural continuities. Both Marshall and Hurston record versions of the folk saying "God don' love ugly and He ain' stuck on pretty." But other sayings, "tumbling big" and "beautiful ugly," for example, have a more specific provenance. So do the rhythms and accents of Barbadian speech and Caribbean speech more generally. The similarities to African American vernacular speech do not transcend the differences, but they suggest a common result. In both communities ordinary people have taken the language available to them and "made of it an art form." Most of the authors discussed in

*Worrying the Line* honor and appropriate the legacy of women like Marshall's poets in the kitchen.

Whereas in some texts authors invent a language that captures the sound of speech, in other texts, the author's challenge is to write beyond the language her characters might have spoken. Scenes in which characters intuit meanings through dreams, visions, and "another way of knowing" signal this challenge. Slavery, not as the institution historians documented but as the experience generations of people lived, has been, in Morrison's phrase, "disremembered." For those who did not live through it, the situation of most of the protagonists of these narratives as well as of their readers, the experience can be approached only through imaginative acts that are figured as dreams and visions. In these states of consciousness, characters meet across generations, encountering ancestral figures who can tell them those aspects of their history that were not written down or even spoken. In most cases, it becomes evident that the communication and the understanding are partial. The character Beloved is the most remarkable example of a figure that at once incarnates the past and signifies the impossibility of recovering it completely. In one passage that represents "unspeakable thoughts unspoken," Beloved retrieves a fragmentary image of the Middle Passage, that rarely written chapter of African American history.[33] Beloved's other ways of knowing facilitate access to that past "disremembered" in the slave narratives and even in oral lore. Writing these alternative epistemologies requires the most experimental prose of the text. The Middle Passage, the rupture that cannot be healed, can at last be written.

The sacred place is another leitmotif. The encounters across generations often transpire in settings that are not sites of religious worship but sites that the characters mark as sacred. For Sethe, it is the keeping room, the parlor where she goes to "talk-think." For Denver it is the bower of boxwood trees where she retreats to make sense of her mother's stories and to find her place in them. For the larger community of black freedmen and women in *Beloved*, it is the Clearing where Baby Suggs preaches her heterodox sermon and presides over a ritual no nineteenth-century church would recognize. In *Mama Day*, Miranda and her sister Abigail hold sacred the "Other Place," the home and burial place of their ancestors. For the blues singers whose line Shug Avery extends, the stage is a ritual space in which both the spiritual and the erotic are celebrated. All of these are sacred places where reconnections are made and where lines get reconfigured.

In *Praisesong for the Widow* and *Zami*, the sacred place is Carriacou, an island in the Caribbean. In Marshall's novel, the protagonist actually visits the island and participates in its ritual of remembrance. In the process of doing so, she reclaims her selfhood and reconnects with a lineage that extends beyond her own family. In Lorde's "biomythography," the protagonist never sets foot on the island, but it serves as an imaginary homeland that helps to connect her to her matrilineage. Tellingly, the ancestry that she claims is mythic, not biological. For Marshall, the impetus is to claim a diasporan family; for Lorde, the impetus is to break free of the constraints of the Western patriarchal construct that defines family as the vertical transfer of a blood line. An expansive sense of geography is critical to both endeavors.

> i have a daughter/mozambique
> i have a son/angola
> our twins
> salvador & johannesburg/cannot speak
> the same language
> but we fight the same old men/in the new world.[34]

These lines open Ntozake Shange's poem "Bocas," the first of a cycle of poems in *A Daughter's Geography*. On one level the speaker of the poem may be understood as the collective "I" that represents the race, much like the "I" in Langston Hughes's "The Negro Speaks of Rivers." Indeed, Shange's title, which means mouths in Spanish, suggests this intertextual connection. But the poem's engendered "I" may also be the mythic African mother, whose "family" has been dispersed throughout the world. This dispersal—under the compulsion of slavery, the pressure of colonialism, and the economic dislocations of postcolonialism—has resulted in a proliferation of languages and cultures that become the daughter's birthright. Whatever the language, the poem conveys the importance of speech in black women's conception of themselves. Conversing in a fusion of tongues, as she travels across borders, the speaker maps a wide terrain, one that contrasts sharply with the constricted sense of movement in earlier writing by black women. For example, metaphors of stasis and claustrophobia in writing by Marita Bonner, Jessie Fauset, and the female poets of the Harlem Renaissance reflect the constraints on women's mobility during that era. But the situation is not limited to the early years of the twentieth century. In her famous choreopoem *for colored girls who have considered suicide when the rainbow is enuf* (1977), Shange gives this plaint to the lady in blue: "i usedta live in the world/then i moved to HARLEM/& my universe is now six blocks."[35] The forces of poverty and sexism in the inner cities of the 1970s, no less than the pull of bourgeois propriety during the 1920s, kept women close to home. In contrast, the daughter in Shange's poem moves easily across a terrain in which "there is no edge/no end to the new world."[36]

Shange's cycle of poems may be a version of the "New World Song" that Ursa Corregidora wants to sing. It recognizes enemies of freedom, figured as the "same old men," but it is confident in the collective power of oppressed people (mainly, but not solely, people of African descent) to resist them. "Tween Itaparica & Itapuã" moves among various locations in Brazil; a pictograph of directional markers helps readers locate themselves in relation to the tourist attractions of Copacabana and the *favela* (shantytown) of Rocinha. "A Black Night in Haiti, Palais National, Port-au-Prince" remembers the triumphant history of the Haitian Revolution as children in the present beg for coins; another poem evokes the Atlanta child murders. Within the sequence, poems that draw the contours of intimate experience—lovemaking and the making of poems ("poets i dreamed abt seduced sound & made history"), pregnancy, and abusive relationships—alternate with poems that map an expansive geographical terrain. They acknowledge that black bodies were treated as commodities during slavery, even as they insist that this history should not prevent twentieth-century black women from claiming their bodies for purposes of their own pleasure as well as procreation.

Like the other texts discussed in *Worrying the Line*, *A Daughter's Geography* evokes the power and the pain of historical memory, memory that can be enacted in dance and washed away in the sea. The last poem in the cycle is "New World Coros." It delights in language that is "tactile, colored & wet" (52). Words can be spoken, sung, and danced. Indeed, this chorus—always "we," never "I"—sings of the New World that must become the daughters' legacy, one in which they can define themselves in terms of their dreams as fully as in terms of their bodies. Theirs is a legacy that includes Africa, the Middle Passage, and multiple locations in the New World (Nicaragua, Costa Rica, Cuba, Puerto Rico, Charleston,

Savannah, and Haiti). The last line of the poem inscribes connection despite physical distance and linguistic difference: "You'll see us in luanda or the rest of us in chicago" (53) restates the common bond. Recognizing that bond depends on both the speaker, who speaks simultaneously for the "us" in Angola and Illinois, and the "you"—similarly positioned in two places—who is addressed, making an imaginative act. These acts of reconnection are instances of worrying the line.

The chapters that follow enact different versions of worrying the line. I look first at the ways in which recent texts revise the tradition of African American autobiography. Morrison gives it fictional form in the blues-inflected *Song of Solomon*, while Lorde in *Zami* invents a genre she names "biomythography." Both texts consider the question of family as biological inheritance and as social and cultural affiliation. Clifton revises autobiographical tradition, as well, by beginning her genealogy with an ancestor born free in Africa rather than enslaved in America. *Generations*, which extends and subverts Whitman's *Song of Myself* in its redefinition of American identity, combines words and images in unexpected ways. Images are also the catalyst for the multiple stories that constitute *Beloved*. *The Black Book*, a scrapbook of African American history, is a crucial intertext for the novel; it represents a model for reconstructing the past that is tropological, improvisational, and communal. The recollections of kin that *Beloved* compels and enables constitute new concepts of lineage and literary tradition.

The blues line informs the language of *Corregidora* and *The Color Purple*; blues aesthetics and ethics reinforce their themes. The blues themselves give the protagonists of these novels access to the structures of feeling that enable them to confront family histories of oppression and sexual subjugation. As Walker writes beyond the blues however, her novel subverts an already subversive discourse.

In a gesture that the social movements of the period make possible, Walker and Naylor respond to texts written by black women, notably Hurston and Morrison, as well as those written by white women and black and white men. In my reading of *Sula* as an intertext for *Mama Day*, I emphasize the discontinuities between them. Marshall explores the theme of lineage in the context of a novel that I read as a song in praise of African American literature. In addition to poetic texts by Robert Hayden, Langston Hughes, and James Weldon Johnson, the novel repeats and subverts themes and metaphors found in fiction by Jessie Fauset. The last chapter of *Worrying the Line*, "In Search of Our Mothers' Gardens and Our Fathers' (Real) Estates," analyzes Walker's essays as they contest and revise the construction and authority of literary tradition. The epilogue, "Moving On Down the Line," uses the film *Daughters of the Dust* to recall and restate this study's conclusions.

The desire to reclaim and reconnect characterizes the project of *Worrying the Line*, but it has multiple modalities. As they survey the remains of history, contemporary black women writers choose differently what to salvage and discard. Even as they reclaim kinship ties, they have distinct investments in the concept of family. Some seek to reform the concept they have inherited, while others extend the definition of family beyond the biological and thus the patriarchal. Just as they redefine lineage, they redefine literary tradition. Here, too, they choose differently what to recuperate and reject. Genre makes a difference, as do generation and location. Black women writers may constitute a chorus, but in each of the following chapters, individual voices offer singular variations on this New World Song.

## two

Reconstructing
Lineage, Revising
Tradition in *Song
of Solomon* and
*Zami*

> What tangled skeins are the genealogies of slavery!
> —Harriet Jacobs, *Incidents in the Life of a Slave Girl*

> Those must have been some times, back then. Some
> bad times. It's a wonder anybody knows who anybody is.
> —Toni Morrison, *Song of Solomon*

> But of course it is out of Chaos that new worlds are born.
> —Audre Lorde, "Eye to Eye"

Toni Morrison's *Song of Solomon* and Audre Lorde's *Zami* are both quest stories in which the quester is trying to find his or her way home. Both seem modeled to some extent on autobiography, which, as Morrison has acknowledged, is "a very large part of [her] literary heritage." "In this country," she writes, "the print origins of black literature (as distinguished from the oral origins) were slave narratives."[1] In the case of *Song of Solomon*, Morrison seeks to recuperate the oral origins of the literature as well—the history that was never recorded. Lorde, while repeating formal tropes and themes characteristic of slave autobiographies, writes her own life as myth. Both works represent the assault on African American families by slavery and colonization, and both reject the ideal of the Western nuclear family. Morrison's novel decenters that ideal by allying the representation of the "Dead" family with capitalist exploitation, racism, and sexism and by proposing a utopian alternative in Pilate's home space. Lorde's text makes an analogous move but locates the utopian alternative in traditions of Yoruban cosmology and contemporary lesbian politics. Both narratives acknowledge the struggles of Africans in the New World to sustain familial connection, even as they propose new conceptions of the family. Worrying the line in these fictions becomes a trope for reconfiguring lineage and for new ways of writing that configuration. The narratives affirm Stuart Hall's observation: "Identity is never finished. It moves into the future by way of a constructive detour of the past." [2] My purpose is less to compare the two texts than to map the detours they take.

So obtuse is Morrison's protagonist, Milkman Dead, that he is on the quest before he realizes it, and when he does become conscious of his journey, he does not know the prize. Looking for gold in Danville, Pennsylvania, he finds the treasure of listening to stories of "his people." Journeying south, he is able to reconstruct his genealogy out of stories, or "lies," as Zora Hurston would deem them, as well as personal testimonies, songs, jokes, and children's rhymes. Only the intervention and piloting of his aunt, Pilate, allow him to continue his quest. Blues singer, conjure woman, bootlegger, and mythical outsider, Pilate has spent a lifetime carrying her father's bones, safeguarding his legacy, and passing on as much of it as she can. But she is missing crucial pieces of the puzzle that Milkman is able to discover. She has nevertheless intuited the lesson he ultimately learns. Without leaving the ground, Pilate can fly.

Morrison's novel is layered with literary allusions to *The Odyssey*, the Old Testament, W. E. B. Du Bois's *The Souls of Black Folk*, Ralph Ellison's *Invisible Man*, William Faulkner's *Go Down, Moses*, Gabriel Marquez's *One Hundred Years of Solitude*, and African American folklore. Even as she recreates the traditionally male quest narrative, Morrison revises the Western classics to give voice to women. Rather than a beautiful enchantress, her Circe is an aged female slave whose supernatural presence provides one of the novel's most striking deviations from realist form. The deviation is necessary to give the protagonist access to his past. In this encounter of Milkman and Circe, the novel creates what Faulkner designates in *Absalom, Absalom* "a might-have-been which is more true than truth."

Faulknerian themes and topoi echo throughout the text: the past that is not past; the mixed bloodlines of Africa, Europe, and (native) America; the hunt as initiation ritual. [3] But in my reading Morrison reaches back past Faulkner to Du Bois and in particular to *The Souls of Black Folk*, the book that by almost every critical reckoning is the preeminent statement of modernist black consciousness. In Arnold Rampersad's assessment, "If all of a nation's literature may stem from one book, as Hemingway implied about *The Adventures of Huckleberry Finn*, then it can as accurately be said that all of Afro-American literature of a creative nature has proceeded from Du Bois' . . . *The Souls of Black Folk*."[4]

A fusion of history, sociology, personal memoir, and collective memory, *Souls* is unique in form and unsurpassed in influence among African American texts. By worrying the line between genres, as it were, *Souls* splinters the opposition between history and memory. As Pierre Nora conceives the terms, history is static, whereas memory is dynamic. "At the heart of history is a critical discourse that is antithetical to spontaneous memory. History is perpetually suspicious of memory, and its true mission is to suppress and destroy it."[5] *Souls* defies this expectation, for Du Bois writes as both historian and poet/preserver of the cultural memory encoded in the spirituals.

In Houston Baker's resonant appraisal, *The Souls of Black Folk* is "a singing book."[6] So, too, is *Song of Solomon*, as its title announces. The first voice we hear is Pilate's powerful contralto singing:

O Sugarman done fly away
Sugarman done gone
Sugarman cut across the sky
Sugarman gone home.[7]

The last voice is Milkman's as he sings verses of the same song to the dying Pilate in the final scene. He has deciphered the history the song encoded. *The Souls of Black Folk* and *Song of Solomon* express a shared belief that the unwritten history of black Americans was encoded in their songs. The protagonist of *Souls* is also a traveler, unsure of his relation to folk who live behind the veil but certain nonetheless that he is connected to them. One of the first texts in the African American tradition to reverse the journey from North to South charted in the slave narratives, *Souls*, like *Song of Solomon*, represents a "cultural immersion ritual."[8] In several of its particulars, *Song of Solomon* echoes its precursor text.

Consider, for example, a comparison of Du Bois's chapter "Of the Black Belt" and Milkman's encounter with Circe and the people of Danville. Dispossession is the primary theme of Du Bois's chapter. Blacks have been robbed of their labor, as Native Americans have been robbed of their land. The narrator directs readers's eyes to the "ancient land of the Cherokees, —that brave Indian nation which strove so long for its fatherland, until Fate and the United States Government drove them beyond the Mississippi."[9] Du Bois's map of the Black Belt uncovers those names lying under the recorded names; it is the kind of map that Milkman ponders on his triumphant return to the South.

Geographically located in Georgia, the state that was home to more than a million African Americans at the turn of the century, Du Bois's "Black Belt" is the center of the black population in the United States. Its rich black soil made it the heart of the antebellum Cotton Kingdom; consequently, the "Black Belt" is for Du Bois "historic ground." Du Bois's idea of "historic ground" is very close to Nora's "site of memory," which exists "where memory crystallizes and secretes itself at a particular historical moment, a turning point where consciousness of a break with the past is bound up with the sense that memory has been torn—but torn in such a way as to pose the problem of the embodiment of memory in certain sites where a sense of historical continuity persists."[10]

The particular historical moment in *Souls* is post-Reconstruction, which, as "Of the Black Belt" illustrates, has proved to be a less decisive break with the past for African Americans than it has been for whites. Blacks' labor was exploited during slavery; their labor then fueled the Confederate war effort when the Black Belt became the granary of the southern troops; and it continues to be exploited during the post-Reconstruction period. Continuing, too, is the struggle of resistance, sometimes in alliance with Native Americans but more often solitary and unavailing. The present is eerily continuous with the past. The vastness of the landscape, the ruins of the corrupt old social order, the harshness of the corrupt new social order, and the isolation of the black population, which outnumbers whites by a factor of five, render this history in the starkest of terms. These terms are at once documentary and poetic, political and prophetic. Du Bois's phrase "the Egypt of the Confederacy" has the force of biblical allusion, connoting both the bondage of the slaves and the peonage to which the putative freedmen and women have been delivered. The chapter as a whole is, to quote Eric Sundquist, "the spiritual center" of the book.[11]

Leaving Atlanta, Du Bois's narrator invites his reader to join him in the Jim Crow car, a gesture that reinscribes the narrator's racial difference vis-à-vis his white audience that he announced in the book's preface, or "Forethought." There he identified himself as "bone of the bone and flesh of the flesh of them that live within the Veil" (2). But the more telling difference in the later chapter is the experiential gap between the narrator and his racial kin. Detraining in Albany, "the centre of the life of ten thousand souls" (95), the narrator observes the transformation the town undergoes on Saturday as black peasants "[take] full possession of the town." The narrator does not comment further on this incipient nationalism. Instead, cosmopolitan to his fingertips, he draws flattering comparisons between the black peasants of Albany and their counterparts of the Rhine-Pflaz, Naples, and Cracow. Stymied by the July heat, the narrator takes several days to "muster courage enough" to explore the "unknown world" that lies beyond the city limits (95).

This unknown world is marked first by the desolated landscape, its once fertile soil now exhausted. Little of beauty remains, "only a sort of crude abandon that suggests power, — a naked grandeur as it were" (99). Throughout the chapter Du Bois extends the trope of the journey so that the reader comprehends the scene through the eyes of the uninitiated narrator/observer. Soon the power of the natural landscape is associated with the ruins that symbolize the power of the fallen slave system. "The whole land seems forlorn and forsaken. Here are the remnants of the vast plantations of the Sheldons, the Pellots, and the Rensons; but the souls of them are passed" (96). In their stead are the souls of black folk.

The transformation from white to black (one day the narrator travels ten miles without seeing a white face) produces odd juxtapositions. Mansions seemingly haunted by the past appear suddenly on the horizon, standing silent amid ashes and tangled weeds. Each scene seems to offer a rebuke to the sins of the past. For example, "the Big House stands in half-ruin, its great front door staring blankly at the street, and the back part grotesquely restored for its black tenant" (97). Another crumbling mansion is "filled now with the grandchildren of the slaves who once waited on its tables" (102). As on those Saturdays when blacks take possession of Albany, these changes are not revolutionary; economic and political power remain in white hands.

Although the narrator expresses sympathy for the heirs of the departed slaveholders ("sad and bitter tales lie hidden back of those white doors" [107]), the text gives voice to the heirs of the slaves, who are left to eke out a living from exhausted land. The narrator stops to interview impoverished sharecroppers, blacksmiths and storekeepers, and a handful of black freeholders. One of the freeholders, a tall, bronzed man who "walks too straight to be a tenant," remarks that cotton is down to four cents. An "old ragged black man, honest, simple, and improvident" is the informant for the history of the Waters-Loring plantation, gutted by the greed of its absentee northern owner. Another "ragged, brown, and grave-faced man" witnesses slavery: "This land was a little hell. . . . I've seen niggers drop dead in the furrow but they were kicked aside and the plough never stopped" (102). On what was once the Bolton estate, worked for years by black convict labor, the narrator meets laborers who are in fact no more free than their slave ancestors. In response to his question of what rent they paid, one turns to his neighbor: "I don't know, what is it, Sam?" Sam's answer captures the pervasive despair: "All we make" (105).

Amid this hopelessness black property owners offer glimmers of promise. The narrator expresses pride in the "gaunt dull-black Jackson," proud owner of a hundred acres, who is also a homespun philosopher: "I says, Look up! If you don't look up you can't get up" (104). Yet even the few success stories become part of the argument Du Bois elaborates against the position of Booker T. Washington throughout the book. In general, the extremity of the suffering "Of the Black Belt" describes evidences the inefficacy of Washington's program. But through the anecdotes of the black freeholders, Du Bois also rejects as insufficient the materialism on which Washington predicated his views. Although Du Bois celebrates examples of economic success among black Americans whenever he finds them, economic indexes are not the ultimate criteria of progress. The figure who is accorded the greatest praise is the preacher Pa Willis, now dead but warmly remembered as "the tall and powerful black Moses" who led his people well (109).

Du Bois's narrator is quick to cite statistics: 150 barons had ruled 6,000 Negroes; 90,000 acres of tilled land in Dougherty County were valued at $3 million. He is also adept at charting geography and quoting historical references. But he is open to other ways of knowing. One moment in the chapter stands out in this regard. In contrast to the often barren landscape, the narrator comes upon a verdant scene in which "spreading trees spring from a prodigal luxuriance of undergrowth; great dark green shadows fade into the black background, until all is one mass of tangled semi-tropical foliage, marvellous in its weird savage splendor" (100). In this setting, the narrator "could imagine the place under some weird spell, and was half-minded to search out the princess" (99). But rather than a fairy tale, the narrator reenvisions history.

The text marks the shift to a different temporal register when the narrator crosses a black silent stream: here he "seemed to see again that fierce tragedy of seventy years ago" when Osceola, an Indian-Negro chieftain, led his warriors into Dougherty County until the whites forced their retreat (101). The narrator's vision is short lived; he recounts it in a paragraph. Moreover, while it is emblematic of the process by which he gains access to the memory of his people, he is mainly concerned in this section with the facts of their social and economic condition.

At the end of the chapter, the narrator seems considerably less estranged from the folk. In Gillonsville, a hamlet that time has passed by, he sits with a homeowner and a storekeeper/preacher, as well as a hapless man who comes by to solicit the preacher's aid, a silent old woman who sits and sews, and the preacher's wife. All who speak tell stories of exploitation and dispossession. Intelligence and industry count for nothing; the talented and the ambitious are cheated as easily as the ignorant. Although the narrator's voice is differentiated by his language and education, for the first time he becomes part of a domestic scene he describes. In the moment he conveys his indignation at the wrong done his fellows, he seems to become aware of the ineffectualness of his hard-won academic knowledge in their world. He explains to the hapless man that the sheriff had no right to take his furniture because "furniture is exempt from seizure by law." But the chapter gives the "ragged misfortune" the last word: "Well, he took it just the same" (110). The world of the Black Belt is one in which neither reason nor law signifies.

Song of Solomon revises and extends The Souls of Black Folk in signal ways. To highlight the links between the chapter "Of the Black Belt" and the chapter that contains Milkman's encounter with Circe, I emphasize the following: the tropological revision of the Black Belt, the revision of an assertion of racial kinship ("Bone of the bone, flesh of the flesh") to the exploration of family history, and the extension of the biblical allusions that inform both texts.[12]

The chapter that relates Milkman's encounter with Circe introduces the second section of the novel. It begins with an allusion to a fairy tale, Hansel and Gretel, that, unlike the similar reference in Souls, predicts the aura of enchantment that will surround the chapter's signal encounter. But, as is true of the novel in general, indirection is the mode of telling.

So before we observe Milkman's meeting with Circe, through whom he will hear vestiges of his ancestor's voice, we watch his preparation for that engagement. While still in Michigan with Guitar, he prepares for a mission he does not pursue. Then, in Danville, in his conversations with Reverend Cooper and other friends of his grandfather's, Milkman begins to understand what he is searching for.

By the time he enters the "dark, ruined, evil" house, now overseen by Circe, Milkman has earned the epithet Du Bois chooses for his persona; he is a "weary traveler." He has flown from Michigan to Pittsburgh, taken the bus from Pittsburgh to Danville, and waited four days to get a ride to the abandoned Butler place only to find that it is inaccessible by car. Milkman emerges from a swamp, "a green maw . . . a greenish-black tunnel, the end of which was nowhere in sight" (238). In the scene in which Milkman encounters Circe, Morrison revisits the bare ruins of Du Bois's text. In her novel these ruins are reinhabited by a singular black soul.

Circe, a figure with a "face so old it could not be alive," presides over the ruins of the Butler mansion; she has been servant to the nouveau riche whites who murdered Milkman's grandfather, the first Macon Dead, in order to steal his land (240). Like the masters of the Black Belt, the Butlers have died or scattered, and the house is left to their onetime retainer. Circe is determined to see the house they lied, stole, and killed for fall into itself. Resolved never "to clean it again," she allows the Weimaraners she tends to foul it to their heart's content (247). Unlike Du Bois's narrator, Milkman gives in to the landscape's weird spell. He meets Circe in a dream, in one of the most conspicuous deviations from the "real" in the novel. As much an agent of transformation as her mythical namesake, she provides the information he cannot obtain otherwise.[13] "Sing" is not a command; it is his grandmother's name.

*Song of Solomon* locates the plantation over which Circe presides outside Danville, Pennsylvania, far from the historical Black Belt. But the novel's geographical shifts extend rather than undermine its relation to *Souls*. At one point Guitar, who tells Milkman that his "whole life is geography," probes the meaning of North and South. The terms depend on each other, but they do not define a difference. As Guitar explains, "But does that mean North is different from South? No way! South is just south of North" (114). All Morrison's novels redraw the symbolic geography of African American literature and American culture. Just as *The Bluest Eye* and *Sula* "nationalize" African American culture by showing how it is carried by blacks from the South—"They come from Mobile. Aiken. From Newport News. From Marietta. From Meridian"—to midwestern towns, *Song of Solomon* represents the nationalization of southern white racism in the post-Reconstruction era.[14]

Yet if Morrison's novel nationalizes Du Bois's major geographical trope, it particularizes the assertion of kinship. The history that engages Milkman's imagination is the history of his family. "It was a good feeling to come into a strange town and find a stranger who knew your people. All his life he'd heard the tremor in the word: 'I live here, but my *people . . .*' or: 'She acts like she ain't got no *people*,' or: 'Do any of your *people* live there?' But he hadn't known what it meant: links" (229). Macon Dead resembles the freeholders that Du Bois's narrator admires, but Milkman's fascination with his grandfather's heroic exploits is fueled by the familial connection. He revels in the stories Reverend Cooper and his buddies tell, and he responds in kind with stories about his father's efforts to buy "the Erie Lackawanna" (236; emphasis in original). One might be tempted to attribute the shift to the narcissism of Morrison's protagonist, but that would overlook the chief benefit the shift produces. Family history makes female characters more central to *Song of Solomon* than they are to the narrative of Du Bois's solitary quester.

Milkman is, of course, the indulged son and heir of a father who is very much a Washingtonian figure and a man whose capacity for love died in the moment he witnessed his father's murder. Macon's materialism and greed are the object of communal censure: "a nigger in business is a terrible thing to see" is the judgment of Guitar's grandmother (22). But his cruel and exploitative spirit have equally dire consequences at home. He encourages Milkman to exploit his sisters and to treat them as his servants. In an emblematic act, Milkman as a young boy urinates on Lena. As an adult his attitude toward his sisters—and his mother—is disinterested contempt. Only when he discovers that Corinthians is involved with Porter, a member of the secret society the Seven Days, does he show any curiosity about her life. He intervenes to break up her romance, thereby prompting Lena to voice the most explicitly feminist sentiments of the novel:

> "You don't know a single thing about either of us . . . but now you know what's best for the very woman who wiped the dribble from your chin because you were too young to know how to spit. Our girlhood

was spent like a found nickel on you. . . . Where do you get the *right* to decide our lives?"

"Lena, cool it. I don't want to hear it."

"I'll tell you where. From that hog's gut that hangs down between your legs. Well, let me tell you something, baby brother: you will need more than that." (215)

His sister's words help to propel Milkman on his journey, but not because he recognizes their rightness. Like the stories his parents tell him about their past lives, Milkman finds Lena's indictment tiresome. It makes him want to leave. That he can embark on his journey, that he has a quest to undertake, is yet another marker of male privilege. Lena and Corinthians cannot leave the house.[15]

As the novel proceeds, Milkman sheds his sexism just as he divests himself of his material possessions before meeting Circe. The giving relationship he shares with Sweet is one example; his willingness to "surrender" his life in response to Pilate's death is another. Milkman is capable of this ultimate act because he has learned well the "other ways of knowing" that Pilate has taught. His lessons begin with his first conscious encounter with the aunt his father has forbade him to see. He espies her first "posed like some ancient mother goddess." The gifts she offers — an apple and lessons in how to boil an egg and how to make wine — carry symbolic significance. Pilate teaches Milkman how to "be" in the world, from the proper way to greet (and treat) other people to the capacity to gain understanding as well as pleasure from sensual experience. Milkman's acquisition of this knowledge confirms that the other ways of knowing the novel privileges are not women's ways of knowing. They constitute, rather, the knowledge that enables one to live wholly in this world and perhaps in the next world as well.

In a telling coincidence, one of the epigraphs to "Of the Black Belt" in *Souls* comes from the biblical "Song of Solomon":

I am black but comely, O ye daughter of Jerusalem,
As the tents of Kedar, as the curtains of Solomon.
Look not upon me, because I am black
Because the sun hath looked upon me:
My mother's children were angry with me;
They made me the keeper of vineyards;
But mine own vineyard have I not kept. (1:5–6)

Dispossession is the key to the passage, as it is to both *The Souls of Black Folk* and *Song of Solomon*. But Morrison's allusions to the biblical text that inspires her title also serve to deepen the representation of female character. These allusions are richly metaphorical: the sensory images of the biblical text infuse the novel. From the wine, which is a source of ecstasy and wisdom in both the ancient and modern texts, to the ginger root and other spices that permeate them, to the vivid evocations of the pastoral, the novel appropriates the song's imagery. Thematically, however, the representation of human relations is key. "What is extraordinary in the *Song*," Alicia Ostriker observes, "is precisely the absence of structural and systemic hierarchy, sovereignty, authority, control, superiority, submission, in the relation of the lovers and in their relation to nature."[16] Pilate is the exemplar of this egalitarian vision in Morrison's novel. She can adhere to it in part because she lives outside societal structures.

Never married, unaffiliated with any social institution, alienated from her only brother, Pilate has created a home for herself, her daughter, and her granddaughter that moves to its own rhythms. They live in a house without electricity, gas, or running water, "as though progress was a word that meant walking a little farther on down the road" (27). Pilate, a woman who makes wine for a living, is as unimpressed with status as with technology. Although she is not naive about social realities (she knows, for example, how to play the "stage Negro" when doing so is necessary to keep Milkman out of jail), she accepts people with equanimity. Macon's money and position, which mean everything to him, mean nothing to her. Music and memory pervade her home.

In the one instance in the novel when Macon visits Pilate's home, he does not enter it. He stands outside, hidden in the darkness, listening to the women sing a song that Pilate leads. She sang "a phrase that the other two were taking up and building on" (29). The counterpoint of Pilate's contralto and Reba's soprano, which will resound for the reader later in the text on the occasion of Hagar's funeral, draws Macon like a magnet. As he "felt himself softening under the weight of memory and music, the song died down" (30). Its effect lingers, however, and Macon cannot bring himself to leave.

Biblical references are especially resonant in the depiction of Hagar. Although named for the bondswoman who becomes Abraham's concubine and the mother of Ishmael in the Old Testament, the Hagar of Morrison's novel is thematically more akin to the "black but comely" woman who has no vineyard of her own to tend. The woman in the biblical "Song of Solomon" searches for her lover through the night: "I will rise now, and go about the city in the streets, and in the broad ways I will seek him whom my soul loveth: I sought him, but I found him not" (3:2). Unlike the biblical lovers, Hagar and Milkman never "find" each other. He takes her love for granted, as long as he experiences gratification in their lovemaking. Then after more than a dozen years, with a coldness that is brutally impersonal, he writes her a note of rejection. Thereafter Hagar roams the streets in search of her lover, but only to threaten his life. Eventually Milkman atones for his callousness, but his repentance comes after Hagar's death.[17]

Pilate has instructed Milkman and Hagar how to treat each other on the occasion of their first meeting, when she introduces Milkman to Hagar as her brother. Reba corrects Pilate and explains that Milkman and Hagar are cousins. Pilate responds as if to a distinction without a difference: "Don't you have to act the same way to both?" (44). Francis Landy asserts that in *Song of Songs* the epithets "my sister, my spouse" suggest "a constant statement of paradoxical relationship which gives assurance, amid the prevailing turbulence, that the object of desire is an intimate part of ourselves."[18] This could serve as a gloss on Pilate's seeming misstatement that Milkman is Hagar's brother or on her later consoling words to Hagar that Milkman must love Hagar's hair because it is the same as his. Theirs is a paradoxical relationship, but one in which Milkman and Hagar fail to recognize that what they desire is an intimate and missing part of themselves. Morrison's novel is consequently a bleak rewriting of the biblical "Song." The biblical book expresses the promise that in the novel goes unfulfilled: "O that thou wert as my brother, that sucked the breasts of my mother! When I should find thee without, I would kiss thee; yea, I should not be despised" (8:1).

"The Sorrow Songs" is the penultimate chapter of *The Souls of Black Folk*. Its importance derives from its rightful estimation of the centrality of spirituals to American culture. Not simply the "sole American music, but . . . the most beautiful expression of human experience born this side of the seas," the spirituals were the slaves' message to the world. Extending the insight of Douglass in his 1845 *Narrative*, Du Bois defines the "heart-touching witness of these songs" as an indictment of the in-humanity of slavery (205, 207).[19] Du Bois's concern is with the words of the spirituals and the function of the songs; he acknowledges his lack of musical knowledge forthwith. He says simply that "the music is far more ancient than the words." To illustrate the point, he does not turn to *The Story of the Jubilee Singers* or to *Hampton and Its Students*, the sources that Eric Sundquist identifies for the book's musical epigraphs, but to his memory.[20] He transcribes the lyrics and the music of an African song passed down in his family from generation to generation. "We sing it to our children, knowing as little as our fathers what its words may mean, but knowing well the meaning of the music" (207). Scholars have been unable to translate the words.[21]

*Song of Solomon*, of course, ends differently. Milkman is able to decode most of the lyrics of the song whose music he has been hearing since the day he was born. He is able to identify the African ancestor and to recognize himself as a son of Solomon. Yet Milkman's quest has succeeded in part at the cost of his sister/cousin Hagar's life. The dark but comely daughter of Solomon, whose beauty Milkman fails to recognize, is sacrificed. Little wonder, then, that despite the honor the novel accords the family's history of resistance and struggle and despite Milkman's belated recognition of his complicity in Hagar's death, this family is always already "Dead."

However, the "spaces" that Morrison has purposely left in the text "can conceivably be filled in with other significances"; the reader can construct a different story.[22] Pilate becomes a model for love of family and community: "I wish I'd a knowed more people. I would have loved 'em all. If I'd a knowed more people, I would a loved more" (336). After years of guarding, unwittingly, her father's bones, she can bury them properly. Having learned the family history, she can lay down the last burden she has carried—the brass box earring in which she has preserved the paper on which her father wrote her name. In the full awareness of self, she can lay claim to her name without his authority or the authority of the Bible, from which he has picked it out. Finally, unlike the male progenitor Jake, son of Solomon, who flew back to Africa leaving his wife and twenty children to mourn his absence, Pilate learns to fly without leaving the ground.

Writing in the 1970s, at what some consider the end of the Second Reconstruction, Morrison is, of course, cognizant of economic and social transformations that were beyond even Du Bois's prophetic powers. Her characters respond to the effects of the Great Migration, industrialization, and two world wars. "There was quite a bit of pie oozing around the edges of the crust in 1945. Filling that could be his. Everything had improved for Macon Dead during the war. Except Ruth" (63). Despite the postwar boom and his own relative privilege, Macon knows that he can hope to catch only the excess of prosperity, what whites do not want or cannot use. For the characters in Song of Solomon the color line is the problem of the twentieth century. Yet, as this passage also suggests, class and gender bias within the black community make that problem much more difficult to overcome.[23] Macon Dead II cannot sustain a relationship with his wife, whom he abuses, let alone with his tenants, whom he exploits; Milkman is a threat rather than a brother to Hagar, who in turn tries to kill him.

Morrison writes against the elitism evident in Du Bois's misplaced sympathy for fallen southern aristocrats; she cannot share his faith that the "Talented Tenth" would lead their kinsmen and women to freedom. In Song of Solomon, his neighbors take pride in Dr. Foster's professional accomplishments, but his success does not predict theirs; his addiction and alienation cast doubt on the satisfaction it has brought him. Neither does Morrison harbor Du Bois's confidence in the liberating power of the liberal arts. Du Bois acknowledges the limits of education in the first chapter of Souls; the educated black men in the book — from the historical Alexander Crummell, to the fictional John, to the protagonist himself — suffer as a consequence of their learning. However, none would accept the judgment on themselves that Morrison's narrator makes of Corinthians that her education had rendered her "unfit for eighty percent of the useful work of the world" (189). The novel itself challenges that judgment in its allusions to Western classics that only an erudite author could make and that only college-educated readers are likely to discern. But the novel's multivocality requires fluency in other cultural codes.

As critics have observed, the novel is created in the "center of [the] irony that oral traditions are preserved only because they have been written down."[24] In "Rootedness: The Ancestor as Foundation," Morrison identifies one of the characteristics of black art as "the ability to be both print and oral literature, to combine those two aspects so that the stories can be read in silence of course, but one should be able to hear them as well." Rather than the silent bars of music in Du Bois's text that only the musically fluent and culturally knowledgeable can hear, Morrison wants the language on the page to resound in every reader's consciousness. "It should try deliberately to make you stand up and make you feel something profoundly in the same way that a Black preacher requires his congregation to speak."[25]

The language of *Song of Solomon* presents the sharpest contrast to *The Souls of Black Folk*. Rather than the monosyllables of the sharecroppers in the Black Belt, one hears the eloquent, hyberbolic, impassioned, and bawdy voices of the men in Tommy's Barbershop. In an early scene Railroad Tommy schools Milkman and Guitar on what things and experiences they are *not* going to have. Beginning with the pleasurable memories of his days as a trainman, he builds up to a litany (no private coach, no governor's mansion, no breakfast tray with a red rose, warm croissants, and a cup of hot chocolate) that in its elaborateness underscores how constricted future opportunities were for black boys in the 1940s. In a later scene, the limitations of the present are dramatized as the group listens to a radio announcement of Emmett Till's murder:

"It'll be in the morning paper."

"Maybe it will, and maybe it won't," said Porter.

"It was on the radio! Got to be in the paper!" said Freddie.

"They don't put that kind of news in no white paper. Not unless he raped somebody."

"What you bet? What you bet it'll be in there?" said Freddie.

"Bet anything you can lose," Porter answered.

"You on for five."

"Wait a minute," Porter shouted. "Say where."

"What you mean, 'where'? I got five says it'll be in the morning paper."

"On the sports page?" asked Hospital Tommy.

"Or the funny papers?" said Nero Brown.

"No, man. Front page. I bet five dollars on front page."

"What the fuck is the difference?" shouted Guitar. "A kid is stomped and you standin round fussin about whether some cracker put it in the paper. He stomped, ain't he? Dead, ain't he? Cause he whistled at some Scarlett O'Hara cunt." (80–81)[26]

To Milkman these are "criss-crossed conversations" because he lacks the historical knowledge and political awareness to understand them (80). The men's rapid-fire responses to the horror of Till's death are in direct proportion to the anger and despair it evokes. They are keenly aware that the dominant society places no value on a black man's life—or death. Till's murder may not even constitute "news" outside the African American community. As the anger and despair intensify, some of the characters leaven it with a humor so mordant that it is chilling. They banter about whether if the murder is reported in the newspapers it would be in the sports section (historically, lynchings were often communal events that took on a festive air; white men on occasion killed black men for sport) or in the funny pages. To an extent, their willingness to place bets on the outcome resists the dominant society's devaluation of black life, but they devalue it themselves in the process. Notably in this scene, Guitar remains too angry to laugh. His rage makes him a prime recruit for the Seven Days, and his ability to reduce women to sexual commodities is further evidence of his qualifications for the group.[27]

Although there is no space comparable to the barbershop for female characters, women in *Song of Solomon* tell some of the most memorable stories. Typically they relate them in private conversations. Often they recount family histories. For example, Ruth as well as Macon gives versions of their marital history. Their son prefers to listen to neither. But Ruth refuses to be intimidated by Milkman's emotional indifference or his anger. In the face of his accurate charge that she has nursed him beyond the appropriate age, she responds: "And I also prayed for you. Every single night and every single day. On my knees. Now you tell me. What harm did I do you on my knees?" (126). A story that Pilate tells about a time before her brother was destroyed by his materialism and greed may be read as a gloss on the novel's representation of a heterogeneous black community:

Hadn't been for your daddy, I wouldn't be here today. I would have died in the womb. And died again in the woods. Those woods and the dark would have surely killed me. . . . We were lost then. And talking about dark! You think dark is just one color, but it ain't. There're five or six kinds of black. Some silky, some woolly. Some just empty. Some like fingers. And it don't stay still. It moves and changes from one kind of black to another. Saying something is pitch black is like saying something is green. What kind of green? Green like my bottles? Green like a grasshopper? Green like a cucumber, lettuce, or green like the sky is just before it breaks loose to storm? Well, night black is the same way. May as well be a rainbow. (40–41)

This poetic image of blackness revises several generations of racial representation. A blues singer as well as a storyteller, Pilate limns a poetic image of blackness that is filled with metaphor and simile. Blackness to Pilate is not a veil but a rainbow. She speaks as one for whom the veil no longer exists, as one determined to construct her own reality and to live fully within it. Pilate is the novel's consummate artist.

AUDRE LORDE'S POEM "125th Street and Abomey" enacts the spiritual reconnection of the severed African American daughter to the African mother/goddess:

> Half earth and time splits us apart
> like struck rock,
> A piece lives elegant stories
> too simply put
> while a dream on the edge of summer
> of brown rain in nim trees
> snail shells from the dooryard
> of King Toffah
> bring me where my blood moves
> Seboulisa mother goddess with one breast
> eaten away by worms of sorrow and loss
> see me now
> your severed daughter
> laughing our name into echo
> all the world shall remember.[28]

The poem collapses distances of time and space, traversing centuries and continents to envision a new symbolic geography. The fabled Harlem thoroughfare intersects with the capital of the fabled West African kingdom of Dahomey. Fragments of history are passed on (King Toffah is a historical monarch), but the source of the speaker's knowledge is a dream. The poem merges dream and reality, history and myth, to create a new sound, the sound of "our name," which "all the world shall remember." Laughing that name and hearing its echo is an act of healing and renewal. It gives the poem's persona "the woman strength of tongue in this cold season."[29]

In this poem and throughout *The Black Unicorn*, the 1978 volume in which it was published, Lorde renews her poetic voice through claiming and revising African cultural traditions and cosmologies. Indeed, the volume's first nine poems introduce the reader to the legendary women and goddesses who, in Robert Stepto's phrase, "inaugurate Lorde's genealogy of timbres and visages." By reengaging these figures, Lorde is able to find a language in which to retell and revise her own history. The orisha of the Yoruba, observes Gloria Hull, gave Lorde a "family that would never fail her."[30]

At the time she published The Black Unicorn, Audre Lorde was engaged in the process of writing Zami: A New Spelling of My Name, her "biomythography" that appeared in 1982. Zami is a companion text to The Black Unicorn; its title inscribes the name the poem foretells. In both texts, Lorde's appropriation of West African cosmology allows her to displace altogether the idea of the patriarchal family. The "age-old triangle of mother father and child, with the 'I' at its eternal core," is "elongate[d] and flatten[ed] out into the elegantly strong triad of grandmother mother daughter, with the 'I' moving back and forth flowing in either or both directions as needed."[31] Zami inaugurates its own genealogy, worrying the line by charting a matrilineage both personal and mythic. This process requires the literary innovations that justify the new generic marker Lorde inscribes.

Entering the discursive field of African American autobiography, Lorde signals immediately that her narrative will deviate from the tradition. Rather than autobiography, she invents the genre of biomythography—biography as myth, myth as biography. She relinquishes the "truth" value that, despite the best efforts of literary theorists, remains a selling point for black autobiographers. In an interview with Claudia Tate in Black Women Writers at Work, Lorde states flatly that Zami is "a biomythography, which is really fiction. It has elements of biography and history [and] myth. In other words, it's fiction built from many sources. This is one way of expanding our vision."[32]

In addition to its innovations, Zami repeats signal features of black autobiography, notably in its emphasis on naming the self and on reading and writing as tools for liberation. In one of her earliest acts of independence, Audre invents a new spelling of her name—preferring the "evenness" of "Audre" to Audrey. By the end of the text, she assumes the name inscribed in the title, one that denotes a change in self-definition rather than orthography. A visually impaired, physiologically tongue-tied child, Audre is as thrilled as Equiano or Douglass when she discovers that letters on a page convey meaning to those who can decipher the code. Her epiphany occurs in the 135th Street Library, probably the most cited reading room in African American literary tradition. Her testimony to the importance of the lesson and of the teacher resonates with similar declarations by black autobiographers through the centuries: "[T]hat deed saved my life, if not sooner, then later, when sometimes the only thing I had to hold on to was knowing I could read, and that that could get me through" (22). Scenes of reading and writing recur throughout the narrative. As a young woman, Audre reflects, "[W]riting was the only thing that made me feel like I was alive" (118). The text also quotes several of the poems that Audre begins to compose as a teenager and that presumably come from the author's journals.

The protagonist's vulnerability to sexual exploitation also echoes and extends a recurrent theme in the slave narratives. As a girl, Audre is molested by a storekeeper, whose trade is in used comic books, and later, when she is ten years old, she is molested by a boy on the rooftop of her building; he threatens to break her eyeglasses if she does not submit. Feeling "dirtied and afraid," she reports neither incident (49). When she becomes pregnant by a high school boyfriend, Audre chooses to have an abortion. She goes alone to the back-alley abortionist on the day before her eighteenth birthday. Her decision marks a turning point: "Even more than my leaving home, this action which was tearing my guts apart and from which I could die except I wasn't going to—this action was a kind of shift from safety towards self-preservation. It was a choice of pains" (111). The action and the language she uses to reflect on it are reminiscent of Harriet Jacobs when she describes a similar turning point in the life of the pseudonymous protagonist Linda Brent. In contrast to Lorde, Brent decides to have her child, one she has conceived with Mr. Sands, the lover she chooses in defiance of her lecherous master, Dr. Flint. Writing with a candor about sexual matters that is even more outspoken for a woman writer in the nineteenth century than Lorde's is for a twentieth-century author, Jacobs explains that she made her decision "with deliberate calculation. . . . It seems much less degrading to give one's self, than to submit to compulsion."[33] Although the decisions were different, the impulse toward self-preservation that compelled them is similar.

"Expanding vision" according to Lorde's perspective means more than participating in a literary tradition; it means, in part, inventing a past to enable a future. It is a past created out of personal history and collective myth and accessed through dreams and visions. Audre Lorde's commitment to this project is intensified by her desire to invent a usable past for black lesbians, to create "against a greater aloneness" (177) what Claudine Raynaud describes as "an empowering tale that women can live by and perpetuate."[34] To do so, Lorde displaces the family story in favor of a coming-of-age narrative that is predicated in part on what Anna Wilson rightly deems "a retrospective connection to a mythicised African past that is not available in the present of the text."[35] Lorde inscribes a dedication to herself:

> To the journeywoman pieces of myself
> Becoming
> Afrekete. (5)

For Lorde the tale begins with "images of women flaming like torches [that] adorn and define the borders of my journey, stand like dykes between me and the chaos." She writes, "It is the images of women, kind and cruel, that lead me home" (3). Drawn in the preface are women who barely figure in the narrative: the Harlem neighbor to whom her mother did not speak, the woman to whom her mother rented a room that became a death chamber, and the white women to whom Lorde is invisible. In retrospect, however, these women model, encourage, or provoke defiance. The women whom readers, along with Audre, the fictive protagonist, actually encounter in the text are variously guardians, lovers, and protectors, rivals, lovers, and adversaries. The home to which they lead is a reimagined version of the one her mother left.

As the daughter of Caribbean immigrants to the United States, Audre is twice displaced. Not only has the African connection been severed, but she knows her Grenadian relatives, the Belmar women, only through her mother's stories. The primary referent to their culture is the food the mother buys in the West Indian markets on Lenox Avenue. Not surprisingly, food supplies the metaphors through which both mother and daughter envision home.

Carriacou, the mother's birthplace, is an island off Grenada, which the British named the Spice Island in recognition of one of its most marketable commodities. For Audre, Carriacou is "a magic name like cinnamon, nutmeg, mace" (14). Spices are important not for their market value but because they conjure up sensory impressions that trigger her mother's memory and her imagination. Carriacou is a home Audre has never seen but that she "knew well out of my mother's mouth" (13). It offers mother and daughter a refuge from Harlem tenements and New York racism.

Its status as motherland is reified by the fact that Carriacou cannot be found on any map. It was not listed in the index of the school atlases; it did not appear in any gazette. A curious child, Audre hunts for what she calls the "magic place" during geography lessons or in free library time, but she never finds it. As an adult, Lorde tells us in a footnote, she fulfills the requirement for her degree in library science by doing an intensive study of atlases; she makes Carriacou a focus of her project and finally locates it in the *Atlas of the Encyclopedia Britannica*, which, as she notes, took special pride in the "accurate cartology of its colonies" (14).

Being unable to fix its location and thus being free of its history of colonization, the young Audre is able to use Carriacou for her own purposes: "But underneath it all as I was growing up, *home* was still a sweet place somewhere else which they had not managed to capture yet on paper, nor to throttle and bind up between the pages of a schoolbook. It was our own, my truly private paradise of blugoe and breadfruit hanging from the trees, of nutmeg and lime and sapadilla, of tonka beans and red and yellow Paradise Plums" (14).

The shift from the collective pronoun to the individual suggests the claim that Carriacou has on Audre's imagination; it functions for her as Shalimar eventually does for Milkman Dead. At the same time, it anticipates the alienation that develops between Audre and her mother. If the smells, tastes, and sounds that ignite memory and imagination are similar, the meanings they assign to home and to lineage are increasingly divergent. The relationship between mother and daughter in *Zami* is fraught with tension and unspoken anger. For much of the narrative, the mother is denied that honorific; she is referred to as Linda.

For all intents and purposes, then, the relationship seems to emblematize a dysfunctional matrilineage. Yet the retrospective narrator credits the mother's voice for enabling her own—and calls attention to the tribute by having the chapter's title, "How I Became a Poet," printed in the boldest type of the volume. "[O]ut of my mother's mouth a world of comment came cascading when she felt at ease or in her element, full of picaresque constructions and surreal scenes" (32). Impassable distances were measured "from Hog to Kick 'em Jenny." Rather than catch a cold, one "got co-hum, co-hum." This mother did not massage her child's backbone; she "raised [her] zandalee." The mother's language, like that of the women Paule Marshall memorializes in "From the Poets in the Kitchen," is a Caribbean patois, which the daughter as a child could not translate. After recording the idioms that coded the sensual content of life, the adult narrator avers, "*I am a reflection of my mother's secret poetry as well as of her hidden angers*" (32; emphasis in original).

The narrative offers dispossession as the key to understanding Linda's anger and reserve. "There was so little she knew about the stranger's country" (11). She had learned what was necessary to survive: she knew how the electricity worked, where the nearest church was, and, in the midst of the Great Depression, the locations where the Free Milk Fund for Babies distributed its charity, even as she refused to accept it. She knew how to bundle herself and her children up against the cold. Much of the knowledge she has acquired from her Belmar foremothers is discredited: how to mix oils for bruises and rashes, how to dispose of all toenail clippings and hair from the comb, and how to burn candles before All Souls Day to keep the soucoyants away. Much more of this knowledge is ineffectual in Harlem. If, for example, she knows how to prepare and apply black-elm leaf to wounds to prevent infection, she learns that there is no black elm in Harlem. Her prayers and her prescriptions are equally unavailing. Neither is there music—the music of Grenada, where everybody "had a song for everything" even if she was taught to disapprove of some of the "song-making as a disreputable and common habit" (11). In New York, she misses the music. To survive the "cold season" of exile, Linda Lorde puts on an armor so stout that her daughter's love fails to penetrate it.

A woman whose daughter bears witness to her power, Linda is also a woman who provokes but does not tolerate any challenge to her maternal authority. When Audre invents a new spelling of her name, the gesture is furtive; even by age four Audre has learned this lesson about her mother: "No deviation was allowed from her interpretations of correct" (24). When in adolescence Audre is entangled by overtly contradictory but intersecting lines of difference—of race, gender, class, and sexual preference—the mother cannot help her negotiate them. Having no words for racism, as in the scene in which Audre names the family's ouster from a Washington, D.C., ice cream shop what it is, Linda would be unlikely to have any words for lesbian. Linda silently disappears from the text.

Moving from her mother's house, where "there was no room in which to make errors, no room to be wrong," Audre resolves to live in a home of her own, where she can claim every aspect of her self (58). Although it is figured through the metaphors used to represent Carriacou—metaphors that are aligned with the mother's secret poetry—this is an inward home.[36] Tellingly, in the many journeys Audre makes after she leaves Harlem, she never attempts to travel to Linda's birthplace.[37] The Carriacou she visits is fictive; it is her "truly private paradise of blugoe and breadfruit hanging from the trees" (14).

Mexico, rather than Grenada, is Audre's geographical destination in *Zami*. Her journey is propelled by the growing political repression in the United States as well as by her personal quest to define who she is. She leaves just after attending a Washington rally protesting the planned execution of the Rosenbergs and at the end of a series of short-lived relationships with young women. Alienated from her family, unhappy with the various factory and clerical jobs she takes to support herself, and failing her courses at Hunter College, Audre is eager to escape. Mexico, "attached" as it is to the United States, seems the most accessible foreign locale. Arriving in Mexico City, she feels immediately revived: "Moving through street after street filled with people with brown faces had a profound and exhilarating effect upon me, unlike any experience I had ever known" (154). Audre feels both "noticed and accepted," a feeling that gives her a "social contour." The phrase is reminiscent of Gwendolyn Brooks's famous sonnet in which a mother asks "What can I give my children?" As she searches for an answer, she asserts that they have not asked for luxuries "[b]ut have begged me for a brisk contour." For Audre, as for Brooks's persona, this contour connotes a sense of racial acceptance and self-definition. Her sense of racial acceptance is also conveyed through an allusion to the best-known American novel of the 1950s; for the first time in her life Audre feels "visible" in Mexico City.[38]

Spurred by this feeling, Audre registers for courses in the history and ethnology of Mexico and in folklore at the university. Forty-five miles south of Mexico City, she discovers the "gift" of Cuernavaca. Here she finds an enclave of American expatriates, mostly women and mostly leftists; a good many are lesbians as well, although Audre is not initially aware of this fact. But she feels "open to anything" in Cuernavaca, and she makes it her home (158). It soon becomes clear how much her art and her sexuality are interwoven. In the following passage she describes the effect the Cuernavaca experience had on her poetry: "The birds suddenly cut loose all around me in the unbelievable sweet warm air. I had never heard anything so beautiful and unexpected before. I felt shaken by the waves of song. For the first time in my life, I had an insight into what poetry could be. I could use words to recreate that feeling, rather than to create a dream, which was what so much of my writing had been before" (160). The passage describes an epiphany familiar to poets in the Western tradition. Some of Lorde's critics find it problematic for that reason. But Lorde as a poet is heir to that tradition as much as to the alternative traditions she seeks to claim. The problem with the passage is its triteness.[39] What seems significant in narrative terms for Zami is that this epiphany becomes available to Audre only once she leaves the United States and finds a new home in Mexico.[40]

Eudora, the woman who becomes Audre's lover in Cuernavaca, is a knowledgeable guide to Mexico and to lovemaking. Journalist, translator (among other books, she has translated textbooks on Mexican history and ethnology), and onetime poet (who remains devoted to Walt Whitman), forty-eight-year-old Eudora calls herself a lesbian. She is the first woman Audre has met who claims this identity proudly. Eudora's ease with her sexuality makes Audre more comfortable with her own. But Eudora is "like the snapdragon," both delicate and sturdy (164). A breast cancer survivor, Eudora is no longer convinced of her physical attractiveness. She is emotionally fragile, a fragility surely heightened in a relationship with a woman so much younger than she. To Audre, however, Eudora's mastectomy scar is the "mark of the Amazon" (169).[41] She loves it fiercely. More significant for Zami, Audre sees her own beauty reflected in Eudora's eyes. The relationship they share marks the transition from childhood to adulthood, as Audre recognizes herself as "a woman connecting with other women in an intricate, complex, and ever-widening network of exchanging strengths" (165).

In place of the mother/daughter dyad, the narrative constructs a mythical matrilineage. It begins with Seboulisa, the goddess of Abomey, who is the "Mother of Us All."[42] Even as Audre decides to "copy from my mother what was in her unfulfilled," she claims retrospectively the "mother goddess with one breast," whom she "was to find in the cool mud halls of Abomey several lifetimes later" (58). (Eudora's racial identity makes her identification with Seboulisa incomplete, but Eudora certainly anticipates Audre's subsequent reclamation of the goddess.) The double gesture allows Audre to acknowledge the alienation and deprivations her biological mother experienced—deprivations that were more psychological than material—while identifying and embracing a mythical mother who can fulfill the daughter's need for affirmation, for love, and for sharing. Consequently, she can take the mother's coded language, which is a function of her displacement and powerlessness, and turn it into poetry. In one of the most lyrical and dramatic episodes in *Zami*, she can sexualize the mortar and the pestle, basic elements of her mother's everyday life, and break the silence surrounding sexuality that signifies the mother's repression.[43] She can become the truthteller who names oppression what it is. She can do so because she is no longer merely Linda's daughter; she is the daughter of Belmar women and of the African women who mothered them.

Linda's character might be identified with what Lorde later defined as "the ascetic" in her influential essay "The Uses of the Erotic." "For the ascetic position is one of the highest fear, the gravest mobility," Lorde wrote. "The severe abstinence of the ascetic becomes a ruling obsession. And it is not one of self discipline, but of self abnegation."[44] Linda's asceticism disrupts her bond with her daughter; it makes her unable to comfort her during the most traumatic experience of her adolescence, the suicide of Audre's closest friend, Gennie. Linda is paralyzed by fear of what her daughter's relationship with Gennie might become. That paralysis prevents her from offering Gennie the protection that she needs (her father is abusing her sexually). When Gennie dies, Linda can only fumble for words. Those she finds mix fear and accusation with sympathy: "Look, my darling child, I know she was your friend and you feel bad, but this is what I been cautioning you about. Be careful who you go around with. Among-you children do things different in this place and you think we stupid. . . . There was something totally wrong there from the start, you mark my words. That man call himself father was using that girl for I don't know what" (101).

Despite her evasiveness, Linda knows exactly what Gennie's father is doing to his daughter. Her inability to say it signifies her inability to stop it. Linda's life becomes for Audre a cautionary tale.[45] In large measure, Linda's self-denial derives from her cultural displacement. By contrast Audre finds in her own cultural displacement a source of power. Even as a high school student, she, like Gennie, joins a group called "the Branded." They wear their status as social pariahs as a badge of honor. It is emboldening. Not only does Audre grow ever bolder in her actions and her speech, but she infuses the idioms through which Linda sought to distance herself from experiences that embarrassed or frightened her with the power of the erotic. On one occasion, as she makes love to Muriel, she whispers in her ear: "In the West Indies, they call this raising your zandalee" (195).

Of course, Linda's fears and repressions are not purely personal. Linda embodies the homophobia that is endemic throughout the society. Audre meets it in the workplace. She loses a friend whose parent objects to her lesbianism. When as part of the Red Scare government agents put the apartment where she is living under surveillance, she is singled out because of her sexuality. Although Audre writes directly about these experiences, her indictment of Linda is indirect. But her mother's homophobia intensifies the need for the daughter to discover a racial and cultural sanction for the life she is determined to lead.

In "Revolutionary Hope: A Conversation between James Baldwin and Audre Lorde," an article that Baldwin and Lorde co-wrote for *Essence* magazine in 1984, Baldwin began by invoking the legacy of self-hatred shared by African Americans and by intoning the names of the heroes, Du Bois, Martin, and Malcolm, who "believed in the American Dream." He counted himself in that number. But when he attempted to include Lorde, she demurred. She spoke colloquially and familiarly at first: "I don't honey. I'm sorry, I just can't let that go past." Then with great urgency, she asserted that "deep, deep, deep down, I knew that dream was never mine." Black, female, and "*out,*" she explained that she had always known, that nobody was dreaming about her.[46]

James Baldwin was born in Harlem the same year that Frederic Byron and Linda Belmar Lorde immigrated there from Grenada. Baldwin's mother arrived from Deal Island, Maryland, shortly before her son's birth on 2 August 1924. She married the New Orleans–born David Baldwin in 1927; he gave her son his name, and their son immortalized him in his writing. Beginning with the classic essay *Notes of a Native Son*, Baldwin penned several portraits of this father in prose, including the novel *Go Tell It on the Mountain*, in which his fictional counterpart is Gabriel Grimes, and the essay "Down at the Cross," which was published in *The Fire Next Time*.[47] Questions of lineage and inheritance recur throughout Baldwin's oeuvre. Indeed, his first novel takes its epigraph from the gospel song that begins, "I looked down the line, / And I wondered."[48] In his nonfiction, questions of lineage can be deeply personal and often begin with the illegitimacy of his birth. Or they can be explicitly political and assert the complicated relation of black Americans to their white kin, who have disenfranchised them in their own country. Inheritance for Baldwin is also a cultural matter, and on occasion an explicitly literary one: the title *Notes of a Native Son* alludes to works by two of his literary precursors, Richard Wright's *Native Son* and Henry James's *Notes of a Son and Brother*.[49] In his early essays — "Stranger in the Village" is the penultimate example — Baldwin was much engaged by the issue of his relation as a black American to Western culture. When he wrote a new preface to the 1984 edition of *Notes*, he distilled the dilemma thus: "[M]y inheritance was particular, specifically limited and limiting, my birthright was vast, connecting me to all that lives, and to everyone, forever. But one cannot claim the birthright without accepting the inheritance."[50] Accepting the racial inheritance, in other words, was the price one paid for the humanity that was one's birthright. For Baldwin, the racial inheritance was shared by white and black Americans.

Ten years Baldwin's junior, Audre Lorde grew up smart and gay in the same Harlem neighborhood, experienced a relationship with her mother as intense and agonistic as Baldwin's with his father, developed high school friendships that crossed racial lines, encountered the raw racism of the industrial workplace in Connecticut as Baldwin had in New Jersey, left the country to find a place that would allow her to become the writer she knew early on she was destined to be, and devoted much of her life to the fight for social and political justice. In their speeches, both Baldwin and Lorde deployed the oracular voice; they were admired — and reviled — for their activism as much as for their art. Despite the striking parallels in their lives and work, Audre Lorde rejected the political assumptions on which Baldwin based his argument with America.

The racial inheritance that Lorde would define for herself goes beyond the bitter cup that was central to, though far from wholly, Baldwin's definition. It goes beyond the peculiar history that generations of black and white kin had lived in the United States. It goes beyond the West. Most profound, Lorde took up the challenge that Baldwin posed in "Down at the Cross." There he wrote: "If the concept of God has any validity or any use, it can only be to make us larger, freer and more loving. If God cannot do this, then it is time we got rid of him."[51] Lorde does just that and finds in the goddesses of Dahomey the deities who will serve the purposes that Baldwin declaims. As a consequence, Lorde can write as a lesbian whose sexuality is the core of her self-definition. For Baldwin, sexuality could be explored only at a considerable remove.

The parallels of their coming-of-age stories are worth considering. If Lorde invents a biomythography in a single volume, Baldwin constructs his biography in essays written across decades. The conflict between father and son, so central to the Western canon from Laertes and Oedipus to Claudius and Hamlet to Thomas Sutpen and Charles Bon, is his theme. Engaged in a contest of wills, the son challenges the father's authority. The father refuses to yield, or he relents. Either way, the son can claim victory. If he does not best the father physically or mentally, he can assert a moral victory. Baldwin alludes to a range of precursor texts, most notably the ultimate father/son story as it is told in the Bible. According to his biographer David Leeming, the theme of the essay *Notes of a Native Son*, as of Baldwin's first novel, is that it is only "through the death of the old prophet of doom that the new prophet of love could be born."[52]

A preacher without a church, a laborer who cannot earn enough money to support his nine children, Baldwin's father, like Linda Lorde, is never at home in Harlem. If Linda wears her stout armor, Reverend Baldwin is "locked up in his terrors" (90). He often took a seat by the window to have a better view of the world that he rejects with the same venom with which it has rejected him. He regularly inflicts his rage on his family; sometimes he only mutters to himself. To his son he looks "like pictures . . . of African tribal chieftains," but the family's tenement apartment is the only arena in which he can exert his patriarchal power (85). He is handsome and proud yet anything but regal. He is instead "ingrown, 'like a toe-nail' " (87), a diminutive comparison that introduces a devastating portrait of a man so cruel and embittered that his son cannot recall even one time that any of his children was glad to see him come home. As his son even as a child understands, David Baldwin fears as much as he hates the white world that denies him the right to the tree of life. The boy is able, therefore, to manipulate the father's fears. Forbidden to attend movies or plays, the child invites a caring white teacher to his home to ask permission on his behalf. The father does not "dare" to refuse, an act that causes his son to despise him all the more. At the time, the son writes in retrospect, "I had no way of knowing that [my father] was facing in that living room a wholly unprecedented and frightening situation" (92).

The incident bears comparison with one in *Zami*, in which Audre has confided in a seemingly sympathetic guidance counselor who is also an

English teacher, who asks if she is having trouble at home. Although Linda Lorde never states her fears for her daughter in the same terms in which Reverend Baldwin does—she does not fear perdition for her soul—she is distressed by her daughter's growing alienation. Ostensibly, she disapproves of Audre's desire to go away to college. When Audre asks Linda to meet with the counselor, the woman repeats everything that Audre has confided. The mother leaves the meeting defeated. Shocked to see evidence of her mother's tears, Audre reports "no fury in her voice, only heavy, awful pain": "All she said to me before she turned away was, 'How could you say those things about your mother to that white woman?'" (85). For Audre, there is no preening, not even a temporary moment of gloating. What Baldwin terms the "really cruel intuitiveness of a child" is altogether absent from this adolescent's tale (91).

To a degree, the difference is the narration: Lorde's narrator is less adept at creating drama and suspense than Baldwin's persona. The scene is too quickly told. In the paragraph that follows, the blame is assigned— rightly—to the guidance counselor, who has perhaps viewed the mother as "uppity" or considered both mother and daughter as part of a sociological experiment. The next paragraph, the last of the chapter, shifts away from the mother and records, with some irony, the plaint of the adolescent to whom a parent's lack of understanding signifies a lack of love. But in a book that strives in significant measure to write what Adrienne Rich described as "the great unwritten story," "the cathexis between mother and daughter," one discerns in this moment a complex fusion of rejection and identification.[53]

In *Notes of a Native Son*, the son identifies with the father only when he recognizes in himself the same bitterness and rage. In part because the identification is so terrifying, he determines to find another way of responding to the assault of racism. "It had now been laid to my charge," he writes, "to keep my own heart free of hatred and despair" (114). With an integrity and deliberateness that prevents him from ever completely succeeding, Baldwin seeks over the course of his writing to supplant that hatred and despair with love and hope. In his writing about the inability of his white countrymen to come to terms with the sensual, Baldwin gestures toward the saving power of sexual love. But for the most part, his writing about the power of the (homo)erotic occurs in his fiction. In *Go Tell It on the Mountain*, for example, the attraction between John and Elisha, the church pianist and John's "big brother in the Lord," simmers until the end, when it culminates in the "holy kiss" that they share after John's conversion on the threshing floor. The bond that they acknowledge is spiritual, and the imagery of the ending reinforces this claim. The rising sun "fell over Elisha like a golden robe, and struck John's forehead, where Elisha had kissed him, like a seal ineffaceable forever."[54] The novel does not contain explicit references to same-sex desire, although it seems coded in this passage and in many others. "The Outing," originally written as part of the novel but published subsequently as a freestanding story, represents John's attraction to another character, "David," as explicitly sexual. The story ends with the characters' embrace; references to "panic" that supplants "peace" and to "danger" where there had been safety accompany it.[55] Located as they are in the culture of the sanctified church, the characters in Go Tell It on the Mountain cannot transgress the fundamentalist Christian proscriptions against homosexuality.

In contrast, as AnnLouise Keating argues, "[B]y rejecting the Judeo-Christian God and reclaiming the prepatriarchal African goddess, Lorde establishes a new relationship to language. She creates—both for herself and for other women—a spirituality wholly rooted in the physical."[56] By embodying the spiritual, Lorde creates a space for sexuality that carries its own moral justification. By contrast, even in the novels that represent the homoerotic explicitly, Giovanni's Room and Another Country, for example, Baldwin's characters are frequently troubled by the moral censure they expect in response to their actions. To create a free space, Lorde reimagines the pantheon of Dahomean deities, which she imbues with powers of her own invention. Seboulisa is the name that residents of Abomey, the capital of Dahomey, gave to Mawu-Lisa, the highest deity of the Fon people. The deity combines Mawu (female) and Lisa (male) valences: Mawu, the moon, is cool and gentle; Lisa, the sun, is strong, tough, and fierce. The balance represents a Fon ideal.[57] The deities served a society in which, according to one historian, women exercised choice, influence, and autonomy, "if not in wholly egalitarian relationships with men, in situations where there was clear recognition of their ability and right to do so."[58] The reference to Seboulisa's severed breast reflects as well the interplay between the spiritual and the social realms. One myth, perhaps derived from Greek mythology, held that Dahomey's female warriors cut off their right breast in order to enhance their ability to hold and discharge their weapons. Lorde appropriates the myth for her representation of Seboulisa. In so doing she imputes a measure of human suffering to the goddess.[59]

No figure is more central to Lorde's cosmology than Afrekete, a goddess that is rarely mentioned in standard books on Dahomean cosmology. As Keating points out, Lorde herself does not mention Afrekete by name in *The Black Unicorn*. She does mention Eshu and Elegba, deities that she identifies as later male versions of Afrekete. Keating quotes a conversation that Lorde had with the poet Judy Grahn in which Lorde claimed that only in the original "old thunder god religion" that preceded Yoruba was Afrekete portrayed as female. Later, according to Lorde, Afrekete was transformed into the male trickster god Eshu/Elegba.[60] Lorde's explanation underscores the syncreticism inherent in the Dahomean belief system, a system that was deeply influenced by the cosmology of the neighboring Yoruba. As Lorde represents it, the cosmology of Dahomey is more than syncretic, of course; it is fictive.

Audre finds the moral sanction for her life choices in the mythical matrilineage the narrative constructs. This matrilineage envisions lovers as maternal surrogates, who provide the affirmation, love, and sharing supplied by Seboulisa and who eventually enable Audre to give birth to herself. Reflecting on her sojourn in Mexico in an interview with Adrienne Rich, Lorde asserts, "I know that I came back from Mexico very, very different, and much of it had to do with what I learned from Eudora. But more than that, it was a kind of releasing of my work, a releasing of myself."[61] By recounting her relationships in *Zami*, Lorde gives fictional form to the tenet she sets forth in "The Uses of the Erotic," which insists on the erotic "as a source of power and information in women's lives." The "sharing of joy, whether physical, emotional, psychic, or intellectual, forms a bridge among the sharers which can be the basis for understanding much of what is not shared between them, and lessens the threat of their difference."[62] Once she leaves her mother's house, the adult Audre lives in a series of communities where women aspire to but seldom achieve the sharing of joy set forth as the ideal.

Until the very end of the narrative, the erotic in *Zami* is more closely tied with the transgressive than with the utopian. To cite the most obvious examples: the lesbian bar is the favored trysting site; its strictly enforced codes for role-playing stifle the possibilities for free expression. Audre's relationships are often furtive and usually short lived. She wages an exhausting struggle to come to terms with the multiple differences that define who she is. *Zami* never loses sight of the political dimension of all these situations. The lesbian bar consequentially becomes, in Katie King's formulation, "a site of the production of historical memory and literary identity for feminist and gay movements."[63] The sexual relationships Audre has become the means through which she develops political and poetic consciousness. Ultimately she learns to embrace the differences that have oppressed her: "It was a while before we came to realize that our place was the very house of difference rather than the security of any one particular difference" (226).

The black women who become Audre's lovers are related imagistically to the mother; it is their images, "kind and cruel, that lead [her] home." Ginger, a historically aware woman who works with Audre in a Connecticut factory, is connected even through her name. The plant from which the spice is derived grows in many places, but the Jamaican variety is especially prized. In addition to the association with the Caribbean, the name speaks to Ginger's mettle. Despite Audre's superior education, Ginger has to teach her the rudiments of black American history; she begins by telling her that Crispus Attucks, for whom the neighborhood community center is named, was a black Revolutionary War hero. Ginger is further associated with African American culture when she is described as resembling Fats Domino. More important, in the descriptions of their lovemaking, Audre's sexual pleasure is imaged through metaphors of food in a reversal of the erotic fantasy involving her mother in which food is described through metaphors of sex. Eventually the narrative literalizes the connections between food and desire, the maternal and the sexual, as food, tropical fruits in particular, becomes part of the lovemaking the text recounts. The protagonist's gloss on this moment reinforces these connections: "Loving Ginger that night was like coming home to a joy I was meant for" (139).

Although the narrative contains mythic elements from the beginning, its conclusion seems to transpire entirely in the realm of myth. The conclusion begins just as the longest-lasting relationship Audre has had comes to an unhappy end. Her affair with her white lover Muriel, a woman who is mentally unstable and jealous of Audre's sense of purpose, is riven with sexual betrayal and unexpressed racial tensions. As she attempts to beat back despair, Audre has an epiphany that, like the moment in Cuernavaca, draws on all-too-familiar tropes; this time the moment is salvaged by its insistence on simile and by its sly wit. Audre hears "music swelling up into [her] head as if a choir of angels has boarded the Second Avenue bus directly in front of [her]." The choir is singing an old spiritual, "I'll die this death on Calvary / aint / gonna / die / no / more!" Appropriating the discourse of Christianity, Lorde rewrites it to fulfill a personal, spiritually heterodox vision. She "hears the sky fill with a new spelling of my own name" (239).[64]

Shortly after this signal moment, Audre meets a black woman at a party. Initially, she appears to be an ordinary woman, dark skinned with high cheek bones, Georgia-born and bred, who reminds Audre of a former co-worker. She gives off a "spicy herb-like odor" that the text attributes to coconut oil and lavender hair pomade. She sings occasionally at a club on Sugar Hill. Soon, however, the character is invested with more profound meanings. Shorn of makeup, her "chocolate skin and deep, sculptured mouth" resemble a Benin bronze (244). It becomes increasingly clear that this character, Kitty/Afrekete, is a mythic figure, at once Audre's lover, spiritual guide, and double. Lorde appropriates the figure of Afrekete to write herself as capable of traversing time and space, centuries and continents, not only to envision but to inhabit a new symbolic geography.[65]

With its profuse collection of green plants and its "glowing magical tank of exotic fish," Kitty/Afrekete's apartment simulates the new geography. Like Linda, Kitty/Afrekete shops in the West Indian markets on Lenox Avenue or in the Puerto Rican bodegas "under the bridge," that is, under the railroad tracks elevated above Park Avenue. Under the bridge, as the narrator explains, was a way of saying "that whatever it was had come from as far back and as close to home . . . as was possible" (249). Here Kitty purchases the cocoyams and cassava, the red delicious pippins, the green plantains, and red finger bananas that the women feed each other in and out of bed. If on the level of story *Zami* moves from the realistic to the mythic, on the level of discourse it moves from the metaphorical to the literal.

Kitty/Afrekete teaches Audre (who, we as readers remember, was earlier in the narrative given the nickname Kitty) "roots, new definitions of our women's bodies—definitions for which I had only been in training before" (250). Unlike Linda, who could not give up her armor, Audre sheds the "carapace" with which she has protected herself and allows herself to be emotionally vulnerable. Consequently, she gains access to the spirituality intertwined in the erotic. With a supple lyricism the poet writes the conclusion to this romance as ritual: "We had come together like elements erupting into an electric storm, exchanging energy, sharing charge, brief and drenching. Then we parted, passed, reformed, reshaping ourselves the better for the exchange" (253).

Having passed through the storm, the narrator takes a new name, Zami, which she identifies only in the epilogue as "a Carriacou name for women who work together as friends and lovers" (255). Kitty/Afrekete disappears as mysteriously as she arrives. But for Audre their encounter marks at once a reconciliation with her maternal inheritance and a move beyond it. While Linda Lorde would not recognize the gift, Audre preserves the ideal of Carriacou as if it were a gift from her mother, like the Christmas candies. Audre identifies within the mother's heritage the cultural sanction for her own sexuality, aesthetic, and spirituality. "Once home was a long way off, a place I had never been to but knew out of my mother's mouth. I only discovered its latitudes when Carriacou was no longer my home" (256). Home for this narrator is not a place to return to but one to journey toward.

In the end, Audre Lorde in Zami, like Toni Morrison in Song of Solomon, makes a constructive detour of the past while journeying toward a freer future. That trajectory is one shared by all the texts discussed in Worrying the Line. Zami ends on a more celebratory note than Song of Solomon, but its new configuration of family leaves uncharted the relation of brothers and sons to sisters and mothers or of "cousins" like Milkman and Hagar to each other. Morrison's novel points toward the possibility of egalitarian and loving relationships within families of biological kin, while Lorde's biomythography boldly envisions families that are not defined by biology but by affiliation.[66] In the chapters that follow, Worrying the Line examines texts that explore both kinds of possibilities; black women writers reimagine the past as they look steadily ahead.

# three

## On the Line to Dahomey: Charting Generations

in populated air
our ancestors continue
i have seen them.
i have heard
their shimmering voices
singing.
—Lucille Clifton, *Two-Headed Woman*

The past and present wilt—I have fill'd them, emptied them,
And proceed to fill my next fold of the future.
—Walt Whitman, *Song of Myself*

Dedicated to the memory of her father, Lucille Clifton's *Generations* (1976) recounts the events surrounding his death and becomes a meditation on the meaning of his life and the lives of the author's extended family. Published the year before Alex Haley's *Roots* and Toni Morrison's *Song of Solomon*, the memoir anticipates the intensifying desire among African American writers to reconnect with an African past. Clifton's ancestor figure is her great-great-grandmother, Caroline Donald Sale, who was born in Dahomey. In subject and form, *Generations* marked a departure for Clifton, whose first recognition had come with the publication of *Good Times* (1969), the volume of spare lyrics on the lives and in the voices of contemporary black urban dwellers. In one of a handful of critiques of Clifton's art, poet Alicia Ostriker identifies Clifton rightly as a "minimalist" and advises readers to "experience the craftsmanship of the minimalist as a set of unerring gestures governed by a constraining and shaping discipline, so habitual that it seems effortless."[1] The apparent effortlessness of *Generations* is the result of a careful conjunction of media and a seamless synthesis of formal and vernacular poetic influences.

Family photographs are key elements of the text. As it charts the family's lineage, *Generations* represents the images of African American elders as well as their voices. Juxtaposing their faces and their speech is one way *Generations* enacts worrying the line. Another derives from the fact that no poetic influence is more important to this volume than Walt Whitman, whose words are regularly invoked. But if Clifton acknowledges her debt to her foremost white literary ancestor, her volume tells the story that Whitman could not tell, a story that moves slavery to center stage and makes the slaves and their descendants central to American memory.

*Generations* is the only memoir and the only extended narrative in an oeuvre that includes nine volumes of poetry and almost twenty children's books.[2] From the beginning, however, elusive references to family history recur in Clifton's poetry. The first lines of the second and third poems in *Good Times* begin respectively "my mama moved among the days" and "my daddy's fingers move among the couplers."[3] Born only two generations after slavery, Clifton's parents, Samuel and Thelma Moore Sayles, had heard its terrible stories from those who had lived them. They had themselves migrated from the rural South to the industrialized North. ("Couplers" denotes machines in the steel mills where Samuel labored to support his family.) But, unlike millions of African Americans who made similar journeys in the twentieth century, Samuel Sayles carried with him a recollection of a past more distant than slavery. In Clifton's memoir, the heroic memory of the ancestral journey from Dahomey to America, then from New Orleans to Virginia, becomes a talisman for later generations to stave off pain and grief.

Initially, the elegiac tone of *Generations* seems out of character for the poet of *Good Times*, but in fact that tone dominates most of Clifton's writing. Loss, or more particularly, the ability to survive loss, is Clifton's major theme. The speaker in the frequently anthologized poem "miss rosie," for example, addresses the ruined figure of a bag lady and proclaims that she will "stand up / through your destruction" (19). The imperative to remember resonates through *Good Times* from the final lines of the title poem, "oh children think about the / good times," to the second stanza of "ca'line's prayer" (24). Notably, this poem identifies no familial connection between the subject and author, yet to readers of *Generations* it becomes immediately recognizable as the call to which the later volume responds:

> remember me from wydah
> remember the child
> running across dahomey
> black as ripe papaya
> juicy as sweet berries
> and set me in the rivers of your glory
>
> Ye Ma Jah.[4]

*Generations* maps the ancestor's journey not across Dahomey to Wydah, a port of embarkation for the Middle Passage, but across the United States. Caroline "walked North from New Orleans to Virginia in 1830."[5] In the narrative present the volume's narrator, Lucille, makes "the journey back" to Buffalo to bury her father.[6] That journey awakens her memories of the stories her father has told about Caroline Sale. The book's Lucille likewise travels north, from Maryland to New York. But her spiritual journey follows a different trajectory. She traces her line, her lineage, back to its African source. Through her identification with her dead kin, enabled both by her father's remembered voice and by family pictures, beginning with the photograph of Caroline Sale and her son that is the memoir's frontispiece, Clifton memorializes her dead. Gradually, she comes to terms with their loss, a loss that finally has less to do with Africa than with an acutely personal grief; grief gives way to acceptance, renewal, and no small measure of triumph.

Among memoirs in the African American tradition, *Generations* is distinctive in terms of its form as well as its content.[7] Each section of the text is introduced by a photograph that, like the words that follow, must be "read." Taken together, the photographs and words constitute the family's documentation of its history. Family photographs, Susan Sontag asserts, are "a portable kit of images that bear witness to [a family's] connectedness." Metonymically, photographs are "ghostly traces" that "supply the token presence of dispersed relatives." Often they are all that remain of an extended family. Photography, Sontag concludes, "is an elegiac art."[8] *Generations* is an elegy in which prose and pictures combine to create a singular text.

Handed down through generations of her family, the photographs are both a source that allows Clifton to reconstruct a history from the images her ancestors preserved and a crucial component of the text she creates. Writing of the importance of photographs in the documentation of black life, bell hooks avers that "when the psychohistory of a people is marked by ongoing loss, when entire histories are denied, hidden, erased, documentation may become an obsession." For African Americans, for whom illiteracy was one of slavery's legacies, photographs became a way to document a history that they could not write down. Preserved not only in photograph albums but displayed on the walls of the most humble homes, these "pictorial genealogies" were one means by which black people "ensured against the losses of the past." "As children," hooks writes of herself and of those African Americans who grew up under segregation, "we learned who our ancestors were by endless narratives told to us as we stood in front of pictures."[9]

The interaction between words and images in *Generations* replicates the process hooks describes. The photographs evoke the stories that Clifton has been told and that she distills for her memoir. Capturing what Walter Benjamin described as the aura emanating from "the fleeting expression of a human face" and conveying a "melancholy, incomparable beauty," these photographs participate in the volume's ritual of remembrance.[10] They evoke the melancholy, incomparable beauty of Clifton's poetry/prose.

In keeping with its ritualistic purpose, some of the text's language is designed to re-create the language spoken by Clifton's ancestors. Like Toni Morrison, Paule Marshall, and Alice Walker, Clifton explores and preserves the elders' language. Walker has written that it is "truly astonishing how much of their language is present tense, which seems almost a message to us to remember that the lives they lived are always current, not simply historical."[11] Not only is Caroline's experience alive to the narrator, but by representing her father's voice as the medium through which her ancestors speak, Clifton closes the gap between the past and the present for her reader. Other members of Clifton's family speak in the volume's present tense as well. As a poet, Clifton creates the effect of orality through repetition, assonance, and rhyme, as well as through direct and indirect discourse.

The language of the text has its own complex genealogy. Two of its roots are signaled by the volume's paired epigraphs. The first is from the

King James Bible, the cadences of which inform much African American literature.[12] Taken from Job, the Bible's supreme book of suffering, tribulation, and reward, the epigraph recounts Job's response to his friends' charge that he has brought his travails on himself. Job would reason with God, but he will not defend himself to his friends. "Lo, mine eye hath seen all this, mine ear hath heard and understood it. What ye know, the same do I know also; I am not inferior to you" (Job 13:1, 2). For Clifton and her kin, slavery is the original, inexplicable travail. But a scourge of tribulations follows the family's passage to freedom. *Generations* is a volume that documents without apology what this family has seen, heard, and understood. The second epigraph is attributed to

> [t]he woman called Caroline Donald Sale
> born free in Afrika in 1822
> died free in America in 1910.

It commands: "Get what you want, you from Dahomey women." Thus, it sets the tone for the volume: while it records the suffering of slavery and beyond, *Generations* resonates with the spirit of resistance and survival. The placement of the epigraphs establishes an equivalence between them: the King James Bible and African American oral tradition are both literary influences and repositories of wisdom. Caroline Sale, no less than Job, is a source of spiritual guidance and inspiration.

Throughout *Generations*, in repeated allusions to Whitman's *Song of Myself*, Clifton pays homage to her precursor. Whitman and Clifton share aesthetic, political, and spiritual affinities. For both, colloquial speech and popular music are key poetic referents. Dedicated to producing in *Leaves of Grass* "the idiomatic book of my land," Whitman argued that "great writers penetrate the idioms of their races and use them with simplicity and power." Clifton has declared her pride in using "a simple language."[13] What Italian opera and Anglo-American folk music are to Whitman, blues and other forms of African American folk music are to Clifton. The influences of speech and music, rather than the conventions of English poetry, led Whitman to write what was symbolically as well as technically "free verse." Sherley Anne Williams points to techniques in Clifton's poetry that "approximate or parallel various blues devices." For Williams, poetry like Clifton's marks "the beginning of a new tradition built on a synthesis of black oral traditions and Western literate forms."[14]

Their politics, like their poetics, demonstrate the democratic convictions that Whitman and Clifton share. The persona of *Song of Myself* declaims that "through me the many long dumb voices, / voices of the interminable generations of prisoners and slaves" speak. Such sentiments have inspired many African American poets, in addition to Clifton, to count themselves among Whitman's literary descendants.[15] In fact, although Whitman stood apart from most white Americans in his recognition of black people's humanity, his egalitarianism was tinged with the racism endemic to his time.[16] If Whitman's sympathies did not wholly extend to the slaves, however, they were profoundly working class. The son of a displaced farmer who struggled to support his family as a carpenter, Whitman came by his class consciousness honestly. So does Clifton.[17] Whitman's affinity for photography reflected an understanding of its democratic potential. Dedicated to the creation of a gallery of American images, he saw in the photographer's art an analogue to his own. Clifton's album of family photographs acts as the call to which her narrative responds.

More important, both poets are mystics whose spiritual beliefs transcend religious orthodoxy. *Song of Myself* embraces all faiths "ancient and modern and all between" (sec. 43, l. 3). Clifton's oeuvre includes cycles of poems inspired by Old Testament prophets, Jesus, and Kali, the Hindu goddess.[18] Both poets perceive what Clifton deems "the Light" in the miracle of ordinary things and the divinity of ordinary people. Armed with the insights that mysticism provides, both poets adopt personae who transcend time and space. The exuberant "I" of *Song of Myself* declares, "I skirt sierras, my palms cover continents, / I am afoot with vision" (sec. 33, ll. 7–8). Linking the acquisition of vision to the process of writing, the "I" of *Generations* reflects: "I type that and I swear I can see Ca'line standing in the green of Virginia, in the green of Africa, and I swear she makes no sound but she nods her head and smiles" (79). Clifton's persona becomes the witness who will write/right the story of her ancestors. In letting an allusion to *Song of Myself* stand as the final words of *Generations*, Clifton seals the bond between her project and Whitman's: "I have no mockings or arguments. I witness and wait."

But her narrative begins with questions. A prologue introduces the contrasts between written and oral, free and slave, South and North, past and present, and white and black that *Generations* contemplates. At the same time the prologue overturns the hierarchical relationships these contrasts assume. It opens with a telephone call from a white woman in Virginia who is a descendant of the white Sale family. An amateur genealogist, she assumes the right to write the family history. But the scene, not to mention the volume readers hold in their hands, identifies her as an amateur. She calls Clifton in response to a notice Clifton has put in a local Virginia paper soliciting information about the Sale/Sayles family. In placing the notice and citing it in her text, Clifton takes control of the written word. In a similar act of negotiation, her forebears had signaled their emancipation in writing by changing the spelling of the surname to Sayle. As a young man, Clifton's father added the "s" because he was sure there would be more than one of him.

The very first words of the text—"She said"—refer to the white woman whose only authority inheres in her voice. She has to learn what Clifton already knows: the Sales/Sayles are black as well as white. This recognition comes through the white woman's failure to recognize even the names of most of her black kin. She becomes speechless in the face of the reality of slavery; her silence confirms Clifton's moral advantage as well as her status as author and authority. Clifton's book will mark the unmarked graves of her ancestors.

The end of the phone call severs the connection between Clifton and her reluctant informant. Later the woman, whose voice has been "sweet and white over the wires," sends Clifton her written history (5). None of the white woman's written words appear in Clifton's text. They are first subordinated to the stories of "Ca'line" that Samuel Sayles has told his daughter, then to the stories stimulated by the photographs of the kin Clifton claims as her own. Unlike the representation of the white woman's "she said" in the past tense, the text uses the present and continuous present tense to represent the voices of the volume's black speakers. In a final irony, the white woman's genealogy identifies her as "the last of her line. Old and not married, left with a house and a name" (7). In response, Clifton's persona refers to her husband and their six children, then reflects: "I feel the Dahomey women gathering in my bones."

Although the prologue displaces the hierarchies of race, it risks recuperating gender hierarchies and patriarchal values. But several textual moves worry the line. First, in this genealogy the female ancestor is the progenitor. Not only is Caroline the first of the Sales, but, as a midwife, she has birthed generations of children of other families. Second, patronymics do not define family. In the story that concludes the prologue, the narrator's father remembers that Caroline would not divulge her African name, despite his warning that "it'll be forgot." Caroline reassures him beneficently, "Don't you worry, mister, don't you worry" (7). Although Clifton's text is unable to retrieve her African name, it confirms her ancestor's belief that she will not be forgotten. Spillers argues that the loss of the patronymic to cultural memory is the "ground" on which the captive African is "symbolically broken in two—ruptured along the fault of a 'double consciousness' in which the break with an indigenous African situation is complete, but one's cultural membership in the American one remains inchoate."[19] What *Generations* effects is a healing of that rupture by demonstrating African American membership in the web of kin.

In Spillers's phrase, the "line of inheritance from a male parent to a female child is not straight."[20] The narrator's father passes the legacy of memory to his daughter but emphasizes its female progenitor. Belatedly, the narrator inserts her mother into the family genealogy handed down by her father and thus overrides patriarchal concepts of lineage. In the end, she charts familial descent as neither patrilineage nor matrilineage but a fusion of both.

Stories, not photographs, provide the narrator's link to Dahomey, the ancient African nation fabled for its female warriors. Dahomey in *Generations* is more dream than destination in this journey to understand the past. In "The Black Writers' Use of Memory," Melvin Dixon observes, "[I]f family disruption and loss of precise genealogy distance black Americans from more solid, or literal, connections to an African identity, they nonetheless increase our predilection for the way figurative connections become charged with increasing symbolic importance."[21] At a moment of failure in *Generations*, after she has flunked out of college, Lucille explains to her disappointed father that she does need a degree to become a poet. She feels authorized to write poems because she is "from Dahomey women" (41). His reply that she does not even know where Dahomey is, let alone what it means, provokes her to tears. As the narrative unfolds, however, Lucille gains the necessary knowledge. The symbolic importance of Dahomey to Lucille's sense of her self and her art becomes clear. Only as she is on the line to Dahomey can the narrator conjure up the relatives she has never known and come to terms with those she has not known well enough.

The voice that initiates the action of *Generations* is the narrator's sister's, but before we learn her identity, we read a transcription of her words. Unpunctuated, they run together like a torrent. "[H]e finished his eggs and his bacon and his coffee and said Jo get me one of them True Greens and I got him his cigarette and went upstairs to get a ashtray and when I got back he was laying on the floor and blood was all on his mouth like when Mama used to have her fits and I hollered Daddy Daddy Daddy" (9). Not only does the representation capture the immediacy of the moment—one sister calls another to report the death of their father—but in its rush of detail it begins to sketch the portrait of the man and the history of the family. So, for example, the use of the conjunction "and" replicates its use in colloquial speech. The speaker assumes the auditor's knowledge of the mother's "fits," even as the reference sparks the reader's curiosity. The sisters' common response to the news of the father's death (members of the rescue squad summoned to the scene tell Punkin, as Punkin tells "Lue") is disbelief. In the interior monologue that follows, the text begins to convey the aura of the man his daughter refers to as "Mr. Sayles Lord," "Old Brother Sayles," and "the Rock." When Lue begins to address the dead father directly, the image of strength is softened by the terms of endearment the father's memory elicits from his child.

Within the space of four paragraphs, the news is reported, the initial grief recorded, and the narrator's journey to Buffalo for the burial begun. While making that journey in a car driven by her husband, accompanied by her brother, Lucille, or "Lue," remembers the stories her father has told about Caroline, who walked north from New Orleans to Virginia as part of a coffle when she was eight years old. Accounts of the journeys of the bereaved daughter in the narrative present and the motherless slave girl remembered through the father's words alternate. "Mammy Ca'line" becomes the model for coping with the inconceivable.[22] Her great-great-granddaughter gives voice to what had been inexpressible.

Critic Karla Holloway coins the term "(re)membrance" to denote the cultural inscriptions of memory in texts by women across the African diaspora. "These are works that claim the texts of spoken memory as their source and whose narrative strategy honors the cultural memories within the word."[23] *Generations* illustrates Holloway's point; it enacts the process of (re)membrance as it represents the daughter's efforts to recall the father's words and through them the ancestor's deeds. Repetition for the text's characters serves as a mnemonic device; it is also a primary structuring tool.

The phrase that triggers the memory is " 'Mammy Ca'line raised me,' Daddy would say." Having established the fact that the father's stories were told and retold, the narrator recalls more of his words. He would describe the woman's physical posture ("tall and skinny and walked straight as a soldier") and her voice (she spoke with "an Oxford accent"). To the father, the different accent and vocabulary—she would chastise him by saying, "[S]top the bedlam"—are markers of intellectual superiority (11). But by embedding Caroline's Britishisms in the father's black American vernacular soundings, the text refuses this reading. It honors the intelligence and strength of the parent as well as the ancestor. The father's precocity and his grounding in an oral tradition preserve the ancestor's legacy: "She was a dark old skinny lady and she raised my Daddy and then raised me, least till I was eight years old when she died. When I was eight years old. I remember everything she ever told me, cause you know when you that age you old enough to remember things. I remember everything she told me, Lue, even though she died when I was eight years old. And then I knowed about what she remembered cause that's how old she was when she got here. Eight years old" (11–12).

In the tradition of the African griot, Samuel Sayles has preserved the family's history. But the dislocations of slavery disrupt tradition; history becomes what eight-year-old minds can retain. The insistent repetition of the age indicts the system of slavery that robs generations of childhood, even as it honors the spirit that enabled the child Samuel to remember fragments of the past. In another fragment Samuel recites the states through which Caroline walked on her journey from New Orleans, her port of embarkation in the "New World," to Virginia. Walking the land is the means through which she stakes a claim to it for herself and for her heirs. Intoning the names he recalls of the next generations— Lucy (the narrator is her namesake) and Gene—Samuel begins to chart the family tree. The use of the conjunction "and" in this telling replicates patterns of speech. More important, it stresses the links through which a family genealogy is constructed despite the gaps in the line.[24]

Interwoven with Samuel's story is the narrative of Lucille's journey to Buffalo. Repeating the pattern by which he catalogs the states through which Caroline walked, Lucille narrates her journey north, state by state. Pennsylvania, she notes, seemed greener than Maryland, and "it smelled like spring." An encounter with a "whiteboy driver in a cowboy hat" hints at the racism simmering beneath the surface, but it is hardly the blot on the social landscape that slavery was. Indeed, these travelers cloak their grief in giddy laughter. As they approach the New York border, however, they leave "spring there in the high ground" of Pennsylvania. The land takes on the pallor of winter and of death; it "turned slowly grey and hard and cracking." "The promised land" is a cruelly ironic epithet for New York (15–16).

The last section of this chapter narrows the distance between the two stories. In the ancestor's narrative Caroline and her sister (Aunt Margaret Brown in her only appearance in the volume) reflect on the loss of their mother, while in the narrative present Lucille and her brother arrive at their father's home. The figure of the father links the two stories. In the former he is the child who asks Mammy Caroline if she misses her mother. She does not answer, but he overhears her and Aunt Margaret Brown wonder aloud about their mother's fate. In the latter narrative Samuel is the missing parent. His death elicits his son's whispered assertion to Lucille: "[W]e are orphans" (18). But the thematic link is about survival as much as loss. As Caroline and Margaret mourn their mother, they sit and rock themselves into a semblance of healing. Their example anticipates the healing Lucille and her brother have yet to undergo.

The family pictures that introduce each section of the text belie the assertion that these two are orphans. The stories that each of the photographs relates and provokes likewise become instruments of healing. Formally posed and professionally taken, a photograph under the heading "Caroline and son" precedes Chapter 1. Two seated figures occupy the foreground. The female figure, an elderly woman wearing a plaid gingham dress and a small hat, holds her left arm at her side; in her right hand, resting on her lap, she grips an object that appears to be either a small purse or a cameo. The younger male figure's attire is more formal; he wears a jacket with white shirt and tie and broadcloth pants. His left leg is crossed over his right, and his fists are clenched. Their clothing and their posture signify their self-possession.

The caption borrows the famous opening lines of *Song of Myself*: "I celebrate myself, and sing myself, / And what I assume you shall assume, / For every atom belonging to me as good belongs to you." [25] As in Whitman's poem, the pronoun references are ambiguous; they may refer to the subjects of the photograph, the narrator of the volume, or the reader. To be sure, the subjects celebrate themselves in the very act of recording their images. As nineteenth-century African Americans (judging from

Caroline and son (From Lucille Clifton, *Generations:*
*A Memoir* [New York: Random House, 1976];
reprinted courtesy of Lucille Clifton)

their dress and the information that Caroline Sale died in 1910 at the age
of eighty-eight, the photograph predates the turn of the twentieth century), they rejected the degrading images the society defined for them
and forged their own self-representation. Their descendant, the narrator,
celebrates them as well. She and they are connected, even if, as seems
likely, she does not know which of Caroline's four sons is depicted in
the photograph. Connected, too, are the readers who share the national
identity that Whitman claims in his poem and that Clifton, by quoting it
in this caption, claims here as well. The Sales/Sayles history, fragmented
as it is, is ours as "Americans" as well. We are all imbricated in the genealogy represented by this picture.

"Photographs are relics of the past," John Berger has written. Clifton's
volume asks the reader, no less than the writer and her subjects, to participate in the process of making these relics meaningful. If, as Berger
continues, "the past becomes an integral part of the process of people
making their own history, then all photographs would acquire a living

Lucy (From Lucille Clifton, *Generations: A Memoir* [New
York: Random House, 1976]; reprinted courtesy of
Lucille Clifton)

context, they would continue to exist in time, instead of being arrested
moments."[26] The next sections of Clifton's text exemplify the creation of
a living context for the images of two ancestors whose lives were cut short
long before Lucille was born. Reproducing their images invites readers
to imagine details of the histories the memoir can only sketch.

As readers have learned earlier in the text, Lucy is Caroline's daughter. But Lucy's photograph surprises. It is the most formal portrait in the
volume. The drapery and the side chair on which the woman's right arm
rests are typical trappings of the nineteenth-century photography studio.
The subject's elegant gown completes the bourgeois ambiance. But one
is reminded that for African Americans in the late nineteenth century, upward social mobility and political resistance often went hand in hand.[27] If
the difference in the way they dress to be photographed suggests a social
distance between Lucy and her mother, the erectness of Lucy's carriage
substantiates a psychological affinity. Lucy, too, is a Dahomey woman.

The photograph's caption, citing Whitman, underscores the spirit of resistance: "I do not trouble my spirit to vindicate itself or be understood, / I see that the elementary laws never apologize" (19–20). Finally, even if only a result of aging, the lights and shadows of the photograph create the effect of Lucy's standing in a circle of light. The rhetoric of the image and the verbal text combine to suggest the analogy between her and an elemental force.[28]

Later in her career, Clifton becomes fascinated by the etymology of the name "Lucille," which is derived from the Latin for "bright light." In a poem first published in *An Ordinary Woman*, she honors her foremother and her name:

> light
> on my mother's tongue
> breaks through her soft
> extravagant hip
> into life.
> Lucille
> she calls the light,
> which was the name
> of the grandmother
> who waited by the crossroads
> in Virginia
> and shot the whiteman off his horse,
> killing the killer of sons.
> light breaks from her life
> to her lives . . .
>
> mine already is
> an afrikan name.[29]

Although the drama of Lucy's story is as striking as the light in which she is figured, the text defers its telling. Instead, much like nineteenth-century slave narratives, it interpolates narratives of slaves whose treatment has been more severe than the protagonist's. Specifically, *Generations* records stories of slaves who have been bought as gifts for their masters. The first vignette ends with lines that summarize the chapter's theme: "'Oh slavery, slavery,' my Daddy would say. 'It ain't something in a book, Lue. Even the good parts was awful'" (22). What is awful in the present narrative is the father's death and Lue's grief. She views his corpse, sleeps in the room that was hers as a teenager, and, inevitably, remembers her father's stories. Lucy was the "first Black woman legally hanged in the state of Virginia" (27). Her crime was murdering the white father of her son.

As the narrator recites the story, it assumes the quality of a ballad of which Lucy is the heroine. If the words (printed on the page as prose) are arranged into verse form, their balladic effect becomes clear. "Harvey Nichols was a white man," the song begins, and a story of lost love unfolds:

> And this Harvey Nichols saw Lucy and wanted her
> And I say she must have wanted him too
> Because like I told you, Lue,
> she was mean and didn't do nothing
> she didn't want to do. (33)

Born under the shadow of slavery, Lucy and Harvey's son, Gene, is disfigured: "But oh, Lue, he was born with a withered arm / Yes, Lord, he was born with a withered arm" (34). These lines recur like a refrain. In the section devoted to Gene, it becomes clear that his maiming is psychological as well as physical. Here, however, more emphasis is placed on Lucy's victory. She was tried for her act and hanged, rather than lynched, a rare example of due process that the narrator attributes to Caroline Sale's standing in the community. The limitations of Caroline's status become painfully clear (and even the "good parts" of a slave's life are revealed as "awful") as the text represents her as a witness to her daughter's hanging. "And I know she made no sound but her mind closed around the picture like a frame and I know that her child made no sound and I turn in my chair and arch my back and make this sound for my two mothers and for all Dahomey women" (35).

Sounds and pictures and the sounds pictures evoke are precisely the theme this section develops. The photograph of Lucy is the catalyst for the story that is told through the sound of the father's remembered voice. The effect of the balladlike structure heightens the artifice of the tale. Despite the narrator's profession of knowing, she cannot know the facts of her foreparents' lives. Lucy remains "a shadow," which coincidentally was a popular term for photographs in the nineteenth century. In

Gene (From Lucille Clifton, *Generations: A Memoir*
[New York: Random House, 1976]; reprinted
courtesy of Lucille Clifton)

two paragraphs that constitute a coda to Lucy's story, her great-grand-daughter Lucille confronts the question of evidence. Neither her father nor her husband can provide the proof she desires: they tell her in effect what Caroline Sale has told her great-grandson about her missing name: "not to worry." But Fred Clifton goes further when he adds "that even the lies are true. In history, even the lies are true" (35). He reiterates the problematic of written and oral texts, history and legend, with which *Generations* wrestles. Pursuing what Morrison calls "another way of knowing," a way that depends on sounds and pictures, Lucille Clifton creates a literary text that recovers what history cannot. If it is no more or no less "true," it is no more or less a "lie."

The picture of a handsome, mustached black man wearing a derby, white shirt with bow tie, and a double-breasted jacket is surrounded by a thick black border. The torn border is probably the remnant of a frame pasted in a photo album, but it creates the visual effect of a bull's-eye. The target is Gene, the now grown child of tragedy. The caption quotes Whitman: "What is a man anyhow? what am I? what are you?" (38). Whitman's questions call the reader as much as Gene to account. Even more pointedly they echo the volume's dedication—"for Samuel Louis Sayles, Sr. / Daddy / 1902–1969 / who is Somewhere, / being a Man." Appropriately, Samuel's story, including his definition of manhood, opens this section.

As the memoir chronicles the lives of the generations the narrator has known firsthand, its gaps and omissions are no less evident but far more troubling. Here the impediment is not what the narrator does not know but what she cannot tell.

"Every man has to do three things in life, he had said, plant a tree, own a house and have a son" records the pronouncement Samuel makes on the occasion of buying a house (39). Given the volume's poignant references to the home as it stands at his death, one expects its purchase to add luster to his character. Yet the description of the event renders it more selfishly arrogant than heroic. Without consulting his wife, he purchases a home just as his last daughter, Lucille, is about to leave for college. No one is nearly so well pleased by his act as he is. Earlier revelations about Samuel Sayles had complicated his representation as heroic. For example, within a brief span of time he fathered three daughters by three women who had all been friends. His first wife died shortly after giving birth to Punkin, and then he married Lucille's mother; six months after Lucille was born, a third woman gave birth to Jo. Moreover, from the evidence of the text, Samuel Sayles failed to shelter the spirits of his children. At the moment he buys his house, Punkin is "walking the line" between her two natal families and the one she is procreating; Jo has begun "the slow dance between the streets and the cells" that she "practiced" for many years, and the coveted son had started the "young Black boy's initiation into wine and worse" (40). Only Lucille seems destined for success, having won a scholarship to Howard University. Almost as soon as this information is disclosed, however, the reader is told that Lucille loses her scholarship after two years and returns home in disgrace. Her father's stinging judgment of her becomes her judgment of him: her idol has feet of clay.

Nonetheless, his daughter remains reluctant to censure him. Samuel's weaknesses are clarified when his narrative is placed side by side with his father's. As Samuel recounts the story of Gene's life, he emphasizes the penchant for wild living that he attributes in large measure to his good looks (in particular the light brown eyes and cinnamon skin bequeathed Gene by his white father) and his misinterpretation of Caroline's dictum to do whatever he wants since he is from Dahomey women. Samuel will not condemn his father's "craziness" because he recognizes the burden his parents' death imposed. Nowhere is the psychological weight of that burden more tellingly betrayed than in Samuel's remembrance of his father: "Gene called me Rock, my Daddy would say" (47). The roles of protector and protected, nurturer and nurtured, parent and child are turned inside out. The son is the rock on whom the father leans. Samuel grows up believing what Caroline has said of the family: it produces strong women and weak men. Nevertheless, Samuel's final statement about Gene radiates compassion: he "didn't hardly get to be a man. He wasn't much past thirty years old when he died" (44).

Samuel, we are told in the lines that immediately follow these, is thirty-five when Lucille is born. Clearly he is not altogether wrong in asserting that he has broken the mold by becoming a strong man. But the pattern of children assuming adult responsibilities too soon and adults becoming too maimed to discharge their duties to their children leaves its mark on the generations that follow. If children cannot comprehend the lives of fathers like Gene who are defeated, even less can they understand the lives of fathers like Samuel who survive. "Once I asked him," Lucille recollects, "why he was so sure that he was going to heaven. God knows me, he said. God understands a man like me" (45). His daughter muses that her mother certainly had not. Neither does she.

The parents, we are told, do not sleep together for twenty years. At one point the narrator recollects that "we children were not close to Daddy in those days" (40). The nearest the narrative comes to an explanation is: "Now, he did some things, he did some things, but he always loved his family" (75). If Generations does not account for the fissures between husband and wife, father and daughter, several of Clifton's later poems explore the legacy of Samuel Sayles as a father who sexually abused his children. For example, the poem "June 20," published in The Book of Light in 1993, begins: "I will be born in one week / to a frowned forehead of a woman / and a man whose fingers will itch / to enter me."[30] The daughter, targeted even before her birth, is destined to suffer her father's compulsions, while the distraught mother looks on helplessly.

The situation that the poem describes is typical of the family dynamic reported in clinical studies of incest. According to Judith Herman, abused daughters view their fathers "as perfect patriarchs. They [are], without question, the heads of their households. Their authority within the family [is] absolute, often asserted by force. They [are] also the arbiters of the family's social life and frequently succeed in virtually secluding the women in the family." Yet, even if the members of the family fear them, they "[impress] outsiders as sympathetic, even admirable men." Such discrepancy deepens the daughter's confusion, since she may not only fear *and* admire the father but loves him as well. In Herman's studies, mothers were often ill or incapacitated and consequently powerless to protect their daughters. "At best, the daughters viewed their mothers ambivalently, excusing their weaknesses as best they could. . . . At worst, the relations between mother and daughter were marked by active hostility." Whether ambivalence or hostility, the rift between mother and daughter cannot be healed because its cause cannot be admitted. If they are fortunate, daughters become what another study of the subject calls "secret survivors," whose inability to name the abuse committed against them lingers into adulthood.[31]

The lingering compulsion to keep the family's secret may well explain the silence surrounding incest in *Generations*.[32] Nonetheless, one is struck by the similarity between the story Clifton does not tell and those stories that she does. Incest follows a pattern established in earlier generations of this family whereby children assumed roles that were rightly their parents'. Of course, the transgression of familial boundaries was one of slavery's gravest crimes. In Spillers's words, "the original captive status of African females and males in the context of American enslavement permitted none of the traditional rights of consanguinity."[33] Slavery undermined "Father's Law," as children legally followed the condition of the mother. At the same time, it rendered the social identities available to women under patriarchy—"mother," "daughter," "sister," "wife"—tenuous for Africans in the Americas. If the incest taboo polices the boundaries between adults and their children in sexual matters, what happens under conditions in which boundaries between adults and children—between the duties of adulthood and the entitlements of childhood—have long been blurred?

Unlike several of her contemporaries, notably Morrison and Gayl Jones, Clifton chooses not to address this question.[34] But her understanding of the history that surrounds it may inform the representation of her father in *Generations* and in subsequent poems. In "album," dated "12/2/92," she pens a portrait of her father as "this lucky old man." It reveals much more than the photograph of Samuel Sayles in *Generations*. The first stanza of "album" pictures him spiffily dressed, "waving and walking away / from damage he has done." Then, in an echo of the dedication to the memoir, the poems ends with this stanza of long-deferred resolution:

> today
> is his birthday somewhere.
> he is ninety.
> what he has forgotten
> is more than i have seen.
> what I have forgotten
> is more than he can bear.
> he is my father,
> our father,
> and all of us still love him.
> i turn the page, marveling,
>    jesus christ
>       what a lucky old man! [35]

Rather than a studio portrait, Samuel Sayles's photograph in *Generations* is a snapshot, as befits a subject who could only belong to the twentieth century. Gazing directly into the camera, a hint of a smile creasing his face, he stands erect; but the hand in his pocket suggests a bearing less than military. Suavely dressed, replete with vest, suspenders, tie, and sharply creased trousers, he looks like his father's son. The layout of the photo marks him as his daughter's father. Snapped outdoors in early spring, to judge from the budding trees, the photograph poses him equidistant between two houses. It is impossible to tell to which, if either, he belongs. That he owns himself seems an incontrovertible fact. In retrospect, it confirms Susan Sontag's observation that "the camera's rendering of reality must always hide more than it discloses." [36]

The passage from *Song of Myself* that serves as the epigraph to this section in *Generations* does not speak to who Samuel Sayles was—elsewhere he is described as the "first colored man to own a dining room set in Depew New York" (66)—but to what has become of him: "All goes onward and outward, nothing collapses, / And to die is different from what any one supposed, and luckier" (64). What follows is the briefest chapter in the book. Two pages recount the rituals of his funeral and burial, and a third charts the genealogy he passed on to Lucille. As the epigraph foretells, the experience of death, incomprehensible as it is, has left Samuel's

Samuel (From Lucille Clifton, *Generations: A Memoir*
[New York: Random House, 1976]; reprinted
courtesy of Lucille Clifton)

spirit intact. His spirit, rather than his misdeeds, is what the poet memorializes. In death he has been lucky indeed.

In her remembrance, Clifton dramatizes a particular moment wherein her father passes his spirit on to her. Fittingly for a poet, the medium is a letter, which Lucille receives during her first week away at college. What renders the deed wondrous to the poet is that the father is illiterate: he could write only his name. As represented in the text, the letter bears markers of illiteracy: "Dear Lucilleman, I miss you so much but you are there getting what we want you to have be a good girl signed your daddy" (69). A second letter from the mother underscores the effort writing the letter required ("Your daddy has written you a letter and he worked all day") and the love that it reflects (69). Interestingly, Samuel's letter constitutes a direct transcription of speech into writing. But turning speech into poetry is not a matter of mere transcription. Samuel's letter reminds the reader of how skillfully Clifton has transformed the voices of her people into literary art. Her craft is indeed, as Ostriker asserts, "a set of unerring gestures governed by a constraining and shaping discipline, so habitual that it seems effortless" (79). Perhaps this same "constraining and shaping discipline" allows Clifton at once to honor the father's memory and to challenge it.

The volume's final section is devoted to Clifton's mother, Thelma. Twelve years younger than her husband, she died a decade earlier, when she was only forty-four. By that time she had long suffered debilitating illnesses, the exact nature of which were apparently not diagnosed but which impaired her mentally as well as physically. In several of Clifton's short lyrics, Thelma Moore Sayles is an elusive figure, a dreamwalker moving through life in her own rhythm ("seemed like what she touched was hers / seemed like what touched her couldn't hold").[37] Her life is described as ineffably sad, yet her spirit is somehow "magical."

As if to illustrate the elusiveness of her personality, Thelma's section is introduced by two photographs. The larger one, a snapshot, depicts a brown-skinned woman with a full face and short hair seated next to a window; the top of her head is almost even with the bottom of the window, which is propped open by a book. Through the window, which dominates the photograph, one can detect only shadows, as if the window faced another building. Open venetian blinds create the effect of bars. The woman is seated left of center (the photograph has been cropped, and one wonders whether another figure had been posed on the other side of the window). She looks away from the camera, and she does not smile. Inset in the left-hand corner is a head shot of what appears to be the same woman when she was younger. It could well be a photo taken in a self-service booth of the kind that were once common in dime stores. Wearing a coat and a felt hat set at an angle over her shoulder-length hair, this woman looks directly into the camera, grinning.[38]

Whitman's words preceding this section proclaim, "They are alive and well somewhere, / The smallest sprout shows there is really no death" (62). Extending the theme of generativity announced in the epigraph, this last section begins with the mother's birth in Rome, Georgia, in 1914. Her father had migrated to the North on the same train that carried Samuel Sayles. Both men sought work that the steel mills promised; they were hired as strikebreakers. Although the section describes the environment

Thelma (From Lucille Clifton, *Generations: A Memoir*
[New York: Random House, 1976]; reprinted
courtesy of Lucille Clifton)

of the small industrial town, populated mainly by Polish immigrants, in
which these men and their families settled, it recounts few incidents in
Lucille's life. In part the various stories contained within the section illustrate the speaker's claim that "the generations of colored folks are families" (64). But they also highlight the extent to which Thelma is absent
from the narrative one expects to be devoted to her life.

When she is present at all—in the briefest of anecdotes—she is the
figure of the first photograph: a woman whose life is off center and whose
spirit is confined. For a woman who is not mythically strong, the cost of
sustaining the family narrative is psychological isolation and sexual de-
privation. Thelma escapes into romantic fantasies at the movies, where
it is safe to do so. When she attempts to actualize the fantasy by buying
herself a wedding ring, for example, she is humiliated. The daughter in
the text recounts odd behavior of her own in an apparent attempt both to
identify with the mother and to make the mother seem less peculiar. But
the mother does not seem peculiar: what she seems instead is physically
ill and mentally and physically abused by her husband. Despite what it
shows, the text tells readers that everybody loved the mother and that she

"adored" her husband. To a discomfiting degree, the speaker reenacts the child's desire, so typical of incest victims, "to make things right" by declaring that the mother was "magic." In an unremarked irony, the speaker cites as an example Thelma's ability to jiggle locks loose. Yet death is the only escape she can finagle for herself.

What the text has shown us in both its words and images—and sometimes seemingly despite itself—amplifies the penultimate declaration: "Things don't fall apart. Things hold. Lines connect in thin ways that last and last and lives become generations made out of pictures and words just kept" (78). Revising Yeats's dire prophecy, Clifton pronounces a hard-won victory. The worst has already happened: her people have survived the anarchy and the "blood-dimmed tide" that in Yeats's vision were portents of a twentieth-century apocalypse.[39] No "center" survived the nightmare of slavery, but "things" held. So it is that his sister stands at Samuel Sayles's grave and addresses Caroline: "Mammy, it's 1969, and we're still here" (59). "Thin" lines connote the limited documentation that survives of their experiences as well as the fragility of the ties that bind this family together. Yet out of pictures and words, Clifton's speaker can perceive connections and create a history. Hers is an act of meditation, not documentation. Through contemplating their images and recreating their voices, the speaker intuits the meaning of her ancestors' lives. Through this meditative act, she becomes a moral witness who does justice to the memory of her kin and charts a path to the future for her daughters as well as her sons.

Like the other texts examined in *Worrying the Line*, *Generations* illustrates the meanings of the line as lineage and as literary tradition. At the same time that Clifton reconstructs her family history and uses her imagination to fill in the gaps in that line, her text inserts itself into the lines of American and African American literary history. *Generations* constitutes Clifton's "Song of Myself." The words and images through which she represents the genealogy of her family revise and extend representations of the nation's family inscribed in Whitman's poem. Clifton's memoir also revises and extends African American literary tradition. It builds on the foundation of the slave narrative. However, by extending the genealogical line to Africa, it evokes a history that starts in freedom rather than slavery. It maps the fitful journey to an official "freedom" that is circumscribed by racism, sexism, and poverty. Its exploration of family secrets anticipates the novels *Beloved* and *Corregidora*. Like those novels, *Genera-*

tions represents the ways that the scars of slavery imprint themselves on the psyches of people born long after the peculiar institution passed into history. Yet it holds out the promise that, as heirs of those who have survived the traumas of the past, the children of the late twentieth century will lay claim to a free future.

## four

Recollections
of Kin: *Beloved*
and *The Black*
Book

There is no place you or I can go, to think about or not
think about, to summon the presences of, or recollect the
absences of slaves; nothing that reminds us of the ones who
made the journey and of those who did not make it. There is
no suitable memorial or plaque or wreath or wall or park or
skyscraper lobby. There's no 300 foot tower. There's no small
bench by the road. There is not even a tree scored, an initial
that I can visit or you can visit in Charleston or Savannah or
New York or Providence or, better still, on the banks of the
Mississippi. And because such a place does not exist
(that I know of), the book had to. —Toni Morrison,
"A Bench by the Road"

With a chilling eloquence, Toni Morrison explained to an interviewer the
raison d'être for her novel *Beloved*. "There is no place you or I can go,
to think about or not think about, to summon the presences of, or recollect the absences of slaves; nothing that reminds us of the ones who
made the journey and of those who did not make it. . . . And because
such a place does not exist (that I know of), the book had to." It was
to fill a void in the historical memory, a void that was itself a moral indictment of the nation. Despite the 250 years during which Africans and
their descendants were enslaved in the United States, no monument of
any kind commemorated their lives or deaths. Neither those who had enslaved them nor those who were descended from them had been able to
give public acknowledgment to their existence. *Beloved* was to memori-

alize those who had been held captive on U.S. soil as well as those who perished on the voyage here. It was "to summon" or to invoke their presence as well as to "recollect" their absence. That recollection was at once a gathering together again and a call to memory. In both senses, *Beloved* compels and enables recollections of kin.[1]

Beginning with the story of a single slave, then an enslaved family, the novel interpolates stories of a community whose members have lived through bondage and who will be bonded together through an ethic of caring and love. The process of bonding requires the willingness of characters to share stories about what they do not want to remember, stories that frequently focus on lost kin. Most dramatic, the protagonist Sethe calls her murdered daughter to mind and then unintentionally summons Beloved in the flesh. But Sethe also remembers the African-born mother (her "ma'am") who speaks in an unknown tongue, bears the mark of another country, and dances the "antelope," a memory that connects her to her other granddaughter Denver, to whom Sethe gives the epithet "the little antelope" in the womb. Reluctantly, Stamp Paid recalls the wife he has been forced to hand over to his master's son, who has chosen her as a concubine. In telling the story, Stamp recognizes that in holding on to his anger toward his oppressor, he has failed to forgive the wife who was equally the oppressor's victim. Paul D remembers his kinsmen, the four other Sweet Home men and the forty-six men to whom he was chained in a box in Alfred, Georgia, and attempts to convey their courage and bravery to Sethe. These stories are told by characters who are in the present of the novel free black men and women living in a small community on the outskirts of Cincinnati, Ohio, in 1873. In the process of the telling, the characters begin to rid themselves of the invisible chains that have left them locked in psychological bondage almost a decade after slavery was legally abolished. Bound neither by slavery nor by blood, they choose to claim the freedom to love and protect each other.

"Recollection" in Morrison's novel also partakes of less familiar definitions of the word. According to the *Oxford English Dictionary*, it denotes "a religious or serious concentration of thought [and] conduct regulated by such concentration" as well as "composure, calmness of mind, and self-possession." A concentration that is at least serious and often spiritual, if not religious, is modeled by the novel's characters for its readers. Indeed, the place that is set aside for those moments of concentration or contemplation is named the "Clearing." But characters may seek these moments in places that they find or fashion individually. Sethe retreats often to the "keeping room," or the parlor, to "talk-think," the mode of spiritual expression that she has adopted in place of prayer. Denver finds her bower hidden by post oaks and five boxwood bushes planted in a ring, where, "veiled and protected by live green walls, she felt ripe and clear, and salvation was as easy as a wish." [2] Paul D hides in the breast of "this land that was not his" and is "astonished by its beauty" (268). At the end of a prolonged and difficult process, some of these characters achieve the self-possession that is, in the words of Baby Suggs, grandmother, former slave, cobbler, unlicensed preacher, and the novel's prophetic voice, "the prize."

Beloved is Morrison's fifth novel and the first to take up the challenge of the topic of slavery directly.[3] Writing as a novelist rather than a historian, she has explained that she was not concerned with slavery as a subject with a capital "S." She was concerned instead with the lives of those who lived the experience. "It was about these anonymous people called slaves." She found incredible "what they do to keep on, how they're able to make a life, what they're willing to risk, however long it lasts in order to relate to each other."[4] The sense of responsibility she felt toward "these unburied, or at least ceremoniously unburied, people made literate in art" was overwhelming. Writing about them, she told Gloria Naylor in their published "conversation," she was aware of "the inner tension, the artistic inner tension" those people created in her: "[T]he fear of not properly, artistically, burying them, is extraordinary."[5]

As Avery Gordon observes, "Morrison names and remembers the anonymous slave and in so doing she also inscribes within each unique individual name a genealogy of the anonymous. Denver is named after the white girl who helped deliver her; Sethe is named after the only man her mother 'put her arms around'; Baby Suggs names herself after her husband; Stamp Paid signs himself all accounts paid." Each name is "a sign of life, a set of memories, a history. Yet each name also offers a story of why the people who hold these names are anonymous, why they have not counted, even if they have against all odds counted for themselves."[6] What the novel demonstrates as well is how these people have counted for each other.

Although Beloved is the first of Morrison's novels to make slavery its central focus, all her previous work reveals a preoccupation with history as lived experience. The Bluest Eye re-creates life in Lorain, Ohio, the small midwestern steel town where Morrison grew up in the 1930s. The novel takes us inside the houses and the lives of black southern migrants whose children try to define themselves in a world that gives them no reliable self-images. *Sula* looks back to World War I, lingers in the 1920s, and then rushes forward to the 1960s in the Bottom, a fictional neighborhood where Morrison limns the "elaborately socialized world of black people."[7] But, as the opening paragraph makes plain, the world that the novel describes no longer exists, and it cannot be regained. In *Song of Solomon*, by contrast, the legacy of the past is a puzzle that can, with great effort, be put back together. For Milkman to reconstruct that legacy, he must go to the places where his ancestors lived, meet the people who knew them, and identify their names in the lore that constitutes the folk history. Son and Jadine, the protagonists of *Tar Baby*, struggle to debate and define the usefulness of the past: whether as it continues in the static existence of Son's hometown of Eloe, in the tethered lives of Jadine's surrogate parents and their employer, Valerian Street, or in the mythic stories of the blind horsemen of Iles des Chevaliers.

In 1974 Toni Morrison wrote an article for the *New York Times Magazine*, describing a book she had just finished working on. Before detailing the process of its production, she outlined the vision that inspired it:

> Like every other book, it would be confined by a cover and limited to type. Nevertheless, it had to have—for want of a better word—a sound, a very special sound. A sound made up of all the elements that distinguished black life (its peculiar brand of irony, oppression, versatility, madness, joy, strength, shame, honor, triumph, grace and stillness) as well as those qualities that identified it with all of mankind (compassion, anger, foolishness, courage, self-deception and vision). And it must concentrate on life as lived—not as imagined—by the people: the anonymous men and women who speak in conventional histories only through their leaders. The people who had always been viewed only as percentages would come alive in "The Black Book."[8]

Many commentators and the author herself have characterized Morrison's greatest novel in quite similar terms. Not only is *The Black Book* a source for *Beloved* in a very specific sense; it also represents a model for reconstructing the past that is tropological, interactive, and communal. A fictional reimagining rather than a historical reconstruction, *Beloved* shares these same qualities. Both challenge conventional historical discourse. Both determine to excavate the lives of the anonymous black folk who have been "disremembered and unaccounted for" (*Beloved*, 274). Both reflect what Morrison views as the necessity for black people "to find some way to hold on to the useful past without blocking off the possibilities of the future" ("Rediscovering," 14).

Published after the civil rights movement had gone into eclipse and in the waning years of the Black Power movement, *The Black Book* was intended in part as a corrective, particularly to rhetoric that had grown more and more disparaging of "the Negro" and "his" history.[9] It sought to bring honor to those whose courage and bravery had been dismissed, overlooked, or misunderstood. It sought, moreover, to honor those who had not perceived themselves to be heroic. Their self-understanding could be summed up in the words of the epigraph preceding a photograph of a black cowboy, "we was mostly 'bout survival / 'Bout living anyhow."[10] Although it included artifacts belonging to the famous (such as a handwritten letter from Frederick Douglass to an acquaintance who wished him well on the occasion of his controversial second marriage to a white woman and a letter to W. E. B. Du Bois from a white academic who inquired whether the Negro sheds tears), its focus was on those whose lives and deeds had been lost to history. To its readers, *The Black Book* was a call to remember.

Generically, *The Black Book* can be described as a scrapbook; it documents the history of African Americans through posters, newspaper articles, letters, speeches, bills of sale, spirituals and blues, work songs and folktales, children's rhymes, drawings, advertisements, photographs (both family pictures and documentary photographs of quilts, tools, furniture, and other artifacts), recipes, patent applications, sheet music, playbills and movie stills, formulas for conjure, and dream interpretations. In a Whitmanesque conceit, *The Black Book* subsumes the experience of the group within a collective "I." Neither a vehicle of social protest nor a compilation of individual achievement, the volume announces itself on the back jacket as "everything I have hated . . . , all the ways I have failed . . . , all the ways I have survived . . . , all the things I have seen . . . , and all the things I have ever loved." It becomes, in other words, a "memory book" for African Americans.[11]

If it documents the creativity of black Americans as expressed through story and song, *The Black Book* records their victimization during and after

# SUNLIGHT SOAP

"So Clean and White"

Advertisement for Sunlight Soap (From Middleton Harris, *The Black Book* [New York: Random House, 1974])

slavery. If it celebrates African American ingenuity as documented by patents filed for the fountain pen, clothes dryer, airship, lawn sprinkler, egg beater, hot comb, and corn harvester, it documents the ways in which African American bodies and personae were debased and caricatured to sell products from Sunlight Soap to Aunt Jemima pancakes. If it documents political resistance in black communities from nineteenth-century slave uprisings to abolitionism to twentieth-century civil rights activism, it also reproduces pages from the family Bible of black slave owners. The evidence of self-hatred and betrayal it offers intensifies the power of the final selection of photographs and drawings of individuals and groups of individuals, a gallery of family pictures, as it were, that signify love and kinship.

The Black Book is filled with what Morrison once described as "the kind of information you can find between the lines of history. It sort of falls off the page, or it's a glance and a reference. It's right there in the intersection where an institution becomes personal, where the historical becomes people with names."[12] The facts and images in The Black Book do not constitute a narrative; they invite readers to construct narratives of their own.

The book's initial image is a photograph of an African woman, over which is inscribed a quotation from the West African writer Bernard Dadié: "I was there when the Angel drove out the Ancestor. I was there when the waters consumed the mountains."[13] Like the reference to "sound" in the article on The Black Book, the reference here to "ancestor" strikes a note familiar to readers of Morrison's essays and interviews. The ancestral sound echoes on every page of Beloved, inscribed in the speech of its characters, the lullabies and love songs they sing, the work songs they chant and choreograph, the stories they tell, the sermon Baby Suggs preaches, and the voices of the women who finally arrive to rescue Sethe. As they had in the Clearing, the voices of the women outside 124 Bluestone Road "searched for the right combination, the key, the code, the sound that broke the back of words. Building voice upon voice until they found it, and when they did it was a wave of sound wide enough to sound deep water and knock the pods off chestnut trees. It broke over Sethe and she trembled like the baptized in its wash" (261). In Beloved, Morrison writes as much of the "sound" as is translatable; in The Black Book, the reader is invited to supply it.

Significantly, The Black Book, as Morrison emphasizes in "Rediscovering Black History," "was not a book to be put together by writers" but one to be put together by "collectors—people who had the original raw material documenting our life" (16). Authorial credit for The Black Book went to Middleton Harris, "with the assistance of Morris Levitt, Roger Furman, and Ernest Smith." Morrison was the in-house editor. Even though The Black Book does not carry her signature, Toni Morrison's engagement with it was intense. She told one newspaper reporter that "nothing could have interfered with my putting this book together."[14] In "Rediscovering Black History," she begins a passage describing in first person singular the need to recover a usable past and the genesis of the project ("Because of the work I do, my thoughts turned naturally to a book. But a book with a difference"). Then she shifts pronouns: "We called it 'The Black Book'" (16). The "we" included the authors, the designer, the production manager, and Morrison, who "built the book, item by item," producing in the end "an organic book which made up its own rules" (16).

Those "rules" complemented the aesthetic that Morrison was shaping in her fiction. Like Langston Hughes, Zora Neale Hurston, Ralph Ellison, and Amiri Baraka before her, Morrison formulated a literary aesthetic from her study of and appreciation for African American art in general and African American music in particular. Her formulations, shared mainly in interviews, have been remarkably consistent for three decades. In one statement, she averred, "If my work is faithfully to reflect the aesthetic tradition of Afro-American culture, it must make conscious use of the characteristics of its art forms and translate them into print: antiphony, the group nature of art, its functionality, its improvisational nature, its relationship to audience performance." [15] To achieve the last and, "having at my disposal only the letters of the alphabet and some punctuation," she explained on another occasion, "I have to provide places and spaces so that the reader can participate. Because it is the affective and participatory relationship between the artist or the speaker and the audience that is of primary importance, as it is in these other art forms that I have described." [16] The Black Book aspires to the same standard.

Morrison's engagement with the project was not only professional but deeply personal as well. An article in Publishers Weekly was headlined: "Editor's Personal Commitment Shapes a Scrapbook of Black History." In the article Morrison proudly cited the book as one "the average black person could relate to on a personal level" and consequently an example of "real black publishing," in contrast to the academic studies that had begun to appear with some frequency. Her tone was joyous as she detailed the process of working on the project: "Everyone I knew was sending me material. I even called my mother!" She recounted several favorite entries and their provenance: "I got a recipe for tun mush, a 19th century cornmeal concoction from a cook I know; my aunt wrote up a story on how her sharecropping family escaped North in 1919 with only $30. cash; a friend of mine gave me her uncle's 'dream book.'" Then, in parentheses, the reporter captures the particularly personal tone to which Morrison had referred. Thinking about the dream book, Morrison wondered: "(Did you know that if you dream about bed bugs it means your friends are unfaithful and the number to play is 522?)."[17]

The published book contains traces of her personal investment. Morrison's parents, Ramah and George Carl Wofford, are among those acknowledged for their contributions to the text "with stories, pictures, recollections and general aid." A small oval photograph of her mother appears on the cover, surrounded by a playbill from a show starring Ethel Waters and two other images of Waters from early and late in her career as well as a Sambo doll; Ramah Wofford's photograph is also among the family pictures reproduced on the closing pages.

The book has no chapters, but quotations from African and African American oral and written literature introduce the basic themes. While the organization of *The Black Book* is not strictly chronological, the first section reproduces documents and images of Africa; the second section focuses on slavery. The heading of the latter is a quotation by Aimé Césaire: "And they sold us like beasts, and they counted our teeth . . . and they felt our testicles and they tested the lustre or dullness of our skin" (7). Following are documents, arranged in no discernible order, that include a poster advertising a slave auction in Charleston in 1833; three images of a black man, identified only as Gordon, including one of his scarred back; an image of a group of fugitive slaves escaping across a river; accounts of George Washington and Thomas Jefferson as slaveholders; documents from black slaveholders; and stories and songs of resistance that circulated in slave communities.[18] Reprinted in this section is an article titled "A Visit to the Slave Mother Who Killed Her Child." It is a contemporary account of Margaret Garner's crime and punishment, the historical event that is the kernel of the plot of *Beloved*. Written by P. S. Bassett, a Baptist clergyman, the article claims to record the unnamed, imprisoned mother's own "detailed account of her attempt to kill her children." Acting on his abolitionist sympathies, Bassett writes that he "inquired if she was not excited almost to madness when she committed the act. No, she replied, I was as cool as I now am; and would much rather kill them at once, and thus end their sufferings, than have them taken back to slavery, and be murdered by piece-meal" (10). The article cites as well the words of her mother-in-law, who witnessed the act "but said she neither encouraged nor discouraged her daughter-in-law, —for under similar circumstances she should probably have done the same." In "Rediscovering Black History," Morrison recounts her response to the

## Forty Dollars Reward.

WHEREAS a certain CHARLES TRAVIS, on the 11th Ult. ran away with FRANCES DE BAPTIST, lawful Wife of JOHN DE BAPTIST, of Fredericksburg, Virginia, and stole, from said Baptist, a Sky-blue superfine Broadcloth Coat with double-gilt Buttons, a Pair of black Velvet Breeches with Basket Buttons of the same Colour, and rode away a large roan Horse : Whoever apprehends the said CHARLES TRAVIS, and brings him to this Town, or lodges him in any Gaol of the United States, shall, in Addition to the Rewards offered in the Virginia Herald, and Maryland Journal, receive FORTY DOLLARS, and all reasonable Expenses, paid by                                       JOHN BOYES.

Fredericksburg, Virginia, July 6, 1790.

## Twenty Dollars Reward.

ABSCONDED, from his Master's Service, about Six Weeks ago, a MULATTO MAN, named WILL; he is about 35 Years of Age, short in Stature, bow-legged, but otherwise well made; he is addicted to Drunkenness, and, when sober, his Eyes have the Appearance of his being in Liquor; his Address is awkward, and attended with a considerable trembling of his Hands: He formerly belonged to the late Mr. JONATHAN HUDSON, and used to attend at his Table and travel with him; from which Circumstances, he is, probably, well known in the State—he has lived with me a few Years. Whoever will deliver him to the Subscriber, shall receive a Reward of TWENTY DOLLARS, including what the Law allows.                     HARRY DORSEY GOUGH.

Perry-Hall, June 29, 1790.

## Twenty Dollars Reward.

RAN AWAY, on the 13th Instant, from the Subscriber, living on Elk-Ridge in Ann-Arundel County, a NEGRO MAN, named HARRY, about 40 Years of Age, near 6 Feet high, has Knots on his left Leg, which is larger than his right, and on his great Toes, and has red Eyes: Had on, and took with him, a Tow-Linen Shirt and Trousers, brown Cloth Coat, brown Corduroy Jacket and Breeches, Two Pair of Yarn Stockings, one white and the other blue mixed, a white Shirt, Felt Hat, and red Silk Handkerchief. Whoever takes up said Negro, and secures him in Gaol, so that his Master may get him again, shall receive, if 20 Miles from Home, *Eight Dollars*; if 40 Miles, *Sixteen Dollars*; and, if out of the State, the above Reward, including legal Fees, and reasonable Charges, if brought Home.                     NICHOLAS DORSEY.

July 19, 1790.

Notices for runaway slaves (From Middleton Harris, *The Black Book* [New York: Random House, 1974])

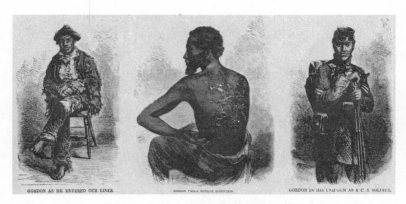

Gordon, "a typical negro" (From Middleton Harris, *The Black Book* [New York: Random House, 1974])

article: "I . . . lived through a despair quite new to me but so deep it had no passion at all and elicited no tears" (16).

In her essay "The Site of Memory," Morrison lauds the achievement of the slave narratives, those texts by writers such as Frederick Douglass, William Wells Brown, and Harriet Jacobs that laid the foundation of modern black literature. She asserts that "no slave society in the history of the world wrote more—or more thoughtfully—about its own enslavement." However, she goes on to note the tremendous pressure on the slave narrators to shape the experiences they recorded in order "to make [them] palatable to those who were in a position to alleviate them." Over and over, the writers pull the narrative up short with a phrase such as, "But let us drop a veil over these proceedings too terrible to relate."[19] As a twentieth-century black writer who has taken slavery as her subject, Morrison views her own task very differently: "My job becomes how to rip that veil drawn over 'proceedings too terrible to relate'" (110). These proceedings involved in the main the experiences of women—their sexual exploitation and the rupture of the mother/child bond, the very experiences that Morrison places at the center of her novel.

"Moving that veil aside" requires Morrison to trust her own recollections and those of others; but, she writes, "memories and recollections won't give me total access to the unwritten interior life of these people. Only the act of imagination can help me" (111). Using the term "literary archeology," Morrison describes her method as journeying to a site and surveying the remains that were left behind. Through this process, she can "reconstruct the world that these remains imply." The catalyst for the imaginative act is an image, a picture that enables "an exploration of an interior life that was not written" and "the revelation of a kind of truth" (112). She emphasizes that unlike some writers, the approach that is "most productive and trustworthy" for her "is the recollection that moves from the image to the text" (115).

This concept of the image is the point at which the historical method implicit in *The Black Book* and the narrative strategies operating in *Beloved* intersect. A scrapbook reproduces a series of images in response to which readers construct their own narratives. Images elicit different stories from different readers at different times. Images in *The Black Book* provoke a kind of storytelling that is participatory, improvisational, and collective. The number of possible stories is infinite, but their sum would total a black history "truer" than that available in archival documents or scholarly texts. In their collectivity, these stories would indeed constitute the "black book."

*The Black Book* was marketed to a mass audience: the paperback edition was priced at $5.95, and the book contained an introduction, conversational in tone, by television star Bill Cosby. Cosby began with a conceit of his own: "[S]uppose a three-hundred-year-old black man had decided, oh, say, when he was about ten, to keep a scrapbook." His description of the book as "a folk journey of Black America" underscored its nonacademic appeal (v). "Folk" also suggested that the book was more than merely a commercial venture; it was hoped that *The Black Book* would reach an audience beyond the traditional book-buying public.[20] Finally, the adjective "folk" aptly conveyed the sense that this book not only documented a shared experience but could be read as one as well. Even the dimensions of the book (8¼" by 11½") welcomed more than one reader at a time. Not intended for reading as a solitary practice, *The Black Book* was instead designed to replicate the interactive dynamic of storytelling. This dynamic is, of course, evident throughout *Beloved*. As she relates the narrative of her birth, Denver, who is one of the novel's finest storytellers, enacts the process: "Denver was seeing it now and feeling it—through Beloved. Feeling how it must have felt to her mother. Seeing how it must have looked. And the more fine points she made, the more detail she provided, the more Beloved liked it. So she anticipated the questions by giving blood to the *scraps* her mother and grandmother had told her—and a heartbeat. The monologue became, in fact, a duet" (78; emphasis added). If its producers were collectors, readers of *The Black Book* were invited to recollect, to give "blood to the scraps" it contained. They could fill in the gaps, add fine points, and provide details that were part of no official history, the details to which only they and their relatives were privy. Told in response to a book that provided countless occasions for recollections of kin, their narratives become the book's "heartbeat."

According to Morrison, images inspired the narrative that became *Beloved*. In her conversation with Gloria Naylor, Morrison identified specific "fragments of stories" and images. Along with the Garner story was a James Van Der Zee photograph, published in *The Harlem Book of the Dead*, a collection that documented what Morrison described as "this fashion of photographing beloved, departed people in full dress in coffins or in your arms."[21] The picture that caught Morrison's attention was of a beautifully dressed young girl lying in a coffin, with a bouquet of roses on her chest and a crown of roses in her hair. According to Van Der Zee, the girl had been shot at a party and refused on her deathbed to identify the shooter, perhaps a jealous ex-boyfriend, saying instead, "I'll tell you tomorrow." The juxtaposition of this image and the Garner story catalyzed Morrison's imagination. Indeed, it was only after seeing the image that she said she understood her obsession with the clipping. The novel that resulted has been described as an "image-text."

Within the novel, the triggering of memory by image is a recurrent motif. The novel's characters do not merely fail to remember the past; the past is what they work actively to forget. Sethe, who in the beginning wants mainly to "keep the past at bay" (42), is constantly ambushed by her memories. "She might be hurrying across a field, running practically, to get to the pump quickly and rinse the chamomile sap from her legs. Nothing else would be in her mind. . . . Then something. The plash of water, the sight of her shoes and stockings awry on the path where she had flung them; or Here Boy lapping in the puddle near her feet, and suddenly there was Sweet Home rolling, rolling, rolling out before her eyes, and although there was not a leaf on that farm that did not make her want to scream, it rolled itself out before her in shameless beauty" (6). The reiteration of "rolling" signifies the absence of control that Sethe has over her memory; it threatens not only to ambush but to overwhelm her. The conflicting emotions that she feels about Sweet Home intensify her need *not* to remember it.

Then Paul D's unexpected arrival, which follows immediately after the scene just discussed, forces Sethe to remember Sweet Home in the same complicated way. She remembers the beauty of the love that the Sweet Home men had for each other and for her, and she remembers the violation she suffered. When Sethe responds to Paul D's question, "What tree on your back?" she begins to tell the story of the boys who abused her and stole her milk. She answers Paul D as she makes a pan of biscuits. At one point she stops speaking, and the narrator observes: "Now she rolled out the dough with a rolling pin" (16). Ordering her experience as she arranges the circles of dough in rows, she begins to exert control over her recollections by arranging them into a story that can be told.

In fiction, Morrison argues, the "act of imagination is bound up with memory" ("Site," 119). Sethe uses the term "rememory" to bracket the two. She describes it as "a picture floating around there outside my head. I mean, even if I don't think it, even if I die, the picture of what I did, or knew, or saw is still out there" (36). Rememory is, in my view, the process of bringing that picture to consciousness, a process that requires an act of imagination. As Deborah McDowell glosses Sethe's "really interesting locution," "[E]very revisitation of an actual event recreates or re-members, puts back together that which was, but that putting back together doesn't bear a uniform relation to what was there before: memory is a creative process."[22] Mae Henderson suggests that "rememory is something which possesses or haunts one, rather than something which one possesses." It is, she continues, "that which makes the past part of one's present."[23] To master it, rememory requires that one relive the painful experience that one has tried, in vain, to forget.[24]

The novel's characters are not alone in their refusal to remember: slavery is the experience everyone wants to forget. Black people do not want to remember it any more than whites do. Morrison has referred to the "national amnesia" that surrounds the subject.[25] Margaret Garner's story was, after all, once a national cause célèbre. The fugitive escaped from a Boone County, Kentucky, plantation with her husband, four children, and mother- and father-in-law in January 1856. After crossing the frozen Ohio River, the family sought refuge with relatives in Cincinnati. They were quickly discovered. As the slavecatchers surrounded the house where the family hid, Margaret Garner slashed the throat of her three-year-old daughter. She was immediately jailed for murder. Abolitionists took up her cause: the most prominent antislavery lawyer in Cincinnati, John Jollife, defended her in the courtroom, and Levi Coffin and Frederick Douglass agitated for her release. Garner's owner, Archibald

Gaines, belonged to a politically prominent family, and proslavery apologists were equally engaged. Press attention was intense. An impassioned speech by women's rights activist Lucy Stone made headlines; Stone intimated that Gaines had fathered the murdered child. Novelists, painters, and poets memorialized the slave mother who killed her child. Frances Watkins Harper recited "The Slave Mother" from lecterns throughout the "free" states and later alluded to the Garner case in her 1892 novel *Iola Leroy*. Mathew Brady's photograph of Thomas Satterwhite Noble's painting "The Modern Medea" was widely circulated.[26] The publicity helped win Garner's acquittal, but the surviving members of the family were sold "down the river" to a slaveholder in Arkansas. Despite the hue and cry her act evoked, once slavery was abolished, Margaret Garner virtually vanished from the national imaginary.

Clearly, Morrison's novel does not document the facts of the case.[27] Neither can it recover the "interior life" of the slaves. *Beloved* itself is rememory; it imagines the pictures that women like Margaret Garner might have carried around in their heads and the stories they might have told about them had there been anyone able to listen. Moreover, in Caroline Rody's persuasive reading, "by dramatizing the psychological legacy of slavery, it portrays that 'interior' place in the African-American psyche where a slave's face still haunts."[28] *Beloved* is a meta–black book that explores the crucible of the African American experience.

Once Sethe finds an audience eager to listen to the stories these images inspire, she begins to take pleasure in sharing them. So when Beloved asks Sethe to "tell me your diamonds" (the image that for Beloved unlocks part of the past), Sethe complies and discovers a perspective on the past that is new not only for her but also for the novel's whole community of ex-slaves. Mae Henderson asserts that "lacking a discourse of her own, Sethe's task is to transform the residual images ('rememories') of her past into a historical discourse shaped by narrativity." Drawing an analogy between the challenges faced by the protagonist and those faced by the author, Henderson goes on to observe that "like Morrison, Sethe must learn to represent the unspeakable and unspoken in language— and more precisely, as narrative." For Sethe, "re-memory functions to re-collect, re-assemble, and organize into a meaningful sequential whole through . . . the process of narrativization."[29] "Amazed" by the "profound satisfaction Beloved got from storytelling," Sethe is equally astonished by the satisfaction she derives from it herself. She learns that the past—the mention of which was so painful that she and Baby Suggs "had agreed without saying so [that it] was unspeakable"—can be remembered and reclaimed (58).

One reason is that the past is not unrelievedly bleak: Sethe remembers the small victories she won in her struggle to retain her humanity under a system designed to dehumanize her. She recalls them as she sits in her kitchen, surrounded by the daughter she claims and the daughter who would claim her. As they perform their tasks of sorting peas and stewing rutabagas, doing "intimate things in place," as Morrison once termed women's work, Beloved prevails upon Sethe to remember.[30] The image of diamonds is the catalyst for a narrative that evinces Sethe's determination to have beauty and ritual in her life. The diamonds are actually crystal earrings that Mrs. Garner has given Sethe for a wedding present. When Sethe discovers that as slaves she and Halle will have "no ceremony, no preacher" to mark their marriage (58), she is determined to improvise some ritual of her own. She fashions a wedding dress out of stolen fabric, mainly remnants that Mrs. Garner has put aside for mending: torn pillow cases, a burned dresser scarf, and mosquito netting. Mrs. Garner is bemused by Sethe's request. Her response reflects the historical reality that since slaves as chattel could not make contracts, marriages between them were not legally binding.[31] Mrs. Garner is too moved by Sethe's gestures to be angry, and she proffers the gift of the earrings. Sethe's impulse accords with the principles Zora Neale Hurston set forth in "Characteristics of Negro Expression": "There is an impromptu ceremony always ready for every hour of life. No little moment passes unadorned."[32] Sethe and Halle exchange their vows and consummate their marriage in a cornfield. Sethe has refused to accept the definition of marriage that is available to her as a slave, just as she will later refuse to accept the definition of motherhood available to her as a slave.

If the image of the earrings retrieves a memory that Sethe welcomes and laughs about, recounting it unlocks memories that Sethe has long ago repressed. Beloved continues to ask questions, and as the three women run inside out of the rain and Sethe begins to comb Denver's hair, the questions become more familiar.[33] Beloved asks whether Sethe's mother had ever "fix[ed] up her hair," and Sethe begins to recount a series of incidents that reveal how thoroughly slavery disrupted the maternal relation (60). The incidents begin with the forced separation of mother and infant two to three weeks after birth, when the mother was sent back to the rice fields. The daughter's recollection of the mother's absence ("she never fixed my hair nor nothing. She didn't even sleep in the same cabin most nights I remember") is embittered. When she remembers the "one thing she did do," it is a memory of the mother showing her a scar, "a circle and a cross burnt right in the skin" (61). Her memories are sketchy in part, she realizes, because she cannot repeat any of the words her mother spoke; they were in a different language. Then Sethe recalls the act that severed forever the daughter's relation to her mother: the mother's hanging. And finally, she remembers "something she had forgotten she knew" (61). Nan, a woman from the mother's country who spoke the mother's language and who was the mother's friend and the daughter's wet nurse, has told Sethe that the mother threw her other children into the sea. She has kept Sethe alone and named her only because she is the child of the black man whom the mother "put her arms around" (62). The disruption of the maternal, meaning both the loss of the mother and the loss of the mother tongue, makes it impossible for Sethe or anyone else to reconstruct the complete family genealogy. But Beloved, as a consequence of her otherworldly knowledge, has asked the right questions. Denver, who has heard none of these stories before, takes note of the answers. Together they summon the presences and recollect the absences of their kin. In the process, they reconstruct as much of the family history as can be apprehended.

The first story that Denver tells is also triggered by an image: "[A] white dress knelt down next to her mother . . . its sleeve around her mother's waist. . . . And it was the tender embrace of the dress sleeve that made Denver remember the details of her birth" (29). The image of two female figures in a gesture of caring and concern anticipates the account of two women, Sethe and Amy Denver, who do something together "appropriately and well" (84). For Denver the story of her teenaged mother and the white girl who acts as her midwife is so familiar that she "steps into it" easily. In the conceit that follows, the story is a place, like the bower that is Denver's refuge and like 124 Bluestone Road, which she always regards not as a haunted house but as "a house peopled by the living activity of the dead" (29).[34] Denver takes pride in the way people condemn her family for its strangeness. She glories in "the downright pleasure of enchantment, of not suspecting but *knowing* the things behind things" (37). She happily enters the story that is a place, where she remembers and reimagines the history of her mother. In an interpolated narrative, Sethe tells the story of her motherlessness.

The extremity of Sethe's circumstances as she acts on her determination to give birth to her baby in freedom makes hers a profile in maternal courage. For Denver the story is important initially because it is about her; only gradually does she realize that in the telling she begins to understand her mother's feelings, her "interior life," as she endured the experiences. As readers, though, we are privy to Sethe's feelings immediately: the image of the antelope and its connection to her mother, whom she remembers through a synecdoche ("this particular back" atop which was a cloth hat as opposed to a straw one), through the mother's speaking her name ("Seth-thuh"), and through song and dance (30). The dance is called the antelope, perhaps as a gesture toward the tradition of African American dances that are named for animals—the monkey, the dog, the chicken—and that imitate their movements. Paradoxically, in the performance of the dance, the enslaved folk "shifted shapes and became something other. Some unchained, demanding other" like the baby in Sethe's womb, who will be born a free child (31).

Attending that birth is Amy Denver, who is, like Sethe, motherless, desperate, physically abused, and a runaway; she has been an indentured servant. In many of its details, their meeting on a riverbank echoes The Adventures of Huckleberry Finn, arguably the greatest nineteenth-century American novel of slavery.[35] Like Huck and Jim, Sethe and Amy are both on the run; their racial difference intensifies mistrust. Amy has been taught the racist codes of her culture: when she first sees Sethe, she proclaims, "Look there. A nigger. If that don't beat all" (32). Sethe, for her part, has heard Amy's voice and decided that she is a white boy. When she sees how raggedly she is dressed, Sethe decides that Amy is "trash." She is, however, relieved to discover Amy's gender; still, to be safe, Sethe uses an alias. The gender reversal, the use of an alias, and the stereotyped racial references all evoke scenes in Huckleberry Finn. In a textual gesture both humorous and unmistakable, Amy is looking for huckleberries when she meets Sethe.

More striking than these echoes are Morrison's revisions. Not only does she change the gender of her characters, but she gives the narrative authority to Sethe and her daughter. The evil of slavery does not become a crisis of conscience for a single white boy; it is a struggle for physical survival as well as for moral integrity for black adults and their families. Sethe and Denver judge the white character's morality, and Amy easily passes the test. She overcomes the racism she has been taught, and she saves Sethe's life. Neither woman expects nor wants a sustained relationship: Amy is on her way to Boston to buy velvet in the hope that she can experience beauty in her life. Sethe is on her way to what she believes is freedom in Cincinnati. Before they part company, though, Sethe acknowledges Amy's succor and sacrifice by giving her name to the baby. Through that act of naming, Amy becomes part of Denver's line.

In "Rediscovering Black History" Morrison writes, "[I]n spite of this tendency to have one set of rules for black history and another for white history, I was, in completing the editing of 'The Black Book,' overwhelmed with the connecting tissue between black and white history. The connection, however, was not a simple one of white oppressor and black victim." She cites a white man "branded" for helping a slave escape and the Jewish hospital that opened its doors to the black wounded during the Civil War Draft Riots. "The two histories merge in the book, as in life, in a noon heat of brutality and compassion, outrage and satisfaction" (20). Brutality and compassion are certainly prominent in *Beloved*. Schoolteacher and his charges represent the worst of plantation slavery; apologists for slavery often referred to the plantation as a school. Scenes of brutality recur in the narratives of all the novel's black characters. But the novel refuses simplistic categories of good and evil, victim and oppressor. In the narrative of Sethe and Amy is evidence that compassion could reach across the boundary of race, and when it did, it brought the participants the deepest satisfaction. They knew they had acted appropriately and well.

Paul D is surely the novel's most reluctant storyteller. He has deliberately locked the people, the places, and the images that could trigger his memories in a tin box. "It was some time before he could put Alfred, Georgia, Sixo, schoolteacher, Halle, his brothers, Sethe, Mister, the taste of iron, the sight of butter, the smell of hickory, notebook paper, one by one, into the tobacco tin lodged in his chest. By the time he got to 124 nothing in this world could pry it open" (113). The images are on deposit, as it were, and Paul D begins to draw down on his assets when he tells Sethe what has happened to Halle.[36] Even then he is not sure he can tell her his own story. He has never talked about his pain. "Not to a soul. Sang it sometimes, but I never told a soul" (71).

Early on he is described as "a singing man." He has an extensive repertoire: work songs, prison camp songs, and songs he has learned during the war. Some of the lyrics belong to the storehouse of African American secular song: "Lay my head on the railroad line, / Train come along, pacify my mind" and "Hard work ain't easy, / Dry bread ain't greasy" (40). But, as he becomes part of the household at 124 Bluestone Road, he improvises new songs to fit his new tasks and his new feelings. Morrison's characterization borrows a page from blues history; Paul D resembles the itinerant singers who were the creators and disseminators of the music. William Barlow describes the historical bluesmen as "cultural rebels" who "acted as proselytizers of a gospel of secularization in which the belief in freedom became associated with the personal mobility—freedom of movement in this world here and now, rather than salvation later on in the next."[37] Fittingly, the song that becomes Paul D's signature begins with a verse that describes his reunion with Sethe. For a traveling man like Paul D, making a home is a poignant possibility. The song's images convey both the intimacy of the welcome he was offered when he arrived and the anger that accompanied his departure:

> Bare feet and chamomile sap
> Took off my shoes; took off my hat.
> Bare feet and chamomile sap
> Gimme back my shoes; gimme back my hat.

The song ends with a couplet that in typical blues fashion combines the "floating lines" of the tradition and a reference specific to Paul D's personal situation: "Stone blind; stone blind. / Sweet Home gal make you lose your mind" (263). By the time he sings the final version of the song, Paul D has reconnected with the emotions that fueled the music the men made at Sweet Home, "where yearning fashioned every note" (40). For most of the novel, however, Paul D struggles toward the same goal as Sethe; he, too, wants to "keep the past at bay."

Consequently, Paul D remembers stories about the past that he does not tell. For example, Sethe crosses her ankles, and the gesture stirs Paul D's memory of Sixo and the Thirty-Mile Woman. Just as Sixo constitutes Paul D's standard for heroic resistance, the bond between Sixo and the Thirty-Mile Woman represents Paul D's romantic ideal. Sixo has twice walked the thirty-four-mile round trip to meet Patsy when he spots a trysting place two-thirds of the way; he asks permission from the Native

Americans whose structure it is to use it. Patsy agrees to walk part of the way to meet him. But they miss each other. Sixo walks past the destination they have agreed on, calls out her name, and, with the bravado that defines his character, instructs her not to move but to "breathe hard" and he can find her (24). He does. Theirs is a union Paul D envies but one he cannot imagine for himself. Two months is as long as he believes he can live with any woman. Even though women perceive "something blessed in his manner," Paul D is convinced that he is not the man Sixo was. Neither is he the storyteller: what he remembers in this instance is not the event itself, of course, but Sixo's narrative of the event. Sixo had told the story in "the particular way that made [the Sweet Home men] cry-dance" (25).

In order to set the record straight and to assuage the resentment that Sethe harbors toward the husband who has not joined her in their planned escape, Paul D decides to tell as much as he knows of Halle's story to Sethe. The image of butter smeared across Halle's face is almost too much for his wife to stand. Only when Sethe asks if Paul D has spoken to Halle is he forced to say something about his own situation. He tells her that he has been unable to speak because of the bit in his mouth. This image is too painful for Sethe, and her recitative interrupts the scene. When the dialogue resumes, Paul D extends a gesture of comfort and explains that he had not planned on telling Sethe about the bit. She responds that she had not planned on hearing it. Then, sensing that Paul D wants to say more about how the bit felt, she encourages him to speak. Sethe tells him: "Go ahead. I can hear it." He responds, "Maybe. Maybe you can hear it. I just ain't sure I can say it" (71). But he begins with the indirection that the novel suggests again and again is the only way that such painful stories can be told at all. Paul D starts by talking about Mister, the rooster from Sweet Home, who looked at him as he walked past with the bit in his mouth. The rooster's look was worse than the bit. "Mister, he looked so . . . free. Better than me. Stronger, tougher. Son a bitch couldn't even get out the shell by hisself but he was still king and I was . . . Mister was allowed to be and stay what he was. I wasn't allowed to stay what I was" (72). He breaks off the story abruptly and resolves to "keep the rest where it belonged," in the tobacco tin that takes up the space in his chest where his heart once was.

One impediment to the telling is that in a world where family counts for so much, Paul D is a solitary man. He does not remember his mother and has never seen his father. The youngest of three half brothers (Paul A, Paul F, and Paul D, sons of one mother and different fathers), he has been sold to Garner and kept at Sweet Home for twenty years. Apart from the family that he finds there, the only kinship he has known is in the prison camp at Alfred, Georgia. The omniscient narrator tells Paul D's story of his experiences in the camp. The story, with its emphasis on song and gesture, illuminates Paul D's reticence.

At the prison camp, Paul D is on a chain gang whose forced labor is made more efficient as well as bearable by the music and movement the men create. They "sang it out and beat it up, garbling the words so they could not be understood, tricking the words so their syllables yielded other meanings." They sang about the women they had known and the children they had been as well as of "bosses and masters and misses; of mules and dogs and the shamelessness of life" (108). With their hands, they beat out the rhythms of their work and their rage. In *Black Culture and Black Consciousness*, Lawrence Levine writes that "creating a rhythm for work—issuing instructions which helped laborers to synchronize their efforts, supplying a beat which timed work and controlled body movements—" was one important function of song during slavery. Equally important were the "psychic benefits" the singing afforded. In the novel "Hi Man" shows how invaluable the role of song leader was.[38] Not only does he set the rhythm for work; he creates and sustains the fraternal feeling that links the men psychically to each other. The sense of connection is not a luxury. The men understand that "if one pitched and ran—all, all forty-six, would be yanked by the chain that bound them and no telling who or how many would be killed. A man could risk his own life, but not this brother's" (109). To survive, they endure physical and sexual exploitation. A mudslide enables the entire line to escape. The men find refuge among a camp of Cherokee whose illness has prevented them from continuing on the Trail of Tears; the Indians cut the black men's chains. For Paul D, the experience of being unlinked is disorienting. He is the last to leave the camp because he can think of nowhere to go; he has no one he wants to find.

Initially, Paul D empathizes with Beloved because he assumes that she, too, is homeless. Indeed, if Sethe's response to the young woman in the black dress is to evacuate her bladder and replicate the process of giving birth, his is to offer a recitative on lost kin. Beloved reminds him of the many black people he has seen drifting in the aftermath of the Civil War. Many are trying to reunite their families, though a few are hoping to escape from unwanted relatives. "Odd clusters and strays of Negroes wandered the back roads and cowpaths from Schenectady to Jackson. Dazed but insistent, they searched each other out for word of a cousin, an aunt, a friend" who had offered to be someone they could call on. The women and children moved in groups, and the families they formed took on unusual configurations. The men traveled alone. For their safety "they followed secondary routes, scanned the horizon for signs and counted heavily on each other" (52–53). Paul D has been one of these men. Beloved's circumstances (her youth, her aloneness, and her new shoes) strike him as odd, but he tries to understand her in the context of this experience.

For eighteen years, Paul D lives on the road, yet his yearning for family is a recurrent theme. "Once, in Maryland, he met four families of slaves who had all been together for a hundred years: great-grands, grands, mothers, fathers, aunts, uncles, cousins, children. Half white, part white, all black, mixed with Indian. He watched them with awe and envy, and each time he discovered large families of black people he made them identify over and over who each was, what relation, who, in fact, belonged to who" (219). Paul D's increasing discomfiture around Beloved derives in part from his inability to identify her. The sexual relationship that develops between them discomfits the novel's readers, as it does Paul D. He insists that Beloved forces him to meet her in the cold house. She makes two requests: one, that he touch her "on the inside part," and second, that he call her by her name (116). Both are acts of radical reclamation, and both require, in the context of a history that has denied them the ownership of their bodies, the most intimate, physical connection. Only by joining with Beloved, the incarnation of the collective lost kin, is Paul D able to pry open the tin box and begin to narrativize his past. His ability and willingness to do so are conveyed in his desire at the end of the novel "to put his story next to [Sethe's]" (273). He is finally free to tell it.

Imagistically, the discourse of the novel reinforces the bond between Paul D and Sethe. Paul D's association with iron images, notably the iron bit that silences and dehumanizes him and the hand-forged iron of the chain that binds him to his brothers, is complemented by the novel's references to Sethe. When he first sees her scarred back, Paul D reads it as a sculpture, "the decorative work of an ironsmith too passionate for display" (17). More important, throughout the novel, Paul D remembers Sethe as the iron-eyed girl whom he has loved since first glimpsing her at Sweet Home. Their characters are irrevocably linked.

As the incarnation of lost kin, Beloved is the novel's figure for inexpressible loss. Caroline Rody's gloss of the name points out that it "names everyone in the official, impersonal rhetoric of the church and names everyone who is intimately loved, but does not name the forgotten." Rody asserts that "Morrison has the name perform precisely this last function; the novel's defining conceit is to call the unnamed 'beloved.'"[39] The images that swirl around the novel's most mysterious character—that reside in her unconscious and in the community's collective unconscious—cannot be shaped into coherent narratives. The four chapters that represent these images constitute what the novel names "unspeakable thoughts unspoken." They seem at first to represent the unspoken thoughts of Sethe, Denver, and Beloved sequentially; each character recollects the absences of those she has lost. But the references in the third chapter extend beyond experiences any of the characters could have had. Worrying the line in this novel shifts the narrative to another dimension. The history that is unknowable is conveyed through Beloved's consciousness. By the fourth chapter of the sequence, the voices blend into each other; readers cannot differentiate among the characters' thoughts. Together the chapters enact the inexpressibility of the grief for the "sixty million and more" to whom the novel is dedicated.

Sethe begins by offering an explanation to the daughter she insists needs none. Her recollection is part justification, part confession, and part plea for forgiveness and reconciliation.[40] Sethe remembers the experiences of her mother and her determination that her child would be treated as the daughter she never got to be. She remembers Baby Suggs and muses about the solace she took in pondering color after everything that she believed in failed her. She remembers Mrs. Garner, a woman she has treated as kindly as she would have treated her own mother; yet she wonders whether her dedication to Mrs. Garner as she prepared to escape Sweet Home made her miss a signal from her husband. She remembers Paul D and his harsh judgment that her love was "too thick." She reiterates her love for Beloved. Worrying the line that opens the chapter ("Beloved, she my daughter. She mine"), Sethe offers a clarification: "[W]hen I tell you you mine, I also mean I'm yours" (203). Sethe has wanted to take her children to the "other side," but having them with her has kept her from the despair and desperation of the "Saturday girls," who sell themselves to men who work at the slaughterhouse.

Denver's recollection also begins with Beloved. She claims her as her sister and cites as evidence that she "swallowed her blood right along with my mother's milk" (205). The image suggests how much more complicated Denver's feelings for her mother are than for her sister. Her mother inspires love and fear in equal amounts. Denver misses her brothers, but she yearns for the father she has never known. She treasures the memories that Baby Suggs has shared with her about the man who loved soft fried eggs and knew how to count on paper. Her grandmother has also taught her not to fear the sister's ghost and to think of her own life as "charmed."

Beloved's thoughts defy linear expression. They begin with a variation of the line used by Sethe and Denver ("I am Beloved and she is mine") that is the only complete sentence in the chapter. Images of flowers, leaves, grass, and round baskets—all evocative of both Africa and the low country of the Carolinas, which was the point of disembarkation for many Africans in the New World—are associated with an unnamed maternal figure, but the speaker's inability to separate herself from that figure causes the language to break down syntactically. Images of crouching figures, corpses, "men without skin," and rats evoke the Middle Passage. The rhythm of the language imitates the rhythm of the ocean ("I am not big small rats do not wait for us to sleep someone is thrashing but there is no room to do it in if we had more to drink we could make tears" [210]). The sensory images reinforce both the horror of the crossing and the longing for the maternal figure. A man sings "of the place where a woman takes flowers away from their leaves and puts them in a round basket" (211). Then he, too, is gone, and only the image of his "pretty little white teeth" remains (212). Allusions to rape and death are reminiscent of the refrain in Robert Hayden's poem "Middle Passage": "Voyage through death / to life upon these shores."[41] But the lines in the novel end with the speaker alone, in a transitional space, that is, neither life nor death but the bridge between them. There she waits and needs "to find a place to be" and a way of reuniting with Sethe, the mother whom she finally names (213).

The fourth chapter begins in Beloved's unconscious. She specifies Sethe as "the one that picked flowers, yellow flowers in the place before the crouching" (214). This misidentification confirms the sense, articulated by Denver, that Beloved is *more* than Sethe's lost daughter. Yet the major impulse in the passage that opens the chapter is to insist on an identity between Beloved and Sethe. Beloved yearns for reunion: "I wanted to join. I tried to join. . . . I lost her again, but I found the house she whispered to me and there she was smiling at last. . . . She smiles at me and it is my own face smiling. I will not lose her again. She is mine" (214). Then a colloquy begins that includes all three voices. As if to signal the merging of the characters, the final pages of the chapter are written as poetry rather than prose. They are words to be chanted, rather than simply read:[42]

> Beloved
> You are my sister
> You are my daughter
> You are my face; you are me
> You are mine
> You are mine
> You are mine. (216)

These chapters bear comparison with the biblical *Song of Songs*, a text to which Morrison has been repeatedly drawn. The repeated variations of the phrase "Beloved. She is mine" allude directly to the King James Version of the Bible, but the parallels go deeper. In his discussion of the biblical text, Francis Landy asserts, "[T]he discourse of love, of which the Song is a distillation, is created not only by the lovers, is not only the basis of a community predicated on love, first developing from the family, the mother-child relationship, and then the society of lovers to which the Song appeals, but also draws into its orbit things, plants, animals, geography. It can do nothing else: lovers can communicate only through the world, through metaphor."[43] Through the metaphors of these four chapters, the novel's characters express a discourse of love so intimate, intense, and painful that it is unspeakable. Landy later suggests that the Hebrew poets chose words for their beautiful sounds. The poetry that resulted he terms "verbal magic, whose extreme is glossolalia, . . . very close to incantation."[44] To the community outside 124 Bluestone Road, the women's voices sound incantatory. Stamp Paid describes them as "a conflagration of hasty voices—loud, urgent, all speaking at once so he could not make out what they were talking about or to whom. The speech wasn't nonsensical exactly, nor was it tongues. But something was wrong with the order of the words and he couldn't describe or cipher it to save his life. All he could make out was the word *mine*" (172). Hearing the voices and declining to knock on a door that had always been open to him, Stamp Paid turns away from 124.

When he returns, he interprets what he hears differently. The discourse of love develops first from the family and then extends to a community that in the novel includes both the living and the dead. As Stamp Paid recognizes, the voices that he hears as he stands outside 124 do not belong just to three women; they belong to "the people of the broken necks, of fire-cooked blood and black girls who had lost their ribbons. What a roaring" (181). Their stories cannot all be recuperated; their histories cannot all be reconstructed. But their voices must be heard and their lives must be commemorated.

As a novelist, Morrison creates the spaces for readers to experience recollection as the serious concentration of thought. She shapes a language that invites her reader to ponder philosophical questions.[45] What is the meaning of freedom? Is it the ability to claim one's own hands, as Baby Suggs ascertains in a moment of simple but dazzling clarity? Is it not to need permission for desire, as Paul D avers? What constitutes history? What is love? Can it be "too thick"? Is it safer to "love small," as Paul D determines? What brings one to say with Ella, "Don't love nothing"? How do a people define themselves? How does one recollect one's kin?

> I will call them my people, which were not my people;
>     and her beloved, which was not beloved.

The epigraph to *Beloved* is taken from Paul's letter to the Romans (Rom. 9:25). The apostle preaches that God will return his love to his people, who now exist in a condition of spiritual estrangement. He rejects the idea of a chosen people and argues instead, as scholar Charles Scruggs explains, that "the real 'Israel' . . . is not a historical people defined by a written covenant of the law, but a spiritual people created anew by the spirit of *caritas*, a Beloved Community that contains within it the figura of the heavenly city."[46] The verse that follows reads: "And in the very place where it was said unto them, 'You are not my people,' they will be called sons of the living God."

Baby Suggs's sermon, the novel's most virtuoso act of speech making, appears a third of the way through *Beloved*. Significantly, it is represented through Sethe's recollection. After learning Halle's fate from Paul D, Sethe returns to the Clearing for an act of mourning and commemoration that is a metonym for the novel's overall project. "[W]ords whispered in the keeping room were too little." Halle's noble life (his willingness to give up "five years of Sabbaths" to work and buy his mother's freedom) and his destruction (driven into madness by being forced to watch the abuse of his pregnant wife) "demanded more: an arch built or a robe sewn. Some fixing ceremony" (86). Sethe revisits the place where the community had gathered for the Saturday meetings led by her mother-in-law. An unchurched preacher, Baby Suggs carries no title before her name but allows the epithet "holy," "as a small caress after it" (87). Revisiting the site, Sethe surveys the remains, including, for example, Baby Suggs's old preaching rock; she remembers the smell of leaves simmering in the sun and recollects the sounds from the one meeting she has witnessed.[47] So vivid are her memories that she recounts them in the present tense.

At Baby Sugg's direction, the people come together: men, women, and children. Initially they assume the posture she assigns: the children laugh, the men dance, and the women cry. Then everyone trades places and assumes the stance of everyone else. Children dance, women laugh, men cry, and all partake of the community's joy and its sorrow. When their energy is spent, Baby Suggs rises and begins to exhort her flock. The text of her sermon, a term she rejects in favor of "call," could be Romans 9:25, but her message is far from Christian orthodoxy. Indeed, just before the sermon proper begins, the narrator recounts what Baby Suggs did not say and lists instructions that one expects to hear from conventional preachers.[48] She does not tell her congregants to repent and sin no more; neither does she offer them the Beatitudes. Rather than telling them to mortify the flesh, she tells them to love it. Rather than proclaiming a faith that is the substance of things unseen, she insists that "the only grace they could have was the grace they could imagine. That if they could not see it, they would not have it" (88). Rather than gathering together in the name of Jesus, she entreats them to gather together in their own name. Rather than instructing them to love an(other), Baby Suggs implores her people to love themselves.

As if to indicate how difficult a task this would be for people who have been defined as chattel, Baby Suggs asks them to reclaim themselves, part by part: flesh, skin, eyes, hands, mouths, necks, and then "the inside parts"—the internal organs that regulate the flesh, that reproduce it, and that pump its lifeblood. Trudier Harris observes that "having given up seven of her eight children to slavery, Baby Suggs knows what it means to have put the heart back together after it has been torn apart valve by valve."[49] Echoing Sethe's reflection that in her dreams she sees only the parts of her lost kin in trees, Baby Suggs commands her people to love themselves whole. After issuing the imperative "love your heart," she dances what she lacks the language to command. In response to her call, "the others opened their mouths and gave her the music. Long notes held until the four-part harmony was perfect enough for their deeply loved flesh" (89).

As powerful an exhorter as Baby Suggs is and as attuned as her congregants are to her message, they fail to live up to its dictates. No sooner do they leave the Clearing after the sermon and partake of a feast prepared by Baby and Sethe to celebrate Sethe's escape from slavery—an escape that denotes her freedom in the body as well as the flesh—than their Beloved Community is riven by "pride, fear, condemnation, and spite" (171).[50] Their neighbors fail to warn the family at 124 Bluestone Road of the approaching slave catchers; their failure contributes to the tragedy that unfolds. Not only does Sethe murder her child, but Baby Suggs, holy, loses her faith. For the next eighteen years, the members of the family live as pariahs; none of their neighbors enters their house.

But Baby Suggs's message resounds throughout the novel. Sethe's memory of it brings her back to the Clearing. She recognizes in retrospect that "freeing yourself was one thing; claiming ownership of that freed self was another" (95). Having come to the Clearing to make peace with the past, she leaves determined to move forward and to make a life with Paul D. "More than commemorating Halle, that is what she had come to the Clearing to figure out, and now it *was* figured" (99). It takes Sethe the next two-thirds of the novel to act on her decision, but when she does, she will have internalized the meaning of Baby Suggs's call.

That call is not only to gather together those who are related by blood. The novel's vision of kinship or family is not defined by bloodline alone but also by loving commitments and mutual ties binding biologically unrelated people within and across generations. As Scruggs argues, the quest in this novel is for the "Beloved Community," "one based on common understanding and *caritas*, balanced between individual respect for communal ties and communal respect for individuality."[51] Baby Suggs is its prophet, but it is the next generation that brings the Beloved Community into being. Stamp Paid's love for Baby Suggs, "the mountain to his sky," compels him belatedly to knock again on the door of 124 (170). Stamp has shared Baby Suggs's vision of a community of free Negroes: "to love and be loved by them, to counsel and be counseled, protect and be protected, feed and be fed" by them (177). He has lived according to its tenets. Conductor on the Underground Railroad, neighborhood scribe, and moral agent, Stamp believes with good reason that he owes no debt to anyone. But, having shown Paul D the newspaper clipping, he has to reassess his moral accounts. Stamp rededicates himself to Baby Suggs's vision when he asks Paul D first to forgive him and then to forgive his neighbors for not taking him in after he leaves 124. Baby Suggs's spirit, which laughs "clear as anything," gives Denver the strength to go out of the yard of 124 and to save her mother's life. It, too, speaks from the "other side":

> "You mean I never told you nothing about Carolina? About your daddy? You don't remember nothing about how come I walk the way I do and your mother's feet, not to speak of her back? I never told you all that? Is that why you can't walk down the steps. My Jesus my."
> But you said there was no defense.
> "There ain't."
> Then what do I do?
> "Know it, and go on out the yard. Go on." (244)

Denver goes for assistance first to Lady Jones, the "colored" school-teacher and a gentlewoman whose light skin has gotten her "picked" to receive an education, a privilege she repays "by teaching the unpicked" (247). When Lady Jones addresses Denver as "baby," the word "inaugurated her life in the world as a woman" (248) by reconnecting her to her dead grandmother. Whether consciously or not, Lady Jones begins the process of restoring community. Soon gifts of food, some with names and some without, start appearing in the yard of 124.

As Denver reveals more about the declining condition of her mother and the presence of the young woman who has no lines in her hand, the women of the community decide to take action. They refuse to allow the past to overwhelm the present and determine to rescue Sethe. Thirty women join the mission; they are convinced that the evil they are fighting against is not of this world. Consequently, "some brought what they could and what they believed would work. Stuffed in apron pockets, strung around their necks, lying in the space between their breasts. Others brought Christian faith—as shield and sword. Most brought a little of both" (257). What they see when they first arrive outside the yard of 124 Bluestone Road is themselves. In their rememory, they return to the feast that Baby Suggs has prepared to celebrate Sethe's freedom. The sensory images are vivid. "Catfish was popping grease in the pan and they saw themselves scoop German potato salad onto the plate. Cobbler oozing purple syrup colored their teeth" (258). They remember themselves as free of envy and spite. They are free, therefore, to revise the history that has divided them.

They pray. The text does not record the call—only the response: "Yes, yes, yes, oh yes. Hear me Hear me. Do it, Maker, do it" (258). It does reveal Ella's thoughts. She remembers the slave owners, father and son who abused her as a teenager, the men whom she deems "the lowest yet," and she remembers the infant she bore and let die. At the thought of that child coming back to haunt her, Ella lets loose a holler. Her scream is echoed by the other women, each in touch with both her own pain and that of her sisters. They all "took a step back to the beginning. In the beginning there were no words. In the beginning was the sound, and they all knew what that sound sounded like" (259).

The women sing. "For Sethe it is as though the Clearing had come to her with all its heat and simmering leaves, where the voices of women searched for the right combination, the key, the code, the sound that broke the back of words" (261). As the sound washes over her, she trembles like the newly baptized. When Mr. Bodwin, whose approach to 124 the narrator has deliberately charted, arrives, he is lost in recollections of his own. The house is his homestead and "the place that continued to surface in his dreams." The memorabilia of his childhood is literally buried there. As he retrieves it mentally, he reflects on the triumphs of his adult life, the greatest of which came when he stood on the front lines of the abolitionist movement. In language that resonates with Baby Suggs's teaching, he formulates his core belief: "[H]uman life is holy, all of it" (260).[52] That belief is almost of no consequence. For when he, a white man with a hat, rides in the yard of 124, Sethe relives the scene of eighteen years before when Schoolteacher in his black hat arrived with his three horsemen to reenslave her and her children. But this time, rather than attacking her child, she lunges toward Bodwin. Then Denver, buoyed by the sound of the singing women, stops her mother's attack. History does not repeat itself. The ghost of Beloved is exorcised. The hold the past has had on Sethe, Paul D, and Denver is broken.

In "The Site of Memory," Morrison attests, "[I]f writing is thinking and discovery and selection and order and meaning, it is also awe and reverence and mystery and magic" (111). The novel is replete with moments that convey the latter qualities. The rescue is only one. But the awe and reverence, mystery and magic constitute one of the novel's key historical interventions. Like The Black Book, Beloved was composed in the aftermath of the civil rights movement. The quest for the "Beloved Community" that Martin Luther King envisioned in eloquent sermons had ended in despair.[53] The national culture was obsessed with profits rather than prophets. Whites in the mainstream were no longer interested in the problems of their black compatriots. Calls to end the affirmative action that had just begun increased. African American communities seemed under assault by crime, drugs, and nihilism. A significant number of blacks no longer lived in the traditional communities; the civil rights movement had enabled them to move up and out. For those who remained, the pull of cultural separatism intensified. By 1987, obituaries for the communities, as for the ideals of the movement, were commonplace.

In a nation that had always preferred to look to the future, there seemed to be no point in looking back. Beloved, of course, argues otherwise. One cannot embrace the future until one has confronted the past. That past in the United States means coming to terms with the history of slavery—not as an institution but as an experience that millions of people whose names we do not know lived through. In order to apprehend their experience, individuals may partake of recollections of their kin; they may peruse the images and facts of the kind compiled in The Black Book. But ultimately, they must make their own imaginative act. Readers of Beloved are invited to do so through listening to a chorus of voices and responding to their call. Their call entreats readers to be open to the awe and reverence and mystery and magic that the novel inscribes. Having made a creative detour of the past, readers can perhaps move beyond it.

# five

## Trouble in Mind: Blues and History in *Corregidora*

I started humming the part about taking my rocking chair down by the river and rocking my blues away. What she said about the voice being better because it tells what you've been through. Consequences. It seems as if you're not singing the past, you're humming it. Consequences of what? Shit, we're all consequences of something. Stained with another's past as well as our own. —Gayl Jones, *Corregidora*

Reclaiming that from which one has been disinherited is a good thing. Self-possession in the full sense of that expression is the companion of self-knowledge. Yet claiming for myself a heritage the weft of whose genesis is my own disinheritance is a profoundly troubling paradox. —Patricia Williams, "On Being the Object of Property," *The Alchemy of Race and Rights*

Worrying the line encapsulates both the form and the content of Gayl Jones's 1975 novel *Corregidora*. Blues singer Ursa Corregidora struggles to comprehend the history of her maternal forebears and to free herself of the burdens that history imposes. Dominating that history is "the Portuguese slave breeder and whoremonger" Corregidora, who fathered both Ursa's grandmother and mother. Passing down the story, "leaving evidence" of unacknowledged crimes, becomes the bounden duty of three generations of Corregidora women. Ursa's great-grandmother has given her this imperative when she was only five years old: "And I'm leaving evidence. And you got to leave evidence too. And your children got to leave evidence. And when it come time to hold up the evidence, we got to have evidence to hold up. That's why they burned all the papers, so there wouldn't be no evidence to hold up against them."[1] Because the evidence is the spoken story, it must be passed down from generation to generation. When, as a result of an act of physical violence committed by her husband, Ursa becomes unable to have children, she must achieve both a profound understanding of the story and a new way to tell it.

As she attempts to overcome her individual trauma, Ursa is repeatedly ambushed by the memories—the stories as well as the instructions—that her maternal ancestors have passed down. These memories recount a trauma that is collective and historical. Yet Ursa remembers only fragments of what she has been told. Ultimately, her continual recollection of these fragments forces her to figure out *how* the trauma she has heard about all her life is related to the particular emotional and physical pain that the breakup of her marriage inflicts.

What Ursa needs to do is to learn the story of her family's past, not to recite it (as her foremothers have instructed) but to understand it so that she can break the cycle. The repetition of the story for them has resulted in the repetition of its effect. In slavery, black bodies are objects of exchange, commodities, just like the gold, coffee, and tobacco that their labor mines and cultivates. This reality is embedded in the discourse of the novel: Ursa's great-grandmother has been Corregidora's "coffee bean woman," his "gold piece." In slavery every aspect of the captive's body was commodified, including and perhaps especially the female's reproductive organs. Throughout the novel, men beginning with the slave owner claim ownership of black women's genitalia: "[I]t's *my* pussy." In "freedom," black men stake an all-too-similar claim on black women's bodies.

Sexuality becomes the locus of identity in this novel.[2] The legacy of incest and sexual abuse is the worse legacy of slavery in *Corregidora*, for it destroys the possibility of love between black women and men. The novel is unsparing in its depiction of the rawness of the hate that develops instead of love. Perhaps unconsciously, the Corregidora women have imposed the role of stud on the men with whom they "make generations." Perhaps unconsciously, men like Ursa's husband, Mutt Thomas, have expected women to behave like prostitutes. His jealous rage ends their marriage for twenty years.

The pain it represents and the tone of despair it often conveys make *Corregidora* a difficult book to read. James Baldwin, who admired the novel, described it as "the most brutally honest and painful revelation of what has occurred, and is occurring, in the souls of Black men and women." Critic Addison Gayle's disdain for Jones's writing led him to write the author out of the race: "[I]f Gayl Jones believes that Black men are what she says they are, she ought to get a white man." A sympathetic reader, scholar Claudia Tate, remarked in her conversation with Jones that when she read the novel she sensed that she "was hearing a very private story, not to be shared with everyone."[3]

The blues offer a way of contextualizing the "private story" *Corregidora* relates. In African American culture, the blues have been the vehicle for discussing and analyzing people's most private concerns. In the musical tradition, the persona of the individual performer dominates the song, which centers on the singer's own feelings, experiences, fears, dreams, acquaintances, and idiosyncrasies. As Amiri Baraka (then LeRoi Jones) argued in *Blues People*, "[E]ven though its birth and growth seems connected finally to the general movement of the mass of black Americans into the central culture of the country [during and after Reconstruction], blues still went back for its impetus and emotional meaning to the individual, to his completely personal life and death."[4] Robert Palmer makes a similar point when he writes that pioneering bluesman Charley Patton "found public events meaningful only insofar as they impinged on his private world—his perceptions, his feeling."[5] Patton sang in the early twentieth century in the Mississippi Delta—in that time and place the unjust socioeconomic system seemed impervious to change; political protest would have been beside the point. Moreover, in a system that denied his humanity, Patton's insistence on the significance of his feelings was, as Palmer argues, a heroic act. That heroism was available to women as well. "Bessie Smith's ability to communicate human emotion in public and make whites and Blacks *hear* the humanity was a victory," writes Michele Russell. The terms of that victory had much to do with transforming black women from sexual objects to sexual subjects in their own regard—if not always in the regard of the larger society.[6]

Although blues exist about a wide range of situations, male-female relationships are the most frequent focus. As Sterling Brown observes, "[T]he blues singer sings of the unrequited love and lost lover. Women sing of men as mistreaters, two-timers, no-gooders, soon-leavers."

Rather than everlasting love, the blues singers that Zora Neale Hurston celebrates sing of "love made and unmade. . . . Love is when it is."[7] Jones has identified the relationships she invents in *Corregidora* as "blues relationships" that come "out of a tradition of 'love and trouble.'" Even when "blues lyrics address themselves directly to negative economic, political, and judiciary circumstances," Albert Murray avers, "more often than not, the main emphasis is likely to be placed on the victim's love life."[8] Rather than denying the importance of public events, this emphasis reflects, again, the premium placed on the singer's own feelings and perceptions.

Blues poet and scholar Sherley Anne Williams describes the blues as "a ritualized way of [black people] talking about ourselves and passing it on." The tradition offers writers "form and setting."[9] The call-and-response form of the blues is well suited to express the contradiction, conflict, and tension that is usually its subject. Those contradictions and conflicts are simply stated—or dramatized—in the blues; they are neither repressed nor resolved. According to Ralph Ellison's oft quoted definition: "[T]he blues is an impulse to keep the painful details and episodes of a brutal experience alive in one's aching consciousness, to finger its jagged grain, and to transcend it, not by the consolation of philosophy but by squeezing from it a near-tragic, near-comic lyricism. As a form, the blues is an autobiographical chronicle of personal catastrophe expressed lyrically."[10]

For good reason, then, blues is the form to which Ursa turns to understand and give shape to her experience. Twenty years of blues singing gives her a perspective and a vocabulary of emotion as well as verbal expression that allows her to work through the emotional debris of her personal and familial history. But beyond its utility for character formation, blues as an art form and a cultural force informs the entire novel. *Corregidora* is a nonrealist and nonlinear novel. Meaning is conveyed through images as much as or more than through narrative. When, for example, Ursa's mother calls the blues her daughter sings "devil's music" and asks where she got them from, her daughter replies that she got them from the mother. But the words are the daughter's own. In words that go unspoken, the protagonist insists that she be allowed "to give witness" the only way she can. "I'll make a fetus out of grounds of coffee to rub inside my eyes. When it's time to give witness, I'll make a fetus out of grounds of coffee. I'll stain their hands" (54). The image inscribes the connection between Ursa's maternal legacy and her own experience. It enacts her determination to make that legacy the subject of her art and to make her art the legacy that she will leave instead of the children her ancestors commanded her to bear. The art is the product of a history of exploitation that will indict the exploiters ("I'll stain their hands") but will cause the artist excruciating pain. Equally important, the image of the coffee grounds being rubbed inside the eyes suggests the difficulty of seeing the past clearly. The artist insists, nevertheless, on her right to keep trying to do so in her own way, even as she confirms her willingness to inflict pain on herself in the process. Rather than a child, she gestates a vision of the past that will both convict and liberate.

The blues are central to Ursa's self-definition. When she comes home from the hospital, she worries that the injury has affected her voice. Her friend Cat encourages her to sing. Ursa begins: "Trouble in mind, I'm blue, but I won't be blue always." She stops, starts again, and when she finishes the song, she worries that her voice does not sound the same. Cat's response is a key to the way that blues functions in the text: "Your voice sounds a little strained, that's all. But if I hadn't heard you before, I wouldn't notice anything. I'd still be moved. Maybe even moved more, because it sounds like you been through something. Before it was beautiful too, but you sound like you been through more" (44). Cat is the first of several characters to comment on how Ursa's painful experiences deepen her art. She compares Ursa's development as an artist to Ma Rainey, asserting that "after all the alcohol and men, the strain made [her voice] better, because you could tell what she'd been through" (44). Later, another character, Max Monroe, tells Ursa that she has "a hard kind of voice" and compares it to "callused hands" that are "strong and hard but gentle underneath." Her singing voice, he observes, is the kind that can hurt you: "hurt you and make you still want to listen" (96). The same can be said of the novel's narrative voice.

For Ursa, the blues offer a way to confront and express the pain she has experienced. In a conversation she remembers having with Mutt, she tells him that the blues help her "to explain what I can't explain" (56).[11] She imagines a conversation with her mother in which she describes finding in blues "the explanation somewhere behind the words" (66). The blues represent a past that is there, even when one is not conscious of it. As Ursa put its, "[I]t seems as if you're not singing the past, you're humming it" (45). The past, this observation suggests, is inescapable; it is like a song one does not consciously remember but finds oneself humming. It is always already there. But as a blues singer, Ursa can exert some control over *how* she sings once she recognizes the song.

"Trouble in Mind" is a folk blues whose most familiar verses alternately express despair and hope: "I'm blue, but I won't be blue always." Its best-known images offer variations on this theme. The singer declares, for example, "I'm gonna lay my head on some lonesome railroad line, / let the two nineteen train satisfy my mind." The image in the line of the verse that Ursa begins but does not finish is equally well known: "I won't be blue always / The sun's gonna shine in my back door some day." In the influential version of the song recorded by Bertha Chippie Hill in the 1920s, this is the penultimate line, and Hill ends her performance on an exultant note. With Louis Armstrong's cornet blaring above the steady beat of Richard Jones's piano, the musical accompaniment reinforces this cathartic shift. Understandably, at least one blues scholar considers "Trouble in Mind" the "anthem" of the classic blues.[12]

The line that *Corregidora* alludes to in the passage quoted later in this paragraph ("I'm goin' down to the river and get me a rockin' chair / If the Lord don't help me, I'm gonna rock away from here") stops short of catharsis. The act of singing and the song combine instead to convey the commingling of pain and pleasure: "I bit my lip singing. I troubled my mind, took my rocker down by the river again. It was as if I wanted them to see what he'd done, hear it. All those blues feeling. That time I asked him to try to understand my feeling ways. That's what I called it. My feeling ways. My voice felt like it was screaming. What do they say about pleasure mixed in the pain? That's the way it always was with him. The pleasure somehow greater than the pain" (50).[13]

Whereas some of her songs are traditional blues like "Trouble in Mind" and "See See Rider" and popular rhythm-and-blues tunes like "Open the Door, Richard," Ursa also composes her own blues. The novel refers to two of these more than once. One is a song about a train going through a seemingly endless tunnel when suddenly the tunnel tightens around the train like a fist. The other is about a bird woman whose eyes were deep wells; she would take a man on a journey from which he would never return. Clearly, these lyrics can be read as expressions of female domination; many critics have done so.[14] But the image of the bird woman suggests emotional fragility rather than power. A subsequent reference to Ursa's mother being closed up like a fist reinforces the association with emotional repression. Ursa is singing her songs when she first meets Mutt, who comments, "[Y]ou try to sing hard, but you not hard" (148). As is true in many of her conversations, Ursa's response is silence. She defines herself through her music. Consequently, her self-definition is fragmented, subject to revision, and open to multiple interpretations.

The song that Ursa wants to sing does not exist, and she strives to create it: "A new world song. A song branded with the new world" (59). This song would express the realities and the longings of Ursa's life as well as the lives of her foremothers that intertwine themselves with hers. She goes in quest of "a new world song" in part because she has no biological way of fulfilling the dictate of her family to "make generations." She feels compelled as a result to question the relation between biology and destiny on the one hand and the cultural (as well as the familial) injunction for women to be mothers on the other. Her questions threaten to silence her music and then become the poetry that is her music. "The center of a woman's being. Is it? No seeds. Is that what snaps away my music, a harp string broken, guitar string, string of my banjo belly. Strain in my voice" (46). Through her poetry, Ursa improvises her own imperative that ultimately allows her to loosen the bonds of Corregidora's legacy.

All the novel's characters are troubled in mind, and most of them speak with a blues accent. The dynamic of call and response is used to structure conversation and interior monologues. Repetition is a primary characteristic, as is the practice of worrying the line. In another exchange between Ursa and Cat, Ursa injects herself into a conversation that had been about her but had not included her:

> "If that nigger love me he wouldn't've thrown me down the steps," I called.
> "What?" She came to the door.
> "I said if that nigger loved me he wouldn't've throwed me down the steps."
> "I know niggers love you do worse than that," she said. (36–37)

With repetitions that mimic the twelve-bar blues form, this exchange extends the novel's thematic of the inextricability of love and pain. Cat's question ("What?") invites the repetition that the blues form requires. Ursa's variation ("I said") neatly worries the line. Cat's response to Ursa's call resounds with a "truth" that Ursa must both acknowledge and move beyond.

As Jones explained in an interview with her mentor, poet Michael Harper, "I used to say that I learned to write by listening to people talk. I still feel that the best of my writing comes from having *heard* rather than having *read*." Jones's work as an artist is to create a stylized language out of the speech she has taken such pleasure in hearing. The result is what she calls "ritualized dialogue," a term by which she extends the understanding of blues as ritualistic. While based on speech she has heard, this dialogue, Jones notes, changes either the words or the rhythms of language that people ordinarily use. Both changes "take the dialogue out of the naturalistic realm—change its quality."[15] Jones adds that the novel contains both naturalistic and ritualistic dialogue; the conversations between Ursa and Mutt, italicized in the novel, are mostly the latter.

> *"Come over here, honey."*
> *"Naw."*
> *"I need somebody."*
> *"Naw."*
> *"I said I need somebody."*
> *"Naw."*
> *"I won't treat you bad."*
> *"Naw."*
> *"I won't make you sad."*
> *"Naw."*
> *"Come over here, honey, and visit with me a little."*
> *"Naw."*
> *"Come over here, baby, and visit with me a little."*
> *"Naw."*
> *"You got to come back to your original man."* (97–98)

As this passage illustrates, *Corregidora* is a novel of yearning and missed connections. Ursa is never certain whether the men who desire her are going to love her or abuse her. "Sometimes I found myself not knowing how much men did meant friendly and how much meant something else. Or maybe I was just kidding myself" (94). Molested as a child, she remembers thinking the molester's advances were friendly. As an adult, she distrusts her lover's motives and her own. The italicized passage recounts her dream of an encounter with Mutt; it is one of many in which Ursa tries to revise the history of their courtship and marriage. The tonal variations of the blues echo the complex shadings of Ursa's feelings. Characteristically, she does not act on what she feels; often she is unable to feel anything at all.

The reference to her "original man" reiterates a central ambiguity of the novel. Both Mutt and Corregidora stand in that role. In conversations with other characters, Ursa mistakes pronoun references and assumes a reference to Corregidora when the speaker refers to Mutt. In another dream, a nightmare in which she has become literally Corregidora's woman, she remembers Mutt's anger at what he perceives to be her disloyalty: "Ain't even took my name. You Corregidora's, ain' you? Ain't even took my name. You ain't my woman" (61). What Ursa struggles to figure out is how to become her own woman, even when she is not singing on stage. Without having the words to describe the effort, she struggles to figure out how to tap into what one character who listens to her sing describes as "something powerful" about her (93).

The novel's use of blues connects Ursa's individual pain to the history of Africans in America. Angela Davis argues that "the blues . . . incorporated a new consciousness about private love relationships, which had been denied to Black people, except in a rudimentary way, as long as they were slaves. In many ways, in fact, interpersonal relationships functioned as metaphors for the freedom they sought: trouble in the relationship was trouble in the overall social universe." [16] Davis's argument depends on the premise that social references in the blues are implicit. Blues encode the history of oppression, slavery, peonage, and segregation, even when that history is not represented. *Corregidora* makes explicit this relation between the individual and the collective, the immediate and the historical, the private and the public aspects of experience. [17]

In keeping with the blues tradition that informs it, *Corregidora* is a nonlinear narrative. The protagonist's description of her mother's talking applies as well to the structure of the text: "[I]t sounded almost as if she were speaking in pieces, instead of telling one long thing" (123). From the story of the original Corregidora to the stories of the characters who exist in the narrative present, the novel represents only fragmentary narratives. *Corregidora* does not fill in details. Within the novel, the voices of Ursa, her mother, grandmother, and great-grandmother contend with the internalized voice of the slave owner Corregidora. Their voices give the novel its major themes. Other voices ring in with harmony or dissonance, especially those of the black men the Corregidora women take as their lovers. Although some are victims and victimizers, others are figures of caring and resistance. Black female characters speak narratives that recount their own experiences of sexual violence and abuse; these characters also represent the unrealized possibilities for sisterly and even sexual bonding between women. Each voice speaks a piece of history. Ultimately, Ursa, who as first-person narrator becomes the filter through whose voice all these voices are heard, speaks/sings the pieces of this remarkable novel.

The novel's structure is analogous to the structure Jones as critic attributes to Sherley Anne Williams's cycle of poems, *Someone Sweet Angel Chile*. In her scholarly monograph *Liberating Voices: Oral Tradition in African American Literature*, Jones suggests that Williams anchors her work, "a poetic biography" inspired by the life of Bessie Smith, in the twelve-bar blues. Williams then constructs an open-ended form that synthesizes diverse voices and histories. Rather than a "poetic biography," *Corregidora* takes the form of a poetic autobiography and a collective blues dialogue "containing fragments of experience (event and speech), abrupt changes (thematic and structural), shifts in perspective . . . , hesitations, repetitions, worrying the line." The flexibility with which she handles form allows Jones to interpolate narratives on the themes of sexual abuse, economic exploitation, resistance to oppression, and the unreliability of the written historical record that documents neither the exploitation nor the resistance. The novel explores these themes, without losing sight of Ursa's individual situation. The use of repetition is key in sustaining this focus. Indeed, the commentary that Jones offers on Jean Toomer's prose sketch "Karintha," which Jones labels a "blues-ballad," applies as well to her novel: "Repetition, as part of the thematic and verbal architecture of the story, sets off the lyrical beginning (the problem introduced), middle (its complications and consequences) and end/beginning (the open end of blues ritual). The experiences of sexual dilemma and tyranny, plus Karintha's [read Ursa's] own involvement in acts of cruelty, reinforce the blues theme."[18] The novel's spare blues-inflected prose is a marvel; the reader can ignore neither the pain it conveys nor the pleasure it affords.

Ursa is a blues singer, but she is not a blues queen. Although the novel contains references to famous blues and jazz singers—from Ma Rainey to Della Reese to Ella Fitzgerald, and especially Billie Holiday—it resists the popular myths that glamorize these women's lives. One reads nothing of furs, gowns, coiffures, and other trappings of fame in *Corregidora*.

Indeed, Ursa never leaves the tightly bound bluegrass region of Kentucky in which the novel is set.[19] She sings in only three local venues, Preston's, Happy's Café, and The Spider. And she refers to only one trip (to Detroit) that she takes in her life. Fixed within geographical borders, this novel's characters speak exclusively in regional vernacular. Yet the novel betrays no hint of "the folk." What Jones writes of Zora Neale Hurston in *Liberating Voices* is even truer of her own work: "[F]or Hurston, dialect as regional vernacular can do and contain anything: subject, experience, emotion, revelation."[20]

Moreover, through references to place-names in the narrative present as well as the ancestral past, the novel locates Ursa in a very wide world. By using the names of actual Kentucky towns like Versailles and Midway, for example, the novel suggests that the histories of local communities are connected to large-scale historical movements.[21] If in the novel's story a character who comes from Hazard, Kentucky, is an outsider, the discourse of the novel implies that the residents of Versailles are shaped by the main currents of Western history. They may be themselves only aware of pieces of that history, however.

The twenty-two years spanned by the plot include the most intense years of the Cold War as well as the landmark events of the civil rights movement. Yet the novel's characters rarely refer to any events that were covered in the newspaper. What Jones terms the "significant events" of their experience transpire in private.[22] As she has written, her principal interest is in "the psychology of characters—and the way(s) in which they order their stories—their myths, dreams, nightmares, secret worlds, ambiguities, contradictions, ambivalences, memories, imaginations, their 'puzzles.'"[23] But her characters act out these interior dramas against an expansive backdrop. The genealogy of the Corregidora women expands the novel's symbolic geography as well as its chronology. The family oppressor and patriarch Corregidora is a Portuguese slave owner in Brazil. The women's memories evoke the eighteenth-century slave revolts in Palmares and the Africans who waged them. Ursa's nightmares summon Brazilian plantations as easily as small-town Kentucky neighborhoods.

When asked why Brazil figures so prominently in *Corregidora* and elsewhere in her writing, Jones explained that exploring Brazilian history and landscape helped her writing by "getting away from things that some readers consider 'autobiographical' or 'private obsessions' rather than literary inventions. . . . In addition, the Brazilian experience (purely literary and imaginative since I've never been there) helped to give a perspective on the American one."[24] In the first instance, Jones saw how shifting the setting of her work heightened its fictionality for readers and made her work less vulnerable to being read as if it mirrored social—or worse, the author's personal—reality. In the second statement, she suggests how her work participates in an ongoing social and political conversation.

Brazil has, of course, long been crucially important in comparative studies of slavery in the New World. Next to the United States, it was the largest slaveholding nation in the Western Hemisphere. For decades historians argued over the meaning of demographic and cultural differences between the two nations. Their interpretations differed regarding the impact of the Roman Catholic Church on the laws and culture of Brazil, the reliance on the slave trade to replenish the African population in Brazil, and the development of an economic system in Brazil that depended on plantation economies. Scholars such as Gilberto Freyre and Frank Tannenbaum concluded that these factors produced a more benevolent system of slavery than the one that developed in the American South. The church offered the rites of baptism to slaves, thereby acknowledging their humanity; the continuous importation of Africans over three centuries and the plantation economies fostered a much greater degree of African cultural retentions.[25]

Recently, more scholars have concluded that, partly as a consequence of the continuation of the slave trade long after it was outlawed in the United States in 1808, "physical conditions endured by slaves in Brazil made life there considerably more precarious . . . than it was for slaves in the United States." Owners in the United States had a vested financial interest in the physical survival of their slaves. For female slaves, the contrasts were even sharper than for males. Not only was the practice of concubinage more widespread and socially acceptable in Brazil than in the United States, but "slave masters in Brazil also prostituted slave women."[26] A line in the novel, "I have a birthmark between my legs," signifies how sexualized identity was for enslaved women in Brazil (45). Finally, despite the laws against teaching slaves to read and write, literacy was much more common among the enslaved population in North America than in Brazil. One reason may be that slaves in the United States lived in closer proximity to their owners. In any case, many more records survive in the United States that document slavery from the slave's point of view.

*Corregidora* comes down on neither side of the scholarly debate. What it does instead is heighten the conditions common to both histories and invent situations in which those conditions impinge on the development of individual characters. Whether or not concubinage was a historical fact on the small farms on which most slaves lived in Kentucky in the eighteenth and nineteenth centuries, conceptions regarding the sexuality of African people were very much like those in Brazil.[27] The novel's characters internalize these attitudes. Whether or not more "free-floating literacy" existed among blacks in the United States than in Brazil, their testimony, both on the page and in the courtroom, did not count. Whether or not more blacks in Brazil had been welcomed into the religion of their masters or allowed to retain their ancestral system of belief, the existential condition for New World blacks—particularly in the twentieth century—could be expressed more honestly through the blues than through European or African ritual. The characters of *Corregidora* have no gods to which to turn; they can rely only on themselves.

Rather than a realistic depiction of history or geography, *Corregidora* is a poetic exploration of the consequences of history. In what appears to be an offhanded moment in conversation, Ursa avers, "[M]y veins are centuries meeting" (46). The moment reveals what Toni Morrison, who was Jones's editor at Random House, describes as "that incredible kind of movement which yields an artistic representation of something that one takes for granted in history." Morrison views *Corregidora* in these terms, noting that in the novel one sees "the weight of history working itself out in the life of one, two, three people." As Morrison analyzes the achievement of the novel, Gayl Jones took "a large idea" and "brought it down small, and at home, which gives it a universality and a particularity which makes it extraordinary."[28]

The particular and defining trauma in the protagonist's personal life occurs just before the narrative proper begins. Despite her husband's disapproval and his willingness to support her financially, Ursa has insisted on continuing to work as a singer in Happy's Café. For her, singing is "something I had to do" (3). Although she never identifies herself as one, hers is an artist's explanation. The explanation does not compute for Mutt because for him Ursa has only one role as his wife. The only identity he can conceive of for Ursa is sexual object. Consequently he assumes that other men undress her with their eyes as she sings: "'I don't like those mens messing with you,' he said. 'Don't nobody mess with me.' 'Mess with they eyes'" (3). The couple's home is a room in the Drake Hotel. The conflation of hotel, a commercial establishment that is frequently the venue for commercial sex, and home reinforces the status of sex as commodity. They have been married only five months when Mutt, in a fit of jealousy, pushes Ursa down a flight of stairs. Unbeknownst to either, Ursa is one month pregnant; she is forced to undergo a hysterectomy as a result of her injuries. The result, in Ursa's words, is "I lost my womb."

Ursa's personal trauma is inextricably bound to the historical trauma of slavery, a condition that depended on the sexual commodification of black bodies. As she understands it, the Portuguese, who enslaved her foremothers in Brazil, "paid attention only to the genitals" when they bought slaves (54). The family history that has been passed down to her is a repetition of sexual abuse. After her breakup with Mutt, Ursa is haunted by the fragments of this history that she remembers. The stories she has been told echo endlessly in her mind; when she sleeps, they haunt her dreams. The novel's italicized passages that represent these stories etch them in the reader's mind. "I thought of the girl who had to sleep with her master and mistress. Her father, the master. Her daughter's father. The father of her daughter's daughter. How many generations? Days that were pages of hysteria. Their survival depended on suppressed hysteria" (59). Their hysteria mirrors the protagonist's own.

References to hysteria recur as well in The Alchemy of Race and Rights, the highly regarded volume published by legal theorist and Ivy League law professor Patricia Williams. Williams's book is mainly about the jurisprudence of rights, but it argues that to understand the complexities of the issues surrounding the extension of rights to African Americans in U.S. law, one must explore structures of feeling as well as legal codes. To do so Williams pushes beyond the limits of legal language and improvises "an intentionally double-voiced and relational" mode of writing.[29] Tellingly, Williams traces her interest in the law, and her particular interest in "the intersection of commerce and the Constitution," to a family history that resonates with the fiction of Corregidora (17). Williams's great-great-grandmother was the slave of a Tennessee lawyer, who purchased her when she was eleven and impregnated her when she was twelve. The children she bore, including Williams's great-grandmother, grew up in the master's house, as his servants and his property but not his heirs. The slave owner, whom Williams recognizes but does not claim as her great-great-grandfather, left letters and legal opinions that documented his position in the world. The enslaved woman disappeared from history. But Williams, who learns about her ancestor through what she calls a "matrilineal recounting," strives to imagine her foremother's feeling (17):

> I try to imagine what it would have been like to have a discontented white man buy me, after a fight with his mother about his prolonged bachelorhood. I wonder what it would have been like to have a thirty-five-year-old man own the secrets of my puberty, which he bought to prove himself sexually as well as to increase his livestock of slaves. I imagine trying to please, with the yearning of adolescence, a man who truly did not know I was human, whose entire belief system resolutely defined me as animal, chattel, talking cow. I wonder what it would have been like to have his child, pale-faced but also animal, before I turned thirteen. I try to envision being casually threatened with sale from time to time, teeth and buttocks bared to interested visitors. (18)

These meditations are not explored. Even to mention them in a "legal treatise" is a transgressive act. They are unmistakably private, much too furtive and necessarily fictive to be the subject of academic analysis. Yet they are too striking to serve only to frame the book's examination of race and rights. They highlight in bold the real-life consequences of this intellectual inquiry.

Unlike the black woman who was his property, the white male ancestor left evidence. Williams can study his writing, as well as the legal career that the author's mother tells her ironically is "in her blood." Rather than relying on her imagination, Williams can draw on her own training and position to gain insight into this white man's perspective. As she reads the records that document his life, however, Williams looks for "the shape described by [her great-great-grandmother's] absence in all this." She describes what she seeks in the fusion of legal and literary discourse that distinguishes her prose: "I see her shape and his hand in the vast networking of our society, and in the evils and oversights that plague our life and laws. The control he had over her body. The force he was in her life, in the shape of my life today. The power he exercised in the choice to breed or not. The choice to breed slaves in his image, to choose her mate and be that mate. In his attempt to own what no man can own, the habit of his power and the absence of her choice" (19).

Absent the education and class privilege of Patricia Williams, the protagonist of *Corregidora* struggles with the same queries. To a significant degree, her struggle is framed by the discourse of the law: "evidence," "verdict," "witness," and "consequence" are keywords in this text. Even the name "Corregidore" means "former judicial magistrate." As Melvin Dixon points out, by changing the gender designation, Jones makes Ursa Corregidora "a female judge charged by the women in her family to 'correct' the historical invisibility they have suffered, 'to give evidence' of their abuses, and 'to make generations' as a defense against further displacement and annihilation."[30] The aim of the Corregidora women is to wrest authority from the slave owner, but their strategy is self-defeating. As critics Ann duCille and Janice Harris argue, making generations means making love; but making love for the purpose of making evidence turns what should be a positive act into an act of vengeance. Harris concludes, "[T]he goal of lovemaking subverts the act; the end denies the means."[31]

As a blues singer, Ursa is not without resources. Indeed, the blues are a far more supple instrument for investigating and expressing feelings than is the law. Jones herself has frequently quoted Janheinz Jahn's description of blues as "subjective testimony."[32] The singer bears witness to the experiences of her life. Extending this prerogative, Ursa becomes a witness not only to her own troubles but to those of women whose historical situations she imagines. Reflecting on the alternatives available to her foremothers when the slave master exercised his ownership of their bodies, Ursa articulates their situations in contrasting blues lyrics. In the first, the female slave responds passively to the master's advances:

> While mama be sleeping, the ole man he crawl into bed
> While mama be sleeping, the ole man he crawl into bed
> When mama have wake up, he shaking his nasty ole head. (67)

In the second the woman resists and protects the integrity of her body by threatening the integrity of his. These lines echo throughout the text as Ursa weighs the alternatives in her own life of either being a sexual object or claiming a subjectivity that she is willing to defend with force if that is required.

> Don't come here to my house, don't come here to my house I said
> Don't come here to my house, don't come here to my house I said
> Fore you get any this booty, you gon have to lay down dead
> Fore you get any this booty, you gon have to lay down dead. (67)

Ursa's mother has made it clear that the choice implicit in these lyrics carries serious "consequences." She remembers the fate of a woman on a neighboring plantation. Her master sent her husband away so that he would have free access to his slave. She resisted and exacted retribution by castrating the master. The next day, a posse came for her and her husband. The slave catchers castrated the husband and stuffed his penis in her mouth. After making her watch him bleed to death, the posse hanged her. The horrific details and the matter-of-fact way in which the story is told are typical of *Corregidora*. The horror is intensified as the reader recognizes that this story has been told by a mother to a daughter.

In a powerful gloss on the way the history of sexual violence and abuse shadows the relationships between characters in the present, the sentence that follows the lines "They made her watch and then they hanged her" reads, "I got out of my wedding suit and was sitting on the couch/bed in my slip when Tadpole came in" (67). After divorcing Mutt, Ursa has married Tadpole McCormick, the older man who owns The Spider and who has been her caretaker during her recovery. Rather than a hotel room, Ursa and Tadpole begin their married life in a room above his club. Tadpole acts out of what seems to be a genuine concern for Ursa, but as her employer as well as her lover, his actions can never be free of a commercial taint. At least, that seems to be how Ursa perceives them. Even before her body heals, she begins to sing in Tadpole's club. When she is not singing, she is preoccupied by the Corregidora women's stories. They become topics of her conversation with Tadpole. The first time they come up, Ursa says, "Corregidora. Old man Corregidora, the Portuguese slave breeder and whoremonger. (Is that what they call them?) He fucked his own whores and fathered his own breed. They did the fucking and had to bring him the money they made. My grandmama was his daughter, but he was fucking her too. She said when they did away with slavery down there they burned all the slavery papers so it would be like they never had it" (8–9). The passage introduces a violent, relentlessly brutal history, one characterized by degradation and abuse. But it acknowledges Ursa's basic ignorance of it: she recognizes that she does not know the right terms, but she fails to realize that no terms could be appropriate. More tellingly, the reader notes the tension in this passage between *his whores* and *my grandmama*, a tension that underlines the impossibility of separating the historical abuse from the familial relation.

In response to Ursa's story, Tadpole shares a chapter of his family history that confirms the common experience of exploitation among Africans in the Americas and the unreliability of the written record in the United States as well as in Brazil. Tadpole's father was a blacksmith who bought land after slavery "so the generations after him would always have land to live on. But it didn't turn out that way." When his mother went to the courthouse to claim the land, "somebody had tore one of the pages out the book." The deception is one reason Tadpole leaves home, but he has no will to fight back. As he expresses his resignation, he picks up the image that Ursa has used in her story: "Anyway, they ain't nothing you can do when they tear the pages out of the book and they ain't no record of it. They probably burned the pages" (78).

A third variation on this theme completes this sequence, as Ursa remembers her grandmother's voice telling the story of abolition in Brazil. In contrast to the war that it took to end slavery in the United States, "a pacific abolition" took place in Brazil (76). Isabella, the Brazilian princess whose people crowned her the Redempt'ress, used a jeweled pen to sign the papers that freed the slaves.[33] But more important than the contrasting situations that led to abolition was the similar erasure of slavery from the memory of both nations. In a merging of voices characteristic of the novel, the grandmother's words echo the great-grandmother's recollection and pledge: "*And that's when the officials burned all the papers cause they wanted to play like what had happened before never did happen. But I know it happened, I bear witness that it happened*" (79).

The stories of the Corregidora women are repeated with an accretion of anecdote: Corregidora prefers dark-skinned women (the color of coffee beans); he refuses to allow his women to sleep with black men; he ships black men out to the fields if he wants to have sex with their wives; he forces Great Gram to have sex with both him and his wife. These repetitions function as repetitions function in blues. As Jones explains in *Liberating Voices*, "[R]epetition in this tradition does not mean stasis, but change/new recognition; a turning point or carrying forward of experience follows each repeated line."[34] In the repetition of these stories, something changes in the novel as well.

A crucial turning point occurs when Ursa goes home to challenge her mother to share the mother's own story. Ursa, who has been over-whelmed by memories of the family story, wants an answer to the question: "*How could she bear witness to what she'd never lived, and refuse me what she had lived?*" (103). The mother complies. Tellingly, she begins by correcting the one fact that Ursa thinks she knows. Ursa's father, Martin, "wasn't a man I met at no depot," the mother declares in her own blues cadence and begins to set the record straight (111). The story Correy tells revolves around yearnings and missed connections, too, but also about her inability to acknowledge, let alone articulate, her own desires. She has refused, for example, to admit that she desired Martin for himself and not just as the procreator of her daughter.[35] As Ursa has felt with Tad-pole, Correy remembers feeling numb as she had sex with Martin. Their marital relationship is defined not by love but by money and anger, thus duplicating the axis of the relationship between her maternal ancestors and Corregidora. In relating the violent act that culminates the relation-ship, Correy remembers saying to Martin, "'Don't hurt me' . . . I said, 'Help me Martin, but don't hurt me'" (119). Not only does Martin beat Correy, but he rips her clothes and sends her out on the street "lookin like a whore." This in turn is how the men who accost her on the street perceive her. But, before she leaves, Correy turns the gaze back on Martin and sees "all that hurt there" (121).

Staring down that hurt and understanding the legacy of self-hate that fuels it are the tasks that both mother and daughter are left to complete. Self-hate begins with the hatred of the black body. Embedded in the story Correy tells are remembered stories of how Corregidora forbids his female slaves to sleep with black men. The extent to which these women have internalized the white slave owner's fear and hatred of black men is revealed in the epithets Great Gram hurls at Martin. Martin retaliates with the question that goes to the heart of the fixation three generations of women have with their oppressor: "How much was hate for Corregi-dora and how much was love?" (131).[36] The question and its permutations linger over the rest of the novel.

The legacy of self-hate is not, however, peculiar to the Corregidora women. All the novel's characters partake of it. They are fixated on com-plexion as a measure of beauty and value. Lighter-skinned blacks like Ursa are desired and distrusted. On one occasion Ursa returns to her hometown, and the neighborhood women immediately assume she will steal their husbands. They do not doubt that her lighter skin makes her more attractive than they are. Darker-skinned people are generally devalued, as the name Mutt surely signifies.

Unsurprisingly, once mother and daughter begin their conversation, they do not want it to end. The dynamic quality of the story Correy tells contrasts with the static quality of the legacy Ursa's grandmother and great-grandmother have bequeathed. The metonym for that legacy is the dark mahogany china cabinet that Ursa thinks was imported from Brazil and that was opened only "to be dusted or polished" (123). Like the history they cling to, the Corregidora women think of the heirloom as "the best thing in the house." Like the cabinet, the history is handled with care. It cannot be changed: it can only be dusted off, polished, and handed down by rote memory.[37] By contrast, when Correy and Ursa talk to each other about what has happened to them personally and understand how their personal experiences are connected to the ancestral lore, they seize the power to revise the narratives they can shape in the present.

During a monologue that continues for several pages, Correy slips into and out of her grandmother's voice. "Mama kept talking until it wasn't her that was talking, but Great Gram. I stared at her because she wasn't Mama now, she was Great Gram talking" (124). This time she remembers incidents of resistance. The most dramatic one concerns a young black man who befriends Great Gram. When Corregidora decides that a relationship is developing between Great Gram and this young man, he decides to end it. The young man has told Great Gram about his dream of escaping and rebelling like the slaves in Palmares: "You know, Palmares, where these black mens had started their own town, escape and banded together" (126). The young man escapes, and Great Gram reflects on his choice:

> But maybe he did the right thing to run anyway, because maybe if he had stayed there, the way Corregidora was looking when he seen us talking he might've had him beat dead. I ain't never seen him look like that, cause when he send them white mens in there to me he didn't look like that, cause he be nodding and saying what a fine piece I was, said I was a fine speciment of a woman, finest speciment of a woman he ever seen in his life, said he had tested me out hisself, and then they would be laughing, you know, when they come in there to me. (127)

The spirit of resistance associated with Palmares contrasts with the degradation of the Corregidora plantation. Dating from the first decade of the seventeenth century, Palmares was the largest *quilombo*, or fugitive slave settlement, in Brazil. The settlement developed and thrived during the struggle between the Dutch and Portuguese for Pernambuco, in what is now the nation's northeast region. Under the cover provided by the clash, Bantu-speaking captives who belonged to various ethnic groups ran away in substantial numbers. The network of settlements they established was given the collective name Palmares, literally "palm groves." Eventually Palmares became economically self-supporting and culturally autonomous. As such, it was a beacon to slaves on nearby plantations who could hope to become citizens of Palmares (called *palmaristas*). In addition, *palmaristas* launched raids to rescue captives. Those who were "freed" involuntarily were required to rescue at least one other captive in order to earn the freedom they had been given.

According to one historian, Palmares constituted the "unusual exception, a real government of escaped Blacks on Brazilian soil." For the most part it was a government at war with the government of Brazil. At one point the Africans negotiated a treaty with the Portuguese, but the truce was short lived. Yet, despite frequent attempts by the Portuguese to destroy it, Palmares lasted almost a hundred years. The final assault required a force of six thousand Europeans and forty-two days to defeat the Africans.[38] Although few written documents exist, the history of Palmares was passed down through oral tradition both in folktales and through performances of rituals that honored the heroism of the fugitives. From sources such as these, the young male character in *Corregidora*, who lives long after the defeat of Palmares, could continue to be inspired by its example.[39]

For Great Gram, the young man is important because he wants her to share his dream. She recognizes that his willingness to confide in her signals a profound trust. She could have betrayed him to Corregidora, but she does not. As the posse chases the young man, Corregidora takes Great Gram to his bed. She imagines that the rhythm of his sex is the rhythm of the young slave's running. The posse loses track of the young man at the river. The slaves rejoice. But three days later his corpse floats to the surface of the water.

The language of the text inscribes his death as a victory, through a description that alludes both to the Bible and to the *Narrative of the Life of Frederick Douglass*. The latter allusion reconnects the novel's Brazil to the historical American South. "What happened was they chased him as far as the river and he just jumped in and got drownded. Cause they didn't know nothing till three days after that when he rose" (128). Just as the passage evokes the biblical narrative of the Resurrection, when three days after his crucifixion Jesus rose from the dead, it echoes a passage from Douglass's *Narrative*. Ambushed by the slave breaker Covey, Douglass falls flat on his back. Both he and his attacker assume that he is beaten. "[B]ut at this moment—from whence came the spirit I don't know—I resolved to fight; and suiting my action to the resolution, I seized Covey hard by the throat; and as I did so, I rose."[40] For Douglass the spirit of resistance is the spirit of resurrection: the verb "rose" inscribes his rebirth. Jones's novel echoes this transformative moment. Just as Douglass defeats Covey, this nameless slave escapes the grip of the slave owner Corregidora.

Eventually Great Gram fashions her own act of resistance. But the form it takes is not passed down in the familial lore. Ursa's mother knows only that Great Gram has done something to Corregidora that angered him to the point that he wants to kill her but that he does not. Afterward Great Gram leaves the plantation and does not return until she reclaims her daughter in 1906. In the interim, her daughter has taken her place as Corregidora's lover. For Ursa, the mystery of what Great Gram has done is the last memory to be unlocked. In a situation in which the ultimate subjugation is sexual, the ultimate act of resistance, she determines, must be sexual as well. Ursa ponders aloud, "[W]hat is it a woman can do to a man that make him hate her so bad he wont to kill her one minute and keep thinking about her and can't get her out of his mind the next?" (184). She intuits the answer as she performs fellatio on her long-absent lover.

Like blues variations, the novel's psychological changes occur within a tightly drawn frame. Ursa does not achieve transcendence. She makes a strategic peace with her history and asserts her selfhood in the privacy of the bed she once again shares with Mutt. A blues riff concludes the novel. It offers one final variation on the themes of love and hurt, pain and pleasure. Most directly, it revises the last conversation that Correy has had with Martin and thereby suggests that the daughter will not repeat the mother's life. Although its structure appropriates the repetitions and tonalities of the blues tradition, it takes the form of a duet rather than a solo. Ursa responds to Mutt's call.

> "I don't want a kind of woman that hurt you," he said.
> "Then you don't want me."
> "I don't want a kind of woman that hurt you."
> "Then you don't want me."
> "I don't want a kind of woman that hurt you."
> "Then you don't want me."
> He shook me until I fell against him crying. "I don't want a kind of man that'll hurt me neither," I said. (185)

One revision seems most significant: rather than a beating, the conversation between Ursa and Mutt ends in an embrace.

By worrying the line of blues and history, Ursa achieves at least moments of reconciliation with her lover, her mother, and the generations of Corregidora women. The characters share a recent and distant history that is so violent and debasing that even moments of reconciliation are hard won. The love that they also share strengthens Ursa's resolve to understand their persistent "trouble in mind." The blues provide the structures of feeling that give her access to that part of her family history that was not only unwritten but also unspeakable. She develops the powers of imagination and empathy that allow her to fill in the gaps in the stories her foremothers have passed down. Strikingly, she answers the kinds of questions regarding her great-grandmother that Patricia Williams can only pose about hers. The art of fiction enables such bold imaginative acts.

Corregidora is the "song branded in the new world" that Ursa dreams of singing. The novel represents the many-layered histories of oppression, subjugation, and survival of Africans in the Western Hemisphere. It draws on the history of Brazil to illuminate the history of the United States. It shows how the traumas of the past and present, as of communities and individuals, are intertwined. Slavery commodified black bodies and threatened to destroy the affective bonds between black men and women, parents and children. The destruction was never total. But its lingering effects disfigure the most intimate relationships among the slaves' descendants. Like other texts discussed in Worrying the Line, Cor-

*regidora* both confronts the traumas and represents the longings of individuals. Historically those longings were expressed in and through the blues. *Corregidora* appropriates the blues for literary purposes, to inform a novel that represents the possibility of confronting the past, surviving the present, and constructing a future that moves beyond pain to love.

## six

Writing
beyond the
Blues: *The*
*Color Purple*

In my mind, Zora Neale Hurston, Billie Holiday and Bessie Smith form a sort of unholy trinity. Zora *belongs* in the
tradition of black women singers, rather than among "the
literati," at least to me. There were the extreme highs and
lows of her life, her undaunted pursuit of adventure, passionate emotional and sexual experience, and her love of freedom.
Like Billie and Bessie she followed her own road, believed in
her own gods, pursued her own dreams, and refused to separate herself from "common" people. It would have been nice
if the three of them had had one another to turn to, in times
of need. —Alice Walker, "Zora Neale Hurston: A Cautionary
Tale and a Partisan View"

In her essay "Zora Neale Hurston: A Cautionary Tale and a Partisan View,"
Alice Walker deems Hurston, Billie Holiday, and Bessie Smith "an unholy
trinity." She asserts that Hurston "*belongs* in the tradition of black women
singers." Like Smith and Holiday, Hurston lived a life of "extreme highs
and lows" and was undaunted in her pursuit of adventure, passionate in
her emotional and sexual experience, and constant in her love of freedom. At the end of the essay, Walker avers, "It would have been nice if
the three of them had had one another to turn to, in times of need."[1]
Walker the novelist shifts from the subjunctive to the indicative mood.
She endows the female characters of *The Color Purple* with the attributes
she assigns to the historical figures in her essay. Moreover, the novel is
informed thematically and structurally by the blues ethics and aesthetics

that shaped the singers' art. But at its midpoint the narrative "turns," and Walker introduces a global spiritual consciousness that was historically unavailable to the figures who inspire her text. This spiritual consciousness, which Walker defines elsewhere as a sense "that everything has equal rights because existence itself is equal," enables the sister bonding that Walker desires in her essay, but it subverts the blues ethics that initially inform the novel.[2]

Incarnating two heads of Walker's unholy trinity, Bessie and Zora, Shug Avery is the primary conveyor of these ethical and aesthetic values. What Ralph Ellison wrote of Bessie is true of Shug: "Bessie Smith might have been a 'blues queen' to the society at large, but within the tighter Negro community where the blues were part of a total way of life, and a major expression of an attitude toward life, she was a priestess, a celebrant who affirmed the values of the group and man's ability to deal with chaos."[3] Shug, of course, affirms *woman's* as well as man's ability to deal with chaos. Moreover, although the southern rural black community represented in the novel is one in which blues are integral to the culture, the values Shug propagates are not derived from the blues alone. They partake of African and Native American spiritual traditions and of principles Walker has articulated and defined as "womanist." These principles, like the blues and spiritual traditions, suggest Walker's debt to Hurston, although just as she writes "beyond the blues" in *The Color Purple*, she writes beyond her ancestor's model.

Much has been written about Hurston and her literary texts as models for *The Color Purple*. *Their Eyes Were Watching God* is often cited as a "pretext."[4] Henry Louis Gates Jr. proposes that *The Color Purple* is Walker's love letter to her literary ancestor, and Walker has confirmed that supposition. *The Color Purple* surely extends the line of its precursor text in its themes, especially concerning gender politics; in its use of Black English vernacular; and in its narrative strategies and its metaphors. Walker extracts and boldly proclaims the feminism implicit in Hurston's novel. Both novels chart their protagonists' journey to selfhood. While Janie and her narrator speak themselves into being, Celie writes herself into being. The voice she uses sounds like Janie's voice, however; the two protagonists share a common idiom and diction. *The Color Purple* also repeats and revises key tropes from *Their Eyes*. For example, Janie's metaphor for her narration to her "kissin-friend" Pheoby ("mah tongue is in mah friend's mouf") is literalized in the erotic relationship between Celie and Shug.

"That which is implicit in Hurston's figures," Gates concludes, "Walker makes explicit." [5]

Just as *The Color Purple* makes the gender politics and the rhetorical and figurative strategies of *Their Eyes* more explicit, it extends the implication of that novel's blues ethics and aesthetics. To give Janie Crawford access to the liberating and self-affirming ethics of the blues, Hurston invented a male character to be Janie's mentor. A blues troubadour whose only possession is his guitar, Tea Cake becomes Janie's lover. Their erotic connection fulfills the dream of "marriage" Janie has harbored throughout the novel. Equally important, Tea Cake leads Janie to an understanding of her culture, from which she has been alienated by her class position, and of her self. Although he is a flawed character who at times becomes jealous and abusive, he is an efficacious spiritual guide. He leads Janie to the wisdom she achieves at the end of the novel: "Two things everybody's got tuh do fuh theyselves. They got tuh go tuh God, and they got tuh find out about livin' fuh theyselves." [6]

Shug performs the parallel function in *The Color Purple*. But even more than "Tea Cake," Shug's name evokes Big Sweet, the female exemplar whom Hurston met while doing fieldwork at the Everglades Lumber Camp in Polk County, Florida. An autonomous woman who is respected by her female and male peers, Big Sweet resists any challenge to her selfhood by asserting that "Ah got de law in my mouth." Big Sweet is a woman of the jook, the combination dance hall, gaming parlor, and pleasure house that Hurston called "the incubator of the blues." Scenes in *Mules and Men* show Big Sweet in the jook, signifying and playing cards with a piece of gamblers' lucky hoodoo in her hair. For Hurston, the jook was musically "the most important place in America." [7] But the jook was also a space where black women were free of the bonds of traditional marriage, the constraints of ladyhood, and the authority of the church. They were free to improvise new identities for themselves. Big Sweet, as her name implies, is both physically imposing and emotionally gentle, powerful and sensual. Her lover, Joe Willard, is a blues man, and Hurston represents the tensions and the commitment in their relationship. But the crucial relationship in the text is that between Big Sweet and the narrator, Zora, for whom she acts as protector and friend.

*The Color Purple* restores the female bonding intimated in Hurston's urtext. To represent this bonding, the novel draws not only on Hurston's literary texts but also on the cultural texts in which the lives and art of the blueswomen are inscribed. Like *Corregidora*, it is informed by blues ethics and aesthetics. *The Color Purple* worries the lines of the blues themselves. It also draws on singers' biographies to represent the context in which these women fashioned their art. While Bessie Smith and other blueswomen have long symbolized female creativity and autonomy, Shug Avery is one of surprisingly few characters in African American fiction to be derived from the personae of the classic blues singers.[8] Her invention followed years during which Alice Walker wrote often and eloquently of her quest for artistic models.[9]

Walker's reclamation of her literary foremothers is rightly praised. Throughout the 1970s, at the same time that she was establishing her own career, Walker was recuperating the work of her forgotten predecessors. Not only did she champion Hurston's work, but she offered a catalog of writers whose names were then barely known: Frances Watkins Harper, Nella Larsen, Anne Spencer, Dorothy West; she sought to recuperate the reputation of Phillis Wheatley, whose name was known but whose words were mocked more often than honored. In "Saving the Life That Is Your Own," for example, she offers one of several accounts in her prose of her discovery of Hurston's work. Through a series of interpolated narratives, Walker describes how, by reading Hurston's writing on hoodoo in *Mules and Men*, she was able to make literature out of an old story that her mother had told. Walker claims that her satisfaction with the result owed much less to the prizes the story won than to the process of writing it, which she chronicles. "In that story ["The Revenge of Hannah Kemhuff"] I gathered up the historical and psychological threads of the life my ancestors lived, and in the writing of it I felt joy and strength and my own continuity."[10] Many of those historical and psychological threads could not be traced on the written record. In "In Search of Our Mothers' Gardens," she reminds her readers that for centuries it was "a punishable crime for a black person to read or write." She implores them: "Consider, if you can bear to imagine it, what might have been the result if singing, too, had been forbidden by law. Listen to the voices of Bessie Smith, Billie Holiday, Nina Simone, Roberta Flack, and Aretha Franklin, among others, and imagine those voices muzzled for life."[11] In addition to the freedom to sing, these women had the advantage of having a tradition in which to locate their art. Bessie Smith recognized her link to Ma Rainey, and so did her audience. In contrast to the stories anonymous black women like Walker's mother passed down through the oral tradition, Rainey's songs "retained their creator's name even while blasting forth from Bessie Smith's mouth."[12]

Like many black writers—an arbitrary list might begin with Langston Hughes, Amiri Baraka, Gayl Jones, and Ntozake Shange—Walker sees music as the supreme achievement of African Americans in art. For Walker, musicians as well as writers become important models. As she responded to interviewer John O'Brien, "I am trying to arrive at that place where black music already is; to arrive at that unself-conscious sense of collective oneness; that naturalness, that (even when anguished) grace."[13] With the representation of Shug Avery, who partakes in so many ways of the blueswoman persona, Walker writes her way to that place.

In the early years of the twentieth century, women like Ma Rainey, Ida Cox, Sippie Wallace, and Bessie Smith had invented an art of their own. "Classic blues," the term jazz historians coined to describe the result, refers both to their repertoire—the mixture of the traditional southern folk blues with often bawdy show tunes and Tin Pan Alley songs—and to their innovative vocal styles.[14] As Amiri Baraka (then LeRoi Jones) has written, they achieved a "beautiful balance between the urban and country styles of blues."[15] Their lyrics often reflected the new realities of city life, but they were grounded in the tradition of southern folk blues. At their best, these artists interwove lines from the blues storehouse and lines of their invention to fashion compelling poetry. Surely, Bessie Smith's "Back Water Blues" and "Young Woman's Blues" are among the finest poems written during the period literary scholars call the Harlem Renaissance.

Even when they sang songs that were not of their own making or even of their own choosing, the vocal signature was unmistakably theirs. They were experts at undercutting the trite sentimentality of Tin Pan Alley and remolding its songs to reflect hardscrabble, cynically humorous truths. When, for example, Bessie Smith recorded "Baby, Won't You Please Come Home," she shifted the beats so that the stress was on the word "please." Yet the effect was to mock the plea rather than intensify it. Her interpolated lines "Landlord's getting worse, I got to move May the first / Baby, won't you please come home. I need money" encapsulate her wholly unsentimental perspective. Notwithstanding the power of her words, the artistry of the blueswoman is conveyed most powerfully not through her words but through the timbre of her voice, the subtlety of her phrasing, and her highly sophisticated rhythmic sense. Working alongside such master instrumentalists as Louis Armstrong, Fletcher Henderson, and James P. Johnson, Rainey, Smith, Wallace, and Cox initiated and responded to the musical innovations that became known as jazz. As Daphne Duval Harrison observes, through their performing style, inflection, and emphasis as well as their lyrical improvisations, the blueswomen introduced "a different model of black women," one that was assertive, sexually aware, and independent.[16]

Although, contrary to popular myth, there was not often a direct correspondence between the singer's life and her song—the songs are much less autobiographical than has been thought—there is an ethical identity. Both the singer and her persona believe, for example, that reality once confronted can be survived; indeed, in Sherley Anne Williams's words, "[T]he inability to solve a problem does not necessarily mean that one can, or ought to transcend it."[17] The blueswoman acknowledged her inability to master the circumstances of her life, but she generally refused to be mastered by them. She could not turn back the "bo weevil" or the jailer. Neither could she force a man to love her or compel the mailman to bring some news. She could, however, express her determination to survive anyhow. Acquiring the knowledge that would make surviving this world possible depended ultimately on a true understanding of self; consequently, self had to be affirmed in the face of society's unceasing attempts to devalue it. No exemplum was more useful to the classic blues singer's black female audience.

In an era when stereotypes about black women were virulent and commonplace, the affirmation in Bessie Smith's "Young Woman's Blues" that "I'm as good as any woman in your town" was profoundly resonant. Many blues offered a more qualified declaration. In "Mean Tight Mama," for example, Sara Martin improvises on a folk adage that partakes of both self-hatred and self-assertion: "Now my hair is nappy, and I don't wear no clothes of silk [repeat] / But the cow that's black and ugly, has often got the sweetest milk." The statement does not challenge the prevailing standards of beauty and value, but the counterstatement expresses the speaker's refusal to be bound by them. Moreover, the following verse establishes the sexual sphere as one in which the speaker can assert autonomy. "Now when a man starts jivin', I'm tighter than a pair of shoes, [repeat] / I'm a mean tight mama, with my mean tight mama blues."[18] The song proclaims both the control she exerts over her body and the control she assumes over her art. "Mean" and "tight" counter "black and ugly" and become positive female attributes that define these blues as the singer's own.

In their much fabled personal lives, as in their performances, the blueswomen achieved a measure of freedom, independence, and power only dreamed of by women in their audiences. To a significant degree the blueswomen's lives seemed and were the stuff of legend. Gertrude Pridgett left home at fourteen, joined a group called A Bunch of Black-berries, served a long apprenticeship working tent shows, and emerged in the 1920s as Ma Rainey, the Mother of the Blues. Bessie Smith was the poor motherless black girl singing on Chattanooga street corners who grew up to be the Empress. Then there was Alberta Hunter, who went from a southside Chicago dive to a cabaret, tellingly named Dream-land, en route to London and European fame. These women were wish-fulfillment heroines, and in every aspect of their public lives they played the part. On stage they were always dressed to the nines whether they pre-ferred the understated elegance of the young Bessie's white satin gowns or the elaborately beaded and spangled costumes favored by Ma Rainey. Early blues critics used the blueswomen's personal styles to discredit them; apparently some male writers believed that artists did not adorn themselves in fur boas and silk gowns. To Rudi Blesh, who coined the term, the "classic blues" were "pseudo-blues." Dismissing the singers as "young girls who were vaudeville entertainers" and their songs as blues composed by New York writers, Samuel Charters concluded that in the twenties vogue for the blues "the blues had lost their folk roots."[19] But the critics these singers heeded were the members of their audience. And they knew their glamorous style was part of what made them heroines to their fans, many of whom, like the blueswomen, had migrated from their southern homes.

Moreover, as Hazel Carby asserts, these women's "physical presence was a crucial aspect of their power; the visual display of spangled dresses, of furs, of gold teeth, of diamonds, of all the sumptuous and desirable aspects of their body reclaimed female sexuality from being an objectifi-cation of male desire to a representation of female desire."[20] Some black men who could not see beauty in her Negroid features gave Ma Rainey the epithet "the ugliest woman alive." But the glamour with which she ar-rayed herself rendered their judgment irrelevant. To an extent the women in their audience could only dream of, the blueswomen had wrested con-trol of their lives.

Shug Avery's experience as the woman who left home and succeeded in the world on her own terms replicates the historical experience of Ma Rainey and Bessie Smith. In the relationship between Shug and Celie, *The Color Purple* reifies the relationship between the blueswoman and this audience. To appropriate Hortense Spillers's observation, the novel represents a black woman's translation of "the female vocalist's gestures into an apposite structure of terms that . . . articulate[s] both her kinship to other women and the particular nuances of her own experience." [21] Specifically, the novel depicts the process by which Celie comes to understand Shug Avery as a light giver and life giver whose power derives from her independence, integrity, expressiveness, eroticism, and spirituality. Through this process of translation, Celie acquires self-knowledge.

Signaling the iconic importance of the blues queen to her audience, the novel's initial representation of Shug Avery is a photograph.

> She [Celie's stepmother] git a picture. The first one of a real person I ever seen. She say Mr. —— was taking somethin out his billfold to show Pa an it fell out an slid under the table. Shug Avery was a woman. The most beautiful woman I ever saw. She more pretty than my mama. She bout ten thousand times more prettier than me. I see her there in furs. Her face rouge. Her hair like somethin tail. She grinning with her foot up on somebody motocar. Her eyes serious tho. Sad some. [22]

What is striking in this response is Celie's sense of wonder that a black woman could be so glamorous and so free. Here freedom is suggested by the car against which Shug is so jauntily posed. [23] However, the sadness in Shug's eyes indicates that the glamour and mobility may be unreliable indexes of power. The impact of this picture on the traumatized and isolated Celie is revivifying nonetheless. Other than Nettie and her children, Shug becomes the first person to stir any curiosity in Celie. A subsequent reference reinforces the iconic importance of the blueswoman. Overhearing Pa and Mr. —— bartering—Celie and Nettie being the objects of exchange—Celie takes out the photograph. As Pa heaps insult onto insult, Celie looks into Shug's eyes, which seem to say, "Yeah, it bees that way sometimes" (10).

A flyer announcing her appearance at the Lucky Star provides Celie with a second image of Shug, and here again the Queen Honeybee seems totally self-assured. The novel's introduction of the actual character serves to undercut these images, or rather, to place them in perspective.

Shug enters the narrative dressed to kill, in red and black, in a feathered hat and snakeskin shoes, yet looking "like she ain't long for this world but dressed well for the next" (42). Cast out and reviled by the respectable members of the community, Shug is at this point helpless and totally dependent. When Celie looks at Shug, she sees through the makeup to a "face black as Harpo," with a "long pointed nose and big fleshy mouth" (42). Shug is no longer a woman ten thousand times prettier than Celie; she looks like someone Celie knows. Shug's helplessness narrows the distance between her and Celie, so much so that Celie recognizes Shug's initial meanness ("you sure is ugly") as the defensive reaction it is. Shug's "evil," Celie reflects, keeps her alive.

In this moment the novel translates the meaning of scores of blues songs like "Mean Tight Mama" and "Evil Gal Blues." Moreover, Shug's extreme vulnerability in the early scenes evokes the persona of the classic blues singer who, despite her strength, fell prey to "no good" men, bad habits, and illness. Like them, Shug is a "queen" who, in Mr. ——'s words, has nobody to fight for her. The blueswoman's vulnerability was part of the price she paid for her independence. But it was also part of her appeal; on its account her audience saw in her a soul mate as well as a star. Gospel queen Mahalia Jackson remembered how, as a girl in New Orleans, she listened to Bessie Smith and thought that "she was having troubles like me. That's why it was such a comfort for people of the South to hear her."[24] To a substantial degree, the audience and the singer were traveling the same lonesome road. The parallels in the plots the text develops for Celie and Shug—particularly those that situate them as mothers of lost children—reinforce this connection.

While her dependence makes Shug approachable for the pathologically passive Celie, it is Shug's independent spirit that, in one of the novel's recurrent metaphors, brings light. A series of seemingly minor incidents first reveal the impact of Shug's example. To begin, Shug demystifies Mr. —— by calling him Albert, something only she and Nettie, among the novel's female characters, are strong enough to do. Simply put, to Shug and Nettie, Albert is a man, not a master. Consequently, Shug sees herself as Albert's equal; her comfort is as important as his. For example, she thinks nothing of telling Albert that she does not want to smell his pipe, and he declines to smoke. To Celie such consideration registers as weakness. In fact, as Celie observes Mr. —— agonizing over Shug and even shedding a tear, she thinks only: "I have more chin" (44).

In this instance Albert is acting not out of weakness but out of love. Celie misperceives his motives both because he cannot articulate them and because they are totally inconsistent with his otherwise inhumane behavior. But for a character who devalues herself as completely as Celie does, to compare herself favorably to anyone is a step forward. Moreover, if Celie is to fight, as a chorus of women including Nettie, Sophia, and even Albert's sisters urge her to do, she has got to shed her belief in Mr. ———'s invincibility. This early scene prefigures the transformations both Celie and Albert undergo and the catalytic role Shug plays in each.

If the power of her personality is one important source of Shug's independence, her money is another. The representation of Shug Avery bears out an observation Walker makes elsewhere in reference to Hurston: "Without money of one's own in a capitalist society, there is no such thing as independence."[25] Unbeholden to anyone, Shug runs her own life; she organizes her band and manages her career. In this regard the novel depicts the fact asserted by LeRoi Jones in *Blues People* that the advent of the classic blues marked the African American's entrance into the world of professional entertainment. Blues singing "no longer had to be merely a passionately felt avocation; it could now become a way of making a living."[26] Shug's success allows her to buy the clothes and cars she pleases and to build a big pink house in Memphis. With its fountains and statues, the house is as garish—or, to use one of Walker's favorite adjectives, as "incorrect"—as the costumes the blues queens fancied. Celie describes these possessions in detail, since to Celie Shug's possessions symbolize her autonomy. The text challenges Celie's perspective by indicating that Shug is not truly autonomous. No black person in a racist capitalist society, regardless of the money he or she has, is powerful enough to create a world of his or her own. A subtle indication that Shug's money does not give her total control of her life is reflected in her inability to build the round house she has initially planned. "Everybody act like that's backward," she explains to Celie as she shows her the sketch of her unrealized design (177). Every aspect of Shug's personal style, realized and unrealizable, is an implicit rejection of societal values, including the value accorded money.[27]

Shug inspires Celie's and Albert's transformations because she is the novel's moral agent. Of course, hers is not the received morality; when judged by conventional standards, Shug is deemed profoundly immoral (as were Bessie Smith, Ma Rainey, Ida Cox, and others). But, as the novel asserts continuously, standards that sanction oppression, exploitation, and abuse must be rejected before any valid standards can be devised. Shug is in the process of devising new standards. She makes mistakes and inflicts serious harm when she does—as in her treatment of Annie Julia (Albert's first wife) and her initial treatment of Celie. What matters more, however, is that Shug holds herself accountable and continues to seek and define moral values worthy of her adherence. By the end of the novel, Albert and Celie are able to articulate responses to this aspect of Shug's character. According to Albert, "Shug act more manly than most men. I mean she upright, honest. Speak her mind and the devil take the hindmost. . . . She bound to live her life and be herself no matter what" (228). Albert's assessment is flawed but not negated by his residual sexism, and Celie emends his description by insisting that Shug's stance is "womanly."[28] What Albert and Celie valorize in these comments is Shug's integrity, a core value in blues ethics.

Stories abound recounting the ways in which blueswomen remained true to themselves, no matter what. Whether it was standing up to a recalcitrant lover or standing down the Ku Klux Klan, as Bessie Smith once did, the blueswomen did not compromise their selfhood. Neither does Shug Avery. Although the situations she confronts in the novel are all personal—Walker chooses not to represent her in conflict with a theater owner or any other white person—Shug meets the problems she faces head-on. She does not flinch from unflattering truths about herself, either. When she explains her infidelity to Celie, she attributes her affair with a nineteen-year-old flutist to her insecurity: "I'm gitting old. I'm fat. Nobody think I'm good looking no more, but you" (211). In some ways the tone of the passage in which Shug confides her indiscretion to Celie is so humorous that it seems almost a blues counterstatement to the idea the passage conveys. This is consistent with traditions of blues performance. Indeed, Ma Rainey joked on stage about her penchant for the young men she called "pig meat."

Even when Celie finds it initially impossible to forgive Shug's actions, she respects her for the honesty with which she reports them. By the end of the novel Celie understands that Shug's integrity is both an approach to life and the result of the life experiences she has confronted. "What I love best bout Shug is what she been through, I say. When you look in Shug's eyes you know she been where she been, seen what she seen, did what she did. And now she know" (228). All of Shug's experiences, noble and ignoble, make her the dynamic character that she is.

If blues ethics place a premium on integrity in one's daily life, blues aesthetics place the highest value on integrity in the art. In this as in other ways, blues ethics and aesthetics merge. Truth, blues scholar David Evans asserts, is the essence of the folk blues, and the ability to project sincerity is the standard by which blues singers are judged. This truth need not be unitary or literal; it is contingent instead on varied experiences and perceived from varied perspectives. The experiences are not necessarily the singer's own. And yet, as a Mississippi bluesman explained to Evans: "Sometimes I'd propose as if it happened to me in order to hit somebody else, 'cause everything that happened to one person has at some time or other happened to another one. If not, it will." [29] The ideal, as expressed in an adage beloved of blues and gospel singers alike, remains "to live the life I sing about in my song."

*The Color Purple* uses Shug Avery's life to illumine her art. Few scenes in the novel depict Shug at work, but those few suggest the sources of her blues. The most memorable is her first appearance at Harpo's juke joint. She opens her set with "A Good Man Is Hard to Find," a song identified with Bessie Smith, though not written by her as the novel implies. The reference nevertheless locates Shug's art in the classic blues tradition. The second number is called "Miss Celie's Song" because, Shug says, "she [Celie] scratched it out of my head when I was sick" (65). The words are formulaic, but the feeling the song expresses grows directly out of Shug's season of suffering and renewal. The power of Shug's art is conveyed through Celie's response to it. In a heightened sense, Celie experiences the reaction many in the blueswoman's audience shared: the singer seemed to be singing *their* song. Celie hears in Shug's song, as she sees in her life, the possibilities of her own renewal.

The sexual relationship that develops between Celie and Shug allows Celie to realize those possibilities. What critic Michele Russell writes of Bessie Smith applies as well to Shug Avery: "In a deliberate inversion of the Puritanism of the Protestant ethic, she articulated, as clearly as anyone before or since, how fundamental sexuality was to survival." [30] Under the protection of Shug's love, Celie transforms herself from sexual object to sexual subject. Having attained autonomy in the sexual sphere, Celie is empowered to pursue it in other aspects of her life. Celie's first response to Shug—to the photograph—is subconsciously sexual.[31] The more conscious she becomes of her attraction to Shug, such as when she gives her a bath, the more uncomfortable she becomes. The novel need not explicate the community's homophobia because it represents Celie's internalization of the lesbianism taboo.[32]

Few were more defiant of that taboo than the blueswomen themselves, and even they were adept at subterfuge. Biographers concur that Ma Rainey, like Bessie Smith, was bisexual. But, however widely rumors of their sexual preferences circulated during their lifetime, the singers did not confirm them. Ma Rainey came closest when she teased in one of her songs, "'Cause they say I do it, ain't nobody caught me, / Sure got to prove it on me." [33]

Once Shug redefines her as a virgin, Celie is free to work out her sexual identity. When she and Shug become lovers, Celie describes the experience using the metaphor of rebirth. Although it signals the sentimental gauze that overlays the novel's erotic scenes, the metaphor does not vitiate this scene's meaning. The liberation of her sexual self is a precondition for Celie's freedom. As Audre Lorde argues in her essay "The Uses of the Erotic":

> But when we begin to live from within outward, in touch with the power of the erotic within ourselves, and allowing that power to inform and illuminate our actions upon the world around us, then we begin to be responsible to ourselves in the deepest sense. For as we begin to recognize our deepest feelings, we begin to give up, of necessity, being satisfied with suffering and self-negation, and with the numbness which so often seems like their only alternative in our society. Our acts against oppression become integral with the self, motivated and empowered from within.[34]

This passage analyzes Celie's growth and liberation precisely. Shug is the first to hear the story of the abuse Celie has suffered; Shug initiates the conversation. Before Shug, Celie has confided only in God; unlike God, Shug affirms Celie's right to rage. She empathizes with Celie's pain and shares her own, creating a mutuality that anticipates the reciprocity they achieve in lovemaking. Finally, Shug helps Celie work through the numbness that accompanies her discovery of Mr. ——'s ultimate cruelty, the theft of Nettie's letters. When, at last, Celie declares her independence, she takes her cue from her lover but claims her own voice.

The scene that represents this event exemplifies the way the novel is shaped by blues aesthetics. As Walker orchestrates the scene, one might say that Shug Avery vamps until Celie is ready to sing the lead:

> Celie is coming with us, say Shug.
>
> Mr. ——'s head swivel back straight. Say what? he ast.
>
> Celie is coming to Memphis with me.
>
> Over my dead body, Mr. —— say.
>
> You satisfied that what you want, Shug say, cool as clabber.
>
> Mr. —— start up from his seat, look at Shug, plop back down again. He look over at me. I thought you was finally happy, he say. What wrong now.
>
> You a lowdown dog is what's wrong, I say. It's time to leave you and enter into the Creation. And your dead body just the welcome mat I need. (170)

This dialogue worries the blues line through Shug's repetition, which emphasizes Shug's determination and clarifies the point that Celie is going to Memphis with her, not merely as part of Shug's entourage. Celie's reference to the "Creation" reflects the spiritual lessons Shug has taught, lessons that empower Celie to defy Mr. —— and take control of her life.

The call-and-response pattern of this exchange is only one example of the influence of blues on the novel's form. Not only does Celie respond to Shug's call, but Mary Agnes, a character whose vocal tone and personality suggest Billie Holiday (the third head of Walker's unholy trinity), responds to Celie's. Moreover, like the blues, Celie's letters are laconic, blunt, and poetic; they are written not to communicate so much as to express what the soul cannot hold within.[35] This conclusion is reinforced by the fact that Celie's letters to Nettie are never delivered; nevertheless, Nettie intuits the meaning of Celie's expressive act. Explaining why she continues to write letters she is certain Celie will never receive, Nettie remarks: "I remember one time you said your life made you feel so ashamed you couldn't even talk about it to God, you had to write it, bad as you thought your writing was. Well, now I know what you meant. And whether God will read letters or no, I know you will go on writing them; which is guidance enough for me. Anyway, when I don't write to you I feel as bad as I do when I don't pray, locked up in myself and choking on my own heart" (110).

Despite its worldliness, an important aspect of the blues singers' art was spiritual. To Alberta Hunter blues were "like spirituals, almost sacred. When I sing: I walk the floor, wring my hands and cry / Yes, I walk the floor, wring my hands and cry, What I'm doing is letting my soul out."[36] Comment after comment affirms the connection members of the audience made between their response to the blueswoman and being in church. A typical reaction came from one of Smith's musicians: "If you had any church background, like people who came from the South as I did, you would recognize the similarity between what she was doing and what those preachers and evangelists from there did, and how they moved people. Bessie did the same thing on stage."[37] Choosing his words with care, this man draws an analogy between the spirit that moved Bessie and that animating the preacher; he asserts that their impact, if not their source, was comparable. Houston Baker has proposed a definition of "classic" that clarifies this aspect of the blues singer's art. "A classic in any culture, one might say, is a space in which the spirit works. The very sign 'classic' denotes an absence of temporal and material boundaries and suggests the accomplishment of effects through means outstripping the tangible and immediate."[38]

For blueswomen, the stage sometimes became a ritual space, "a space in which the spirit works." The rituals they enacted celebrated both the erotic and the spiritual. If, on the one hand, their adorned bodies inscribed their sexual subjectivity, on the other, the beaded dresses, feathered headpieces, and ornate jewelry could be perceived as ceremonial dress. Perhaps the most famous ritual opened Ma Rainey's performances. Almost a symbolic enactment of the birth of the blues, the ritual enforced Rainey's maternal claim. As the band played its introduction, the curtain rose to reveal a large replica of a Victrola bathed in blue light. A girl came on stage and put a record on the phonograph, and Ma Rainey's voice emerged from within. When the doors of the Victrola opened, Ma Rainey stepped into the spotlight, and the crowd went wild. In his description of the performance, her pianist, Georgia Tom, who later became Thomas A. Dorsey, the Father of Gospel, emphasized the magical effect of her jewels: "Her diamonds flashed like sparks of fire falling from her fingers. The gold-piece necklace lay like a golden armor covering her chest. They called her the lady with the golden throat."[39]

Whereas her detractors could hear only the erotic or, to their ears, the profane, Ma Rainey's fans could hear something spiritual in her singing, even if they lacked a vocabulary to define it. They had either to rely on references to the religious tradition they knew, Christianity, or to concede their inability to express the inexpressible. As Sterling Brown represents it in his poem "Ma Rainey": "Dere wasn't much more de fellow say: / She jes' gits hold of us thataway."[40]

In *The Color Purple*, Alice Walker attempts to articulate this spirituality. The attempt is complicated by her decision *not* to represent the spirit work in performance but to abstract it from ritual. Shug speaks through the spirit offstage, rather than on. But because the novel has constructed Celie as a metonym for the blues singer's audience, whatever space these characters share becomes a potential site for spirit work. Shug can speak as well as sing that "unself-conscious sense of collective oneness." She has achieved the requisite grace.[41]

Throughout her writing, Walker has asserted the interrelation of spirituality and art. In the classic essay "In Search of Our Mothers' Gardens," Walker seeks to define a tradition of black women's art in which she can locate her own work; in the process, she suggests ways in which black women's art offers possibilities for transcendence other than those offered by organized religion. Walker writes of some of her foremothers: "They were Creators, who lived lives of spiritual waste, because they were so rich in spirituality—which is the basis of Art—that the strain of enduring their unused and unwanted talent drove them insane." These are the women on whom poet Jean Toomer based his characters in *Cane*: "black women whose spirituality was so intense, so deep, so *unconscious*, that they were themselves unaware of the richness they held."[42] Significantly, when Fern, the most intense of these characters, experiences spiritual ecstasy, she cries "inarticulately in plaintive, convulsive sounds, mingled with calls to Christ Jesus."[43] Fern is surely no orthodox Christian (which is perhaps one reason Toomer gives her the Jewish surname Rosen), but the only vocabulary she can employ to discuss spiritual concerns is borrowed from the church she detests.

In *The Color Purple* Alice Walker seeks through Shug to represent this heterodox spirituality brought to consciousness. Shug knows and is unafraid to say that "any God I ever felt in church I brought in with me" (165). Echoing another of Toomer's characters, she dismisses the Bible as "the white folks' white bible" and urges Celie to love the "color purple" rather than the idols men have created. That a classic blues singer would posit definitions of God is wholly credible. But when Shug urges Celie to "conjure up flowers, wind, water, a big rock" when she wants to pray, the novel inscribes a pantheism that to my ear has no resonance in the blues.[44]

Tellingly, Shug's exposition of her spiritual beliefs follows the introduction of Nettie's letters in the text. Not only do the letters that report Nettie's travels to New York, London, and Africa expand the novel's geographical boundaries, but they provide a context for the spiritual revelations that both Nettie and Shug impart. Shug's spiritual understanding is represented as being intuitive, but the novel's complex discourse of spirituality links it explicitly to African traditions—traditions that are interrogated and revised in the text.[45]

The novel's depiction of African culture generally has proved problematic for critics, especially those who assume that the novel is realist fiction. They argue that the novel misrepresents West African culture, that its depiction is static rather than dynamic, and that it fails to consider the impact of colonialism.[46] Certainly, the novel takes liberties in its representation of African spiritual traditions. For example, in her description of the Olinka roofleaf ceremony, Nettie reports, "[T]he roofleaf became the thing they worship" (131). She makes the error, characteristic of Christian missionaries, of mistaking the image of the traditional god for the god itself. Read against scholarly accounts of traditional West African religions, her representation seems incongruous in several other aspects. Most notably, Nettie reports no belief in a transcendent benevolent deity/creator. This omission reflects the extent to which the very concept of god is contaminated by its association with patriarchal constructs in the novel's thematic scheme. Nettie emphasizes instead belief in "the power of spirits animating things in nature to affect the welfare of people."[47] Whatever its historical foundation, this emphasis serves a narrative function. When Nettie reflects, "[W]e know a roofleaf is not Jesus Christ, but in its own humble way, is it not God?" she anticipates precisely the understanding Shug—and through her, Celie—will subsequently achieve.

After several years in Africa, Nettie avers that "God is different to us now. . . . More spirit than ever before, and more internal. Most people think he has to look like something or someone—a roofleaf or Christ—but we don't. And not being tied to what God looks like frees us" (218). This view is, of course, perfectly congruent with Shug's personal liberation theology and with her explanation to Celie that God is not "a he or a she, but a It": "Don't look like nothing, she say. It ain't a picture show. It ain't something you can look at apart from anything else, including yourself. I believe God is everything, say Shug. Everything that is or ever was or ever will be. And when you can feel that, and be happy to feel that, you've found It" (167). As these statements confirm, spirituality in both of the novel's settings is dissociated from institutional structures and ritual practices. By freeing its representation from the dictates of "social reality," the novel fashions a spirituality that, unlike most organized religion, is free of the taint of systems of domination such as sexism and racism. Here, too, *The Color Purple* worries the line and extends the implications of *Their Eyes*, where Janie in a process abstracted from ritual gains the spiritual wisdom she shares with her Pheoby at the conclusion.[48]

Later in the novel (and elsewhere in Walker's writing), the concept of divine interconnectedness that is at the core of Shug's transcendental vision is associated with Native American systems of belief.[49] Although this association provides an important underpinning of the novel's liberation theology, it renders the novel vulnerable to charges of ironing out the specificities of distinct cultures. Nevertheless, readers can identify the threads of the cultural amalgam the novel weaves.

Scholar Paula Gunn Allen uses the Plains Indians concept of the "sacred hoop" as a figure for the "essential harmony of all things" that she argues is fundamental to the worldview of traditional American Indian societies. Gunn points as well to the broad affinities between American Indian belief systems and those of other "sacred cultures," including traditional African societies.[50] The novel expresses these affinities in various ways, both sacred and secular. When, for example, Nettie describes the journey to the Olinka village, she notes the dugout canoes that look like those she has seen pictured in an Indian village (126). Another character, Corinne, and her husband, Samuel, have been missionaries in the Southwest before coming to Africa. Nettie abstracts the qualities of Corinne's "Indianness": "She was so quiet. So reflective. And she could erase herself, her spirit, with a swiftness that truly startled, when she knew the people around her could not respect it" (199). The most important sign of the affinity of "sacred cultures" is the iconography of the round houses preferred by Shug and Nettie, an iconography that is consonant with the sacred hoop.

Yoruban cosmology provides an interesting parallel. In this belief system, the riverain goddesses are represented by round fans, crowns (some with beaded fringes) and earthenware vessels filled with water, rounded stones, and sand. According to the legend (retold in Robert Farris Thompson's *Flash of the Spirit: African and Afro-American Art and Philosophy*), Ifá, the god of divination, quarreled with the river goddesses and departed from the holy city. Thereafter a famine struck the world. Ifá hid in the forest in a round house made of leaves and saplings. Only the river goddesses, including Yemoja, who was noted for her round fan, could persuade him to return. When the female spirits, each with a fan like that of Yemoja, found Ifá, they began to fan him, feasted him, and fanned him again. Their actions persuaded him to return to the city, and the famine ended. According to Thompson, the rounded fan—"like a giant soothing drop of water—restores peace and calm, associating itself with the image of Ifá's cool round house made of herbs and leaves. An indelible current of association links the roundness of habitations to the roundness of things pertaining to riverain goddesses."[51]

The novel's round houses offer solace comparable to that of Ifá's. Nettie realizes her dream of a round house, one that reflects the asceticism and virginal purity of her religious vocation. Unlike the square school building or the open-air church, her mud hut is "round, walled, with a round roofleaf roof" (146). A mere twenty feet in diameter, the interior is adorned with the art of the Olinkas. A stove, bed, writing table, and stool are the only furnishings. It is a room for prayer, meditation, and writing. Like the sacred places identified throughout this study, Nettie's room is an ordinary place that she remakes to serve a spiritual purpose. According to her unrealized plan, Shug's round house is also to be built of mud or concrete, with a wraparound porch festooned with flowers and statues of Shug's familiars, her elephants and turtles. Unlike Nettie's nunlike cell, Shug's house would be welcoming; her table would be set with the elaborate meals she cooks for her friends. In the novel's Memphis, Shug cannot get anyone to build her dream house. People think it is a "backward" idea. But Shug finds the conventional "backward," for, as she puts it: "I just feel funny living in a square. If I was square, then I could take it better" (178). She settles for a round bed.

The cool of Shug's house emanates from her. More than a style (which distinguishes her from the squares), "cool" is inherent in her character. Her generosity, creative goodness, and the grace she exhibits under pressure are manifestations of this "cool." Here, too, the parallels to Yoruban belief, in which "coolness is a part of character," are striking. The attributes the novel assigns Shug are consonant with those valorized in Yoruban tradition. Moreover, the Yoruba associate the "mystic coolness" that Shug manifests with the equally crucial quality of àshe, "spiritual command, the power-to-make-things-happen, God's own enabling light rendered accessible to men and women."[52] Shug, the blueswoman, becomes a messenger of àshe.

The novel's treatment of spiritual discourses is futuristic rather than traditional. The Color Purple does not urge the restoration of traditional African society. Indeed, the traditional society the novel depicts is patriarchal, sexist, and vulnerable to colonial exploitation. Nevertheless, it contains spiritual elements that the novel wants to borrow and build on, elements that in the traditional societal context are conservative. Two examples that suggest both the possibilities and liabilities of the novel's representations of Africa are the sense of harmony with nature and the bonding of women that is often associated with polygamy.

The novel's Olinka have "always lived on the exact spot where their village now stands" (129). Their worship of the roofleaf is the reaction to its sudden scarcity in a land where all things that were valued had been abundant. The scarcity results from one man's desire to plant more than his share of land. His actions upset the balance between nature and humankind. Years pass before that harmony is restored. Shug, the traveling blueswoman, achieves a comparable harmony with nature by following a different path. Her epiphany constitutes a powerful dissent from the religious orthodoxy of her childhood: "My first step from the old white man was trees. Then air. Then birds. Then other people. But one day when I was sitting quiet and feeling like a motherless child, which I was, it come to me: that feeling of being part of everything, not separate at all" (167). Having got man "off her eyeball," Shug is free to glory in her oneness with nature. Unlike the racist, sexist society in which she lives, the natural world affirms her value. The ethic of inseparability Shug posits sets the standard for her relationships with other people as with nature. Significantly, adhering to this ethic of responsibility to and for all of creation requires Shug's continuing nonconformity. Her activist example inspires in Celie the courage to remake her life.[53]

Nettie writes about the intense friendships among Olinka women, friendships that develop out of shared work and shared husbands. Such bonds distress her fellow missionary, Samuel, since they indicate to him the women's contentment with polygamy. But Nettie is persuaded that, though husbands occasion these friendships, the husbands themselves are marginal to the Olinka women's lives. "Their lives always center around work and their children and other women" (141). Although Nettie is disparaging of the male privilege on which these arrangements rest, she is more concerned with the free space that women are able to carve out for themselves. Unfortunately, Nettie as a narrator does not allow the voices of these women to speak through her. Consequently, Olinka characters, both female and male, are not sufficiently differentiated throughout the novel. What the novel enables instead is the appreciation of female bonding from the African American situation that parallels the African one. Celie's and Shug's friendship is also occasioned by their status as unofficial co-wives. They become the nucleus of a circle of women that includes Mr. ———'s son Harpo's co-wives, Sophia and Mary Agnes, and risk their lives for one another. Eventually the circle extends beyond the boundaries of marriage and blood relation. Moreover, rather than remaining outside the circle of women, the redeemed men (Albert, Harpo, Samuel) and the new man, Adam, join it. The "family" that the end of the novel celebrates is a new configuration.

In the process of revising elements of traditional African society and belief, Walker revises the traditional blues ethics and aesthetics that give shape to the first half of the narrative. *The Color Purple* looks forward to a utopian future in which circumstances can be mastered, wrongs righted, and evil overturned. Thus, in sharp contrast to the blueswoman's acknowledgment of her inability to master the circumstances of her life— even as she refused to be mastered by them—no problem defies Shug Avery's intervention. She gives Celie spiritual instruction, and in the next scene, Celie announces her decision to leave Mr. ———. A practical as well as a spiritual mentor, Shug helps Celie take possession of her inheritance and establish her business. Even Shug's infidelity is beneficial; it hastens the reconciliation between Celie and Albert. No situation is beyond her ken. When Nettie and her family are reported missing at sea, Shug goes to the State Department to inquire about their status. As with a blues priestess or a Yoruban messenger, when Shug speaks, her words have "spiritual command."

At the conclusion of *The Color Purple*, Walker imagines a world where personal transformations induce social transformations. In imagining such a world, Alice Walker is writing beyond the blues. When she subverts the blues, however, she subverts an already subversive tradition. The paradoxical result is a degree of sentimentality that threatens to undermine the utopian vision the novel sets forth. Yet for readers attuned to its spiritual frequencies, Walker's text is a new age song. It recuperates the blueswoman's voice and the moral agency that is also her legacy. Then, rising over the familiar beat is an obbligato that partakes of African and Native American melodies and that sings of a future wherein voices like Bessie's have the power to change the world.

The Color Purple worries the line as lineage and as literary tradition. It revises conventional definitions of family; like Audre Lorde's Zami, it offers new configurations in which biological kinship is not the foundation of familial connection. Heterosexuality is not normative. Lesbian bonding is celebrated, even if the sexual relationship between Shug and Celie is relatively short lived. Their bond outlasts their romance. The family that gathers at the novel's conclusion includes lovers and former lovers, biological and adopted children, and relatives born in America and Africa. Celie and Nettie, the reunited sisters, are the family's progenitors. The Color Purple plays multiple changes on the line as literary tradition as well. In addition to its revisions of Their Eyes Were Watching God, it recuperates aspects of Hurston's nonfiction and revisits the blues matrix out of which Hurston wrote. Walker reclaims the blues for herself and then tries with mixed success to write beyond them. In the last chapter, I take up Walker's essays, in which she returns to the blues and redefines them as part of her literary line. In so doing, she revises the concept of literary tradition in compelling and affecting ways. But first, I look at texts in which Gloria Naylor and Paule Marshall critique, revise, and subvert precursor texts by African American writers, both female and male.

## seven

Extending the
Line: From *Sula*
to *Mama Day*

Think about it: ain't nobody really talking to you. We're sitting here in Willow Springs, and you're God-knows-where.
It's August 1999—ain't but a slim chance it's the same
season where you are. Uh, huh, listen. Really listen this time:
the only voice is your own.—Gloria Naylor, *Mama Day*

Lyrical, seductive, and justly celebrated, the prologue of Gloria Naylor's
1988 novel *Mama Day* invites the reader into a fictive world that in its
location, history, customs, and beliefs is a world elsewhere. Belonging
to the United States but part of no state, Willow Springs can be located
only on the map that the front matter of the book helpfully provides. Its
existence is anomalous in the extreme: it is a place that has been black-
owned and self-sufficient since 1823 when an enslaved conjure woman
compelled her master to deed the land to her and her descendants. What
renders this unfamiliar world accessible to many readers is the narrator's
language. The use of Black English vernacular and the direct address to
the reader create an illusion of intimacy that is reinforced by the narrator's invitation to include readers in on a joke that is told at the expense
of a resident of Willow Springs. "Reema's boy" is mocked as a classic example of an educated fool. Schooled on the mainland, Reema's boy, in the
only identity the narrator grants him, has returned with a tape recorder
and an addled brain. He has subsequently published his ethnography of
Willow Springs, in which he identified the island's "unique speech patterns" and specified examples of "cultural preservation."[1] His "extensive
field work" has yielded what seems to those on the island who read even

the introduction of his book an inane conclusion. The "18 & 23s," the all-purpose phrase that encodes something of both the island's history and its philosophy, he has determined, is actually an inversion of the lines of longitude and latitude on which Willow Springs was once located on maps. From this observation, Reema's boy has extrapolated the conclusion that inversion is the key to the worldview of Willow Springs, a place where, in order to assert their cultural identity, people had "no choice but to look at everything upside-down" (8). Such a conclusion may impress his fellow academics, but the people of Willow Springs dismiss him and his findings. They wonder "if the boy wanted to know what 18 & 23 means, why didn't he just ask?" (8). Then they go on to admit that they would not or could not have told him. Had he learned to "listen," however, he would have found out for himself.

Reema's boy is not the only butt of this joke. The buzzwords that the narrator attributes to the ethnographer are at least as common among literary critics. Indeed, the narrator's words might be taken less as a joke and more as a warning to those who would reduce the complexity of the author's vision to catchphrases. But, just as the residents of Willow Springs have had fun with Reema's boy, misleading him as often as telling him "the God-honest truth," Naylor is having some fun of her own. Like all her novels, *Mama Day* is studded with allusions. Critics have identified references to *The Tempest*, *Hamlet*, and *King Lear*; they have discerned as well intertextual connections to William Faulkner's "The Bear," Zora Neale Hurston's *Their Eyes Were Watching God*, and Toni Morrison's *Song of Solomon* and *Tar Baby*.[2] Indeed, Henry Louis Gates Jr. asserts that, "in the history of the African-American literary tradition, perhaps no other author has been more immersed in the formal history of that tradition than Gloria Naylor."[3] A primary intertext that has seldom been cited is Morrison's *Sula*. By repeating and revising, clarifying and inverting the themes and metaphors of *Sula*, *Mama Day* extends the line of African American literary tradition.

*Sula* is more than "a point of reference," as one critic terms it, that suggests a first name for two of the dead daughters of the Days ("Peace") as well as a female-centered family structure. Not only its characters but its sense of place, its perspective on history, its representation of ritual, and its language are in sustained dialogue with Morrison's second novel. Perhaps not coincidentally, critics have frequently interpreted *Sula* as a novel of inversion: a novel in which the Bottom is in the hills, the Peace women know no peace, and the (W)right women are wrong.[4] In *Mama Day*, Naylor pays homage to her precursor, but she does so by revising—indeed, almost inverting—Morrison's complex vision to offer a challenging vision of her own. *Sula* is, preeminently in the African American tradition, the representation of "home" as already and forever lost. To this representation *Mama Day* responds with a loud and forceful rebuttal. "Home. You can move away from it, but you never leave it. Not as long as it holds something to be missed" (50). It cannot be lost. The vision of *Mama Day* is congruent with bell hooks's concept of "homeplace." "Drawing on past legacies," hooks writes, "contemporary black women can begin to reconceptualize ideas of homeplace, once again considering the primacy of domesticity as a site of subversion and resistance."[5] Naylor's novel does not simply assert the value of recuperating African American cultural legacies; it seeks to dramatize their utility in the contemporary world.[6]

In "A Conversation," the often cited Naylor/Morrison interview published in 1985, Naylor expressed her gratitude for the example of Morrison's work because "it said to a young black woman, struggling to find a mirror of her worth in this society, not only is your story worth telling but it can be told in words so painstakingly eloquent that it becomes a song."[7] The metaphor of the mirror recurs throughout *Mama Day*. Perhaps the most critical example occurs when the young female protagonist, Cocoa, suffers hallucinations so severe that her grandmother Abigail covers the mirrors in the house to spare her pain. When Cocoa looks into Abigail's face, she recognizes that it is the true mirror, "a mirror that could never lie" (287).[8] In both the conversation and the novel, mirrors suggest the link between identity and ancestry. Cocoa can confirm who she is because her grandmother and great-aunt, "her living mirrors," show her.[9] As a young black woman writer, Naylor found similar confirmation in Morrison's work. With Morrison she entered into what Mae Henderson calls "familial, or testimonial discourse" as one black woman writer to another.[10] Yet, just as the cultural inheritance that is thematized in the novel is only of use if it can be adapted and transformed, the literary legacy is constantly in the process of revision.

*Sula* is a loving elegy to a way of life that sustained African Americans from emancipation through the civil rights movement. With an understanding as prescient as its prose is lyrical, Morrison's 1974 novel mourns the passing of the segregated communities that nurtured generations of black folk in the United States. It mourns their passing some years before most of those who had called places like the Bottom home began to miss them. From the images of destruction that introduce the text, through a series of deaths by fire and water, to rituals to stave off fear and to bury the dead, to the "circles of sorrow" that close it, *Sula* is suffused with sadness. Leavening a sadness that would otherwise be all but unbearable is the novel's precise rendering of the impromptu ceremonies of everyday life, sassy talk, and raunchy humor. Despite racism so unyielding that it seemed another force of nature, or perhaps because of it, the community's elders bonded together out of kinship and necessity. As the novel begins and ends, their legacy has been destroyed root and branch. White capitalism, cavalier in its indifference, is the agent of destruction; it provides the money and the perceived need for the Medallion City Golf Course, which sprawls over what was once the neighborhood called the Bottom. But it is the forgetfulness of young blacks, a new generation of "deweys" in the novel's cruelest insult, that threatens to obliterate even the memory of the Bottom.

Gloria Naylor's *Mama Day* is a fable for the twenty-first century, one that replaces history as "a nigger joke" with history as liberating myth. It offers a heritage, both to those African Americans who, like the novel's male protagonist, George, are culturally orphaned, cut off from any traditions other than those of mainstream America, and to those who, like Cocoa, are linked genealogically to the wellspring of black American culture. Yet it emphasizes that anyone who can hear the sound of that culture can partake of its balm. Instead of rituals of death, it fashions rituals of life and giving. Unlike Eva Peace, a mother whose love for her children is so fierce that it destroys those it cannot save, the titular character of *Mama Day* has no biological children; she is "everybody's mama." In her vocations as midwife and conjure woman, Mama Day specializes in bringing and sustaining life. Her given name, Miranda, "worker of wonders," bespeaks her power to assist even in the creation of life. Mama Day mediates between the cultures of Willow Springs and Manhattan, as she does between the past and the present. From Willow Springs she mails a letter, fragrant with lavender, that sparks the romance between George and Cocoa in New York. When Cocoa is in Willow Springs, Mama Day tutors her in the family history. Emulating Mama Day's example, the residents of Willow Springs reject lucrative inducements from developers and refuse to allow their property to be turned into a vacation paradise, with the requisite golf course. As a novel whose present is the future—

the prologue and epilogue are set in 1999 — *Mama Day* is optimistic about the prospects of the young.

*Sula* begins with the future already foreclosed. Only the remembered landmarks of the Bottom attest to the fact that black people defined the character of life there. What was most memorable was the pleasure they created for themselves and shared with each other whether it was ice cream at Edna Finch's Mellow House, the singing of the Mount Zion male quartet, or pool at the Time and a Half. White people were barely present. Yet the one road that connected the Bottom to the valley and that, as the River Road and the New River Road, threads its way throughout the text is the sign of whites' invisible power. Theirs is the power that determines when, where, and at what black men can work, that determines in turn when black men like Jude Greene decide to marry black women like Nel. In face-to-face confrontations, white men like the conductor on the train can turn a weak black woman like Helene Wright to custard. But it is in part the more insidious because unseen power of the white world that reduces men to boys ("BoyBoy" is aptly named) and causes a strong black woman like Eva Peace to lay her leg on a railroad track and mutilate herself.

The map of Willow Springs that serves as the endpapers of *Mama Day* is itself a sign of black self-sufficiency. If, as Franco Moretti avers, "a map is . . . a connection made visible," the map of Willow Springs visualizes its disconnection from the United States.[11] A bridge that the text reveals to be fragile is the only link to the mainland. Drawn to a scale that makes the island dwarf the states of South Carolina and Georgia, the map reflects the islanders' sense of their world and the relative lack of importance of the world beyond the bridge. Apart from the dense woods that cover much of the landscape, the map charts relationships in a community that finds its primary connections to each other.[12] Mama Day's trailer sits across the road from her sister Abigail's house, which is north of Chevy's Pass, a key location in the history of their ancestor Sapphira. Their antagonist, Ruby, has a house at the northern tip of the island, just across from the Other Place. The original homestead of Bascombe and Sapphira Wade, the Other Place is a site of transition, both for the ancestors of the Days who are buried there and for all their descendants who are attuned to its soundings. The map establishes the relation of the residents of Willow Springs to each other and to the past. Although relations among the residents of Willow Springs are not always benign, their relationships to each other are far more important than any interaction with outsiders. Inspired by Mama Day's example, the residents feel confident that they can repel the threat from those who want to buy up their land. The property at the southernmost point in Willow Springs belongs to Ambush and Bernice Duvall. "Steady," "genuinely kind," a "virtuoso" at his work, and a man of "infinite patience," whose rectitude is softened by a sly humor befitting his name, Ambush becomes the novel's exemplar of manhood.

The past is an ever present presence in both novels. But the representation of history and the relationship of the primary characters to it could not be more different. The prologue of *Sula* evokes a place that, despite its destruction, is so alive in the narrator's memory that the recollection of landmarks—the Time and a Half Pool Hall, Irene's Palace of Cosmetology, and Reba's Grill—seems to set the long-gone habitués into motion. But the attitude of the novel's central characters toward the past is at best uncertain, at worst dismissive. Moreover, while the music, the dance, the carved spoons—in other words, the expressive culture of the Bottom—haunt the outsiders who encounter them (the valley man who happens upon the scene of "a dark woman in a flowered dress doing a bit of cakewalk, a bit of black bottom, a bit of 'messing round'" to the accompaniment of a harmonica played by a man in "bunion-split shoes" is an example), their meanings are ineffable.[13] Neither characters nor readers, particularly insofar as they are implicitly identified with the valley man, have much hope of unraveling them.

The history of the Bottom begins as "a nigger joke." A white farmer strikes a bargain with his slave that he will grant him his freedom and a piece of bottom land in exchange for his performing particularly difficult chores. When the white man's promise comes due, he persuades the slave that the land up in the hills is bottom land—because "when God looks down it's the bottom." Not only does the slave accept the story, but he pleads for the hilly, infertile land. The white man keeps the rich, fertile valley land for himself. The black man is the butt of the joke in that he is foolish enough to believe the white man, even when he can see with his own eyes what he is being offered. The storytellers know—and imply that the protagonist of their story should have known—that white men do not keep the promises they make to black men. And yet the black man did get the freedom he was promised. It just turned out to be the freedom to do backbreaking work. The laughter that the joke

Extending the Line | 167

occasions—"a shucking, knee-slapping, wet-eyed laughter"—resonates with the proverbial laughing to keep from crying (4).

*Mama Day* opens with the intoned name "Willow Springs." The narrator, through whom the communal voice speaks, makes it clear immediately that the truth of anything about the place will be difficult to discern. Everything depends on "which of us" is doing the telling. But if none can agree on how to describe Sapphira Wade's complexion ("satin black, biscuit cream, red as Georgia clay") or her powers, if none in the present generation can even call her name, all are certain that in 1823 a slave triumphed over her master and secured freedom *and* highly desirable land for her children and their children and *their* children. Sapphira's progeny own the land "clean and simple" (5). A conjure woman, Sapphira is not buried on the island her cunning acquired and her spirit pervades. According to one version of her legend, she has flown black to Africa, "some say in body, some say in mind" (206). Bascombe Wade, the Norwegian who purchased her, married her, and perhaps fathered one or more of her seven sons, is buried in Willow Springs, sent to his grave by Sapphira. Dispossession and slavery have defined the African experience in the New World; the history of enslavement from Jamestown to the Emancipation Proclamation is more than a century longer than the history of freedom. Yet *Mama Day* opens with a myth of ownership and freedom.

Rituals in these fictive communities likewise reflect contrasting worldviews. Both texts depict the funerals of children: Chicken Little in *Sula* and Charles Kyle Duvall (Little Caesar) in *Mama Day*. Both wrench the heart, the former because of the intensity of the emotional release, the latter because of its emotional austerity. The service for the drowned child in *Sula* becomes the occasion for each female congregant to get in touch with her own pain. Nel and Sula mourn separately, their grief deepened by their shared guilt. But the communal response is inscribed in "the hands of the women unfolded like pairs of raven's wings [that] flew high above their hats in the air." As the Reverend Deal delivers his sermon, the women "did not hear all of what he said; they heard the one word, or phrase, or inflection that was for them the connection between the event and themselves" (65). Once that connection is made, the response is visceral: the women stand, speak, sway, dance, and scream. Narrated by George, the outsider best positioned to draw attention to its uniqueness, the ritual in *Mama Day* is not called a funeral but "the standing forth." A ritual without adornment—no flowers, music, or ceremonial dress—the "standing forth" calls on each participant to bear witness to the life of the dead child. The focus is on the mourned, not the mourner. The minister's query "Who is ready to stand forth?" echoes the biblical Jesus, who in defiance of the Pharisees offered healing to a man on the Sabbath (Mark 3:3). But the healing that is implicit in this ceremony defies Christian belief "in an earthly finality for the child's life" (269). Bernice, who is the last to speak, addresses her son and asks for his forgiveness, even as she expresses her conviction that she will see him again. Her neighbors share that faith, and the stoicism of the ritual is its fruit.

Two annual rituals, National Suicide Day and Candle Walk, define the character of these fictive communities more completely. The roster of the dead in *Sula* begins with the soldier whose exploding head traumatizes Shadrack. Absent the angel who watched over his biblical namesake and delivered him, Meshach, and Abednego out of the fiery furnace, the novel's Shadrack is compelled to deliver himself from fear. He cannot do so immediately, but after his return from the French battlefield and his release from the military hospital, Shadrack comes home to the Bottom and "institutes" National Suicide Day. Concentrating his fear of unexpected death on a single day—3 January—Shadrack is able to face the rest of the year. His ritual becomes a way of "making a place for fear as a way of controlling it" (14). Calling people together with a cowbell and a hangman's rope, he announces that on this day and this day alone, they can kill themselves or each other. Although they resist Shadrack's invitation and his logic, his neighbors absorb the ritual into their lives. National Suicide Day becomes a more significant marker of time in the Bottom than the historic events toward which the dates that differentiate the sections of *Sula* gesture.

That the characters of the Bottom accommodate themselves to National Suicide Day is hardly surprising, even if it is only Shadrack in his madness who can articulate a fear that is omnipresent. The unnamed soldier is the first of the novel's many dead. Cecile Sabat, Plum Peace, Chicken Little, Hannah Peace, Sula Peace, Tar Baby, and the others who die commemorating National Suicide Day in 1941 are among the rest. Most die unnatural deaths; few die in the expected order. Only Cecile and Sula die in their beds. Eva outlives her daughter by forty years and survives her granddaughter by twenty. The fear that Shadrack expresses, then—not of death or dying "but the unexpectedness of both"—is a fear that all the novel's characters know well (14).

This fear spurs the conviction of the women at Chicken Little's funeral that "the only way to avoid the Hand of God is to get in it" (66). But it is not assuaged by Christian orthodoxy. The ethic of the Bottom accepts the existence of evil. No one trusts that evil can be overcome with good. Yet evil is not simply a force to which people resign themselves. In a passage that occurs just before the narrator describes Sula's return to the Bottom, the narrator limns the Bottom philosophy. "The purpose of evil was to survive it and they determined (without ever knowing they had made up their minds to do it) to survive floods, white people, tuberculosis, famine and ignorance" (90). Residents of the Bottom see no reason to distinguish between natural and manmade phenomena, between dangers that one might predict and resist and those that are random. The clear-eyed belief that survival is triumph is sustaining. If, however, adherents to this creed see no point in seeking solutions, they enjoy identifying scapegoats, a role that Sula fulfills once she arrives. At the very end of the novel, the residents of the Bottom join Shadrack's procession and for the first time focus their energy on the symbol of their oppression: the New River Road, the road that black men were never hired to build and that led to the just excavated tunnel for which their labor would again be denied. When the tunnel collapses on them and Shadrack is left to commemorate the moment by ringing his bell, the futility of resistance seems confirmed.

Held three days before Christmas, Candle Walk is as local a holiday as National Suicide Day, but its ethic is communal rather than solitary. Going from house to house, their way lit with the candles they hold, the residents of Willow Springs offer gifts to each other; many use the occasion to repay debts of kindness. The practice allows people to help those in need without making them objects of charity. The history of Candle Walk is interwoven with that of Willow Springs, but the details of both are fragmentary. Only a folktale and an aphorism connect the holiday to Sapphira Wade, the island's ancestral figure. Her descendants whisper farewells to each other that repeat Sapphira's promise to God that she had only her poor black hands but she could "[l]ead on with light." Egalitarianism is one value implicit in the folktale; spiritual heterodoxy—God shakes hands with "the greatest conjure woman on earth"—is another

(110). The power one has in one's own hands is sufficient not only to provide for oneself but also to inspire others. Sharing is, of course, a value in the Bottom as well. Mrs. Suggs keeps Eva's three children for a year, and the only thing that surprises either woman about the arrangement is that Eva gives Mrs. Suggs ten dollars when she retrieves her children. But the precarious existence of the Bottom motivates people to honor their fears, while the free history of Candle Walk encourages people to honor their best impulses.

As befits a traditionally agrarian society, the custom at Candle Walk is to give gifts people have grown or made—cured meat or potatoes, candies and cookies made of orange and ginger. Those young people most rooted in the ways of Willow Springs adhere closely to the tradition, Ambush and Bernice, for example, respectively carving a rocking chair and tatting lace for a dress. But many of their peers exchange store-bought gifts, much to the chagrin of their elders. Mama Day, who has witnessed many variations in the holiday since her girlhood, is unfazed. Her recollections of the changes illustrate how the figure of Sapphira Wade has gradually been forgotten. Even in Mama Day's girlhood, people referred to the ancestor obliquely in their farewell: "Lead on with light, Great Mother." In John-Paul's recollections of his childhood, the ritual was dedicated to Sapphira: "a slave woman who took her freedom in 1823" (111). Although the reason for the tradition has been forgotten, the practice continues. What the novel shows across its several representations of Candle Walk is that living traditions continually yield new meanings. When they cease to do so, they die. "It'll take generations [Mama Day says of Candle Walk] for Willow Springs to stop doing it at all. And more generations again to stop talking about the time 'when there used to be some kinda 18 & 23 going-on near December twenty-second.' By then, she figures, it won't be the world as we know it no way—and so no need for the memory" (111).

Valerie Lee's interpretation of "18 & 23" is suggestive: "Whatever happened between Bascombe and Sapphira Wade in 1823 is but an historical springboard for an 18 & 23 epistemology. '18 & 23' is many things: the history of Willow Springs; the way blacks manipulate the system; a type of deep black skin color; a rite of passage, anything the community wants it to be and to mean . . . 'the God-honest truth: it was just our way of saying something.' This floating, unstable and changeable trope certainly qualifies as a type of hieroglyph, [a term that Barbara Christian identifies as] 'a written figure which is both sensual and abstract, both beautiful and communicative.' "[14] Reema's boy has not understood that its meaning cannot be fixed, a concept that is applicable to Naylor's and Morrison's novels.

Even among the singular characters of the Bottom, the "magnificent" Eva Peace stands out. Her magnificence inheres in the greatness of her achievement (she keeps her children alive despite the societal odds), the grand scale of her expenditures (she is "creator and sovereign of [an] enormous house"), the splendidness of her appearance (her dresses stop at midcalf "so that her one glamorous leg was always in view"), and the arrogance of her ambition (she takes it upon herself to choose death for her son). Her neighbors stand in awe of her; they turn her life into legend. Tales about her lost leg circulate: "Somebody said Eva stuck it under a train and made them pay off. Another said she sold it to a hospital for $10,000—at which Mr. Reed opened his eyes and asked, 'Nigger gal legs goin' for $10,000 a *piece*?' as though he could understand $10,000 a *pair*—but for *one*?" (30–31). Not only in the neighborhood legend but in the novel's exquisitely drawn vignettes of Eva in the outhouse easing her child's pain and years later in his room releasing him from the adult pain of addiction in a baptism of fire, Eva's sacrifices defy comprehension. As Hortense Spillers aptly observes, "Eva behaves as though she were herself the sole instrument of divine inscrutable will."[15]

Least of all do her children, on whose behalf the sacrifices were made, understand them. Hannah, grown and a mother herself, wonders aloud to Eva, "Mamma, did you ever love us?" Eva is quick to label this "an evil wonderin' if ever I heard one." In the conversation that follows, Eva and Hannah continue to speak past each other:

> "Mamma, what you talkin' about?"
> "I'm talkin' about 18 and 95 when I set in that house five days with you and Pearl and Plum and three beets, you snake-eyed ungrateful hussy. What would I look like leapin' 'round that little old room playin' with youngins with three beets to my name?"
> "I know 'bout them beets, Mamma. You told us that a million times."
> "Yeah? Well? Don't that count? Ain't that love?" (69)

Eva has repeated her story numerous times, but her daughter has never understood it. Eva cannot explain it because to her the explanation is self-evident. Her once starving daughter is now bountifully fed. Tellingly, the scene is framed by Hannah's entering her mother's room with "an empty bowl and a peck of Kentucky Wonders" (67). When she gets up to leave, the bowl is full. The sound of the beans snapping provide the scene's background music. The riffing on the word "wonder" adds to its poetry. "Kentucky Wonders" works metaphorically as well as musically. Pole beans, which in the process of growing wrap themselves around a stalk, are an image of interdependence. Eva is baffled by Hannah's failure to see her own survival as proof of her mother's love. In "Maternal Narratives," Marianne Hirsch identifies a pattern of missed communication in the novel. "Mothers and daughters never quite succeed in addressing each other directly; mothers fail to communicate the stories they wish to tell."[16] When Eva leaps from a second-story window in a vain attempt to save Hannah's life, her actions bespeak the fierceness of her love. But it is too late.

Mama Day's larder is always full, as is her sister's. Mama Day chides her great-niece for doing nothing "with your grandma's pole beans doubling over to the ground" (149). The young woman her elders call "Baby Girl" has never doubted their love. Mama Day does not assume an intimidating posture. Indeed, at eighty-five, she is diminutive and frail enough that she needs her father's cane to lean on as she makes her way through the woods she knows so well. She lives in a trailer. Compared with Abigail, she has a quick temper and a sharp tongue. But Mama Day is feisty, rather than fierce like Eva. Skilled in the domestic arts, she bakes, quilts, and gardens. In each of these arts she excels, but only gradually does it become evident how extraordinary her talents are.

She is a midwife who has delivered generations of babies in Willow Springs and a practitioner of herbal medicine so accomplished that she has the professional respect of the physician from the mainland. "Being a good doctor," the young African American Dr. Smithfield "knew another one when he saw her" (84). Her knowledge of the healing properties of plants is extensive: ground raspberry to tone the insides, choke-cherry bark for pain, foxglove to regulate the heart. She perceives "differences in leaves of trees, barks of trees, roots" (207). The domestic and the medicinal arts are as closely linked as the gardens that she plants and the tonics, poultices, and healing teas that she makes up in her kitchen. When she cannot find a cure in her pharmacy, she knows enough psychology to "disguise a little dose of nothing but mother-wit with a lot of hocus-pocus" (97). Houston Baker provides a more elegant explanation of the conjurer's trade when he writes that its secret "is imagination, which can turn almost anything into a freeing mojo, a dynamic 'jack,' or a cunning conjure bag."[17] Readers discern the quality of Mama Day's gifts from the respect her neighbors accord her. The daughter of the seventh son of a seventh son, she has been so attuned to nature as a child that her neighbors called her "a spirit in the woods" (79). Later having found her vocation as midwife, she is recognized for "gifted hands" (88). The gift has come at a price. Forced to raise her sister after their grieving mother committed suicide, she becomes "little mama" when she is still a child. As "Mama Day," she is the island's most respected elder.

Her vocation is more midwife than conjurer, but in the latter capacity the character recalls a character from Sula that Morrison never brings on stage. The mother of Ajax—and the only interesting woman her sensual, foul-mouthed, and irresistible son had ever met in his life—is a conjure woman. Indeed, she is an evil conjure woman and the mother of seven sons; Ajax is the eldest. The novel limns her portrait in a paragraph: she is "blessed with seven adoring children whose joy it was to bring her the plants, hair, underclothing, fingernail parings, white hens, blood, camphor, pictures, kerosene and footstep dust that she needed, as well as to order Van Van, High John the Conqueror, Little John to Chew, Devil's Shoe String, Chinese Wash, Mustard Seed and the Nine Herbs from Cincinnati." With the utmost economy, the novel gestures to the mixture of the mundane and the supernatural, the homemade and the exotic that define the conjurer's art. Readers may latch on to whatever details seem familiar and use their imagination to understand the work that the character performs. Additionally, readers are told that this woman "knew about the weather, omens, the living, the dead, dreams and all illnesses and made a modest living with her skills" (126). The dissonance created by her possession of this profound, if subjugated, knowledge and the modest living it affords encapsulates the novel's political critique. But the character herself makes no further appearance in the text.

Miranda Day is her lineal descendant, and she is frequently on center stage. Yet the challenges a character like "Mama Day" poses for a novel are serious. On the one hand, the character threatens to turn into an icon of virtue and endurance and thus a bore. On the other hand, the emphasis on her beneficence when coupled with her magical power could render the character incredible. In the main Mama Day avoids these pitfalls. Most of the character's miracles are explained by her intimate knowledge of her environment and by her psychological insights. For example, she describes the assistance she initially gives Bernice: "The mind is a funny thing, Abigail—and a powerful thing at that. Bernice is gonna believe they are what I tell her they are—magic seeds. And the only magic is that what she believes they are, they're gonna become" (96). Later, of course, Miranda does perform "supernatural" deeds. Two in particular stand out: the ceremony during which Bernice conceives, a ritual that is represented as unrepresentable, and the destruction by lightning of Ruby's house. By the time these scenes occur, the very qualities that render Miranda unintimidating have led most readers to a willing suspension of disbelief. As to the first pitfall, Miranda's humor and the testiness of her relationship with her great-niece prevent her from turning into a plaster saint. She is no saint at all. The revenge that she takes against Ruby reveals that Miranda can use her power to destroy as well as to create.

Both strong-willed women, both inheritors of Sapphira's mantle, Miranda and Cocoa/Ophelia have a fractious relationship. Miranda recognizes in Cocoa what she cannot see in herself. She believes that she and Abigail "take after the sons . . . the earth men who formed the line of Days, hard and dark brown. But the Baby Girl brings back the great, grand Mother . . . it's only an ancient mother of pure black that one day spits out this kinda gold" (48; emphasis in original). Cocoa/Ophelia can "read between the lines," but her perception is limited by the immaturity that her pet names connote. Her elders have shielded her from the work that Miranda does. She knows that her great-aunt possesses "second sight," but beyond that her knowledge of conjure, as of her history, is limited. Chafing under Mama Day's protection during a visit to Willow Springs, she calls her "an overbearing and domineering old woman" and protests that she is not a child anymore. At twenty-seven, she is not. Gradually she negotiates a new respect from Miranda, who appreciates in turn Cocoa/Ophelia's deepening apprehension of their past. Tellingly, over the course of the plot, the young woman earns a degree in history, a goal she seeks because "coming from a place as rich in legend and history as the South," she is "intrigued by the subject" (126). Mama Day scoffs at the young woman's naïveté. "Baby Girl did have something lost to her, but she weren't gonna find it in no school" (150). Cocoa/Ophelia has not yet learned to read the texts of her own family, inscribed, for example, in the walking stick that John-Paul has handed down to Miranda and the quilt that Miranda and Abigail send Cocoa and George for a wedding present. But before the novel ends, she learns how to "listen" to texts of a different kind.

History as well as legends of the South inform Naylor's novel. The history of the Sea Islands suggests alternatives to the dominant stories of segregation—the black bottoms, the Buttermilk bottoms, the black sides of U.S. cities in the South and North—that are the factual counterparts to the setting of Sula. Stretching almost four hundred miles from the southern border of North Carolina to the northern border of Florida, the Sea Islands by virtue of their geographical isolation became repositories of African survivals and New World creativity. Johns Island and Hilton Head, St. Helena and Daufuskie, Sapelo and St. Simons are among the islands that for generations were accessible only by sea. Just since the 1930s have many of the islands been connected to the mainland by bridges or causeways. Some, like Hilton Head, have become havens for wealthy tourists, while others, like Daufuskie and Sapelo, remain rural and largely inaccessible. As Twining and Baird point out, that lack of access and the concomitant barriers to outside influences made the islands "a matrix of African American family tradition."[18] Extended families established compounds or communities of kin and after the Civil War acquired ownership of their land. Indeed, Jones-Jackson identifies the custom of "heir's land," an unwritten contract that allows land, if it must be sold to relatives, to be sold for only one dollar. The practice in Mama Day of willing land to the second generation stems from a similar impulse. In the preface that Charles Joyner contributes to Jones-Jackson's When Roots Die, he observes that "for generations folk medicine of both the pharmaceutical and the psychological varieties continued to heal the sick on the Sea Islands, and natural phenomena continued to serve as signs foretelling the future, whether changing weather or impending death."[19] Naylor's healer is one with this tradition. Literary critics explore other connections between the historical Sea Island culture and the fictive culture of Willow Springs. Strikingly, even historians acknowledge the difficulty of separating legend from fact.[20] History in places like Sapelo has been preserved in legend. This is a truth that Miranda Day divines for herself.

Even without knowing the history of Willow Springs, Mama Day understands it intuitively, in part because it is so deeply intertwined with the history of her family. The great-granddaughter of Sapphira Wade,

Miranda Day has learned the family genealogy from her father. When saving Cocoa/Ophelia's life requires her to learn the older communal history, she uses her heightened power of perception to apprehend it. At the Other Place, the realm of unearthly time and space, she is able to divine the historical knowledge she needs. The written record is inadequate. The ledger she finds in the attic has only fragments of fact. "Water damage done removed the remainder of that line with the yellowish and blackened stains spreading down and taking out most of the others as well" (280). "Line" here gestures both toward Sapphira's name and her legacy. Enough of the damaged bill of sale—reprinted in full in the novel's front matter—is intact to confirm that a "negress" was sold to Bascombe Wade. But only the letters "Sa" remain of her name. Mama Day tries in vain to guess the right name: "Sarah, Sabrina, Sally, Sadie, Sadonna—what?" The inadequacy of the written record is an insuperable obstacle for the rationalist. George has doubted even the existence of the woman sometimes described as the "great great grand mother." "Places like this island," he maintains, "were ripe for myths" (218). Mama Day cannot give up. Her mission is to save her great-niece. She "falls asleep murmuring the names of women. And in her dreams Miranda finally meets Sapphira" (280).

Even before she does, Mama Day extracts all the meaning she can from the written record. She revises the bill of sale so that it relates something of who Sapphira was: a nurse, who was tender and kind. Along with the land, Sapphira has bequeathed an ethical legacy in which healing, nurturing, and kindness are values to be passed on.[21] Armed with this knowledge, Miranda pursues other fragments of her family history, and in so doing she learns how to look past pain, to assuage the hurt that has led her sister Peace and her niece Peace to their graves, and to devise a strategy that will save Cocoa's life.

The dream work that this process requires ("Miranda opens door upon door upon door") offers further evidence of the intertextual connections between Mama Day and Sula. Mama Day has to revisit the sites of her ancestors' loss. Looking down the well in which her sister has thrown herself after losing a child, Mama Day sees "circles and circles of screaming" (284). But unlike Nel's cry that ends Sula ("a fine cry—loud and long—but it had no bottom and it had no top, just circles and circles of sorrow"), the pain of the past here inspires resolve rather than mourning. Not only does Mama Day resolve to save Cocoa/Ophelia, but the lesson that she intuits from her male ancestors — "those men *believed* — in the power of themselves, in what they were feeling" — is embraced by the community of Willow Springs (285). In sharp contrast to the inhabitants of the Bottom, the characters who dwell in Willow Springs refuse to be defeated. Taking control of their future, the men of Willow Springs band together to rebuild the bridge to the mainland. Despite George's importuning, they insist on building it on their own terms. Figuratively, the bridge the novel builds is, as Lindsey Tucker asserts, "between the scientific and the intuitive, the rational and non-rational, the secular and the sacred." [22]

As the prologue's repeated invitation to the reader "to listen" suggests, the knowledge of Willow Springs is available to anyone who is willing to make the effort to acquire it. It is significant that the island is separated from the mainland by "The Sound." While the noun "sound" is defined as a relatively narrow passage of water between larger bodies of water or between the mainland and an island, it has other meanings: (1) the sensation produced by stimulation of the organs of hearing by vibrations transmitted through the air or another medium, (2) auditory effects, and (3) spoken utterances. All these meanings resonate in the novel. The novel's representation of Willow Springs aspires as well to the goal that Morrison, in "Rediscovering Black History," articulated for *The Black Book.* It seeks "a very special sound . . . made up of all the elements that distinguished black life" as well as "those qualities that identified it with all of mankind" (16). The novel's creation of a world elsewhere encourages both possibilities.

At many points in *Mama Day*, characters instruct readers in the art of listening. Readers are advised to listen to noises made by wind, water, birds, and denizens of the woods that define the landscape of Willow Springs. Mama Day becomes the model for this kind of listening. "She can still stand so quiet, she becomes part of a tree" (81). She can hear approaching storms. Listening "under the wind," she can hear the movements of history: "the sound of a long wool skirt passing. Then the tread of heavy leather boots. . . . And the humming — humming of some lost and ancient song" (118). These sounds compel her to search her memory for the stories her father has told, the stories that have conveyed the history of Willow Springs. At the climatic moment, they prepare her to meet Sapphira. The novel suggests that the ability to hear not only words but vibrations is a necessary life skill. George, for example, has become expert in decoding the sounds of his own heart. Sounding is also a necessary interpretive strategy. As a verb, "sound" means to measure or try the depth of, or more broadly, to examine or investigate, seek to fathom or ascertain. Readers are invited, then, to "sound" the world of Willow Springs.

In order to do so, they must pay close attention to the speech of those characters who, like the narrator of the prologue, seem to speak barely above a whisper. One is reminded of the comment Naylor made to Morrison regarding the latter's use of language: "Your books just whisper at the reader and you move in, you move in and then you finally hear what's being said, and you say to yourself, 'Oh, my God.'"[23] For example, when Miranda and Cocoa/Ophelia visit the family graveyard, they put moss in their shoes to facilitate their ability to "listen" to the voices of their ancestors, who tell Cocoa the stories of two women who are not buried there, Sapphira and Ophelia, the great-grandmother for whom she is named. Later, when Cocoa/Ophelia returns to the "family plot" with George, she hears the "whispers" in the wind that predict that she is destined to repeat the fate of those two women, who broke men's hearts and were unable thereafter to find peace. Her response is to grow agitated and despondent. But when Mama Day hears the same message, she is determined to intervene, to revise the "family plot"; as a result of her intervention, only the first part of the prophecy comes true. Listening in this novel is not a passive activity.

Indeed, the novel confirms that both George and Ophelia learn to be active listeners. Although George cannot surrender to the ways of Willow Springs in time to save himself, he learns to listen after crossing over, so that his spirit remains on the island and from there carries on the dialogue with Ophelia that structures the text. George has become another of the voices of history that Ophelia has learned to heed. Willow Springs makes those voices and that history tangible in a way that commands attention. Given a "heritage intact and solid enough to be able to walk over the same ground that your grandfather did" counts for something, as George attests (219). Ophelia, having heard the stories of the past, is able to move past her own pain and the pain of her ancestors. Heir of the Days, both female and male, she will extend the line.

In her revisions of American and African American literary tradition, Naylor extends those lines as well. Beginning with the map of Willow Springs, she decenters the traditions of American history and literature. In her countermyth, the history and rituals of the Sea Islands, like the character of Sapphira, the great *grand* mother, loom larger than the myths of the nation's Founding Fathers. The egalitarian and communal values of the island realize ideals that have so often been dishonored in mainstream society. Neither race nor gender nor class separate people from each other in Willow Springs. Just as the novel revises the national story, it revises the story of African Americans so that it begins not with slavery but with freedom. Although the novel's characters remember and honor the past, the novel's vision has more to do with the present and future. The prologue announces as much; set as it is in 1999, it looks forward to the twenty-first century. *Mama Day* offers lessons from a fictive agrarian past to readers who negotiate the demands of fast-paced, heterogeneous urban societies. The figure of the bridge that links Willow Springs to the mainland and the characters Cocoa/Ophelia and George, who mediate between the novel's two worlds, represent their interconnectedness.

Unlike Walker, who had to become a literary detective to unearth the writing of Zora Hurston, Nella Larsen, and Rebecca Cox Jackson, Naylor encountered Morrison's novels in a college classroom. Morrison had secured her own reputation; she was not in need of rescue. *Sula*, her second novel, is a favorite of critics from a broad spectrum of perspectives and methods. Its protagonist is as fiercely original a character as any in African American literary tradition. The representation of motherhood, embodied most memorably in Eva Peace, is as unsettling as any in American literary tradition—at least before the invention of Sethe. Despite moments that are laugh-out-loud funny, the novel's sensibility is tragic. Home, a site of scarcity, danger, and love, is always already lost. *Mama Day* is, by contrast, a comedy. Its protagonist is likely to remind many young middle-class readers of themselves. The representation of motherhood, embodied in the title character, is gently ironic: Miranda has no children of her own. Home, a site of abundance, safety, and love, is something one takes with one wherever one goes. Drawing on these strengths as well as the examples of subversion and resistance women at home demonstrate, one can move boldly into the world. The challenge is to remake the world's values so that they reflect those of home.

## eight

Bare Bones and
Silken Threads:
Lineage and
Literary Tradition
in *Praisesong for
the Widow*

And the single, dark plangent note this produced, like that
from the deep bowing of a cello, sounded like the distillation
of a thousand sorrow songs. . . . The theme of separation
and loss the note embodied, the unacknowledged longing
it conveyed summoned up feelings that were beyond words,
feelings and a host of subliminal memories that over the
years had proven more durable and trustworthy than the
history with its trauma and pain out of which they had come.
. . . The note was a lamentation that could hardly have come
from the rum keg of a drum. Its source had to be the heart,
the bruised still-bleeding innermost chamber of the collective
heart. — Paule Marshall, *Praisesong for the Widow*

Among the most vivid scenes in Paule Marshall's 1983 novel *Praisesong for
the Widow* are the flashbacks to the early years of the marriage of the titular protagonist, Avey (born Avatara) Johnson, and her husband, Jay (officially Jerome). As a couple, the two fashion rituals that bind them both
to each other and to their ancestral legacy, although the latter effect is
unintended. At the time, the dances Jay stages for the two of them, as he
pretends their living room is a Harlem dance hall—the Savoy, Rockland
Palace, or the Renaissance Ballroom (the "Renny," as Avey and Jay call
it)—seem more about romance than cultural preservation. But in retrospect, Avey finds the sacred as well as the sensual in the jazz tunes that
inspire their dance: "Flying Home," "Take the A-Train," "Stompin' at the

Savoy," "Cottontail," and "After Hours." If Lionel Hampton, Duke Ellington, Chick Webb, and Avery Parrish provide the soundtrack for Saturday nights, the Southerneers, the Fisk Jubilee Singers, the Wings Over Jordan Choir, and the Five Blind Boys fill the house with spirituals on Sunday mornings. In between the music, Jay recites fragments of the poems he learned as a boy growing up in segregated Kansas: Langston Hughes's "The Negro Speaks of Rivers," Paul Laurence Dunbar's "Little Brown Baby," and James Weldon Johnson's "The Creation." Although she cannot define what it was, Avey later reflects that "something in those small rites, an ethos they held in common, had reached back beyond her life and beyond Jay's to join them to the vast unknown lineage that had made their being possible. And this link, these connections, heard in the music and in the praisesongs of a Sunday: '. . . I bathed in the Euphrates when dawns were / young . . . ,' had both protected them and put them in possession of a kind of power."[1]

When Avey begins the journey back that structures the novel's plot, she has long since lost touch with the power these small rites impart. Indeed, the rituals themselves have become an unwelcome distraction from the relentless pursuit of upward mobility in which Avey and Jay have been engaged. Moreover, although both husband and wife have become unrecognizable to themselves or each other in the process, they have won the material success they sought. Now widowed, Avey, like Morrison's Milkman, finds herself on a quest before she realizes it. Fleeing a cruise ship (the Bianca Pride) in response to physical and emotional symptoms of dis-ease, she disembarks in Grenada in the eastern Caribbean. Soon she finds herself caught up in the rituals of the out-islanders, people who have migrated to Grenada in search of employment. Speaking patois, which Avey does not understand, they seem to think that Avey is one of them. On the spur of the moment, she joins their annual excursion to Carriacou, the same island that looms so large in Audre Lorde's imagination but that her protagonist does not visit in Zami. Avey finds the people more familiar than mythic, and that very familiarity gives her access to spiritual transcendence. After a purging and purification that prepare her to participate, Avey takes part in the Big Drum, the dance that is the culmination of the excursion. Entering the circle, she dances the Carriacou Tramp, whose steps she recognizes in retrospect as the same ones she has learned watching the ring shout with her great-aunt Cuney in the Sea Islands of South Carolina. With Cuney guiding Avey in her dreams and the equally intuitive Lebert Joseph taking her physically by the hand, the protagonist reclaims herself and her cultural legacy.

Most critics have read the novel as a journey toward wholeness. In Abena Busia's eloquent interpretation, *Praisesong* is a novel of the African diaspora in which, "through the healing of one of Africa's lost daughters, a scattered people are made whole again."[2] She argues that the reader, like the protagonist, must develop "diaspora literacy" and learn to read the various cultural signs and performances that signify an underlying bond.[3] Other critics echo Busia's emphasis on cultural and spiritual wholeness.[4] Yet *Praisesong* is also a novel that equips its readers to live in a world in which cultural knowledge will remain fragmentary, African Americans will never be able to recuperate the past completely, and individuals must continually compromise between the demands of material well-being and spiritual idealism.

At its most accessible level, the novel depicts the story of a black Everywoman, a striver whose family traces its U.S. roots to Tatem, South Carolina, who grows up in Brooklyn, has a civil service job (in the state motor vehicle department), marries, and raises three children, and whose husband works two jobs, goes to night school, and, with extraordinary determination, moves himself and the family into the middle class. As the final symbol of their success, Avey and Jay move to the suburbs, to a destination that is the polar opposite of rural South Carolina: North White Plains.

To represent the process through which Avey reverses the trajectory of her life, the novel employs a narrative strategy that might be called "triple exposure." In Marshall's 1991 novel *Daughters*, the protagonist Ursa begins to perceive the events of her present, to wit, the urban desolation and political corruption that pervade Midland City, a fictional New Jersey town, through the prism of the urban desolation, rural poverty, and political corruption of her Caribbean birthplace, the fictional Triunion. Standing in one location, she frequently imagines herself in the other; she dubs the effect "double exposure." In *Praisesong* there are three primary locations: Tatem, New York City, and Carriacou. In each setting the protagonist goes on a voyage (even if only mentally) and becomes initiated into the rituals of a particular community. In each setting the protagonist perceives events in the present that have taken place in the past. Triple exposure produces a structure that risks becoming schematic. But the frequent crosscuttings between the locations, the sudden interjections of dreams and memory, the shards of music, and the vital descriptions of dance mitigate against this effect. Most important, so does Avey's uncertain and discontinuous progress throughout the text.

*Praisesong for the Widow* seeks to honor the history of Africans in the New World; it does not attempt to reconstruct it or even to suggest that it can be reconstructed. At best, whether on the U.S. mainland or the out islands of the Caribbean, only the bare bones of the story of the journey to the New World and the almost four-hundred-year existence of African people here remain. What the characters of Marshall's novel enact is the importance of creating rituals of remembrance for that story: rituals that consist not only of organized public events but of expressions that are personal and private as well. Not surprisingly, the more assimilated the individual is to Western culture, the more private the expression is likely to be. To sustain the remembrance, however, the individual must find ways to connect his or her personal ritual to a more collective expression. Silken threads are the novel's metaphor for the tenuous but meaningful ties that bind black people to each other. Rituals of remembrance keep those ties alive. Music and dance are key elements of these rituals, and the novel makes the point emphatically that commercially recorded music may be as inspired and as useful equipment for living as that created by folk in isolated communities. Storytelling is the principal means through which family and communal history are passed down. Poetry is key as well, whether the poems come from the literary or oral traditions. Indeed, *Praisesong for the Widow* is a novel rich in allusions to other African American texts, so much so that it would be fair to call it a song in praise of African American literature. Were it not for the literature, the novel insists, even the bare bones of the story would be lost. Reading becomes a ritual of cultural preservation. I read the metaphor of the "silken threads" as an analogue for the written texts to which the novel so often alludes. These words preserve cultural memory by weaving together its fragments into new, heterogeneous poetic texts like the novel itself.

In Marshall's own telling, *Praisesong* began with a place, Ibo Landing, that she read about in *Drums and Shadows*, a book of interviews conducted during the 1930s by Works Project Administration employees with elderly residents of the Sea Islands, some of whom had been slaves. Referring to that place, several told the story of the Africans who turned around and walked back home across the Atlantic Ocean. "That's how *Praisesong* began," Marshall averred, "with that folktale." As Barbara Christian points out, the folktale, whose variants include the story of the flying African that informs *Song of Solomon*, "is a touchstone of New World black folklore."[5] But Marshall, like most of her readers, had to read in a book the story that for generations had been passed down orally.

Although its inspiration was the folktale, the novel begins with a scene in which belief in the myth of Ibo Landing seems anomalous. Its opening juxtaposes the middle-aged, thoroughly bourgeois widow always dressed in muted colors, perfectly coiffed, and radiating "Marian Anderson poise and reserve" with her idealistic and high-spirited ten-year-old self. Now cruising the Caribbean on a luxurious ocean liner, the mature Avey dreams of the summer vacations she spent in the Sea Islands with her aged aunt, where their walks to Ibo Landing, a long, narrow spit of land jutting into the Atlantic, were the highlights of her week. The social comedy of the present (as Avey jousts with her traveling companions, especially Thomasina Moore, the former chorus girl whose racial attitudes shift from a determination to get equal treatment, to an exotic primitivism she might have imbibed in the Cotton Club, to a racial self-hatred that she turns on her friends as easily as on herself) contrasts with the austere yet vibrant recollections of Avey's childhood summers. Material excess defines the present experience: the ship is "huge, sleek, imperial, a glacial presence in the warm waters of the Caribbean" (16). The larger meaning of the *Bianca Pride* may be understood in the context of what Carole Boyce Davies terms the "tourist ideology" that perceives the Caribbean as "'prostitute,' as source of pleasure and relaxation," within a system of economic and political domination and exploitation.[6] The ship's Versailles dining room is laden with gilt, silver, and crystal, and the narrator refers to treaties signed in the Hall of Mirrors it imitates, treaties "*divvying up India, the West Indies, the World?*" (47; emphasis in original) The signature dessert, "Peach Parfait á la Versailles," is sated with calories. Overeating disrupts Avey's sleep, but Great Aunt Cuney's nightly visitations disorient her completely.

Long since dead and buried, Aunt Cuney was a commanding woman who both named and claimed her great-niece. As a child Avey has been in awe of her; yet in her dreams as an adult, she resists her aunt's pleas to join her and even raises her hand against her elder. The dreams stir memories that haunt Avey's days as well as her nights. She remembers that twice a week, with great ceremony, the old woman would don a field hat and put on two belts—one at the waist and the other strapped low around the hips—and call "Avatara" to join her on a walk. The attire is traditional for Sea Island women; the second belt allowed them to hoist their skirts as they worked in the low-lying fields. The novel gives an alternative explanation for the second belt: "worn in the belief that it gave them extra strength," the belt is "strapped low around their hips like the belt for a sword or a gun holster" (32). In this description, the belts are reminiscent of the bandolier worn by Congo Jane, the co-leader of a slave revolt in *Daughters*. Like Congo Jane, Aunt Cuney breathes the spirit of resistance. But in her case, the spirit expresses itself through the story she shares with her niece.

The myth of Ibo Landing recounts the initial disembarkation of a shipload of Africans in the New World. In fact, according to some historians, shiploads of enslaved Africans first set foot upon U.S. shores in Charleston and the islands that surround it.[7] In the version of the myth the novel elaborates, the new arrivals are Ibo people, who are taken from the white-sailed ship to shore in smaller boats. Once on land they look around and, endowed with the capacity to "see in more ways than one," envision their bleak future in the New World.[8] They turn back and head for home. The myth as it is told in the novel draws on the rhythms and repetitions of the spoken story. The child Avey interrupts Aunt Cuney's performance in a way that both heightens the drama for the reader and confirms for the teller that she has successfully passed the story down.

> "They just turned, my gran' said, all of em—" she would have ignored the interruption as usual: wouldn't even have heard it over the voice that possessed her—"and walked on back down to the edge of the river here. Every las' man, woman and chile. And they wasn't taking they time no more. They had seen what they had seen and those Ibos was stepping! And they didn't bother getting back into the small boats drawed up here—boats take too much time. They just kept walkin' right on out over the river. Now you wouldna thought they'd of got very far seeing as it was water they was walking on. Besides they had all that iron on 'em. Iron on they ankles and they wrists and fastened 'round they necks like a dog collar. 'Nuff iron to sink an army. And chains hooking up the iron. But chains didn't stop those Ibos none. Neither iron. The way my gran' tol' it (other folks in Tatem said it wasn't so and that she was crazy but she never paid 'em no mind) 'cording to her they just kept on walking like the water was solid ground." (38–39)

Walking—and singing—the Ibos begin the heroic march home. Much like the ending of the myth of the flying African and of *Song of Solomon*, the myth of Ibo Landing ends ambiguously. Yet Aunt Cuney, who is both the story's teller and its "ideal reader" or auditor, shows that it does not matter whether Africa or death was the Ibos' ultimate destination. Telling the story thrills Aunt Cuney, as it had the great-grandmother who has told it to her, the ancestor for whom Avatara is named. Both tellers end with the declaration that, although their bodies might remain in Tatem, in their minds they have left with the Ibos.

Aunt Cuney's one moment of impatience with Avey comes when the child questions whether the Ibos had not drowned. With disappointment and regret, Aunt Cuney asks whether Avey has voiced similar doubts about Christ's ability to defy gravity. The truth here, Aunt Cuney teaches, is likewise spiritual rather than factual. Avey quickly atones for her failure of belief and begins to act out the implicit meaning of her name. The etymology of *avatāra*, derived from the Sanskrit, carries the meaning of a passing down or a passing over. Avey, "short for Avatara," is the character who passes down the ancestral knowledge that Aunt Cuney bequeathed before she passed over. Like her foremothers, Avey might remain earthbound, but "her mind [is] long gone with the Ibos" (39).

The novel's representation of Tatem is Edenic. Lushly vegetated with air so thick it is almost visible during the day, with nights almost eerily black and still, Tatem is, like Willow Springs, a world elsewhere. The community has it own history and rituals that have been preserved long after they have died out on the mainland. Shad Dawson's wood and the houses of Doctor Benitha Grant (the local herbalist), Pharo Harris, and Mr. Golla (read Gullah) Mack are tangible markers of local history. National history leaves a less legible imprint; a fallow field was "last cultivated before Sherman's march to the sea" (39). Great Aunt Cuney, much like Caroline Sale, possesses the land in the process of walking it. Walking alongside her, Avey is able to lay her own claim to the land. She is also introduced to the rituals that preserve the island's cultural inheritance. To a greater extent than the fictive rituals in *Mama Day*, the rituals in *Praisesong* are grounded in history. Chief among them is the ring shout.

Considered the earliest type of African American religious song, the ring shout was widely performed during slavery. After emancipation, the ritual survived only in culturally isolated parts of the southern United States, like the Sea Islands. In keeping with the West African traditions from which it is derived, the dancers in the ring shout shuffle round and round single file, moving in a counterclockwise direction, clapping out the beat in complex polyrhythms. Rhythmic complexity may be variously enhanced, such as by the stomping feet of those who stand outside the circle or with the participation of a "sticker," who beats a broom handle on the floor. The tempo and revolutions of the circle accelerate during the course of the movement. The rules governing the ritual are strict. No matter how rapid the movement, participants are forbidden to allow their feet to cross because such a movement denotes dancing rather than shouting; the Protestant churches to which many religious African Americans belonged by the late nineteenth century deemed dancing a sin. More than an accompaniment, singing is integral to the movement. The singing is antiphonal, employing the overlapping call and response characteristic of West African music. Women's voices rise in jagged harmonies as the shout intensifies. The ring shout achieves what one scholar/composer designates the "heterogeneous sound ideal" that results from "the timbral mosaic created by the interaction between lead voice, chorus, rattle, metallic gong, hand clapping, various wind or string instruments, and drums, which exist in greater or lesser degrees of complexity in almost all African ensemble music."[9]

In his seminal study *Slave Culture: Nationalist Theory and the Foundations of Black America*, historian Sterling Stuckey argues that "the ring in which Africans danced and sang is the key to understanding the means by which they achieved oneness in America." In Stuckey's estimation, the ring shout was not only the principal ancestral ritual of the slave era but the single most important ritual to come out of Africa to inform the culture of black people in North America. Published four years after *Praisesong*, *Slave Culture* deepens and extends the thematic meaning of the novel's representation of the ring shout, even as it confirms its historical accuracy. Stuckey documents the ubiquity of circle dances in Congo-Angola, Nigeria, Dahomey, Togo, the Gold Coast, and Sierra Leone, that is, throughout the regions of Africa from which the majority of slaves came. He maintains that the convergence of these rituals and the values they encoded allowed Africans from various ethnic groups to become one people in the United States. In Africa the circle dances, often distinguished by their counterclockwise direction, were elements in burial ceremonies that were intended to foster reunion with the ancestors. The climax of the ceremony was the spiritual possession of the celebrants by their ancestors. In Stuckey's words, "[T]he achieving of spiritual peace involved a complex ritual essential for harmony between the living and the dead, command of a symbolic world in which the circle steadily appears."[10]

During the nineteenth century, black people were able to syncretize their traditional beliefs with the Christian theology that many were adopting; some did not convert to Christianity. Among those who did, participants in the ring shout might be possessed by the spirit of the Holy Ghost rather than the spirits of their ancestors. Whereas before participants shuffled their feet in accordance with the traditions of African dance, in which the ability to move various parts of the body *other* than the feet was admired, now the proscription against the crossing of the feet was attributed to church dogma. As organized religion took hold among African Americans, as worship moved from praise houses to more formal edifices, and as church leaders imposed greater authority over the worship practices of their congregants, the ring shout began to disappear.[11]

The ritual depicted in *Praisesong* exists as a vestige. The very name of the island (Tatem) suggests how the ring shout becomes one of the *totems* through which New World Africans identify with one another. If it is a hereditary mark or emblem, it suggests a connection that binds many peoples. In particular, the ritual that Avey learns as a child, then carries dormant in her memory, eventually allows her to achieve the peace with her ancestor that, unbeknownst to either Great Aunt Cuney or her descendant, is its traditional goal.

In *Praisesong* Aunt Cuney breaks the prohibition against crossing her feet during the ring shout and is put out of the church. After she leaves, her neighbors accuse her of making Ibo Landing her religion. But the novel suggests an unbroken circle. As they dance the ring shout, participants sing: "Got your life in my hands / Well, well, well." These lyrics come from "Run, Old Jeremiah," a ring shout that John A. Lomax and Alan Lomax recorded in Jennings, Louisiana, in 1934.[12] The lines suggest a communal ethic that corresponds to Christian belief *and* to the belief systems that predate Christianity in West Africa, where it is the ancestor's life as well as one's own for which one is responsible. Aunt Cuney's heresy excludes her from the church but not from the community of Tatem or from the larger community for which it stands.

That Avey returns not to Tatem and Ibo Landing but to Carriacou, a place she has never been, forestalls nostalgia and complicates the narrative. The depiction of Carriacou is much less romanticized than that of Tatem. There are, to be sure, underlying commonalities. Even though Avey cannot understand the patois she hears on the wharf in Grenada, the "peculiar cadence and lilt" call the speech of Tatem to mind. Indeed, she realizes in retrospect that it was the same "vivid, slightly atonal music underscoring the words" that she has heard on the first stop the *Bianca Pride* makes in Martinique that initially summoned Aunt Cuney to her dreams (67, 196). But if their voices are reminiscent of Tatem, the out-islanders' circumstances seem different. They are not farmers; they have immigrated to the capital of Grenada to pursue material success. Avey's taxi driver, who is from the main island, tells her that when the out-islanders are not going on the excursion, they speak the "King's English" as well as anyone. Begrudgingly, he concedes that they are "serious" and "hardworking." Then, in a statement that echoes frequent jibes that U.S.-born blacks once directed at Caribbean immigrants, he avers, "[T]hey come to live here and before you know it they're doing better than those like myself that's born in the place. . . . They have a business mind, you know, same as white people" (78). In short, the out-islanders' lives are no less fragmented and no less driven by economic imperatives and social ambition than the life of the African American protagonist. Their success provokes similar resentment and suspicion. Significantly, they too are going on a voyage, an excursion, but one that is restorative rather than alienating. That difference remains for Avey to understand and to emulate.

Critics have focused on the differences but have too often missed the parallels the novel draws between the out-islanders and the African Americans. To appreciate the significance of the parallels, I compare the novel with Marshall's 1967 short story "To Da-duh: In Memoriam," clearly its precursor text. Like Avey, the story's protagonist travels by ship and lands in a world that bears slight resemblance to the one she has left. Like Avey, too, the protagonist is initially convinced of the cultural superiority of the world she has left behind. But the story's narrator is not a tourist. She is kin, the daughter who returns to the land of her parents' birth. Significantly, Marshall describes it "as the most autobiographical of [her] stories," one that is largely a reminiscence of a trip she took to Barbados as a nine-year-old.[13] The most significant aspect of the journey was meeting her grandmother, whose nickname was "Da-duh." The grandmother inspired several of Marshall's characters, including Mrs. Thompson, the hairdresser and elder in *Brown Girl, Brownstones*; Carrington, the silent cook in *The Chosen Place, the Timeless People*; Celestine, the family retainer in *Daughters*; and, of course, Aunt Cuney. Da-duh is, in Marshall's reckoning, "an ancestor figure, symbolic for me of the long line of black women and men—African and New World—who made my being possible, and whose spirit I believe continues to animate my life and work" (95). Indeed, in *Praisesong*, Da-duh's memory informs Lebert Joseph, the old man who becomes Avey's guide, as surely as it informs Aunt Cuney. It is altogether fitting that the novel's dedication reads, "for my grandmother, Alberta Jane Clement ('Da-duh')."

In fact, the author's sojourn in Barbados lasted a whole year, during which time both the child and her elder recognized a special bond between them. Marshall describes it in terms that resonate with the premise of *Worrying the Line*: "[I]t was as if we both knew, at a level beyond words, that I had come into the world not only to love her and to continue her line but to take her very life in order that I might live" (95). The author takes her grandmother's life in the sense that she makes it the subject of her writing—preserving in her fiction what the older woman might have preferred to go unrecorded. At the same time, that writing is what gives meaning and purpose to the author's life; she cannot imagine her life without it. To a significant degree, the grandmother's love and her recognition early on of the author's gift give her the strength to pursue her craft.

Written thirty years after the visit and told from the now-grown child's perspective, "To Da-duh" recounts a nine-year-old's first visit to her mother's birthplace and ancestral home. The visit seems much shorter than a year. But as she narrates the story retrospectively, the granddaughter draws the grandmother and her culture from a respectful distance. At the same time, she leaves largely undrawn the world she has known in New York. The story gestures toward the sociopolitical conflict between the metropole and the rural colony, but it does not explore the psychological ramifications the conflict produces. On one level, "To Da-duh" represents a child's relationship with her grandmother and a classic conflict between youth and age. At another level of meaning, the story represents a woman's encounter with history as apprehended through her matrilineage. But, although "To Da-duh" conveys some of the complexities of a character, a woman whose life has been stunted by political and economic oppression, it mainly does what its title promises: it memorializes an idealized ancestor.

From the initial welcome, the old woman is eager to impress her spirited grandchild with the beauty of her island and the value of her way of life. With an innocent bravado, the child deflates the grandmother's effort by boasting that she has visited the Empire State Building, which is "hundreds of times" as tall as the royal palm her Da-duh has been showing her (95).[14] Even as she regrets the effect her words have on her grandmother, the child insists on the accuracy of her facts. She wants to prove them to Da-duh. But before the child, now home in New York, has a chance to mail the picture postcard of the building Da-duh cannot believe exists, Da-duh is dead. In the coda to the story, the granddaughter/narrator refers to her later experience as a young woman trying and failing to capture with paints the beauty of the "seas of sugar cane and the huge swirling Van Gogh suns and palm trees" (106). Unlike the narrator, the author succeeds in capturing this beauty in words.

From the opening line, "I did not see her at first I remember," the discourse of the narrative emphasizes the difficulty of perceiving the grandmother clearly. The darkness of the disembarkation shed, as well as the blinding sunlight, obscures the child's vision. The repetition of the phrase "I did not see her" compels readers to question the accuracy of the narrator's representation once the grandmother does come into view. One cannot but be skeptical of such idealized descriptions as "perhaps she was both child and woman, darkness and light, past and present, life and death—all the opposites contained and reconciled in her" (96, 97). This mythicization of the grandmother is reinforced by other references: her face is "as stark and fleshless as a death mask." Da-duh's "name sounds like thunder," and she becomes the child's "anchor" in the crowd of relatives who, "like a nervous sea," circle the newly reunited family. Later she sits on a trunk in the lorry and seems a "monarch amid her court" (96–99). Such perceptions reflect the perspective—if not the language—of the young protagonist.

Yet, even by the second page of the story, the reader may develop a more complicated assessment and thus a clearer understanding of all it means that Da-duh "brought a sense of the past that was still alive in the present." The narrator's mother—who is otherwise barely mentioned—speaks anxiously about the initial meeting with Da-duh because she knows Da-duh prefers male, light-skinned grandchildren. Da-duh's reactionary values are further reflected in the rebuke she offers her Barbadian relatives who are awestruck by their New York kin: "You all ain't been colonized" (98). Unlike the explicit critique of tourism as a component of postcolonialism in *Praisesong*, the impact of colonialism is thus introduced ironically in the story; it becomes an important theme in the narrative.

The history of Barbados offers a microcosm of the history of English colonialism in the New World. Slavery and the sugar plantation were first perfected in the seventeenth century by British planters in Barbados. Just two years after the British landed on the island in 1625, the first African slaves arrived. The number of slaves was small at first, but after sugarcane became the island's chief commodity, the slave population grew exponentially. The cultivation of sugarcane was highly labor intensive. As early as 1685, enslaved Africans outnumbered British colonists four to one. To control the slaves, a series of repressive codes were enacted. A planter elite, enriched by the enormous profits of the sugar industry, solidified its hold on the economic, legislative, and political affairs of the island. That grip continued after slavery was abolished in 1833. The authoritarian style with which the white minority ruled Barbados was admired and emulated by European colonists throughout the Caribbean. Despite efforts to develop political resistance, blacks remained subjugated until the island gained its independence in 1966. A caste system in which racially mixed individuals were accorded lower social status than whites but higher social status than blacks helped maintain the repressive regime. Periodically resistance would intensify. The decade of the 1930s was one such period of activism, particularly on the part of workers.

"To Da-duh," set during that decade, evokes this history in several ways; one example is the references to sugarcane in the narrative. These references work to critique the perspective both of Da-duh—who boasts of the canes cultivated in her parish, "they's cane's father, bo"—and of the narrator when she tells of painting seas of sugarcane. The author is aware, as neither narrator nor character seems to be, that the Barbadian landscape is not completely natural; the land and the people's labor have been exploited to produce it. This exploitation accounts in part for the alienation of the narrator's parents from their home. The mother is returning for the first time in fifteen years, and the father, at home in Brooklyn, has told his daughter that the trip is "blowing good money on foolishness" (99). Da-duh feels a nameless and profound fear toward the technology of the West. The story never mentions the growing social unrest. It simply reports that Da-duh dies in an air strike on Barbados in

1937. That was the year in which black workers in Barbados, like their counterparts throughout the Caribbean, went on strike to demand higher wages. The government's response was swift and violent and included attacks of the kind that kill the character in Marshall's story. "To Daduh" hints at the history of slavery and colonialism and at the social and political forces that have further dispersed members of a family. But it does not explore the ruptures and psychic fissures that these dispersals produce. *Praisesong for the Widow* does. Ultimately the ancestral figures of the novel, Aunt Cuney and Lebert Joseph, serve, in Stuart Hall's words, to "restore an imaginary fullness or plenitude, to set against the broken rubric of the past."[15] Rather than an elegy for the dead, the novel is a song in praise of the living.

The novel's title confirms this reading. According to Busia, a praisesong "is a particular kind of heroic poem" for Africans. She notes that praisesongs are "sung in communities over the entire continent." Although they "embrace all manner of elaborate poetic form," they are always "specifically ceremonial social poems, intended to be recited or sung at anniversaries and other celebrations, including . . . funerals." But important as their ceremonial and communal functions are, praisesongs "can also be sung to mark social transition. Sung as a part of rites of passage, they mark the upward movement of a person from one group to the next."[16]

The novel marks Avey's successful transition into widowhood, a status determined in relation to the dead. Her ability to create a life for herself requires that she come to terms with her dead husband. Through the intervention of Great Aunt Cuney, Avey is compelled as well to come to terms with the many thousand gone who constitute her lineage. The first two sections of the novel, "Runagate, Runagate" and "The Sleeper Wakes," represent the process of recognition, reconciliation, and mourning. Tellingly, coming to terms with the collective loss precedes the reconciliation with the individual. The first section takes its title from the powerful poem by Robert Hayden; an epigraph quotes the poem, thus making the allusion explicit. The second echoes the title of a novella by Jessie Fauset; whether or not Marshall evokes this text deliberately, her novel revisits themes and personae reminiscent of her literary precursor.

Runs falls rises stumbles on from darkness into darkness
and the darkness thicketed with shapes of terror

and the hunters pursuing and the hounds pursuing
and the night cold and the night long and the river
to cross and the jack-muh-lanterns beckoning beckoning
and blackness ahead and when shall I reach that somewhere
morning and keep on going and never turn back and keep on
going

   Runagate
     Runagate
       Runagate.

From this opening stanza, Hayden's modernist masterpiece captures
the swift and disorienting transitions in the fugitive's escape from slavery
to freedom. Borrowing lines from the storehouse of spirituals, interpo-
lating documentary material such as advertisements for runaway slaves,
fashioning free verse equal to his subject, the poet represents the in-
destructible will to be free. The poem invokes the heroic figures of the
abolitionist movement, most notably Harriet Tubman, "woman of earth,
whipscarred," who is "a summoning, a shining." The runagate or rene-
gade slave travels the freedom train toward the mythic North and beyond
("*first stop Mercy and the last Hallelujah*").[17]

*Praisesong* begins with a desperate Avey, furtively plotting her escape;
but unlike the fugitive slave, she cannot explain what she is escaping
from.[18] Ambushed by her memories of Halsey Street and her dream of
Aunt Cuney, she grows more discomfited. Literally and figuratively at sea,
she sees things that are not there: golf balls go hurling into the water,
shuffleboard players begin to brawl, and the sound of quoit, a game being
played on deck, strikes her ear "as the sound of some blunt instrument
repeatedly striking human flesh and bone" (56). She remembers a scene
she and Jay witnessed on Halsey Street in which a police officer beat a
man with a nightstick before pushing him into the back of a patrol car.
Powerless to help or to protest, she and Jay sat up for the rest of the night.
Unlike the dream of the little girls murdered in the Birmingham church
that Avey counts as the last dream she had for decades, these memories
cannot be closed down. Images of slavery and racial oppression continue
to invade Avey's consciousness as she "runs falls rises stumbles from
darkness to darkness."

"The Sleeper Wakes" is the most interior section of the novel; all the
action of the plot takes place in Avey's consciousness. Physically, she is in

a deluxe hotel room in Grenada; psychologically she is reliving her past, particularly her marriage. As Christian describes it, "The Sleeper Wakes" is "a wake for the past as well as awaking from the past" (77). Avey has not achieved freedom when the section ends, but she at least recognizes what she seeks to be free of. Tellingly, as the section opens, Jay's voice is resounding in Avey's head; it calls her to account first for her recklessness in leaving the cruise and more generally for her failure to appreciate and safeguard the legacy he has left. Appraising that legacy is one of the primary tasks Avey goes on to perform.

Avey recognizes the value of the security, both financial and psychological, that Jay's hard work (and her own) afforded the family. She recognizes that their sacrifices created opportunities for their daughters, who have grown up to be a teacher, a physician, and a stay-at-home mother. But she also recognizes that their sacrifices cost too much. As she remembers the early years of her marriage, Avey realizes the extent to which the couple's ambition was fueled by fear, fear of conforming to racist and sexist stereotypes. The figure who embodies this fear is a woman who goes out every Saturday morning, a house dress or a coat thrown over her nightgown, to bring her man home from the bars; her profane soliloquies wake the neighborhood. In the quarrel that determines the trajectory of their lives, Jay accuses Avey of sounding like this woman. Avey in turn imagines the woman standing over her bed. Both project their fears and anxieties onto this desperate figure. In order not to emulate this woman's life, the Johnsons begin a relentless pursuit of success. They cease performing their private recitals of music, poetry, and dance. For Jay these black cultural expressions now connote the racist stereotypes he seeks to transcend. It is no longer possible for Jay and Avey to claim these expressions for themselves and to fashion their own rituals of remembrance.

In the fourth chapter of the section Avey describes these "small rituals and private pleasures" in loving detail. Her memory serves up extended allusions to "The Negro Speaks of Rivers," "Lil' Brown Baby," and "The Creation," three famous poems that affirm African American identity. Hughes's poem inscribes a racial lineage that harks back to Africa; the lines that Avey recalls evoke the Euphrates, the Congo, and the Nile. Dunbar celebrates the love of family in "Lil' Brown Baby," and Johnson's speaker, a preacher in the black folk tradition, represents God, "[l]ike a mammy bending over her baby," "[t]oiling over a lump of clay" and making man in his image. Johnson's figure suggests an anthropomorphic god made in the image of black Americans. Avey remembers Jay reciting Dunbar as he lifts their daughter in his arms, and Avey recalls that same daughter learning to perform "The Creation," just as her father had. The recital that "enthralled" that child is an act of cultural transmission. To gloss the meaning of the memory, Avey cites a line from Lucille Clifton: "[O]h children think about the good times" (126; emphasis in original). In retrospect, Avey understands the discontinuance of these rituals as part of an imperceptible process by which every other aspect of life is sacrificed to the demands of work. The couple finds no time to take either the annual trips to Tatem or the boat rides up the Hudson that Avey has loved as a child. Jay and Avey withdraw from the Brooklyn community where they live. By the time they move physically to North White Plains, they have long since become spiritual residents of a culturally arid location.

They have also become sexually estranged. The novel connects the pleasure the characters take in music and poetry to the pleasure they take in each other. Avey's memory of their lovemaking is as much aural as physical. Jay's sweet talk is amplified by the voices of Billy Eckstine and Lil Green on the phonograph. The narrator describes a silence during intercourse that she fills in with references to African deities: "Erzulie with her jewels and gossamer veils, Yemoja to whom the rivers are sacred; Oya, first wife of the thunder god and herself in charge of winds and rains" (127).[19] As she comes to the end of her reverie, Avey remembers the feelings of desperation and anguish that later characterized the couple's sexual intercourse: for his part, "love like a burden he wanted rid of," and for hers, feelings of anger, sympathy, and rage. She then hears a voice in the present—standing on the balcony of a luxury hotel in Grenada— that she recognizes belatedly as her own. In it she hears first "a hint of the angry, deep-throated cry she might have uttered as she rushed forth slashing and slaying like some Dahomey warrior of old" (130). That utterance is quickly suppressed. However, Avey's full-throated cry ends the section in a refrain that punctuates several pages of interior monologue. She asks herself hard questions ("Couldn't they have done it differently? Hadn't there perhaps been another way?" [139]). She recognizes that just as Jay has lost himself by becoming Jerome, she, who begins the cruise not recognizing herself in the mirror, no longer even thinks of herself as Avatara. "*Too much! Too much! Too much!*" (144; emphasis in original) is the final refrain that indicts both her and her husband and <u>allows her</u> to <u>begin</u> to explore another way to live.

The allusions to Jessie Fauset encoded in the title "The Sleeper Wakes" are apt. In her class status, her sense of reserve and propriety, and ultimately her moral consciousness, Avey bears a strong resemblance to Fauset's heroines. Like Joanna Marshall in *There Is Confusion*, Avey is the child of an upwardly mobile working-class family. Like Laurentine Strange in *The Chinaberry Tree*, she is as fastidious about her appearance as about her behavior, wearing linen shirtdresses on the cruise "in place of the shorts and slacks favored by other women her age on board, no matter what their size" (13). Like Angela Murray in *Plum Bun*, Avey is complacent in the security of her middle-class life until she declares her commitment to the race. But unlike Olivia B., the middle-aged antiheroine of *Comedy: American Style*, Avey finds a purpose to her life larger than sustaining bourgeois comfort.

At first glance, Avey has even less in common with Amy Marshall, the flighty young protagonist of Fauset's "novelette" "The Sleeper Wakes."[20] An orphan whose race is indeterminate, Amy is raised by a Negro family. The plot recounts her move to New York City, her marriage to a wealthy white southerner, and the dissolution of that marriage when, to save a colored employee who reacts to her husband's racist vitriol, Amy claims to be colored, too. As dissimilar as the plot is, Amy's awakening strikes notes in common with *Praisesong*. The novella's detailed description of clothing, its recurrent scenes of the protagonist gazing at herself in the mirror, and the interiority of the drama anticipate elements of the novel. Amy's recognition that she has been vain and shallow, "caring nothing for realities, only for externals," is echoed in Avey Johnson's cry "*Too much! Too much*" as she rues the choices she and Jay made and wishes they had found another way. Similar, too, is the commitment to racial uplift expressed at the conclusion of both texts.

To reach the conclusion of *Praisesong*, however, Avey undergoes experiences that Fauset would not have imagined. Fauset was not uninterested in the Caribbean: she translated Haitian poetry and met with intellectuals from throughout the diaspora at the Pan African Congresses that she attended and documented during the early decades of the twentieth century. But Fauset's Pan-African perspective was more political than cultural, more cerebral than experiential. The ritual aspects of the last two sections of *Praisesong*, "The Lavé Tête" (literally "to wash clean") and "The Big Drum," are more reminiscent of Hurston's writing than of Fauset's. *Praisesong* makes the kind of cultural encounter that Hurston as a professional ethnographer and a woman of uncommonly bold spirit reveled in available to a protagonist as prim and proper as any that Fauset invented.

Remorseful over the fact that Avey has grown ill on the excursion, Lebert Joseph comes with an offering: coconut water and a drop of rum. He recognizes Avey as one of the diasporan children, including his own grandchildren, dispersed throughout the world *and* in Grenada itself who do not know their nation. He reels off a list of names of nations, relates myths, and sings songs in order to incite a spark of recognition in Avey. As in *Song of Solomon*, history is encoded in songs. For example, children learn the story of the enslaved parents sold in chains, one to Trinidad and the other to Haiti. This song names the children rather than the parents and associates the islands' torrential rains with their parents' tears. Avey knows none of this. But the word "juba" sparks a tinge of recognition. Avey recognizes the word, although she cannot remember its meaning. To Avey it is "only something you might hear or read about," to which Lebert retorts, "*We* still dances it" (178; emphasis in original).

Juba denotes one of the earliest forms of African American secular music and performance. Dancers would form a circle, repeat a rhyme in call-and-response fashion, and pat their feet in rhythmic time as they repeated the words of the rhyme. According to Thomas Talley, an African American professor at Fisk University and the compiler of the earliest collection of African American secular songs, as participants danced the juba, their feet "beat a tattoo upon the ground answering to every word and sometimes to every syllable of the rhyme." Like the ring shout, juba is a ring dance that symbolizes "community, solidarity, affirmation and catharsis." [21]

Joseph knows juba as a dance but believes that the term means something more. The narrator notes that Lebert might have referred to Juba, "the legendary city at the foot of the White Nile," the city that is now a "forgotten backwater" (178). But he cannot. He has never heard of it. All Lebert knows for sure is that in Carriacou juba is a dance that women do. He can do all the steps nonetheless and exclaims that he "needs a real skirt" to show Avey how it is really done (179). The moment echoes the earlier one in which Avey first dreamed of her great-aunt. Cuney is as free from gender constraints as Lebert; she wears brogans like "seven-league boots" (33).[22] In Avey's dream, Cuney beckons with a hand "that should have been fleshless bone by now: clappers to be played at a Juba" (40). This eerie image invokes the tradition, common throughout the African diaspora, of bones played as instruments and the specific tradition of "patting juba," "an extension and elaboration of simple hand clapping that constitute a complete and self-contained accompaniment to the dance," a performance practice that is described by Solomon Northrup in his 1853 narrative *Twelve Years a Slave*.[23] The references to juba suggest again how the two elders in *Praisesong* stand in for each other: it is as though Cuney has played the music for the solo part of Avey's journey. Lebert Joseph urges Avey to continue her journey by joining the community at the Big Drum.

The novel represents Lebert Joseph as an ancestor, not only to Avey but to the community at large. When they meet in his grog shop, a site the novel imbues with sacred meanings, he tells Avey that nearly everyone in his home village on Carriacou is "family to me. They all got to call me father or uncle or grandfather, granduncle or great-grandfather or cousin or something" (163). But the discourse of the novel suggests a wider circle of kin. Despite Lebert's claim that he knows his nation (a Chamba from his father's side and a Manding from his mother's), the passages that introduce him give him a transnational identity: "lines etched over his face like the scarification marks of a thousand tribes" (161). Initially, Avey is put off by his descriptions of rituals practiced in Carriacou and dismisses his frequent interpolations of Creole expressions: "What was this voodoo about lighted candles, old parents, big drums and the rest?" (166). But the movement of the plot makes the spiritual and cultural practices increasingly familiar, in just the way that the out-islanders become as recognizable to Avey as she is to them.

Lebert Joseph is the figure that facilitates this back-and-forth movement. As several critics have remarked, the name "Lebert" evokes the West African deity called Legba among the Fon in Benin and Esu-Elegbara in Nigeria.[24] Known variously as Exú in Brazil, Echu-Elegua in Cuba, Papa Legba in Haiti, and Papa La Bas among hoodoo adherents in the United States, this trickster figure turns up throughout the black Atlantic world. He is the messenger of the gods, and as Robert Farris Thompson notes, "the very embodiment of the crossroads," "the point where doors open or close, where persons have to make decisions that may forever after affect their lives." "Outwardly mischievous but inwardly full of overflowing creative grace," Legba is the "ultimate master of potentiality."[25] Gates, who uses Esu-Elegbara as "the indigenous black metaphor" for the literary critic, emphasizes the figure's interpretative role: it interprets the will of the gods to humans and carries the desires of humans to the gods. Not only the guardian of the crossroads, Esu is "master of style and stylus, the phallic god of generation and fecundity, master of that elusive, mystical barrier that separates the divine world from the profane." Represented in art and mythology as a figure with one leg shorter than the other, Esu is said to keep one leg "anchored in the realm of the gods while the other rests in this, our human world."[26]

Lebert Joseph is described as "a stoop-shouldered old man with one leg shorter than the other" (160). A purveyor of rum in a shop with a dirt floor that feels as hard and smooth as terrazzo, Lebert moves easily between the profane and the sacred. He adheres to the old ways. As he explains to Avey, the first act he performs when he arrives home in Carriacou is to roast an ear of corn, put it on a plate, light a candle next to the plate, and sprinkle rum outside the house as a libation in tribute to his ancestors. He also functions successfully in the modern society of Grenada. Most significant, he meets Avey as she reaches her personal crossroads, where she must decide whether to settle for the materially rich but spiritually arid existence she has or to open the door to a meaningful life.

Lebert's surname is equally resonant, for it alludes to the biblical character, fabled as an interpreter of dreams.[27] Avey asks Lebert Joseph to interpret her dreams of the night before, the dreams that have taken her back to Halsey Street. She sees in his look the mark of "someone who possessed ways of seeing that went beyond mere sight and ways of knowing that outstripped ordinary intelligence" (172). Although he demurs, she is convinced that he knows "the Gethsemane" she has experienced the night before without being told. The reference to Gethsemane, the scene of Jesus' agony and betrayal, signals the spiritual syncretism that shapes the rest of Avey's journey. Lebert Joseph acts as her guide.

To travel to Carriacou, they board the *Emmanuel C*, a name that alludes to the Christian deity (God with us + Christ). Its sails call to mind the "huge ecclesiastical banners" that Catholics display on feast days (195). Two elderly women are on board, one stout, with large hands and a "gold-rimmed smile," and the other so thin that her face "was simply bone and a lined yellowish sheeting of skin." They are discursively associated with Cuney and Lebert Joseph, as "old people who have the essentials to go on forever" (194). They remind Avey of the church mothers of her child-hood, who held the place of honor in the front pews, whose "Amens" propelled the sermon, whose arms steadied those overcome by the spirit, and whose exhortations helped bring the sinners through. As she takes her seat beside the Grenadian women, Avey slips into a reverie that takes her back to the Mount Olivet Baptist Church. When it ends, these women perform the very ministrations Avey attributes to the church mothers.

Her memories take Avey back to an Easter Sunday morning service. Rather than the ring shout or juba, a sermon is the ritual performed here. The charismatic preacher takes his text from Mark 16:1–5, the scripture that recounts the arrival of Mary, the mother of James and Joses, and Mary Magdalen at the tomb of Jesus only to discover that the tomb is empty and the stone, on which an angel now sits, has been rolled away. The subject of the sermon is resurrection, the theme is redemption, and the aim is catharsis. The minister begins by describing the women as "af-frighted and filled with wonder," a condition he attributes to his congre-gants and one that also defines Avey at this stage of her journey. She is fearful of her future and awed by both the natural beauty of Grenada and the boldness of the acts that have brought her aboard the Emmanuel C. To move forward, she needs to access spiritual power. The preacher ex-horts his congregation "to roll away the stones sealing up our spirits, our souls from the light of redemption" (200). His performance builds to an impassioned call and response and to the cathartic release that the wor-shipers experience in the past and that overwhelms Avey in the present. The Grenadian women minister to Avey, but hers is hardly a Christian conversion experience.

Tellingly, the narrator expresses admiration for the minister's perfor-mance but questions his integrity: "[H]is hands made like a croupier's stick raking in the money and chips on a gaming table" (201). The perfor-mance itself rings false at the end, as the preacher seems to embody the word not of the New Testament but of the Old. This "choleric old God, hurling the exhortations like some cosmic stones" over the congregants' heads, instills new fear (a theological terror) to replace the fears that had been released (202).

Ultimately, the novel's heterodox spirituality allows Avey to purify her spirit and to embrace her flesh. The memory of the sermon produces a physical and spiritual catharsis, a purging first of the "overly rich, indi-

gestible food" and then of the values, figured in the sermon as sto
that have burdened Avey's spirit. Intercut through the scene are visi
that partake of the Middle Passage: "other bodies lying crowded with
in the hot, airless dark . . . their moans, rising and falling with each r
of the schooner" (209). For Avey, like other protagonists discussed in
*Worrying the Line*, the only way to go forward to the future is to go all the
way back to the past. After soiling herself, she is given a ritual bath by
Lebert's daughter, Rosalie, who follows the bath with what the narrator calls a "laying on of hands," a ceremonial gesture of healing and affir-
mation. The laying on of hands as a spiritual practice among women is
represented in several contemporary texts by black women including
Bambara's *The Salt Eaters*, Naylor's *The Women of Brewster Place*, and Ntozake
Shange's *for colored girls who have considered suicide when the rainbow is enuf*.[28]
For the long celibate Avey, the experience is a resurrection of the flesh.
At its conclusion, cleansed and prepared like Zora, the protagonist of
Hurston's *Mules and Men*, as she is made ready for a spiritual initiation,
Avey is ready to participate in the Big Drum, the novel's preeminent ritual.

The epigraphs to the Lavé Tête section suggest a literary syncretism.
One is written in Haitian Creole, a Vodun introit, "*Papa Legba, ouvri barrière
pou' mwê*" (italic in original). The other comes from the white modernist poet Randall Jarrell, "Oh, Bars of my . . . body, open, open!" Not
only do the epigraphs reinforce the spiritual and physical dimensions of
the freedom Avey seeks, but they also reflect the heterogeneous sources
that inform this novel. In addition to containing many allusions to African American poetry, the novel quotes white American writers including
Susan Sontag and Randall Jarrell. Indeed, it twice evokes Jarrell's "The
Woman at the Washington Zoo." During Avey's agon with Aunt Cuney,
she also dreams the lines "*at any moment the beast may spring, filling the air
with flying things and an unenlightened wailing*" (45; emphasis in original).
Here the speaker of the dramatic monologue identifies with the caged
animals around her: her frustrations threaten to break through the quiet
surface of her daily life. When the poem is quoted again in this epigraph,
its lines provide a rough translation for the Vodun introit. As Avey prepares to enter a sacred space, the invocation of the two statements suggests how the spiritual and the psychological, the ancient and the modern, convey a common desire: to break down the barriers to a free and
fulfilling life.

## The Big Drum

Like the ring shout, the Big Drum is a historic practice. Marshall witnessed the ceremony when she visited Carriacou in the 1960s. Significantly, the ceremony is not ancient; it dates only from the 1950s, when, owing to the economic collapse of the island's sugar-based economy, most of the owner class left. The descendants of enslaved Africans took possession of the land. Like the residents of the Black Belt and the Sea Islands, they developed a distinctive culture. In the Big Drum, songs and dances "are attributed to the African 'nations,' or tribes, from which the slave population of Carriacou was drawn." They are "combined with secular songs and a cult of ancestor-worship" that the islanders practice along with Christianity.[29] The Big Drum was created to mark a moment of social and cultural transition; in the novel it occasions Avey's spiritual transformation.

After her initial excitement, Avey takes a more measured look at Carriacou. Rather than the grand extravagance that Lebert Joseph has led her to expect, she sees the depleted soil, the wreck of a house that is the backdrop to the dance, and the rum kegs that serve as drums. The last detail is the most striking, for it conveys the cultural loss the New World passage signified for Africans, even as it encapsulates the economic imperatives of the Triangular Trade. Through Avey's unblinkered eyes, the ceremony constitutes "the bare bones. The Big Drum—Lebert Joseph's much vaunted Big Drum—was the bare bones of a fete. The burnt-out ends" (240). And yet, to her considerable surprise, Avey is not disappointed. As she continues to observe the scene, she concludes:

> It was the essence of something rather than the thing itself she was witnessing. Those present—the old ones—understood this. All that was left were a few names of what they called nations which they could no longer even pronounce properly, the fragments of a dozen or so songs, the shadowy forms of long-ago dances and rum kegs for drums. The bare bones. The burnt-out ends. And they clung to them with a tenacity she suddenly loved in them and longed for in herself. (240)

What Avey begins to understand is that, like her, the out-islanders retain only fragments of their heritage, but they know how to treasure what they have. Most of those attending the fete are like Avey in another way:

they do not know their nation. Only when the Creole dances begin and the invitation to participate extends to everyone does the yard fill up. For the first time during the evening, younger people participate. In this moment *Praisesong* is not valorizing racial hybridity; neither is it clinging to a notion of racial purity. It is acknowledging the reality for people of African descent in the New World in the late twentieth century. As Christian points out, the Big Drum ceremony "combines rituals from several New World African societies: the Ring Dances of Tatem, the Bojangles of New York, the voodoo drums of Haiti, the rhythms of the various African peoples brought to the New World" (82). Just as the ceremony fuses music from the rituals of various geographical and cultural locations to create a "heterogeneous sound ideal," the community it creates is characterized by a unity that honors difference. Each voice makes its own sound; each person draws on his or her particular well of experience.

The drumming becomes more intense, and "the bottle-and-spoon boys" add their rhythms to the mix. Their makeshift instruments signify the determination of a people to beat out the rhythms of their culture even when the drum was prohibited. Just as in the ring shout, the tempo and revolutions of the circle accelerate during the course of the dance. Voices rise in mingled tongues and jagged harmonies as the ritual grows more intense. Finally, the swollen thumb of the lead drummer knifes across the goatskin at an angle. His movement produces the "single, dark plangent note . . . that sounded like the distillation of a thousand sorrow songs" (245).

The single note is the novel's most powerful metaphor for the collective mourning that *Praisesong*, like *Generations* and *Beloved*, both represents and enacts. "The theme of separation and loss the note embodied . . . summoned up feelings that were beyond words" (245). Here again the memory encoded in music captures more truth than any written history; the music has already outlasted the distortions of the previous centuries' written official records and will endure beyond the corrections of the present. Alluding to Du Bois and to Douglass before him, Marshall invests the collective memory in the music of the sorrow songs. By using the term to apply to music created in the Caribbean, she expands the scope of Du Bois's assertion that the sorrow songs were "the most beautiful expression of human experience born this side of the seas" (*Souls*, 205). They were also the most plaintive. Intensifying the connection between the music of the New World and the music of the Old, the note is played on a drum. The drum is both a sign of slavery and a sign of the people's will to overcome its legacy. But the process of mourning and consequently of overcoming is incomplete. The sound of the drum, the "lamentation," is the expression of the "bruised still-bleeding innermost chamber of the collective heart" (245). Images of blood that flow through this novel refer to the shared grief and mourning that bind the people of the African diaspora in the New World.

Avey responds to the sound, both with her heart (making the sorrow her own) and her body (as she recalls the movements to the ring shout she had observed through the window of the church in Tatem). To that memory she adds another, the sense of belonging and connection she felt on the 125th Street pier as she waited with her family to board the *Robert Fulton*. The annual boat ride up the Hudson from Harlem to Bear Mountain is an excursion sponsored by a neighborhood social club. Its ostensible purpose is pleasure, for adults as well as children. The delight that Avey takes in the event is heightened by her awareness of the changes it produces in her parents. Her dandified father and her mother, with marcelled hair and wearing a brand-new dress, dance and speak their private language. The glimpse of the erotic connection between her parents anticipates the charged relation to the group at large: "[S]he would feel what seemed to be hundreds of slender threads streaming out from her navel and from the place where her heart was to enter those around her" (190). For Avey this excursion, like the one in Carriacou, takes on larger meaning. The picnic becomes a holy repast; the destination is no longer a secular camp but a spiritual campground. These deeply freighted meanings would be more than the passage could bear were they not embedded in the narrative of the voyage of the *Emmanuel C*. The meanings that Avey extracts from one experience are transposed to the other.

In an extended passage Avey elaborates on the image of the threads that connect her not only to the people aboard the boat but to all the people in the neighborhood, those she knows and those she has not met, to southern migrants and West Indian immigrants.

> She visualized the threads as being silken, like those used in the embroidery on a summer dress, and of a hundred different colors. And although they were thin to the point of invisibility, they felt as strong entering her as the lifelines of woven hemp that trailed out into the water at Coney Island. If she cared to she could dog-paddle (she

couldn't swim) out to where the Hudson was deepest and not worry.
The moment she began to founder those on shore would simply pull
on the silken threads and haul her in. (191)

The colors repeat patterns of the "myriad colors" of the clothes and um-
brellas of the women on the excursion. They also echo images recurrent in the African American literary tradition, from Langston Hughes's
"Harlem Sweeties" to Robert Hayden's "Kaleidoscope." The image of the
silken threads is at once fragile and fine, as the reference to embroidery
suggests. The fragility describes the ties that bind this disparate group
of people together. Avey wonders whether it is a childlike fantasy, the
desire of "a mere girl in a playsuit," "someone small, insignificant, outnumbered," to become "part of, indeed the center of, a huge wide confraternity" (191). Such thoughts at the end of the novel suggest how the
middle-aged woman has regained the idealism of her youth. But the embroidery also recalls Hurston's concept of the "will to adorn," the insistence on beauty as a cardinal value, an insistence that the novel's literary
allusions reaffirm.

Avey's connection to the out-islanders has been foretold—when the
people on the wharf mistake her for one of them. More tellingly, the cab
driver's description of the pride with which the out-islanders embark on
their journey—they are *stepping*—echoes Aunt Cuney's evocation of the
Africans at Ibo Landing: "They had seen what they had seen and those
Ibos was stepping!" If in the myth the action was a courageous defiance
and determination to escape the enslavement that lay ahead, in the late
twentieth-century New World Africans who retain a modicum of pride
and a sense of cultural belonging can live with dignity even as they negotiate the demands of postindustrial capitalist society.

Hesitantly, Avey begins to do the Carriacou Tramp. She joins the elders
on the periphery of the circle and recognizes the steps performed in the
ring shout in Tatem. As she dances, she feels for the first time since
her girlhood the sensation of the silken, brightly colored threads leaving
her body and entering the bodies of those gathered around her. The
text repeats the passage that describes Avey's membership in that "far-
reaching, wide-ranging confraternity." But in this repetition with a difference, Avey's perspective reflects the wisdom she has attained through
the process of purification and rebirth. The metaphors that complement
the silken threads convey both the frightful cost of history and the sense

of wonder with which those who survived it look back: "Now, suddenly, as if she were that girl again, with her entire life yet to live, she felt the threads streaming out from the old people around her in Lebert Joseph's yard. From their seared eyes. From their navels and their cast-iron hearts. And their brightness as they entered her spoke of possibilities and becoming even in the face of the bare bones and the burnt-out ends" (249). Giving herself fully to the rhythms, Avey dances the Carriacou Tramp as if she has done it all her life. Led by Lebert and Rosalie, the other dancers bow to Avey, thereby turning the ritual of the Big Drum into a praisesong for her.

The continuous parallels established between Avey's spiritual conversion and narratives of Christian conversion culminate in this moment. For readers who can believe in the possibility of the latter, the possibility of the former may be more easily imagined. For those who cannot, the novel offers the solace of literature. The allusions in *Praisesong* are chiefly to African American literary texts that posit an identity for readers that is neither commodity nor consumer. Rather, readers live within a history that they have the power to affect. After her participation in the Big Drum ceremony, Avey is changed. She goes home and sets up a camp for children on Ibo's Landing, where her schoolteacher daughter can teach the poetry of Gwendolyn Brooks. The novel does not suggest that its privileged protagonist will give up the material possessions she has or promise to buy no more. It is not that idealistic. It is heuristic, however, in its plea to its African American readers that they perform rituals of remembrance that connect them to a history they too often ignore or dismiss. Even if not always a defense against racism, sexism, and other systems of domination, historical knowledge and acknowledgment ensure a sense of personal integrity. Finally, *Praisesong* challenges all its readers to find a purpose to life larger than sustaining bourgeois comfort. It encourages them to become agents of change; it maintains that even small acts of rebellion and reconstruction, like Avey's camp, improve the future of all our children.

## nine

In Search of
Our Mothers'
Gardens and
Our Fathers'
(Real) Estates:
Alice Walker,
Essayist

The will to adorn is the second most notable characteristic
in Negro expression. Perhaps his idea of ornament does not
attempt to meet conventional standards, but it satisfies the
soul of its creator. . . .

Whatever the Negro does of his own volition he embellish-
es. His religious service is for the greater part excellent prose
poetry. Both prayers and sermons are tooled and polished
until they are true works of art. The supplication is forgotten in the frenzy of creation. The prayer of the white man is
considered humorous in its bleakness. The beauty of the Old
Testament does not exceed that of a Negro prayer. —Zora
Neale Hurston, "Characteristics of Negro Expression"

In absence of fixed and nourishing forms of culture, the Negro has a folklore which embodies the memories and hopes
of his struggles. Not yet caught in paint or stone and as yet
but feebly depicted in the poem and novel, the Negroes' most
powerful images of hope and longing for freedom still remain
in the fluid state of living speech. . . . Negro folklore remains
the Negro writer's most powerful weapon, a weapon which
he must sharpen for the hard battles looming ahead, battles
which will test a people's faith in themselves. —Richard
Wright, "Blueprint for Negro Literature"

Whatever she planted grew as if by magic, and her fame as a
grower of flowers spread over three counties. Because of her
creativity with flowers, even my memories of poverty are seen

through a screen of blooms—sunflowers, petunias, roses, dahlias, forsythia, spirea, delphiniums, verbena . . . and on and on.—Alice Walker, *In Search of Our Mothers' Gardens*

None of the writers examined in *Worrying the Line* has been more engaged by issues surrounding the construction and authority of literary tradition than Alice Walker. *In Search of Our Mothers' Gardens: Womanist Prose* (1983) charts what Susan Willis calls a "motherline" through which Walker connects her work to writing by women of the Harlem Renaissance, especially Zora Neale Hurston and Nella Larsen, and extends its lineage to precursors as distant as Phillis Wheatley and Rebecca Cox Jackson.[1] Walker vigorously protests the exclusion of women from the line of African American tradition, but she also revises and extends that tradition as it has been articulated by black men. For example, she acknowledges Richard Wright, whose sexism she abhors, as a major influence on her writing. But the traditions in which Walker locates her work are multiple. She writes about Flannery O'Connor and Virginia Woolf as well as Langston Hughes and Jean Toomer. Always insistent on uncovering the "whole story," Walker explores the connections between the African American tradition and the Anglo-American one, which has both excluded and distorted the experiences of black people. As a writer who is black and southern, she is keenly aware of the points at which these lines of tradition intersect. Finally, Walker recognizes the shaping influence on her writing of men and women who did not write at all but whose stories and songs worry the lines of her prose.

Few late twentieth-century essayists have been more widely read than Walker. Published in magazines and journals including the *American Scholar* and *Ms.*, her earliest essays circulated among audiences devoted to intellectual inquiry and political activism. As they were reprinted in textbooks for undergraduate courses, not only in literature and women's studies but also in composition, Walker's essays reached audiences far beyond their initial readership. When collected in a volume, the pieces continued to attract wide notice. In addition to the essays on literary topics, *In Search* reprints a number of essays and speeches whose subjects are social and political: the civil rights movement; the dissolution of community, the rise of crime and spiritual despair in urban black America; the antinuclear movement; and womanism, a concept that is defined in the prologue and elaborated on throughout these essays. Several pieces in the volume, notably the title essay and "Looking for Zora," are among Walker's best-known and most memorable works.

Indeed, I would make the case that Walker, despite her reputation as a novelist, short story writer, and poet, has done her best work in the essay, a genre that has at present little critical currency. Consequently, few critics have commented on the lucidity of Walker's prose, the richness of her humor and irony, and the power of her passion in these pieces. She shifts discursive registers with ease: vernacular voices speak through her essays as eloquently as through her fiction. She is also able to draw on her skill as a fiction writer to interpolate the narratives that sometimes advance and other times complicate her arguments. The form of the essay, which strives to produce the effect of the spontaneous, the tentative, and the open-ended, lends itself to exploring the complex and contentious issues that Walker addresses.[2] She invites readers to puzzle the issues out with her and welcomes them to share those epiphanies she achieves. Yet writer and readers have to accept the reality that most of these issues have no easy resolution.

Among the group of black women writers who have remade the literary landscape of our time, Walker is by many accounts the most controversial. Perceived in some quarters as the exemplar of political correctness, Walker is often accused of sacrificing art to politics. But if she is deemed politically correct by more conservative white critics, within the African American literary community, not to mention among African Americans generally, her politics are often considered heretical. In the essay "Reading Family Matters," Deborah McDowell analyzes incisively the critical reception of Walker's fiction.[3] Her analysis clarifies the extent to which the debates over aesthetics and ideology remain gendered debates. In contrast to the situation faced by black women writers before her, the charge in Walker's case is not that her work lacks ideas or seriousness; it is, rather, that Walker in her commitment to feminism has endorsed the wrong ideology. Interestingly, Walker in her essays anticipates repeatedly the attacks that have been leveled at her and her work. She determines early on to

Be nobody's darling;
Be an outcast.
Take the contradictions

In Search of Our Mothers' Gardens | 211

Of your life
And wrap around
You like a shawl,
To parry stones
To keep you warm.

Watch the people succumb
To madness
With ample cheer;
Let them look askance at you
And you askance reply.

Be an outcast;
Be pleased to walk alone
(Uncool)
Or line the crowded
River beds
With other impetuous
Fools.

Make a merry gathering
On the bank
Where thousands perished
For brave hurt words
They said.

Be nobody's darling;
Be an outcast.
Qualified to live
Among your dead.[4]

Richard Wright, as well as Zora Neale Hurston, is among Walker's "dead." She recuperates and revises both their positions on politics and aesthetics in her endeavor to unify the quest for freedom and beauty.[5] This quest is the theme of In Search, and Walker's revisions of her precursors' views may be read even in her manipulation of the image the title encodes. The garden is the initial signifier of the beautiful. In the title essay, Walker writes vividly of her mother's garden, "so brilliant with colors, so original in its design, so magnificent with life and creativity" that strangers drive out of their way to view it.[6] Writing is for the daughter what gardening is for the mother: "work her soul must have." The mother in her garden, like the daughter at her desk, is "ordering the universe in the image of her personal conception of Beauty" (241). Both, Walker insists, are artists. They adhere to the tenet set forth in Hurston's "Characteristics of Negro Expression" that in African American culture "there can never be enough of beauty, let alone too much."[7] But in a stance that diverges from her female precursor's Walker refuses to allow the beauty of the garden to blind her to the poverty and racism that have scarred the family's life. If "memories of poverty are seen through a screen of blooms," they are seen nonetheless. The perspective through which Walker remembers is akin to the perspective Wright called on black writers to develop.

Walker's title essay alludes directly to Virginia Woolf's *A Room of One's Own* in its discussion of Phillis Wheatley, who, Walker observes, did not own herself, let alone the room (with key and lock) Woolf maintained the woman writer required. But Woolf's room contrasts as well with the mother's gardens. Because of the itinerant life the Walkers as sharecroppers lived, the mother planted many gardens. Their beauty nurtured Walker's spirit, but the family's dispossession—and that of the generations of black women artists whose legacies Walker wishes to recuperate—motivate her political commitment. In the tradition of Richard Wright, Walker wants her writing to serve political ends.

In 1934 Zora Neale Hurston published an essay, "Characteristics of Negro Expression," that set forth the aesthetic principles she believed undergirded African American oral performance, music, and dance. First among them was the heightened sense of drama that marked every phase of black life. "Everything is acted out," she asserted. "There is an impromptu ceremony always ready for every hour of life. No little moment passes unadorned" (830).[8] This concept of ritualized improvisation was reflected in casual conversations, customs of courtship, and worship practices. Its complement was the "will to adorn," which was expressed through both the form of the ceremonies and their linguistic content.

Drawing on her notes and transcriptions from years of ethnographic fieldwork, Hurston enumerated the contributions African Americans had made to the English language; she listed examples of the distinctive metaphors and similes, double descriptives, and verbal nouns. Then, in one of the most detailed descriptions of the essay, she connected the linguistic practices with the worldview that produced them. The object described was a room Hurston had observed in Mobile, Alabama. Furnished with an overstuffed mohair living room suite, an imitation mahogany bed, a chifforobe, and a console Victrola, the room was papered with Sunday supplements of the local newspaper. Seven calendars and three wall pockets, one decorated with a lace doily, were hung along the walls. For Hurston, no gesture was more telling than the lace doily adorning the wall hanging: a decoration of a decoration. In her interpretation, it bespoke the feeling that "there can never be enough of beauty, let alone too much" (834). Despite, or perhaps because of, the fact that the gesture did not conform to "conventional standards," it exemplified Hurston's assertion that the expression of beauty, whether through action or words, was a cardinal principle of African American vernacular culture.

Surveying the same body of oral expression, though appalled by the material culture in which it was embedded, Richard Wright saw and heard not the will to adorn but the will to be free. In "Blueprint for Negro Literature," published in 1937, Wright maintained that Negro folklore contained "in a measure that puts to shame more deliberate forms of expression the collective sense of the Negro's life in America."[9] He argued, moreover, that black writers ought to tap the "racial wisdom" distilled through what he later designated "The Forms of Things Unknown."[10]

Given the subversive content and political implications of this wisdom, which Wright designated "nationalist," its expressions were necessarily veiled. Consequently, and perhaps in contradiction of our expectations, Wright privileged private discourse over the culture's public social dramas with which Hurston was more concerned. Indeed, he rendered the public private when he extolled the "blues, spirituals, and folk tales recounted from mouth to mouth, the whispered words of a black mother to her black daughter on the ways of men, the confidential wisdom of a black father to his black son, the swapping of sex experiences on street corners from boy to boy in the deepest vernacular, [and] work songs sung under blazing suns" (6). For Wright the conception of these expressions as private suggested both the sense that whatever happened in the African American community, behind the veil in terms of Du Bois's famous metaphor, was necessarily private—the white world was the public sphere—and the sense that blacks could communicate the anger and rage that their oppression provoked only furtively and in language too coded to be understood by those outside the race.

From the perspective of a half century later, it might seem most notable that in essays published only three years apart Zora Neale Hurston and Richard Wright concluded that oral lore could and should be the "generative source" of African American literature.[11] Wright states so explicitly when he claims folklore as the black writer's "most powerful weapon" (8). Although Hurston does not discuss formal fiction and drama in the context of her ethnographic writing, she operates according to the principle and employs the mode of ritualized improvisation throughout her literary work. In the case of each writer, his or her own fiction has provided the best textual evidence for these conclusions.

Whatever the similarity between their conclusions, the more vivid and certainly profound differences in their conceptions have gained critical currency. If for Wright the "folk" culture is defined by absence (7), for Hurston it is an overflowing presence. Wright's metaphors encode physical constriction; Hurston's convey psychological and spiritual expansiveness. Where he sees provisions of bare sustenance, she sees a banquet of verbal riches. In one telling contrast, the prayers that to her signified beauty were to Wright evidence of the lamentable fact that for millions of African Americans their only guide to personal dignity, as well as their only sense of the world outside themselves, came through "the archaic morphology of Christian salvation" (6). Hurston was quick to observe that the "Negro is not a Christian really" and leave it at that (836).

The definitions of culture on which their analyses depended were fundamentally at odds. For Wright, the forms of culture had been already fixed, and blacks were shut out of them. While he urged writers to recognize the value in life as the folk lived it, he saw in that recognition the emergence of "a new culture in the shell of the old." The writers' larger mission was to make people realize a meaning in their suffering: for at the moment they begin to do so, Wright predicted, "the civilization that engenders that suffering is doomed" (8). To achieve their mission, writers had to develop a perspective on the world, a sense of the interconnectedness of the suffering and hopes of black Americans and other oppressed people. Marxism provided one source for that perspective as well as a means, ultimately, to transcend the nationalist consciousness that was the legacy of Jim Crow.

For Hurston cultural forms were not fixed. African American folklore, she averred, "is not a thing of the past. It is still in the making"

(836). Her essay was much more concerned with analyzing the process of cultural production than with its products. Consequently, she valorized adaptability, variety, and dynamic suggestion as foundational principles of black expressive forms from speech to music to dance. In their forced encounter with Western culture, Hurston argued, Africans in America had seized the Europeans' language and remade it so compellingly that European Americans changed their way of speaking.[12] African American music and dance had likewise transformed the national culture in the 1920s.

The arena for struggle and resistance that Hurston defines is cultural. Rather than awaiting writers and intellectuals to lead it, as Wright desired, Hurston maintained that the struggle had long since been joined. The intellectual's role was to analyze the ways in which the culture of the "Negro farthest down" had pervaded the national culture. It was to devise, in other words, a deconstructive practice to refigure and reinterpret the centrality of the margin. To do so meant rejecting "conventional standards," which obscured black people's cultural contributions. One needed instead to formulate alternate standards that would, for example, validate the jook as, "musically speaking," the most important place in America.[13] Hurston did not comment on the fact that southern jooks, like all other public places in the U.S. South, were segregated.

In the longstanding debate over the relation between aesthetics and ideology in black literature, African Americanist critics have deployed the contrasting positions of Hurston and Wright with their respective emphases on beauty as a cultural value and on the priority of political struggle. Versions of that debate have fueled the "culture wars" that have roiled the academy for the past several decades. Critics of what was once known as the mainstream have been forced to acknowledge the ideologies at work in the construction of even the "masterpieces" of English and American literature and to confront the concurrent loss of "enduring" criteria by which to assign aesthetic value. Their situation is an inversion of that facing critics of African American literature.

From its beginnings in the United States, black writing has been defined as having only an ideological importance. Houston Baker argued in a 1972 essay that most black American texts "have been considered excessively didactic, and when they have been acknowledged for their utilitarian quality, white critics have felt compelled to point out that such *utile* has been purchased 'at the expense of the *dulce*.'"[14] Evidence for this conclusion is abundant. For example, historians and an occasional critic valued slave narratives not as literature but as documents of the abolitionist crusade. W. E. B. Du Bois in *The Souls of Black Folk* and a shelf full of additional volumes revealed himself to scholars as merely a brilliant "polemicist." Routinely, critics read novels by Wright, Ann Petry, and James Baldwin as sociology and dramas by Lorraine Hansberry and Amiri Baraka as protest or propaganda. Departing from the work of mainly white scholars and critics of an earlier generation, much of the work in African American literary study over the past quarter century has been devoted to defining aesthetic principles and to demonstrating the dual quests for freedom and for beauty in black writing.

Walker's first essay, "The Civil Rights Movement: What Good Was It?," was published in the *American Scholar* in the fall of 1967. The backlash to the movement was already in full effect (Langston Hughes's poem "The Backlash Blues" appeared the same year), but Walker answered her question without anger or cynicism. Simply put, the movement has awakened black "people to the possibilities of life" (*In Search*, 121). In a gesture that would become characteristic, she invites witnesses to present evidence. Comparing the movement to herself, an old woman who is described as "a legendary freedom fighter" in her small Mississippi Delta town testifies that "if it's dead, it shore ain't ready to lay down!" (120). The essay contrasts this testimony to the views — always expressed by the white man in the media he controls — that the movement is dead. But the primary witness in her first essay is Walker herself.

She writes that in effect her life began with the movement. In terms that resonate with Du Bois's metaphor of double consciousness, she describes the split between her perceptions of herself and her perceptions of how others saw her. In her mind she had ambitions to be an author or a scientist that the color of her body denied. Consequently, she measured herself against the views of others. "I had never seen myself and existed as a statistic exists, or as a phantom. In the white world I walked, less real to them than a shadow; and being young and well hidden among the slums, among people who also did not exist — either in books or in films or in the government of their own lives — I waited to be called to life. And, by a miracle, I was called" (122).[15]

Walker's language renders the call a spiritual awakening. But in the next paragraph she tells readers that the call was delivered on television, a medium that transformed her family life in negative as well as positive ways. The Walkers acquired a television in 1960, at the beginning of the decade that would transform American life. In Walker's telling, the representation of whites on television—upper class, glamorous, and neurotic—heightened the insecurity of black viewers. She was especially dismayed by the impact on her mother, whom she considered "a truly great woman" (123). As a spectator, the mother identified with the white characters—never the black maids who served them—and concluded that whites were "jest naturally smarter, prettier, better" (123).[16] Walker maintained a more critical perspective, but it was not one on which she could act. That changed when she found that, unlike the soap operas that fed insecurity and self-hatred, the news brought a message of liberation. Many historians have asserted the importance of television to the success of the civil rights movement, but most emphasize its impact on white viewers. Walker tells another story.

"Like a good omen for the future, the face of Dr. Martin Luther King, Jr., was the first black face I saw on our new television" (124). His message allows Walker to resolve the dilemma of double consciousness. He does not require that blacks become "carbon copies" of whites, but he tells them they have "the right to become whatever we wanted to become" (125). Rather than a shadow, Walker is able to claim a self. Life becomes more than the struggle to eke out an existence. For blacks in general, the answer to the question the essay poses is that the civil rights movement gave them each other. Although she does not mention it, the fact of the essay's publication is evidence that the movement authorized Walker to pursue her ambitions. As a writer as well as a citizen, she is indebted to the cause.

The timing of Walker's initial publication was not fortuitous. If the backlash to civil rights was gaining force in the white community, the forces of Black Power were gaining momentum among African Americans. The term "Black Power" had been used earlier by Richard Wright and Adam Clayton Powell, among others, but in 1966 leaders of the Student Nonviolent Coordinating Committee (SNCC), including Stokeley Carmichael, brought it into wide circulation. Invoking it in a speech in Greenwood, Mississippi, Carmichael was surprised by the enthusiastic response. At rallies and on campuses, the slogan soon supplanted the former cry of "Freedom Now."[17] The artistic and critical analogues of Black Power were, respectively, the Black Arts movement and the Black Aesthetic. As a black woman married to a white man, as an activist committed to nonviolence, and as a writer dedicated to the exploration of rural southern life, Walker was not welcomed by either.

The Black Aesthetics movement of the 1970s embraced the definition of black literature as didactic or ideological; indeed, despite its label, it marks one of the most intensely ideological moments in African American literary history. Stephen Henderson charged that "Black poetry in the United States has been widely misunderstood, misinterpreted, and undervalued for a variety of reasons—aesthetic, cultural, and political."[18] Only by devising a critical practice that took all these reasons into account could black poetry be well read. Addison Gayle wrote in the introduction to the movement's signal anthology, *The Black Aesthetic*, that "the question for the black critic today is not how beautiful is a melody, a play, a poem, or a novel, but how much more beautiful has the poem, melody, play, or novel made the life of a single black man?"[19] Few critics then or now would venture to evaluate a text in terms of this question; its usefulness was rhetorical and inherent in the asking. It aimed toward an ideal whereby ethics and aesthetics were one.

Black Aestheticians treated concerns that were more conventionally viewed as aesthetic largely by analogy to the sister arts, especially music. In *Black Fire*, an anthology edited by Amiri Baraka and Larry Neal, as in *The Black Aesthetic*, extended sections were devoted to music. Moreover, in their most imaginative gestures, like Henderson's theorizing in *Understanding the New Black Poetry*, the Black Aestheticians derived their theories from black speech and black music.[20] Although their efforts might have gained impetus from the work Hurston had done in the 1930s, her work was rarely cited.[21] By contrast, Richard Wright, widely regarded as the most influential black writer of his time, continued to represent an ideal that the next generation strove to emulate. A 1968 article in *Black World*, "Black Writers' Views on Literary Lions and Values," celebrated "a spirit of revolution" abroad in the world of black letters. Wright, who was pictured on the cover, was seen as its guiding light. More than half of thirty-eight writers polled rated him as the most important black writer in history.[22]

In the early 1970s, "Blueprint for Negro Literature" was reprinted in two influential anthologies. *Amistad 2*, edited by John A. Williams and Charles F. Harris, was dedicated to Wright; "Blueprint," published for the first time in its original version, was its lead essay. Editor Addison Gayle chose a slightly different version to introduce the section on fiction in *The Black Aesthetic*. In the preface to the volume, Gayle represented the black artist at war with society; Richard Wright was the prototypical warrior/writer.

Gayle reconferred on Wright the mantle of heroic manhood, which Wright had claimed for himself in "Blueprint." There he referred contemptuously to the black writing of earlier generations in images of humiliation and emasculation. Black writing "had been confined to humble novels, poems, and plays, decorous ambassadors who go a-begging to white America. They entered the Court of American Public Opinion dressed in the knee-pants of servility, curtsying to show that the Negro was not inferior, that he was human, and that he had a life comparable to that of other people" (4–5).

Although it is difficult at first to see how Hurston's texts could be subsumed within Wright's description, since they seem hardly decorous or humble—and curtsying is not a cultural practice they record—Wright's review of her novel *Their Eyes Were Watching God* shows clearly that he included her writing in his indictment. The novel, in his view, lacked a theme and any claim at all to seriousness. He located it instead in the tradition of minstrelsy and described its characters as caught "in that safe and narrow orbit in which America likes to see the Negro live: between laughter and tears."[23] He defined it, in other words, as a novel of feeling rather than of ideas. In so doing, he placed its author in the sphere of the feminine.

Wright's bias is apparent throughout this review, in which seriousness and ideas are masculine-coded terms.[24] But nowhere is the sexism more telling than in Wright's remarks on the language of Hurston's text. Her prose, he charges, "is cloaked in that facile sensuality that has dogged Negro expression since the days of Phillis Wheatley" (25). The reference to sensuality is egregious. Wright's invocation of Wheatley serves mainly to link Hurston to a politics he deemed reactionary and to a quest for the beautiful that, to him, served no "serious" purpose. Most readers will see—or better yet, hear—little resemblance between Hurston's blues-inflected prose and Wheatley's neoclassical poetry.

Wright's review of *Their Eyes* and Hurston's review of his *Uncle Tom's Children* exemplify the extent to which the debate over aesthetics and ideology in African American literature is a gendered debate.[25] The beautiful is perceived to be ornamental and superfluous. At best, the beautiful distracts attention from the overriding goal of social and political liberation. At worst, it undermines and trivializes that struggle. What enables both of these conclusions is the unspoken assumption that the beautiful is ascriptively feminine and that the goal of the struggle is the liberation of the black man.

Hurston betrayed a gender bias of her own when she wrote that *Uncle Tom's Children* contained "perhaps" enough killing "to satisfy all black male readers."[26] Or perhaps she was just signifying—that is, employing the African American rhetorical device of communicating by indirection; the purpose is often to ridicule.[27] The object of ridicule in the foregoing quotation might be Wright, the fantasies of his black male readers, and/or the images of black men running through the minds of white readers of the *Saturday Review*, which published her critique. Surely signifying is the impulse behind her dismissal of Wright's rendering of black vernacular speech. She pretended to wonder if he was "tone-deaf." Her point was that Wright's dialogue captured none of the drama or the adornment she viewed as characteristic of black expression. She was willing to grant that he was not deaf to beauty elsewhere. "But aside from the broken speech of his characters, the book contains some beautiful writing. One hopes that Mr. Wright will find in Negro life a vehicle for his talents" (32). As is often the case with signifying, this last remark scores a rhetorical point while misstating fact: Wright's stories were obviously representations of African American lives. The remark does contain a certain truth, however. From Hurston's perspective, Wright's misinterpretation of those lives was too profound to be credible. Critics and readers disagreed; after the success of *Uncle Tom's Children*, Wright went on, with the publication of *Native Son*, to the greatest success theretofore achieved by a black writer. His contemporaries, even those like James Baldwin and Ralph Ellison, whose aesthetic and ideological assumptions were substantially different from his, responded to Wright's example. Hurston's books went out of print. No one did more to bring them back than Alice Walker.

Walker has described her discovery of Zora Neale Hurston many times. Most frequently she has told the story of finding her name in a footnote as she researched the background for her story "The Revenge of Hannah Kemhuff." Writing with an expansiveness that resembles Hurston's own response to her fieldwork, Walker exults in "Saving the Life That Is Your Own" that "Zora had collected all the black folklore I could ever use" (*In Search*, 12). Through her commentary, Hurston provides the key that unlocks its meanings. Walker also praises *Their Eyes Were Watching God* as "one of the greatest novels America has produced" and laments the fact that she had never heard of it. As important as Hurston's work is the example of her life. Rather than Wright the warrior/writer, Hurston becomes the model that Walker the artist needs.

"Saving the Life That Is Your Own: The Importance of Models in the Artist's Life" begins audaciously by quoting a letter that van Gogh wrote a friend decrying the "absolute lack of models" in his life. The letter does not indicate that his art suffers from the lack; it refers instead to "the five size 30 canvasses, olive trees" that he has just completed. But the letter is followed by the information that the painter committed suicide six months after writing it. In contrast to his current reputation, "he had sold one painting during his lifetime." Implicitly Walker compares her situation as an artist to that of the certified European male genius. With its allusion to the title of Flannery O'Connor's famous short story "The Life You Save May Be Your Own," the essay suggests a comparison to a putative white American female genius as well. While Walker recognizes the need for the artist to become her own model, as O'Connor and van Gogh certainly were, she also holds that "the absence of models . . . is an occupational hazard for the artist, simply because models in art, in behavior, in growth of spirit and intellect—even if rejected—enrich and enlarge one's view of existence" (4). Hurston becomes Walker's protection against the occupational hazard. As a black woman raised in the rural South, Hurston is sufficiently *like* Walker that in "Looking for Zora" Walker can claim her not as a mother but as an aunt.

Just as the proponents of the Black Aesthetic fashioned a model out of Richard Wright, Walker drew an empowering portrait of Hurston. Rather than rage, she emphasized humor:

Zora was funny, irreverent (she was the first to call the Harlem Renaissance literati the "niggerati"), good-looking, sexy, and once sold hot dogs in a Washington park just to record accurately how the black people who bought the hot dogs talked. . . . She would go anywhere she had to go: Harlem, Jamaica, Haiti, Bermuda, to find out anything she simply had to know. She loved to give parties. Loved to dance. . . . [S]he loved to wear hats, tilted over one eye, and pants and boots. (I have a photograph of her in pants, boots, and broadbrim hat that was given to me by her brother Everette. She has her foot up on the running board of a car—presumably hers, and bright red—and looks racy.) (88)

As I noted earlier, Hurston is clearly one of the models on which Walker draws to invent Shug Avery. Bold and funny, always on the move, intellectually curious and sexually alive, Hurston is anything but the suffering solitary genius of legend. Despite the fact that Walker quickly learns how controversial Hurston was, how many of her peers rejected and mocked her, Walker clings to the portrait of the black woman artist who would not accept defeat and who never stopped loving herself. She resolves "to fight for Zora and her work; for what I knew was good and must not be lost to us" (87).

At the same time, Walker does not ignore the debt she owes Wright. She invokes his name and legacy specifically in two of her essays, "The Unglamorous but Worthwhile Duties of the Black Revolutionary Artist, or of the Black Writer Who Simply Works and Writes" and "Beyond the Peacock: The Reconstruction of Flannery O'Connor." In the former, she protests the exclusion of Wright and other black writers from the southern writers course she took at Sarah Lawrence College. Having taught such a course herself by 1971, she determines that Wright's Black Boy and "The Ethics of Living Jim Crow" are indispensable. The first duty she has faced as a black writer who eschews the label revolutionary is to teach herself black writing; the second is to teach it to others. The ultimate duty is to write.

In "Beyond the Peacock," Walker proclaims her unwillingness ever to settle for a segregated literature. O'Connor had been on the college reading list, of course, and Walker admired deeply "the magic, the wit, and the mystery" of her writing. She wants very much to reclaim O'Connor's work and to place it alongside that of the black authors whose writing she has had subsequently to seek out by herself. To do so, however, she has to put their lives (and her own) in perspective.

The essay recounts a pilgrimage Walker makes, accompanied by her mother, first to the abandoned sharecropper cabin the Walkers once rented and then to Andalusia, the O'Connor country house, where the author had moved after being crippled by lupus. To Walker's surprise, the houses stand on either side of the same field; the field she had loved as a girl, she now recognizes, was "Flannery's field." This and subsequent revelations threaten to overwhelm Walker's empathy and admiration for

O'Connor. Knocking on the door of the O'Connor house, which is unoccupied but in good repair, Walker reflects bitterly on "the fact that in Mississippi no one even remembers where Richard Wright lived, while Faulkner's house is maintained by a black caretaker."[28] The racial identity of the groundskeeper in Milledgeville, Georgia, can only be inferred; but not only is the house cared for, so are the peacocks. These birds, beloved by O'Connor, become a problematic signifier of beauty and privilege. Walker's mother observes that peacocks "eat up your blooms," and the reader recalls that Mrs. Walker's daffodils bloom still around the long-abandoned cabin. As the essay's title implies, before she can reconstruct O'Connor's legacy, Walker has to get beyond the peacocks. That she does is implied by the essay's invitation to interpret her rage in the terms it uses earlier to gloss "The Displaced Person" as a "moment of revelation, when the individual comes face to face with her own limitations and comprehends 'the true frontiers of her own inner country'" (In Search, 56). The limitations here are both Walker's and O'Connor's, but they are more profoundly those of the society that would segregate two kindred spirits in literature as it had in life.

"Beyond the Peacock" quotes from O'Connor's essays, letters, and short stories; it sketches her biography. Walker interweaves anecdotes from her own life, both as a child growing up in Georgia and as an adult writer. These are often contradicted within the essay by the memories and conclusions of Walker's mother, a woman whose pithy and poetic speech might remind readers of voices they have heard in fiction by both Walker and O'Connor. As much as the essay respects the integrity of Minnie Lou Walker's voice and her experiences, however, it challenges her conclusions, too. No speaker has a monopoly on truth.[29]

"Beyond the Peacock" represents a way of piecing together a new understanding, one that the history of the recently desegregated South makes possible. To comprehend that history, one must survey the (real) estates of the Walkers as well as the O'Connors—not only what they owned but what they valued and what in particular they perceived to be beautiful. Daffodils and peacocks signify the contrast in values, of course, but they also represent Walker's quest for historical and political meaning in the apparently tangential. The essay's elegant digressions extend this thematic.

One seemingly peripheral scene illustrates the point. On the way from their old home to Andalusia, the two "pilgrims" stop at a Holiday Inn.

(Walker is always aware of the relation of her stories to the classic narratives of Western tradition.) Over lunch Walker imagines O'Connor's response to the garishness of the motel and what it suggests about the dilution of southern culture. She shares O'Connor's disdain—to a degree. However tasteless she finds the food, Walker takes a "weary delight" in the fact that in 1975 she can buy lunch for her mother in such a place in Georgia. She asserts, "I believe the truth about any subject only comes when all the sides of the story are put together, and all their different meanings make one new one. Each writer writes the missing part of the other writer's story. And the whole story is what I'm after" (49). The statement might be read as a gloss on Walker's view of history, literature, and the art of the essay.

Like "Beyond the Peacock," "My Father's Country Is the Poor" is among Walker's most exquisitely crafted essays. Although it does not allude directly to Richard Wright, it offers one of several instances in which Walker's writing seems actively in dialogue with his. Racism, poverty, socialist revolution, and violence are central concerns. On one level, the essay presents reportage of a trip Walker makes to Cuba with a group of African American artists. From the vantage point of Cuba, it develops a critique of the treatment of the poor and of people of African descent in the United States. On a philosophical level, the essay is a meditation on the morality of violence as means to revolution—a frequent theme in Walker's writing. On a personal level, the essay records Walker's spiritual reconciliation with her recently deceased father, from whom she had long been estranged. Dispossessed by racism and poverty, Walker's father had no country to claim. He had no estate to bequeath his daughter. She speculates on the difference a revolution might have made in his life and in her relationship with him. In the process, she discerns the legacy that she has in fact received.

Many voices speak through "My Father's Country Is the Poor": Cuban officials (the texts of Castro and Ernesto Cardenal), U.S. revolutionaries (Angela Davis and Huey Newton), individuals whom Walker meets in Cuba, dissenters in the United States who speak of and for the silenced dissenters in Cuba (homosexuals, Jehovah's Witnesses, and political prisoners), members of the tour group, and, through her memories and dreams, Alice Walker's father. Walker speaks plainly for herself: "[M]y own bias, when considering a country like Cuba, is to think almost entirely of the gains of the formerly dispossessed." [30] Yet the range of voices the essay interpolates allows for readers with different biases to enter into dialogue with the writer on the subject at hand.

The essay's form is digressive. A long epigraph from Angela Davis's autobiography describes the performance the Cuban delegation presented at the 1962 World Youth Peace Festival in Helsinki. The essay proper opens with the statement "Perhaps I saw Angela Davis at the festival" and contrasts the political sophistication Davis's memories imply with Walker's naïveté. As a student, Walker did not analyze the political implications of the performance; she was just impressed by the spirit of the multiracial Cuban dance troupe. The contrast produces a second, perhaps unintended, effect: Walker will seem a more credible guide in Cuba because she, unlike Davis, is not a Marxist. Walker dates her desire to visit Cuba from the performance she viewed in Helsinki. She determines to go, not least to ease the despair she felt "due to my sense of political powerlessness, caused to some extent by a lack of living models. I believed poor people could not win. . . . But here at last was a revolutionary people I could respect, and they made it quite clear they did not intend to lose" (202).

Walker is drawn to Cuba also because she "was eager to see the effect on the people of having used violence to liberate themselves." As "a pacifist and a believer in nonviolent means to effect social change," she "needed to know that the use of violence did not necessarily destroy one's humanity." She finds hope for this view in an unexpected source. "I wanted to confirm the truth of one of my favorite lines from Flannery O'Connor: 'Violence is a force that can be used for good or evil, and among the things taken by it is the Kingdom of Heaven'" (202).

Responding to Americans who say that life in Cuba is hard, Walker states, "And it is." But that judgment lacks a context. Walker provides one in her list of the revolution's accomplishments—the elimination of poverty and racism, the achievement of universal literacy and free medical care, and the promise of decent housing for all. What those Americans invoked above do not say, Walker suspects, is what she feels: "[A] hard life shared equally by all is preferable to a life of ease and plenty enjoyed by a few" (203).

At several junctures the essay explores the gaps between the ideal of revolution and the actuality. Huey Newton, the exiled Black Panther leader, is represented as a figure of ambiguity. Walker recounts rumors she hears of dissenters whom the revolution has dispossessed. She questions an official at length regarding discrimination against homosexuals. She wonders, too, about the cost of cultural assimilation for darker-skinned Cubans. Walker's doubts and queries are all restated at the essay's conclusion, but they are suspended at its heart, where revolutionary Cuba helps Walker make peace with her dead father.

"A week before I flew to Cuba, I began to dream about my father," Walker writes, noting that, four years after his death, it was not unusual for her to dream of him. But she could not place the pose he assumed now: "standing by the side of a road in front of a filling station, his hat in his hands, watching me as I moved farther and farther away from him" (212). In a paragraph she sketches her father's physical features and his life: the hard labor, the subsistence wage, and the struggle to support a family of ten. From her adult perspective, she recognizes that his condition was that of "millions of peasants the world over." But, she confesses, "as a child I was not aware of any others. I thought it was my father's own peculiar failing that we were poor" (213).

The essay's most dramatic and riskiest moment comes when Walker, arriving in Cuba, proclaims that her father was waiting for her there. Sustaining the moment of epiphany, she repeats the physical description and announces, "My father's name in Havana was Pablo Diaz" (213). The information that he spoke Spanish, which she did not understand, returns the essay to the realm of the real. Once a peasant like her father, Pablo Diaz is an official historian of the revolution. Lecturing to the group, he speaks proudly and in a steady cadence. Walker watches him and envies his children.

This moment is analogous to that in "Looking For Zora" when Walker stands knee-deep in the weeds of the Garden of Heavenly Rest Cemetery, searching for Hurston's unmarked grave. For the third time, she calls out "Zo-ra," and her foot sinks into a hole. Walker orders a stone monument to mark the site of what she identifies as Hurston's grave. Whether it is or is not is both unknowable and unimportant. The essay is Hurston's monument, just as "My Father's Country Is the Poor" is a tribute to Willie Lee Walker.

The spiritual reunions that occur throughout Walker's essays are highly dramatic, yet they do not require the same suspension of disbelief that those in her fiction demand. In the essays these encounters are understood to be psychic rather than physical. They are Walker's way of coming to terms with her dead: black and white, writers and workers, artistic ancestors and close kin.

After her encounter with Pablo Diaz, Walker is able to interpret the dream about her father. The narrative of her interpretation is, she concedes, a simple story. But its themes (economics, politics, and class) are not. The story recalls the incident that inspires her dream. She is on her way to college and is bidding her father farewell. As she boards the bus, he stands, hat in hand, by the side of the road. If education is her route out of poverty, it comes at the expense of her relationship with her father. "This separation," she concludes, "is what poverty engenders. It is what injustice means" (216).

The narrative of Walker's spiritual reconciliation with her father should be read against the narrative of Richard Wright's failed reconciliation with his father in Black Boy. Wright breaks the chronology of his autobiography to describe his reunion with his father twenty-five years after their bitter parting in Memphis. He draws a pitiable portrait of a defeated man (one that may be hung alongside that of Wright's paralyzed mother, whose suffering becomes one of the book's key metaphors). Aged beyond his years, white haired, toothless, body-bent, and dressed in ragged overalls, the prodigal father stands alone on the Mississippi plantation where he sharecrops. His son, now an author and man of the world, concludes that "we were forever strangers, speaking a different language, living on vastly distant planes of reality."[31]

Having achieved the spiritual reconciliation with her father's memory, Walker draws a different kind of conclusion. Looking back, she remembers not a defeated "peasant" but a "brilliant man," "great at mathematics" and "unbeatable at storytelling" (216). Recognizing his gifts, she can measure their loss. Walker is not content to let her father or any of the "poor" remain abstractions.

In several respects the public positions Wright and Walker occupy are analogous. As was Wright, Walker is identified with a political movement—in his case communism, in hers feminism—that is based outside the African American community. Just as the Left provided Wright with his first publishing outlets, feminist publications supported Walker's early work. Many of the essays in In Search were first published in Ms. magazine. Perhaps in response to Wright's and Walker's situations as black artists within white progressive organizations that gave them a platform—both in the sense of a place to speak from and in the sense of an orthodoxy to speak—the issue of autonomy looms large. Walker addresses it in her subtitle with the designation of her prose as "womanist." Prominent among the volume's front matter is an extended definition.

The definition, with its deliberate borrowing of dictionary form, announces Walker's intention to invent and define her own terms. She defines the word first by establishing what it is not. Its antonyms include "'girlish,' i.e. frivolous, irresponsible, not serious." A womanist is a black feminist or feminist of color, presumably a new phenomenon in the world. But Walker's definition immediately connects the new to the old. The etymology of her word ["from *womanish*"] establishes its derivation from black vernacular speech, as do the illustrations of usage that follow. Walker refers specifically to "the black folk expression of mothers to female children, 'you acting womanish,' i.e., like a woman." Like any good lexicographer, she notes the occasions on which the word might be used by these women, to wit, in response to "outrageous, audacious, courageous or *willful* behavior." The entry goes on to note that the expression from which "womanist" is derived is "interchangeable" with another black folk expression, "You trying to be grown." The first entry concludes with synonyms for Walker's neologism: "Responsible. In charge. *Serious*" (emphasis in original).

Additional meanings for "womanist" denote what one does, including loving other women, sexually and/or nonsexually; appreciating and preferring women's culture; sometimes loving individual men, sexually and/or nonsexually, and being "committed to survival and wholeness of entire people, male *and* female" (xi). Here, too, the definition insists that despite the introduction of political and sexual dimensions not associated with the expression from which "womanist" descends, the concept is traditional in African American history and culture.

This aspect of the definition encapsulates Walker's representation of Zora Neale Hurston as well, particularly the quality that Walker sees as most "characteristic" of her precursor's work: "racial health; a sense of black people as complete, complex *undiminished* human beings."[32] In *Search* is replete with encomiums to Hurston, but a most telling example of Walker's Hurstonian sensibility is reflected in her gloss on the poem "Revolutionary Petunias." The poem's subject, Sammy Lou, has killed her husband's murderer and become a political heroine in the process. But she does not recognize herself in the picture drawn by movement singers and versifiers.

> Sammy Lou of Rue
> sent to his reward
> the exact creature who
> murdered her husband,
> using a cultivator's hoe
> with verve and skill;
> and laughed fit to kill
> in disbelief
> at the angry, militant
> pictures of herself
> the Sonneteers quickly drew;
> not any of them people that
> she knew.
> A backwoods woman
> her house was papered with
> funeral home calendars
> and faces appropriate for a Mississippi
> Sunday School. She raised a George,
> a Martha, a Jackie and a Kennedy. Also
> a John Wesley Junior.
> "Always respect the word of God,"
> she said on her way to she didn't
> know where, except it would be by
> electric chair, and she continued
> "Don't yall forget to *water*
> my purple petunias." [33]

Walker explains that her motive in "Revolutionary Petunias" was "to create a person who engaged in a final struggle with her oppressor and won, but who in every other way, was incorrect." [34] Most important, Sammy Lou refuses to see killing as heroic; she is amused by other people's attempts to make it so. Despite their clamor, she declines to change her life or herself to suit the expectations of others.

The poem's description of Sammy Lou's house is reminiscent of the room Hurston wrote about in "Characteristics of Negro Expression." According to Walker's gloss, "the walls of her house contain no signs of her blackness—though that in itself reveals it; anyone walking into that empty house would know Sammy Lou is black" (266). Anyone would know from her garden that Sammy Lou adheres to the tenet that there can never be enough of beauty, let alone too much. Walker makes explicit the ideology implicit in Hurston's theory. Walker demonstrates, moreover, the ways in which the preservation of cultural values and practices may be the springboard for political action.

The civil rights movement is the historical pivot on which Walker's revision of Wright's and Hurston's worldviews turns. Most of her "models" for behavior are movement activists. She credits one, Mrs. Winsom Hudson, of Harmony, Mississippi, for inspiring her research on black women writers.[35] The movement was, significantly, based in the South; its soldiers were the sons and daughters of the African Americans whose culture Zora Hurston had honored and preserved. Apart from Hurston, Martin Luther King is the book's most haunting and revered presence.

The essay "Choosing to Stay at Home: Ten Years after the March on Washington" opens with a flashback of that historic event. Walker, then a sophomore at Spelman College in Atlanta, journeys to Washington and takes as a vantage point a tree far from the Lincoln Memorial. Perched on this limb, she can see very little, but in the retelling, she becomes her reader's ear; it hears "everything."

As is typical of the skill with which she handles the form, Walker pauses in the essay's narrative of the march to interpolate another narrative. The year before, her speech and drama instructor in Atlanta had sent his class to hear Martin Luther King lecture. He cautioned them to pay attention only to his speech; the instructor was not interested in King's politics. Walker had done as she was told and written a term paper from which she quotes in the essay. "Martin Luther King, Jr. is a surprisingly effective orator, although terribly under the influence of the Baptist church so that his utterances sound overdramatic and too weighty to be taken seriously."[36] Further to mock her younger, more cynical self, Walker repeats her comments about King's clothes, his lack of humor, and his "expressionless 'Oriental' eyes."

At the march, of course, neither Walker nor anyone else is trying to separate form and content, aesthetics and ideology. They are perfectly fused. King's "tone" was as "electrifying as his message." What stirred her most was King's command to the marchers to go back to Mississippi, Alabama, and Georgia—his injunction for them to go back home. The effect on Walker was immediate and prolonged. At that moment, she avers, "I saw again what he was always uniquely able to make me see: that I, in fact, had claim to the land of my birth" (160). Two years later, she decides to forego a trip to Senegal to go to Mississippi. Eventually, she would make her home there for seven years, acting out of the belief that she "could never live happily in Africa—or anywhere else—until [she] could live freely in Mississippi" (163).

King gives her the inspiration and the courage to make this choice. But he is a model for Walker the writer as well as for Walker the woman. He belongs to her literary line. Retrospectively, in this essay written five years after King's death, she describes her response to his voice on that August day.

> Martin Luther King was a man who truly had his tongue wrapped around the roots of Southern black religious consciousness, and when his resounding voice swelled and broke over the heads of the thousands of people assembled at the Lincoln Memorial I felt what a Southern person brought up in the church *always* feels when those cadences —not the words themselves necessarily but the rhythmic spirals of passionate emotion, followed by even more passionate pauses—roll off the tongue of a really first-rate preacher. I felt my soul rising from the sheer force of Martin King's eloquent goodness. (159)

"Eloquent goodness" might also serve as the standard to which Alice Walker the essayist aspires. It is one she often meets. Moreover, by embracing that standard, Walker keeps faith with the best of African American literary tradition.

Throughout In Search of Our Mothers' Gardens Walker reflects self-consciously on the traditions out of which she writes. These include classics of modernist fiction as well as sermons, blues, and stories spun out on southern porches. As she charts her literary lineage, she is ever aware of her position as a black woman, born southern and poor. Her race, gender, class, and location complicate her relation to all the literary traditions she inherits. By grounding her aesthetics in her mothers' gardens, finding in that example her standard for beauty and design, and by grounding her ethics in the civil rights movement, finding in that example the moral capital that constitutes her fathers' (and mothers') real estates, Walker seizes critical authority. Just as she exercises her choice to remain for a time at home in the South, she exercises her choice alternately to love and loathe, appropriate and reject, aspects of the American and African American literary traditions. The result defines and extends an inclusive literary legacy. Alice Walker's essays constitute an elegant example of worrying the line.

*Daughters of the Dust*, the 1991 film directed by Julie Dash, makes extensive and explicit allusions to *Praisesong for the Widow* and to *Beloved*. Set in the Sea Islands, it is attuned to the spiritual beliefs and cultural practices that Gloria Naylor represents in *Mama Day*. It depicts the crafts of quilting and cooking that Alice Walker redefines as art in *In Search of Our Mothers' Gardens*. It appropriates many of the images in these texts, moving its audience, as it were, from text to image. *Daughters of the Dust* is set on the eve of an African American family's migration north from rural South Carolina. Although the family could not have known it, their journey is part of what historians would call "The Great Migration," the movement of hundreds of thousands of black Americans from the rural South to the urban North, and one of the most important events in twentieth-century American history. Within the film, the moment is documented by the taking of family photographs. The film resonates with the statement that I quote from Toni Morrison in the prologue to *Worrying the Line*, that the images that float around her memories of kin are her "route to a reconstruction of a world, to an exploration of an interior life that was not written and to the revelation of a kind of truth." [1]

Two-thirds of the way through *Daughters of the Dust*, a young woman relates the version of the Ibo Landing tale told by Great Aunt Cuney in *Praisesong*; the screenplay credits Marshall's novel. [2] Eula the storyteller has been raped, and she tells the tale to her unborn child. As she speaks, scenes appear of her estranged husband "walking on water" and releasing from a tangle in the marsh the figurehead of an African that had once adorned the prow of a slave ship. The tale effects the reconciliation between the storyteller Eula and her husband; the visual imagery signals the reconciliation of African Americans to their African past. The figurehead, like the mythic Ibos, is free to return home. Those remaining on shore incorporate elements of African culture into the culture of the New World. The result is the legacy the mother/speaker passes on to her daughter.

Long before the tale is told, the film has established its thematic relationship to the novel. One of its initial images is the figure of an older woman rising from the water; a character in the film later explains that she bathes with her clothes on. She is wearing a skirt with two belts. Here and in subsequent scenes, one can see a strong resemblance between the character Nana Peazant and Aunt Cuney in their position as elder of the family and their adherence to a pre-Christian belief system. The film's setting is identified as "Ibo Landing: The Sea Islands of the South, 1902." Indeed, reversing the impulse I have identified in poetry and prose, the film moves from text to image in an act of homage and re-vision. Through the character of the photographer, "a Philadelphia-looking Negro" who travels south to document a pivotal moment in the family's history, Daughters of the Dust suggests what can and cannot be captured on film, even one as visually striking and lush as this one. Conversely, it puts in bold relief the distinctive qualities of the literary texts.

With its announcement on the second of two printed screens that begin the film that "Gullah communities recalled, remembered and recollected much of what their ancestors brought with them from Africa," the film identifies itself not only with the project of Praisesong but also with that of the "community of black women writing" addressed in Worrying the Line. The Unborn Child, who narrates much of the film, evokes the character of Beloved. She, too, mediates between this world and another one from which souls of the unborn come and to which souls of the dead return. As in Mama Day, the graveyard is the site of communication between the inhabitants of these worlds. Daughters of the Dust celebrates the culture of the Sea Islands: its folklore and language, crafts and cuisine. Women weave sea-grass baskets and make indigo dye. Children play the circle games that are characteristic of African diasporan culture, rhyming words in the cadence of the Sea Islands. Overflowing platters of food (crab, shrimp, greens, okra, corn, and tomatoes) featured in the exquisitely filmed ceremonial meal mark the Sea Islands as a site of plenitude. The film elaborates other ways of knowing in images of conjure, bottle trees that memorialize the dead, and Nana's tin can that contains "scraps of memories." As the multiple allusions in Daughters confirm, black women's literary texts have had a wide-ranging influence in various media.

In a conversation with Houston Baker, Dash explained that as a college student in the 1970s she was exposed to African American writers including Morrison, Toni Cade Bambara, John Williams, and the sixties poets. "I believe I was very much influenced by their work." She singled out Bambara's *Gorilla, My Love* as a book that "influenced my whole generation. The way Toni Cade takes an idea, a thought, weaves it for many paragraphs and then brings it back around, it was just like a regular conversation. It was the way your mother used to talk to you, the way your grandparents would speak to you. I would go as far as to say her work even had an influence on *Daughters of the Dust*."[3] Dash's comment brings to mind Sethe's "circling the subject" and Ursa's great-grandmother's "speaking in pieces" as well as moments in Bambara's fiction. The non-linearity of the film is analogous to their approach to storytelling. But what Dash describes as her "mythopoetic film" depends mainly on visual images rather than words to create its meaning. Two clusters of images—the film's representations of Ibo Landing and of the family photographs—suggest the continuities and discontinuities that result.

As the characters approach Ibo Landing for the first time, the audience sees from above a chain of islands, "separated from the mainland by wide marshes and tidal estuaries" ("*Daughters of the Dust*," 76). It looks like a three-dimensional map, analogous to the frontispiece of *Mama Day*. Then the camera moves close in. It lingers lovingly on lush foliage that covers every inch of ground, on trees bending to touch the shore, and on barely rippling water. The audience arrives on Ibo Landing on the same batteau that brings home two of its daughters. The first voice that speaks in the film belongs to Viola, a Christian missionary who is one of two women in the family who have left the island for the mainland. When Viola exclaims "I can't believe it. I had no idea," she is referring to her cousin Yellow Mary, the film's fallen woman. But she may speak for the spectator, who enters a world that he or she did not know existed, one for which the adjective Edenic is apt. The images on the screen express what George, the character in Naylor's novel, cannot find words for. He inquires of the reader: "But how do I describe air that thickens so that it seems as solid as the water, causing colors and sounds and textures to actually float in it?" (175). *Daughters of the Dust* shows us that air.

In her essay on the film, which is included in Dash's "*Daughters of the*

Dust," Bambara analyzes the representation of Yellow Mary in this scene. The actor is dressed in a long white dress and a veiled broad-brimmed hat, thus appropriating a Hollywood convention—deployed in films like *The African Queen*—in which the white missionary or colonist first encounters the "exotic" world of the "native."[4] But here both the woman in white and the missionary are black women coming home. When they arrive, the characters they greet are kin. The spectator who expects to encounter the exotic is disappointed, although the film anticipates the possibility that what he or she does encounter can be misinterpreted.

One of the ways it does so is by asking who can see Ibo Landing: the beauty of the landscape, the beauty of the people, the value of the culture and heritage. The film suggests the difficulty of perception by incorporating different visual technologies into the plot, including Mr. Snead's cumbersome camera equipment, the kaleidoscope he brings to amuse the children, and the stereoscope or viewer through which the Unborn Child watches black and white moving pictures of life in the North. Given the dominant society's opinion of rural black communities, it is not surprising that even some of its daughters are blind to the beauty of Ibo Landing. For example, Yellow Mary considers it "the most desolate place on earth," while Viola deems the move to the mainland a sign of progress toward culture and wealth. Quoting Shakespeare as well as the Bible, she is embarrassed by Nana's beliefs and devotes her life to saving others from paganism. Haagar (whose name may refer to the biblical Hagar), the widowed daughter-in-law who is already estranged from the line of the Peazants, also scoffs at Nana's rituals. In the end the film punishes her, the character who has been most eager to migrate north in search of opportunities for her children, when her daughter Iona refuses to leave Ibo Landing and runs off with her Native American lover. Despite some of its characters' failure to appreciate it, the film insists that spectators perceive the island's beauty. It fixes our gaze repeatedly on the moss-covered oaks, the towering pines and palm trees, the expanse of beaches, and the glistening water that holds endless memory and limitless promise. Moments in the film bring to mind Jean Toomer's prose poem "Karintha," in which the speaker repeatedly poses the question regarding the beauty of an impoverished twelve-year-old black girl in rural Georgia: "O can't you see it?"[5] Only rarely do we see interiors of houses. When we do, as in a scene in the bedroom of the parents of the Unborn Child, we perceive both material poverty and strained relationships. In the exterior scenes, by contrast, the camera not only documents the beauty of the Sea Islands but also celebrates the beauty of its people.

No aspect of the film has drawn more praise than its cinematography.[6] Arthur Jafa's camera captures the dramatic landscape in continuously shifting light. The vivid colors and patterns of the kaleidoscope are refigured in the quilts on which the sumptuous feast is spread. For many commentators and viewers, *Daughters of the Dust* captures the physical beauty of black women in a way no film before it had. It depicts a range of body types—heights, sizes, skin tones—and the camera represents them as being equally attractive. Intricately designed natural hairstyles frame the faces of the female actors; the white dresses they wear for the ceremonial dinner contrast vividly with their dark skin. Some critics take issue with the costumes, noting that historically women in the Sea Islands did not dress in white, and with the scene—families did not eat banquets on the beach. But these criticisms miss the more important point.[7] The film elaborates an argument that many of the writers discussed in *Worrying the Line* engage. So intent have historians and sociologists been on documenting oppression and struggle in African American life that they have neglected those moments that black people took and take to enjoy and celebrate themselves. Aesthetically, *Daughters* accords with the tenet that Hurston extracted from her fieldwork: "There can never be enough of beauty, let alone too much." For writer and filmmaker alike, not only is that beauty a celebration of African American people and culture, but it is an implicit rejection of the official culture that denigrates and marginalizes black life. These women's art simultaneously records and constitutes a triumph of the spirit.[8]

The ritual dinner marks the transitional moment in the family's history, one that is documented within the film by the taking of photographs. Rather than in a studio, Mr. Snead sets up his shots outdoors. Ibo Landing is a backdrop at once more culturally specific and more splendid than the artificial trappings of turn-of-the-century parlors. Viola has "commissioned" the photographer Mr. Snead, and he takes a series of pictures, each formally posed and each featuring a different group of relatives. Men, women, and children are posed in separate groups, and particular elders sit for individual pictures, before the entire clan assembles for the penultimate portrait. As bell hooks asserts, these "pictorial genealogies . . . ensur[e] against the losses of the past." The film's use of flashbacks highlights this point. The audience sees images of the family's

Snead at work (From Julie Dash, *Daughters of the Dust: The Making of an African American Woman's Film* [New York: New Press, 1992])

experiences during slavery, but the characters in the film do not. Only the elders can remember any of those experiences; no one recalls them all. Not surprisingly, Nana recognizes the similar function of Mr. Snead's camera and her tin can. They both promise to preserve the memory of the moment. But rather than "arrested moments," the photographs in the film fulfill the potential that John Berger describes in which "the past becomes an integral part of the process of people making their own history." Family photographs in *Daughters* have "a living context."[9]

Six of the Peazant men pose first. They follow Mr. Snead—his camera hoisted on his shoulder and his face dripping perspiration—onto the beach. Their dress is as formal as, if more old-fashioned than, his. Several wear morning coats; all wear white shirts and vests. One carries a cane, while another holds a bowler hat like the one Gene Sayles wears in his photograph in *Generations*. Two kneel in front of the four standing, and they all strike proud and expansive poses. In the conversation before the camera flashes, Snead remarks that the family sticks to the old ways; one of the men responds that "you have to change with the time." The fact that they are posing in this way indicates that they will. Photographs of small children and giggling teenagers symbolize the potential for change. As if evidence of Viola's claim that the children and elders are the most important members of the clan, Mr. Snead turns his camera on Viola's mother. She sits in a straight-back chair with her head tilted upward next to a field of golden high grass, several feet taller than she and equally regal. "I ain' tink about those old days much lately, but when I start to tink on 'em, lots of things come back to me," she muses. Her photograph is an occasion for remembering, both for its subject and for those who in the future will view it. The penultimate family portrait offers manifold opportunities for the same. Spanning generations, the entire family positioned in groups of two, three, or four fill the screen; Nana sits at the midpoint. In a moment that resonates with Paul D's sense of reverence at the survival of black families through slavery, Mr. Snead senses the import of the family gathered before him. He entreats them all to "Look! Look up! . . . And remember . . . Ibo Landing." For the rest of the film, Mr. Snead is no longer a detached observer; he acts like kin.

Despite their ability to generate intense feelings of identification,

Viola's mother (From Julie Dash, *Daughters of the Dust: The Making of an African American Woman's Film* [New York: New Press, 1992])

there is much the photographs cannot capture. The most striking example comes when Mr. Snead poses the group of men; he sees the Unborn Child in the frame. When he looks again, she is gone. A man of science, Mr. Snead does not believe what he has seen. He wipes his brow, checks the lens, and goes on to take the photograph he has planned. This is just as well, for the camera cannot catch the spirit. Indeed, although *Daughters* represents the Unborn Child more effectively than the film version of *Beloved* represents the novel's character, the invisible is represented more easily on the page than on the screen. On the page these spirits become extensions not only of the author's imagination but also of the reader's. Each act of reading produces the character that both reader and author conjure.[10] The fact that the character cannot be fixed in time or place enhances our understanding of its status as spirit. In Morrison's *Beloved*, it helps us comprehend the different ways in which other characters respond to the spirit. Their responses are as various as ours. The Unborn Child may have been inspired by *Beloved*, but it is less complex a creation. Its influence is totally benign, and its interactions with other characters in the film's narrative are limited.

In addition to the presence of the spirit, photographs also miss the tensions and contradictions that are part of the Peazant family dynamic: the disavowal of the old ways, the vexed relation to Ibo Landing, and the hostility that most of her female relatives harbor toward Yellow Mary are represented in the film but not in the photographs. Mr. Snead's camera cannot capture what he does not see. That observation would apply to the filmmaker's camera as well. The nonlinear narrative, with its noticeable omissions and gaps, reinforces the sense of incompleteness. We are not privy to this family's whole story. We see the physical marks of slavery, imaged in this film by the indigo dye that discolors the skin. But we can only get hints of the psychic disfigurations in the tensions that the camera cannot completely record. The kaleidoscope, with its continually changing symmetrical forms, becomes one metaphor for the shifting and partial truths of its representations. At one point, Mr. Snead explains the etymology of "kaleidoscope": *kal(ós)* beautiful + *eîdo(s)* forms + *skop(eîn)* (to) view. As we look at the beautiful forms and figures that constitute the representations of this family, we recognize that what is partial is not untrue.

The Peazants' migration north is, of course, emblematic of the collective history of African Americans, a fact that the family surname invites the audience to consider. Their status as emblems, however, flattens them out as characters. None of them has the contour of Eva Peace or Shug Avery. The film lacks the verbal complexity of Ursa Corregidora's "poetic autobiography." A few of the characters stand out sufficiently to be recognized by name: Nana, Eula and her husband, Eli, Haagar, Viola, Mr. Snead, Yellow Mary, and Trula, her female companion and lover, but many more just seem to be kin. Perhaps the point is they can be anybody's kin. The range of physical types and the fact that none of the actors is a movie star facilitate the audience's identification with these characters. Their faces look familiar to anyone who has spent any time in an African American community. Images of the family's past—the Middle Passage and slavery—are memories of the collective past; they could and do belong to black families in general. What is particular about the Peazants is what they do with their memories.

They are moving on down the line, but they pause to recall, remember, and recollect. An elder confers a blessing on the Unborn Child, who he believes is destined to be the first in the line born in the North, as "we child of the future." In fact, her destiny is to be born on Ibo Landing after many of her kinfolk depart. Nana prepares them for their crossing. She creates a "hand," a conjure bag, for her children to take with them on their journey. Scraps of memories and locks of hair—her own and her African-born mother's—symbolize the ties that bind them to their past as they embark on their future. The film ends here. We do not know whether the members of the family can put blood to these scraps, whether they will remember the stories Nana has told, and whether there is, in fact, power in the old ways that can sustain them in the fast-moving city. For its viewers, Daughters of the Dust is surely a journey to the past. But the figure of the Unborn Child suggests how this journey is also a detour on the way to the future. She is the film's ideal spectator, the one for whom looking back is moving forward, the one for whom these images will conjure memories and serve—like the "hand" that Nana prepares— as a connection to history and heritage.

Daughters of the Dust invites us to imagine the woman who was the Unborn Child looking back on the photographs taken on Ibo Landing, now yellowed with age. I can hear her saying with Toni Morrison, "[T]hese people are my access to me; they are my entrance to my own interior life." The recollections of kin explored throughout Worrying the Line serve to put the protagonists of fiction, the speakers of poems, and the autobiographical "I" of essays and memoir in touch with themselves. The images that swirl around the memories of their parents and grandparents help them imagine the worlds in which their ancestors struggled, laughed, and lived and give them courage to do the same. Those images inspire the creators of these texts to invent new ways of writing in order to tell stories that have never been told.

The stories evoke new concepts of the beautiful and of the heroic, in which enslaved black women like Caroline Donald Sale set the standard for strength and courage and in which brave fugitives like Sethe confront moral questions more complex than the nation's philosophers could formulate. Blues singers like Ursa Corregidora and Shug Avery become moral arbiters who have earned the right to judge those who have exploited and oppressed them. Their art gives rise to a different concept of the poetic as well as the heroic. The blues inform their stories and their telling. Black women writers at the end of the twentieth century find artistic precursors in the blueswomen whose art redefined American music at the century's beginning. They draw on their example as heroic individuals and as artists who could express truths that could not otherwise be spoken. Within their literary texts, the writers examined in *Worrying the Line* invoke the music of the blues to trigger memories of a history that was more often sung than said—and never written. As the protagonists of these texts confront the traumas of that history, they find in the blues a source of solace and healing.

The blues constitute one way of accessing and confronting history. Family stories, photographs, dreams, and visions are other ways of knowing that convey information that the written record does not contain. In order to fill in the missing links in family genealogies and to reconnect with the past, protagonists learn to "read" these phenomena. After hearing and dismissing the stories his parents have told him, Milkman meets Circe in a dream and learns his grandmother's name. Lucille looks at the photograph of her grandfather and understands chapters of the family history better than her father, who recited it, could. Audre sees her new name—one that ties her to her foremothers—written in the sky. Ursa stops reciting the stories she has heard all her life and by worrying the line creates a new story that liberates her from her history. The irony is that Ursa can liberate herself in the present only by confronting the most painful aspects of her family's past. Her situation is emblematic of all the protagonists in this book.

To represent these situations, the writers studied in *Worrying the Line* revise, subvert, and extend the literary traditions to which they are heir. They reread and revise mainstream American literary texts to put the experience of the slaves and their descendants at the center of the national story. If Walt Whitman's persona in *Song of Myself* could be the channel through whom the anonymous slave spoke, Lucille Clifton in *Generations* can speak her great-grandmother's name and remember what she said. Toni Morrison rereads *Adventures of Huckleberry Finn* and amplifies the moral dilemma of slavery beyond the conscience of an adolescent white boy. The community of newly freed black folk in Cincinnati grapple with their responsibility to the outcast Sethe and to each other. Of course, the writers discussed in *Worrying the Line* participate in the African American literary tradition. But their re-visions present a sharp critique of the way in which that tradition marginalized women's stories and women writers. As they recuperate the legacies of Jessie Fauset and Zora Neale Hurston, Paule Marshall and Alice Walker insist on the beauty and the pain of stories that transpire not across the color line but within black families and neighborhoods. Indeed, the most painful traumas of race are experienced within the family, where they are complicated by differences in gender and class. The conflicts between Macon and Ruth Dead or Celie and Mr. ——, for example, are as soul crushing as any represented in novels by Richard Wright. By worrying the line of literary traditions, contemporary black women writers tell the stories that their predecessors could not. They also suggest how many more stories might yet be told.

# notes

## Prologue

1 In 1973, Stevie Wonder recorded a version of this story in his tune "Living for the City." Some time later scholar Robert Hemenway informed me that numerous versions of this story exist in African American folklore.

2 Morrison, "Site of Memory," 115.

## Chapter One

1 Rich, "When We Dead Awaken," 35.

2 Although its use in *The Souls of Black Folk* is best known, Du Bois first referred to the "color line" in a speech, "To the Nations of the World," delivered at a Pan African conference in London in 1900 and reprinted in Du Bois, *W. E. B. Du Bois*, 639–41.

3 This assertion holds not only for the generation of writers treated in this study but also for many of their twentieth-century predecessors. Jessie Fauset, Zora Neale Hurston, and Gwendolyn Brooks in her novel, *Maud Martha*, come to mind. Although Nella Larsen and Ann Petry represent interracial encounters, their greater concern is with the impact of racism on the personal lives of their characters.

4 Dance, "Interview with Paule Marshall," 5.

5 Rushdy makes a similar point in "Daughters Signifying History," 51.

6 Henderson, "Speaking in Tongues," 35.

7 Perhaps the clearest articulation of Wallace's view is the article "Multiculturalism and Oppositionality," 5–9. See also the essays "Variations on Negation and the Heresy of Black Feminist Creativity" and "Negative Images."

8 Spillers, "Cross Currents, Discontinuities," 245. Even when the commercial and critical success of this fiction broadened its audience, the implied reader in most cases remained an African American woman. See Christian, "But What Do We Think We're Doing Anyway?," 60–69.

9   Morrison, "Rootedness," 340.

10  Wallace, "Blues for Mr. Spielberg," 69.

11  Williams, *Some One Sweet Angel Chile*, 39.

12  Henderson, *Understanding the New Black Poetry*, 41; Williams, "Blues Roots of Contemporary Afro-American Poetry," 77.

13  Marshall, *Praisesong for the Widow*, 250.

14  Baldwin, "Sonny's Blues," 863.

15  Douglass, *Frederick Douglass*, 140. Late twentieth-century African American writers have employed the trope of the family tree, sometimes to ironic effect. Both Gloria Naylor in *Mama Day* and John Edgar Wideman in *Damballah* produce family trees as front matter in their novels. Wideman prefaces his with "A Begat Chart." Unlike in Naylor's novel, ancestors and descendants do not meet in Wideman's stories.

16  Spillers, "Mama's Baby, Papa's Maybe," 218.

17  Susan Willis observes that in Morrison's three-woman households "male domination" is not "the determining principle for living and working relationships of the group." *Specifying*, 106.

18  Stepto, *From behind the Veil*, xv–xvi. Despite the fact that he devotes none of his chapters to narratives by women, the intertextual model of reading that Stepto elaborates can be applied to black women's writing. This includes the concepts of the "narrative of ascent" and the "immersion narrative," as well as the analysis of "symbolic geography" of African American narratives. What cannot be appropriated is the "pregeneric myth." The efficacy of literacy as an instrument of freedom is continually worried in the texts I study here.

19  Gates, *Signifying Monkey*, chap. 1. In a critical gesture that echoes an impulse found in many of the narratives in *Worrying the Line*, Gates identifies continuities between African, specifically Yoruban, and African American vernacular speech and cultural practices. The figurative kinship he proposes between the Yoruban deity Esu-Elegbara and the signifying monkey of African American folk legend is not wholly persuasive. But it resembles similarly controversial gestures in *Zami*, *The Color Purple*, and *Praisesong for the Widow*. Gates's observation that black texts speak to other black texts cannot be gainsaid. He cites bountiful evidence that "black writers read, repeated, and imitated others' texts." The resulting "web of filiation" creates the space for the critic to theorize. Signifying(g) is the process of repeating and revising a "double-voiced tradition," as black writers revise texts in the European and Anglo-American traditions as well as those written by other black writers (xxiii).

20  Smith, "Toward a Black Feminist Criticism," 170, 174.

21  In 1980 (in "New Directions for Black Feminist Criticism") Deborah McDowell was among the first to challenge several of Smith's critical categories, particularly the concept of a specific black female language. Fifteen years later, in "*The Changing Same*" (a title borrowed from Amiri Baraka's volume of essays on black music), she interrogates her earlier critique in a volume of self-reflexive essays. She argues for an intertextual reading of black women's writing that is atten-

tive to the nuances and distinctions that she had faulted Smith for ignoring. Her readings are situated in a larger context of the history of black women's literary production and reception.

22  Washington, "'Darkened Eye Restored,'" xvii; Spillers, "Cross Currents, Discontinuities," 251; Carby, *Reconstructing Womanhood*, 15.

23  These include Christian, *Black Women Novelists*; Willis, *Specifying*; Awkward, *Inspiriting Influences*; and Kubitschek, *Claiming the Heritage*.

24  See, for example, Carby, "Politics of Fiction, Anthropology and the Folk," and duCille, *Coupling Convention*.

25  See, for example, Wilson, "Audre Lorde and the African-American Tradition," and Gilroy, "It's a Family Affair." In "Reading Family Matters," McDowell critiques the use of family metaphors in the literary histories written by black male critics hostile to feminist projects. Responding specifically to an essay by Mel Watkins, she observes, "[H]ere we have a family of *writers* who were unified until contemporary black women decided, in Watkins's words, that 'sexism is more oppressive than racism'" (80).

26  Clifton, *Blessing the Boats*, 25.

27  Baker, *Blues, Ideology and Afro-American Literature*, 2, 7.

28  Snead, "Repetition as a Figure of Black Culture," 67. Snead defines "the cut" as "an abrupt seemingly unmotivated break . . . with a series already in progress and a willed return to a prior series."

29  Gates, *Signifying Monkey*, xxii–xxiii; Henderson, "Speaking in Tongues," 16–37.

30  Williams, *Dessa Rose*, 6. Subsequent references to this work are cited parenthetically.

31  Walker, "Coming in from the Cold," 63; LeClair, "Language Must Not Sweat," 121, 124.

32  Marshall, "From the Poets in the Kitchen," 8.

33  "Middle Passage" is the title and subject of two celebrated African American texts—the poem by Robert Hayden and the novel by Charles Johnson. Metaphors alluding to the Middle Passage figure prominently in Henry Dumas, "Ark of Bones"; Paule Marshall, *Praisesong for the Widow*; and August Wilson, *Joe Turner's Come and Gone*. These texts signal a new chapter in African American literary tradition. The subject of the Middle Passage is seldom broached in nineteenth- and early twentieth-century texts. Hayden's poem represents the experience through the nautical logs of a slave ship's captain; it does not represent the voices of the captive. Morrison refers to "those that died en route. Nobody knows their names, and nobody thinks about them. In addition to that, they never survived in the lore; there are no songs or dances or tales of these people. The people who arrived—there is lore about them—But nothing survives about . . . that." Marsha Darling, "In the Realm of Responsibility," 247.

In "A Conversation on Toni Morrison's *Beloved*," Barbara Christian credits *Beloved* for the increased attention that scholars have subsequently paid to the Middle Passage (204). See, for example, Diedrich, Gates, and Pedersen, *Black Imagination and the Middle Passage*.

34  Shange, *Daughter's Geography*, 21. Subsequent references to this work are cited parenthetically.

35  Shange, *for colored girls who have considered suicide when the rainbow is enuf*, 38.

36  Shange, *Daughter's Geography*, 22.


## Chapter Two

1   Morrison, "Site of Memory," 103.

2   Hall, "Dialogics of Identity in the Age of Globalization."

3   For an extended comparative analysis of *Song* and *Go Down, Moses*, see Weinstein, *What Else but Love?*, 55–65.

4   Rampersad, *Art and Imagination of W. E. B. Du Bois*, 89.

5   Nora, "Between Memory and History," 286.

6   Baker, *Modernism and the Harlem Renaissance*, 68.

7   Morrison, *Song of Solomon*, 6. Subsequent references to this work are cited parenthetically.

8   In *From behind the Veil*, Stepto asserts that "[w]hat is extraordinary and absolutely fresh about this ritual is that, in terms of its symbolic geography, it is a journey both to and into the South" (66).

9   Du Bois, *Souls of Black Folk*, 93. Subsequent references to this work are cited parenthetically.

10  Nora, "Between Memory and History," 284.

11  Sundquist, *To Wake the Nations*, 503.

12  For a discussion of "tropological revisions" in African American literary tradition, see Gates's *Signifying Monkey*, xxv. In their introduction to *History and Memory in African-American Culture*, Fabre and O'Meally point out that a site of memory "may be a historical or legendary event or figure, a book or an era, a place or an idea" and include *The Souls of Black Folk* itself among their examples (7).

13  In *Transformations of Circe*, Yarnall asserts that Morrison's character "is unambiguously a creature of the novelist's own imagination." While finding that she is "as effectively instrumental a character as the enchantress of Aiaia," Yarnall devotes only a paragraph to discussing her.

14  This last quote from Morrison's *The Bluest Eye* links these places with the "sound" of the women's speech. "And the sounds of these places in their mouths make you think of love. When you ask them where they are from, they tilt their heads and say 'Mobile' and you think you've been kissed. They say 'Aiken' and you see a white butterfly glance off a fence with a torn wing. They say 'Nagadoches' and you want to say 'Yes, I will.' You don't know what these towns are like but you love what happens to the air when they open their lips and let their names ease out" (63).

15  In his analysis of Morrison's revision of classical myth, Michael Awkward notes that Milkman's quest is "inspired by an urge to avoid emotional commitment and familial responsibility." However, in a conclusion that I find complements my reading, Awkward argues that although Milkman seeks familial treasure,

"what he finds, after a series of episodes, conforming to traditional mono-mythic paradigms for the male hero called to adventure, is a mature sense of his familial obligations, an informed knowledge of familial (and tribal) history, and a profound comprehension of tribal wisdom." "'Unruly and Let Loose,'" 145.

16   Ostriker, "A Holy of Holies."

17   In "'Unruly and Let Loose,'" Awkward notes that the novel's structure en-courages a contrast between Milkman's journey and Hagar's. In his reading, the novel's thirteenth chapter, "which records the circumstances surrounding Hagar's death, offers a literal—and strategic—breaking of the male mono-mythic sequence" (148).

18   Landy, "Song of Songs," 313.

19   In his introduction to *The Souls of Black Folk*, Gibson quotes Douglass to argue that "Douglass precedes Du Bois in asserting, using nearly the same words, that the 'souls of black folk' are revealed in the 'sorrow songs,' though Du Bois's discussion of the topic is much more detailed and comprehensive than Douglass's" (xxxiv).

20   Sundquist, *To Wake the Nations*, 474.

21   Sundquist argues that a good measure of the song's significance derives "pre-cisely because it cannot be translated. . . . 'Do bana coba' literalizes the vocal-ization as an unknown language beyond words, a cry out of the territory of sound that is transgeographical and Pan-African in the most elemental sense" (ibid., 529–30).

22   "The point is," Morrison continues, "that into these spaces fall the rumina-tions of the reader and his or her invented or recollected or misunderstood knowingness." "Unspeakable Things Unspoken," 29.

23   Alice Walker's sardonic observation comes to mind here. When she glosses Du Bois's prophecy that "the problem of the twentieth century is the problem of the color line—the relation of the darker to the lighter races of men in Asia and Africa, in America and the islands of the sea," she affirms its truth. But she argues that his is "a man's vision. That is to say, it sees clearer across seas than across the table or the street. Particularly it omits what is happening within the family, 'the race,' at home; a family also capable of civil war." "If the Present Looks Like the Past," in *In Search of Our Mothers' Gardens*, 310.

24   See, for example, Middleton, "From Orality to Literacy," 36.

25   Morrison, "Rootedness," 341.

26   Till, a fourteen-year-old black youth from Chicago, was murdered in LeFlore County, Mississippi, in the summer of 1955, allegedly for whistling at a white woman. His mutilated corpse was recovered in the Tallahatchie River. At his mother's insistence, the boy's body was laid out in an open casket, and photo-graphs of it were widely reprinted in newspapers. Outrage at Till's murder was a catalyst for the civil rights movement. Mamie Till understood as well as the characters in the novel the value the dominant society placed on her son's life. Had she not decided to use his corpse as evidence of the horror of his death, it

might have gone unremarked. For a discussion of the impact of the case, see Hampton and Fayer, *Voices of Freedom*, 1–15.

27 In a reference that honors what Ralph Ellison once referred to as the unremarked "free-floating literacy" in Negro communities, Freddie the janitor wonders if Till thought he was in "Tom Sawyer land" (81), a reference that signifies on the disparity between literary representations of innocent American boyhood and the victimization of actual American black boys.

28 Lorde, *Black Unicorn*, 12–13.

29 Ibid.

30 Stepto, "Phenomenal Woman and the Severed Daughter," 316; Hull, "Living on the Line." See also Hall, "Negotiating Caribbean Identities," 3–14, for an analysis of the importance of Africa in contemporary Caribbean culture. Writing of the Rastafarian movement, Hall avers: "You see, it was not the literal Africa people want to return to, it was the language, the symbolic language for describing what suffering was like, it was a metaphor for where they were" (13).

31 Lorde, *Zami*, 7. Subsequent references to this work are cited parenthetically.

32 Tate, *Black Women Writers at Work*, 115.

33 Jacobs, *Incidents in the Life of a Slave Girl*, 54, 55. Elizabeth Alexander writes that "the link between Lorde and Brent is crucial: for both the issue is control over one's own body and the power to see the voice as a literal functioning *member* of the corpus, an organ that works and must be self-tended" ("'Coming Out Blackened and Whole,'" 699).

34 Raynaud, "'Nutmeg Nestled inside Its Covering of Mace,'" 222.

35 Wilson, "Audre Lorde and the African-American Tradition," 83.

36 As Chinasole argues in her essay "Audre Lorde and Matrilineal Diaspora," "home as an image means primarily the place of her most private self" (387).

37 Lorde first visited Grenada in 1978. She returned in December 1983, two months after the U.S. military invasion that toppled the socialist government led by Maurice Bishop. See Lorde, "Grenada Revisited," 176–90.

38 Gwendolyn Brooks's sonnet sequence "the children of the poor" was first published in *Annie Allen* (1949), the book for which she won the Pulitzer Prize, and reprinted in *Selected Poems*, 53. Ralph Ellison published *Invisible Man* in 1952.

39 Sagri Dhairyam asserts, for example, that the passage represents "moments of failed resistance in Lorde's corpus, testaments to the seduction and strength of literary tradition [that] are vulnerable precisely for their *failed* struggles to articulate a politics of identity that challenges dominant literary hegemony." "'Artifacts for Survival,'" 242–43.

40 Lorde, "Interview with Audre Lorde and Adrienne Rich," 85.

41 Throughout her essays and speeches, Lorde refers to the Amazon warriors of Dahomey. See *Sister/Outsider*, 49, 151, and passim. According to Edna Bay, the belief that the female warriors of Dahomey severed their right breast in order to fire arrows at their enemies more efficiently is a myth, one that derives from Greek antiquity. *Wives of the Leopard*, 1–2.

42 The identification comes from a glossary of African names appended to Lorde's *The Black Unicorn*, 121.

43 See, for example, Raynaud's analysis, "Nutmeg Nestled inside Its Covering Mace," 228–29.

44 Lorde, "Uses of the Erotic," 56.

45 Lines from the poem "Black Mother Woman" echo this sentiment: "I learned from you / to define myself / through your denials" (Lorde, *Chosen Poems, Old and New*, 53).

46 Baldwin, "Revolutionary Hope."

47 Leeming, *James Baldwin, a Biography*, 5–9. Baldwin's *Notes of a Native Son* was first published in 1955; "Down at the Cross" was originally published under the title "Letter from a Region in My Mind" in 1962, then as Part II of *The Fire Next Time* (1963). *Go Tell It on the Mountain* was published in 1953.

48 Baldwin, *Go Tell It on The Mountain*, 11.

49 Leeming, *James Baldwin, a Biography*, 119. The third section of Baldwin's *Notes of a Native Son* consists of essays that ruminate on expatriation and American identity; not only in their themes but often in their prose, they evoke James.

50 Baldwin, *Notes of a Native Son*, xii. Subsequent references to this work are cited parenthetically.

51 Baldwin, *Fire Next Time*, 314.

52 Leeming, *James Baldwin, a Biography*, 88.

53 Rich, *Of Woman Born*, 225.

54 Baldwin, *Go Tell It on the Mountain*, 215.

55 Baldwin, "The Outing," 796.

56 Keating, "Making 'Our Shattered Faces Whole,'" 21.

57 Thompson, *Flash of the Spirit*, 176.

58 Bay, *Wives of the Leopard*, 5.

59 Seboulisa's suffering calls to mind Lorde's struggle against breast cancer, which she wrote about often, perhaps preeminently in *The Cancer Journals*, in which she also refers to her friendship with Eudora.

60 Keating, "Making 'Our Shattered Faces Whole,'" 26. Thompson identifies Avrekete as the Fon name for the Ewe sea goddess. "Esu-Elegbara" plays a key role in the theory that Gates proposes in *The Signifying Monkey*. According to Gates, the figure is not only a trickster but "the divine linguist," who "speaks all languages . . . and interprets the alphabet of Mawu to man and to the other gods" (7). In Gates's paradigm, Esu-Elegbara becomes the figure for the "indeterminacy of the interpretation of writing," and his "traditional dwelling place at the crossroads, for the critic, is the crossroads of understanding and truth" (25).

61 Lorde, "Interview: Audre Lorde and Adrienne Rich," 85.

62 Lorde, "Uses of the Erotic," 56.

63 King, "Audre Lorde's Lacquered Layerings," 52.

64 This moment resonates with a description of Kongo ritual identified by Thompson in "The Song That Named the Land." "Kongo writing also included myste-

rious ciphers, received by a person in a state of spiritual possession. This was 'writing in the spirit,' sometimes referred to as 'visual glossolalia,' this was writing as if copied from a 'billboard in the sky'" (101). The transposition of the visual to the aural in Lorde's text is reminiscent of a line in Hurston, *Their Eyes Were Watching God*, when, in response to Janie's signifying, one neighbor says to another: "You heard me, you ain't blind" (75).

65 Other black lesbian writers followed Lorde's example and identified with Afrekete. Selected writings are included in McKinley and De Laney, *Afrekete*.

66 For a discussion of relationships of filiation and affiliation, see Said, "Secular Criticism," 1–30.

## Chapter Three

1 Ostriker, "Kin and Kin," 79. Subsequent references to this work are cited parenthetically. Other critiques of Clifton's poetry include Hull, "Channeling the Ancestral Muse"; Lazer, "Blackness Blessed"; Madhubuti, "Lucille Clifton"; McCluskey, "Tell the Good News"; and Rushing, "Lucille Clifton."

2 The volumes of poetry are *Good Times, Good News about the Earth, An Ordinary Woman, Two-Headed Woman, Next, Quilting, The Book of Light, The Terrible Stories*, and *Blessing the Boats*. *Good Woman* reprints the first four volumes, along with *Generations*.

3 Clifton, *Good Woman*, 16, 17. Subsequent references to this work are cited parenthetically.

4 Ibid., 33. Wydah in the kingdom of Dahomey was one of the most important slave ports in West Africa. Between the 1640s and the 1870s, an estimated 2 million Africans were shipped to the New World from Wydah. It was also the cradle of Vodun, the only African religion to flourish in the Western Hemisphere. "Ye Ma Jah" (also "Yemoja" or "Yemayá") are Yoruban riverain goddesses whose worshipers use round fans as an emblem embodying the coolness and command of these spirits of the water. See Thompson, *Flash of the Spirit*, 72.

Other Clifton poems in dialogue with the narrative of *Generations* include "The Way It Was," "Africa," "An Ordinary Woman," "Speaking of Loss," "Confession," "Forgiving My Father," and two untitled poems beginning with, respectively, "light/on my mother's tongue" and "i went to the valley."

5 Clifton, *Generations*, 10. Subsequent references to this work are cited parenthetically.

6 I take the phrase from Houston Baker's 1980 critical volume *The Journey Back*. For a discussion of the importance of the journey in black women's writings, see Willis, *Specifying*. "If there is one thing that predominates in contemporary writing by black American women," writes Willis, "it is the journey (both real and figural) back to the historical source of the black American community. For contemporary writers, the journey back probably originates with Hurston's flight from the city back to the South to drive the back roads, spend time in

small towns and sawmill camps, and collect the material that comprises her landmark text of Afro-American folklore, *Mules and Men*" (57–58).

7   Brooks's *Report from Part One* anticipates elements of the form Clifton develops in *Generations*. Brooks's volume is more autobiographical; it does not attempt the generational history that Clifton's volume does. But it incorporates photographs into the text in a similar way. It is worth noting that Brooks published *Family Pictures*, a volume of poems, in 1970.

8   Sontag, *On Photography*, 8–15.

9   hooks, "In Our Glory," 48, 51.For a model of "reading" photographs, see the chapter "Truth in Photographs" in Painter, *Sojourner Truth*.

10  Benjamin, "Work of Art in the Age of Mechanical Reproduction," 226. Benjamin notes that the portrait was the focal point of early photography; but as the art form developed, photography lost its ritualistic function. The formal portrait of Caroline Sale and her son, taken before her death in 1910, belongs to that early phase. But all the photographs in *Generations* enact a ritualistic function.

11  Walker, "Coming in from the Cold," 60. See also Marshall, "From the Poets in the Kitchen," 1–12, and Morrison, "Rootedness."

12  See Mays, *Negro's God As Reflected in His Literature* (1938), for a pioneering analysis. In *Conjuring Culture*, Theophus H. Smith demonstrates the wide-ranging influence of the Bible on African American culture.

13  Whitman quoted in Reynolds, *Walt Whitman's America*, 129; Clifton, "Simple Language," 137.

14  Williams, "Blues Roots of Contemporary Afro-American Poetry," 83, 87.

15  Whitman, *Song of Myself*, sec. 24, lines 12–13. Subsequent references to this work are cited parenthetically. See Gibson, "Good Black Poet and the Good Gray Poet," 65–80. Other African American poets who express a debt to Whitman include Amiri Baraka, Sterling Brown, and June Jordan.

16  Like Abraham Lincoln, Whitman criticized abolitionism and accepted the existence of slavery in those areas of the United States where it was already established. He could not envision a nation in which blacks and whites were equal citizens. See Reynolds, *Walt Whitman's America*, 111–53.

17  Biographical parallels, including the incidence of mental illness and epilepsy among their kin, suggest additional connections. One of Whitman's brothers, Jesse, died in an insane asylum. A sister, Hannah, suffered from mental illness. Another brother, Andrew, became an alcoholic whose widow turned to prostitution, and the youngest sibling, Edward, suffered from epilepsy. For varying accounts of the Whitman family, see ibid., 7–51, and Kaplan, *Walt Whitman*, 55–73.

18  Clifton's oeuvre reflects an ongoing engagement with the Bible, from a cycle of poems, "some jesus," in which she retells biblical narratives in *Good News about the Earth*, to lyrics on Old Testament figures and spiritual meditations in *The Book of Light*, to the cycle "From the Book of David" in *The Terrible Stories*.

The "Kali" poems appeared in *An Ordinary Woman*. See Hull, "Channeling the Ancestral Muse," for a discussion of Clifton's mysticism.

19  Spillers, "'Permanent Obliquity of an In(pha)llibly Straight,'" 129–30.

20  Ibid., 127.

21  Dixon, "Black Writer's Use of Memory," 21–22.

22  "Mammy" is a word that carries a lot of freight. Alice Walker has explained that she hoped to use the word "Mammy" in *The Color Purple* "as a word used by turn-of-the-century black people, instead of 'mother,' though already in a somewhat pejorative way." See Walker's "Coming in from the Cold," 60. Clifton's use is similar. The white woman is the first to refer to "Mammy Caroline," but Lucille's father uses the title as well. Lucille, the narrator, does not. In a more recent essay, "Giving the Party," Walker writes, "For many years I did not make the connection that 'mammy' is derived from 'mammae,' that is, breasts" (138).

23  Holloway, *Moorings and Metaphors*, 25.

24  Etheridge Knight's poem "The Idea of Ancestry" provides a compelling counterpoint. Knight's speaker represents his own troubled life as the gap in the family's line.

25  In the 1881 edition of *Leaves of Grass*, Whitman inserted the following lines, stressing his nativist genealogy, just after the opening lines: "My tongue, every atom of blood, form'd from this soil, this air, / Born here of parents born here from parents the same, and their / parents the same." Reynolds asserts that, "in both his life and his writings, Whitman showed a persistent instinct to keep strong [a] succession of links" with his family's past. See *Walt Whitman's America*, 9.

26  Berger quoted in Davis, "Afro Images," 173.

27  See, for example, Tate, *Domestic Allegories of Political Desire*, especially chap. 4, "Allegories of Gender and Class as Discourses of Political Desire."

28  This discussion is informed by my reading of Barthes, "Rhetoric of the Image," 32–51.

29  Clifton, *Ordinary Woman*, 72.

30  Clifton, *Book of Light*, 12. Once she resolves to explore publicly what it means to be an incest survivor, Clifton returns to the theme repeatedly. See, for example, "forgiving my father" in *Two-Headed Woman*, "To My Friend Jerina" in *Quilting*, and "sam" and "my lost father" in *The Book of Light*. Notably, "daughters," the poem that follows "June 20" in *The Book of Light*, charts a matrilineage: "woman, i am / lucille, which stands for light, / daughter of thelma, daughter / of georgia, daughter of / dazzling you" (13).

31  Herman, *Father-Daughter Incest*, 71, 81. See also Blume, *Secret Survivors*.

32  This seems sufficient reason, although the influence of the Black Arts movement with which Clifton was aligned might have reinforced her decision to maintain her silence. To be sure, the seeming exaltation of the father in *Generations* earned approval for Clifton in some quarters. In his essay "Lucille Clifton," Black Arts poet and critic Haki Madhubuti praised her for her "unusually significant and sensitive" treatment of black men. He speculated that "part of the

reason she treats men fairly and with balance in her work is her relationship with her father, brothers, husband, and sons. Generally, positive relationships produce positive results" (152). Madhubuti contrasts Clifton with unnamed black women writers whose negative portrayals of black men allegedly won them critical acclaim and commercial success. For an astute critique of Madhubuti's argument and of the negative response of several prominent black male critics to black women's fiction of the 1970s and 1980s, see McDowell, "Reading Family Matters."

33  Spillers, "'Permanent Obliquity of an In(pha)llibly Straight,'" 129.

34  I think of Morrison's *The Bluest Eye* and Jones's *Corregidora*. Moreover, Maya Angelou, Morrison, and Alice Walker all by stunning coincidence in 1970 published groundbreaking explorations of sexual abuse within black families in the autobiography *I Know Why the Caged Bird Sings* and the novels *The Bluest Eye* and *The Third Life of Grange Copeland*, respectively.

35  Clifton, *Terrible Stories*, 51.

36  Sontag, *On Photography*, 23.

37  From Clifton, "my mama moved among the days," in *Good Woman*, 16. Originally published in *Good Times*.

38  In the first edition, this section contains two additional photographs. One depicts two women of similar age seated with one wrapping her arm around the other's shoulder. The figure on the left is holding a guitar. This photograph is reproduced on the cover of *Good Woman*. Beneath it in *Generations* is a wedding photograph. Fading produces the effect of the subjects standing in the clouds.

39  Yeats, "Second Coming." Chinua Achebe alludes to Yeats's poem in the title of his best known novel, *Things Fall Apart*.

### Chapter Four

1  Morrison, "Bench by the Road," 5.

2  Morrison, *Beloved*, 29. Subsequent references to this work are cited parenthetically.

3  Although *Beloved* is the only novel by Morrison to tackle slavery head-on, the traces of slavery are nonetheless visible in all her works, even those that are set at a significant chronological distance. Retrospectively, the physical scars, the multiple mutilations that recur throughout these novels, may be read as metonyms of slavery.

4  Angelo, "Pain of Being Black," 257.

5  Naylor, "A Conversation," 585.

6  Gordon, *Ghostly Matters*, 188–89.

7  Morrison quoted in Dowling, "Song of Toni Morrison," 58.

8  Morrison, "Rediscovering Black History," 16. Subsequent references to this work are cited parenthetically.

9  Mobley makes a similar point in "A Different Remembering" when she describes *The Black Book* as "a literary intervention in the historical dialogue of the

period to attest to 'black life as lived' experience" (190). My gendered reference to the Negro and "his" history is deliberate. Inevitably, the recovery of Negro history was complicated by its residual sexism. *The Black Book* was published before the paradigm-shifting work of Paula Giddings, Darlene Clark Hine, and Deborah Gray White, to cite three leading scholars of black women's history. Like their studies, Morrison's novels have done much to convey the courage and bravery of ordinary black women (and men) during the century between the Civil War and the civil rights era.

10   Harris et al., *Black Book*, 49. Subsequent references to this work are cited parenthetically.

11   The *Oxford English Dictionary* defines "memory book" (U.S.) as a blank book in which cuttings from newspapers and the like are pasted for preservation; a scrapbook.

12   Morrison, "Toni Morrison," 105.

13   Born in the Ivory Coast in 1916, Dadié is a poet, novelist, and playwright. As a boy he was steeped in the traditional folklore that he would later incorporate into his writing. He served his country for many years as minister of culture.

14   Campbell, "New Book Bridges Gap in Black History."

15   Morrison, "Memory, Creation and Writing," 388–89.

16   Morrison, "Rootedness," 341.

17   Freilicher, "Editor's Personal Commitment Shapes a Scrapbook of Black History."

18   Not all critics found the book's lack of structure satisfactory. Kalamu ya Salaam complained that "to throw all of these images and documents together without a text to explain the meaning, context and original intent does not serve to help us truly understand what our history, our *real history of struggle* is about." He attributed the absence of pictures of political figures and events and the absence of major political documents to a "near total lack of political insight." Review of *The Black Book*, 73.

19   Morrison, "Site of Memory," 109–10. Subsequent references to this work are cited parenthetically.

20   At Morrison's prodding, *The Black Book* was aggressively marketed. Cosby recorded five radio commercials: 160 press kits containing the book, the Cosby tapes and scripts, quotes from an array of black artists and celebrities (including Muhammad Ali, Toni Cade Bambara, B. B. King, Gwendolyn Brooks, Angela Davis, Alex Haley, Paule Marshall, Ishmael Reed, Max Roach, and Alice Walker), and a letter explaining the kit's contents and proposed use were mailed to disc jockeys on black-oriented radio stations across the country. Morrison herself made numerous media appearances to promote the book. Several book parties were held; the star-studded gala at Charles' Gallery, a restaurant on Harlem's 125th Street, on 4 March 1974 was widely reported on local television and radio and in newspapers. The effort paid off: on 15 April 1974, *The Black Book* was number nine on the *New York Times* Trade Paperback Best Seller List. The Ran-

dom House Files, Rare Book and Manuscript Library, Columbia University, box 1146.

21  Naylor, "A Conversation," 584. See also Billops, *Harlem Book of the Dead*. The photograph Morrison refers to below appears on p. 52; Van Der Zee's comment is on 84. Morrison wrote the foreword to the volume.

22  Christian, McDowell, and McKay, "Conversation on Toni Morrison's *Beloved*," 210.

23  Henderson, "Toni Morrison's *Beloved*," 68–69.

24  In "Toni Morrison's *Beloved*," Rody notes that "for Sethe, a 'rememory' (an individual experience) hangs around as a 'picture' that can enter another's 'rememory' (the part of the brain that 'rememories') and complicate consciousness and identity. 'Rememory' as trope postulates the interconnectedness of minds, past and present, and thus neatly conjoins the novel's supernatural vision with its aspiration to communal epic, realizing the 'collective memory' of which Morrison speaks" (101).

25  Angelo, "Pain of Being Black," 257.

26  The most comprehensive reconstruction of the Margaret Garner case is Weisenburger, *Modern Medea*. Drawing from contemporary press accounts, legal records, and other manuscript sources, Weisenburger documents a riveting history. After Margaret Garner was acquitted on charges of child murder, she and her family were sold to a plantation owner in Arkansas. On the voyage, Garner threw a second child overboard. Weisenburger's evidence suggests that both children were fathered by Garner's Kentucky slave owner. Garner died of typhoid in 1858; her husband, Robert, disappeared from the public record in 1870. Even though it is replete with fascinating facts, *Modern Medea* does not offer what the novel does: insight into the interior lives of the African Americans involved. Few contemporary observers even thought to ask the Garners their opinions of the events in which they risked their lives.

27  Morrison told interviewer Marsha Darling that although she had researched "a lot of things in this book to narrow it, to make it narrow and deep," she had not done much research on Margaret Garner because she wanted to "invent her life." Darling, "In the Realm of Responsibility," 248.

28  Rody, "Toni Morrison's *Beloved*," 98.

29  Henderson, "Toni Morrison's *Beloved*," 66–71.

30  Stepto, "'Intimate Things in Place.'" Domestic tasks thread through this extended scene. Sethe cooks, washes, folds laundry, and combs her child's hair as she narrates the stories of her past.

31  Stampp, *Peculiar Institution*, 250. "The slaves' condition was compatible only with a form of concubinage, voluntary on the part of the slaves, and permissive on that of the master. In law there was no such thing as fornication or adultery between slaves, nor was there bastardy, for, as a Kentucky judge noted, the father of a slave was 'unknown' to the law."

32  Hurston, "Characteristics of Negro Expression," 830.

33　In the scene Beloved is referred to as "a familiar," a word that denotes a super-natural spirit or demon supposed to attend on or serve a person. "Familiar" is also defined as "of or pertaining to one's family or household" (*Oxford English Dictionary*).

34　Other instances in the novel in which story and place are conflated include the passage where Paul D asks Beloved what she was looking for when she came to 124; she responds, "This place. I was looking for this place I could be in" (65). The response follows the scene discussed below in which Beloved's hungry listening evokes Sethe's stories about her marriage and about her mother.

35　See Mayer, "'You Like Huckleberries?'" Critics have also noted that Morrison's novel shares a subject and a setting with Harriet Beecher Stowe's *Uncle Tom's Cabin*. For a comparative analysis, see Askeland, "Remodeling the Model Home in *Uncle Tom's Cabin* and *Beloved*."

36　In *The Book of Memory*, Mary Carruthers explicates the "treasure-hoard" and "money-pouch" as figures for memory. W. J. T. Mitchell refers to figures of memory "as a storehouse in which experience is 'deposited' (sometimes to ac-crue 'interest') and the memory technology characterized as a device for 'with-drawing' these deposits on demand." See *Picture Theory*, 195.

37　Barlow, "Looking Up at Down," 5.

38　Levine, *Black Culture and Black Consciousness*, 212. Levine quotes the lines "Hard work ain't easy / Dry bread ain't greasy" from a recording made by John Lomax of song leader Henry Truvillion.

39　Rody, "Toni Morrison's *Beloved*," 104.

40　Recollection is a spiritual practice in the Catholic Church, and its definition suggests ways to understand "unspeakable things unspoken." According to the *New Catholic Encyclopedia*, recollection is "a type of attention whereby the indi-vidual excludes voluntary distractions, internal and external, to concentrate all his powers on introspection. Although there are various types of natural rec-ollection, in the spiritual life recollection signifies a concentration of one's powers on God, or something related to God. It may be a transitory concentra-tion or a habitual practice whereby the individual directs his faculties to God in order to live in the presence of God." Sethe's concentration is directed not to God but to her child. Saint Teresa of Avila classified the prayer of recollec-tion as "acquired recollection." She distinguished it from meditation, which is discursive and intellectual, or affective prayer, which utilizes the will predomi-nantly; "acquired recollection" she defined as a simple loving gaze upon God or some mystery related to God. All the powers are recollected in this unifying activity. Again, for Sethe and her daughters, the quest is simply to gaze on each other as "the beloved."

41　Hayden, "Middle Passage," 118.

42　The passage resembles Pecola's interior monologue in *The Bluest Eye*, in which the child, having lost contact with reality, expresses her belief that she has in fact received the blue eyes for which she has yearned. The resemblance is in part the structure of the passage and in part the intensity of desire it inscribes.

But whereas *The Bluest Eye* represents one character's divided consciousness, *Beloved* represents the merged consciousness of three characters.

43    Landy, "Song of Songs," 305.

44    Ibid., 307.

45    Morrison discusses the significance of philosophical questions in her work in Dreifus, "Chloe Wofford Talks about Toni Morrison," 73.

46    Scruggs, *Sweet Home*, 184. Scruggs gives an extended gloss to the biblical epigraph (179–84).

47    Baby Suggs's preaching rock alludes most obviously to the words of Jesus: "Upon this rock, I shall build my church" (Matt. 16:18). Barbara Christian, exploring the novel's incorporation of African cosmology, notes: "[F]or West Africans, a particular tree, rock, or grove embodies that relationship between themselves as human beings in Nature, and other aspects of Nature that are often seen as separate from human beings. Thus Nature is seen as part of the human and the divine and is considered sacred in much the same way as churches in the Christian religion are considered sacred. In *Beloved*, Morrison uses this aspect of traditional African religions in her representation of the Clearing, that space from which Baby Suggs preached and the place to which Sethe, her daughter-in-law, comes to communicate with her elder when she has passed on." "Fixing Methodologies," 12.

48    Note the similarities and differences between Baby Suggs and historical black female preachers, like Zilpha Elaw and Jarena Lee, who were bold in making the claim to their vocation and in the eloquence of their language but whose theology was orthodox.

49    Harris, "Beloved," 147.

50    In "Mama's Baby, Papa's Maybe," Spillers distinguishes between "body" and "flesh" and "impose[s] that distinction as the central one between captive and liberated subject-positions. In that sense, before the 'body' there is the 'flesh,' that zero degree of social conceptualization that does not escape concealment under the brush of discourse, or the reflexes of iconography. Even though the European hegemonies stole bodies—some of them female—out of West African communities in concert with the African 'middleman,' we regard this human and social irreparability as high crimes against the *flesh*, as the person of African females and African males registered the wounding" (60–61).

51    Scruggs, *Sweet Home*, 170.

52    Bodwin's residual racism leaves him outside the novel's Beloved Community, however. The image of the bank on a shelf by his back door with "a blackboy's mouth full of money" partakes of the minstrel stereotypes that the novel writes against. It is also reminiscent of a cluster of caricatured images reprinted in *The Black Book*. The motto painted on the pedestal of the bank, "At Yo Service," suggests Bodwin's complicated relation to the community of black people in the novel. As a good Christian, he wants to "serve" them, even as he has employed Baby Suggs and Denver, two generations of a family, as servants.

53    The term derives from Josiah Royce, the philosopher and pragmatist, who used

it to describe the city as a social ideal. In 1957, King wrote that "the ultimate aim of SCLC [Southern Christian Leadership Conference] is to foster and create the 'beloved community' in America" (quoted in Scruggs, *Sweet Home*, 3).

## Chapter Five

1   Jones, *Corregidora*, 14. Subsequent references to this work are cited parenthetically.

2   Critics who explore this theme include Melvin Dixon, *Ride Out the Wilderness*; Madhu Dubey, *Black Women Novelists and the Nationalist Aesthetic*; Ann duCille, *Skin Trade*; Janice Harris, "Gayl Jones's *Corregidora*"; Sally Robinson, *Engendering the Subject*; and Ashraf Rushdy, *Remembering Generations*.

3   James Baldwin's comment is the blurb on the 1986 Black Women Writers Series paperback edition published by Beacon Press; Bell, "Judgment," 215; Tate, *Black Women Writers at Work*, 91.

4   Jones, *Blues People*, 67.

5   Palmer, *Deep Blues*, 75.

6   Russell, "Slave Codes and Liner Notes," 132. Hazel Carby argues that "the women's blues of the twenties and early thirties . . . is a discourse that articulates a cultural and political struggle over sexual relations, a struggle that is directed against the objectification of female sexuality within a patriarchal order but which also tries to reclaim women's bodies as the sexual and sensuous objects of women's songs." " 'It Jus Be's That Way Sometimes,' " 12.

7   Brown, "The Blues"; Hurston, *Dust Tracks on a Road*, 132.

8   Harper, "Gayl Jones," 360; Murray, *Stomping the Blues*, 66.

9   Tate, *Black Women Writers at Work*, 208–9. In her interview with Tate, Sherley Anne Williams asserts that "blues [as] a basis of historical continuity for black people" existed until the sixties, when the "continuity of our preserved history in this art form" was ruptured under pressure from the "black-consciousness people." Although the action of *Corregidora* ends in 1969, Ursa's consciousness was shaped in an earlier time. Williams further suggests that the debate over sexism be placed into the blues tradition, where it would be better understood. "People who care about one another argue," she observed and concluded, "[T]hat we are having this debate now ought not to mean we no longer care about each other."

10   Ellison, "Richard Wright's Blues," 90.

11   The character Ma Rainey in August Wilson's play echoes this view: "You don't sing to feel better. You sing 'cause that's a way of understanding life." *Ma Rainey's Black Bottom*, 82.

12   Barlow, "*Looking Up at Down*," 142. The version that Barlow quotes ends with one of the best-known blues aphorisms: "When you see me laughin', / I'm laughin' to keep from cryin'." Gayl Jones's articulation of pleasure/pain is an analogous paradox.

13   Nina Simone includes the "rockin' chair" verse in her rendition of "Trouble in

Mind," recorded in the 1960s and very familiar to blues and jazz fans of Gayl Jones's generation.

Jones explores the theme of pain and pleasure in her most frequently anthologized poem, "Deep Song," in which the persona says of her lover, "Sometimes he is a good dark man. / Sometimes he is a bad dark man. / I love him." Harper and Stepto, *Chant of Saints*, 376.

14  In addition to Bell, "Judgment," see, for example, Barksdale, "Castration Symbolism in Recent Black American Fiction." Barksdale attacks Toni Morrison's *Sula* and Paule Marshall's *Praisesong for the Widow*, along with *Corregidora* and *Eva's Man*.

15  Harper, "Gayl Jones," 352, 359–60.

16  Davis, "Black Women and Music," 12.

17  The premise is disputed. According to Sterling Brown, references to social problems were common in the prerecorded blues; blues about male/female relationships were more commercially successful. As his statement quoted above makes clear, Albert Murray recognizes few social references in the blues of any period. By any reckoning, blues contain many fewer coded references to social reality than do spirituals. Whatever one concludes about the social and political import of blues in general, however, it seems indisputable that *Corregidora* brings the blues and history into fruitful conjunction.

18  Jones, *Liberating Voices*, 38, 72. Originally written as a doctoral dissertation and completed in 1982, this study argues that twentieth-century black American writers from Paul Laurence Dunbar to Ernest Gaines use models from black vernacular forms as well as from European and European American literary traditions. The book explores the "technical effects" that black writers develop as a result and argues that "when the African American creative writers began to trust the literary possibilities of their own verbal and musical creations and to employ self-inspired techniques, they began to transform the European and European American models and to gain greater artistic sovereignty" (1). In the wake of studies by Houston Baker, Henry Louis Gates Jr., Stephen Henderson, Valerie Smith, and Eric Sundquist, this became the critical consensus in African American literary study during the 1980s and 1990s. Had Jones's study been published when it was written, it would have been among the first to assert this argument.

19  Born in Lexington, Kentucky, Jones wrote in "About My Work": "I like the idea of Kentucky in my work, though I don't always place my stories there. But it's like a 'magic word'" (234).

20  Jones, *Liberating Voices*, 68.

21  Although to readers the word looks and sounds like the name of the palace of Louis XIV, its residents pronounce the name of their town "ver sails."

22  In an interview with Rowell, Jones distinguishes between "trivial" and "significant" events (Rowell, "Interview with Gayl Jones," 39–42). Interestingly, the references that characters in *Corregidora* make to the world beyond their small town purview are mainly to performers. Through these references, characters

often reveal a confidence in the validity of their subjugated knowledge. For example, late in the novel Ursa talks with an older bluesman who comments that Ray Charles was acknowledged as a genius only after Sinatra called him one: "'If a white man hadn't told them, they wouldn't've seen it. If I come and told them they wouldn't've seen it. Do you know what I'm talking about? I could've told 'em. You could've told 'em. Like, you know, they say Columbo discovered America, he didn't discover America. You hear that song where Aretha say she discovered Ray Charles. Now tha's awright.' He laughed" (170).

23  Jones, "About My Work," 233.

24  Rowell, "Interview with Gayl Jones," 45. Later in the interview Jones reaffirms the fictionality of her work by noting that "nothing in the Corregidora story really happened" (45).

25  Freyre, *Masters and the Slaves*, and Tannenbaum, *Slave and Citizen*, promulgate the most widely influential arguments for the comparative benevolence of the system of slavery in Brazil.

26  Conrad, *Children of God's Fire*, xvi–xvii. Ashraf Rushdy notes that "while the prostitution of 'slave women as a source of income is virtually unknown in the history of the United States,' Brazilians time and again reported the practice" (*Remembering Generations*, 47).

27  In *Race Matters*, West refers to the U.S. context when he writes that "Americans are obsessed with sex and fearful of black sexuality. . . . [T]he fear is footed in visceral feelings about black bodies fueled by sexual myths of black women and men. . . . The myths offer distorted, dehumanized creatures whose bodies—color of skin, shape of nose and lips, type of hair, size of hips—are already distinguished from the white norms of beauty and whose feared sexual activities are deemed disgusting, dirty, or funky and considered less acceptable." West goes on to argue that "these myths are part of a wider network of white supremacist lies whose authority and legitimacy must be undermined" (83, 91).

28  Stepto, "'Intimate Things in Place,'" 229.

29  Williams, *Alchemy of Race and Rights*, 6. Subsequent references to this work are cited parenthetically.

30  Dixon, *Ride Out the Wilderness*, 110.

31  Harris quoted in duCille, *Skin Trade*, 74.

32  Rowell, "Interview with Gayl Jones," 36.

33  In *Slave and Citizen*, Tannenbaum emphasizes this historical contrast between the United States and Latin American societies: "If in Latin America the abolition of slavery was achieved in every case without violence, without bloodshed, and without civil war, it is due to the fact that there was no such fixed horizontal division [between slave and free man], no such hardening of form that the pattern could no longer change by internal adaptations" (106). For Tannenbaum, the twentieth-century history of racial segregation in the United States and racial assimilation in Brazil are the consequences of this contrast.

34  Jones, *Liberating Voices*, 73.

35  In *Black Women Novelists and the Nationalist Aesthetic*, Dubey comments that "the

denaturalization of her ancestors' reproductive myth enables Ursa to perceive what this myth represses. Her mother's deepest and most inchoate desires cannot be expressed within this reproductive economy" (102). Ursa's recognition of her own subjectivity allows her to develop alternative myths that validate her life as a sexually desiring and desirable woman who is not a mother.

36 In an interesting twist on the significance of family pictures in black women's writing, the female characters in this novel keep a photograph of Corregidora so that they can teach new members of the family whom to hate.

37 Rushdy argues that "the Corregidora story has become a *legend*, assuming the status of an immutable, inflexible, mythical artifact. When a generational memory stops changing, growing, and circulating, that story becomes dead" (*Remembering Generations*, 39).

38 Kent, "Palmares," 170–88. See also Rushdy, *Remembering Generations*, 49–53.

39 See Conrad, *Children of God's Fire*, for transcriptions of these oral texts. Gayl Jones's long-standing fascination with Palmares resulted in the book-length poem *Song for Anninho*. Narrated by Almeyda, an African woman in Brazil, the poem recounts her romance with Anninho, their separation after the Portuguese raid on the settlement at Palmares, Almeyda's suffering after an attack during which her breasts are cut off, and her healing under the care of a "wizard woman" named Zibatra. Throughout the narrative, Almeyda sustains a vision of hope both that she and Anninho will be reunited and that Palmares will be restored. In the 1970s Jones also completed an unpublished novel inspired by the history of Palmares.

40 Douglass, *Narrative of the Life of Frederick Douglass*, 81.


## Chapter Six

1 Walker, "Zora Neale Hurston," in *In Search of Our Mothers' Gardens*, 91.

2 Walker, "Everything Is a Human Being," 148.

3 Ellison, "Blues People," 249–50.

4 Among the critics who analyze intertextuality in Hurston and Walker are Gates, *Signifying Monkey*; Henderson, "Color Purple"; Hite, "Romance, Marginality, Matrilineage"; Sadoff, "Black Matrilineage."

5 Hurston, *Their Eyes Were Watching God*, 6. In *The Signifying Monkey*, Gates argues that Walker "[s]ignifies upon Hurston by troping the concept of voice that unfolds in *Their Eyes*" (239–58).

6 Hurston, *Their Eyes Were Watching God*, 183.

7 Hurston, *Mules and Men*, 124, 148; Hurston writes about the jook in her essay "Characteristics of Negro Expression," 841–45.

8 Two important examples are Harriet in Langston Hughes's *Not without Laughter* and Ida Scott in James Baldwin's *Another Country*. Harriet, one of the first examples of the professional female entertainer portrayed in African American fiction, symbolizes the survival spirit of the blues; she teaches the protagonist its lesson. The beautiful and tough Ida plays a redemptive role in *Another Coun-*

try, a novel in which music and sex are the primary sacraments in the salvation of the human spirit. In this and other aspects, *Another Country* and *The Color Purple* are complementary texts.

9   Among the essays that chronicle her search are "Saving the Life That Is Your Own"; "In Search of Our Mothers' Gardens"; "A Talk: Convocation—1972"; "The Unglamorous but Worthwhile Duties of the Black Revolutionary Artist"; and "Looking for Zora."

10  Walker, "Saving the Life That Is Your Own," in *In Search of Our Mothers' Gardens*, 13.

11  Walker, "In Search of Our Mothers' Gardens," in *In Search of Our Mothers' Gardens*, 234.

12  Ibid., 240.

13  Walker, interview with John O'Brien, in *In Search of Our Mothers' Gardens*, 264.

14  Credit is usually given to Rudi Blesh, *Shining Trumpets*. Blesh and other jazz historians of the 1940s had applied the adjective "classic" to the instrumental jazz created in the 1920s and reiterated it in their analysis of the vocal music of the same era.

15  Jones, *Blues People*, 102.

16  Harrison, *Black Pearls*, 111.

17  Williams, "Blues Roots of Contemporary Afro-American Poetry," 125.

18  Sara Martin, "Mean Tight Mama Blues" [Okeh 8255]. In her 1934 essay "Characteristics of Negro Expression," Hurston quotes jook songs on similar themes, for example: "Oh de white gal rides in a Cadillac, / De yaller girl rides de same, / Black gal rides in a rusty Ford / But she gits dere just de same" (843).

19  Blesh, *Shining Trumpets*; Charters, *Country Blues*, 57. For an important corrective to this bias, see Barlow, "*Looking Up at Down*." Harrison's *Black Pearls*, cited above, is an excellent treatment of the blueswomen's lives and art.

20  Carby, "It Jus Be's That Way Sometimes," 20.

21  Spillers, "Interstices," 167.

22  Walker, *Color Purple*, 8. Subsequent references to this work are cited parenthetically.

23  As Gates notes, this depiction echoes Walker's description of a photograph of Hurston "in pants, boots, and broadbrim hat [that] was given to [Walker] by [Hurston's] brother Everette. She has her foot up on the running board of a car—presumably hers, and bright red—and looks racy" (quoted in Gates, *Signifying Monkey*, 254).

24  Jackson quoted in Barlow, "*Looking Up at Down*," 171.

25  Walker, "Zora Neale Hurston," 90.

26  Jones, *Blues People*, 82.

27  In an interview with Claudia Tate, Alice Walker refers to her "basic antagonism toward the system of capitalism": "Since I'm only interested in changing it," she told Tate, "I'm not interested in writing about people who already fit into it. And the working class can never fit comfortably into a capitalist society" (Tate, *Black Women Writers at Work*, 185). Surely, Shug does not.

28  The judgment of Shug echoes Joe Willard's estimation of Big Sweet in Hurston's *Mules and Men*: "You wuz noble! You wuz uh whole woman and half uh man" (152).

29  Evans, *Big Road Blues*, 54. The intersections of blues and gospel music are exemplified in the career of Thomas Dorsey, who composed a gospel song entitled "I'm Going to Live the Life I Sing about in My Song." Dorsey, whose career in blues reached a high point when he worked as Ma Rainey's accompanist, achieved greater fame as a gospel composer whose songs were frequently recorded by Mahalia Jackson, among many other gospel singers. His most famous composition is "Precious Lord, Take My Hand."

30  Russell, "Slave Codes and Liner Notes," 131.

31  Celie's conscious response to the picture acknowledges its sexuality in a socially acceptable way. To attract Mister's attention sexually, and thus deflect it from Nettie, Celie dresses like the figure in the photograph—in horse hair, feathers, and high heels.

32  Critics have responded to the novel's silence on the community's expected homophobia in varying ways. In "The Truth That Never Hurts," Smith takes the position that the total acceptance of Celie and Shug is "one clue that [*The Color Purple*] is indeed an inspiring fable" (233).

33  See, in particular, the biographies Albertson, *Bessie*, and Lieb, *Mother of the Blues*. The lyrics excerpted from "Prove It on Me Blues" are transcribed from Lieb (124). A newspaper advertisement for the record shows a figure of the singer wearing a jacket, vest, tie, and fedora and flirting with two much thinner, femininely dressed female figures (127). Placed across the street is a uniformed policeman. In the wriest comment of all, a photograph of the singer is interposed between the women and the law. Her image shields the transgression the officer guards against.

34  Lorde, "Uses of the Erotic," 58.

35  Critics have discussed the novel's epistolary form as literary revisionism. Hall asserts that "Walker makes clear the relationship between the emptying of literary space and the fulfillment of female identity through her novel's epistolary structure, which subverts the predominantly male code of the Western literary tradition" ("Towards a Map of Mis(sed) Reading," 89). According to Carolyn Williams, "the novel's epistolary form . . . is the most fundamental representation of a concern with women isolated from one another within the patriarchal network." Williams argues that the shift in epistolary address from God to Nettie is the turning point in the text ("Revision of Epistolary Address in *The Color Purple*," 273–85). As the chapter on her essays will clarify, Walker locates her writing in multiple traditions.

36  Hunter quoted in Shapiro and Hentoff, *Hear Me Talkin' to Ya*, 223–24.

37  Albertson, *Bessie*, 131.

38  Baker, *Workings of the Spirit*, 74.

39  Dorsey quoted in Lieb, *Mother of the Blues*, 30.

40  Brown, *Collected Poems*, 63.

41  In this regard, too, the novel echoes *Their Eyes Were Watching God*. Janie's spiritual fulfillment comes not through the rituals of the church or conjure but through her experience during a storm. Even then, Janie's response is not made explicit; rather, the novel represents it as part of a collective experience. Consider, for example: "The wind came back with triple fury, and put out the light for the last time. They sat in company with the others in other shanties, their eyes straining against crude walls and their souls asking if He meant to measure their puny might against His. They seemed to be staring at the dark, but their eyes were watching God" (150).

42  Walker, "In Search of Our Mothers' Gardens," in *In Search of Our Mothers' Gardens*, 233, 231–32.

43  Toomer, *Cane*, 17.

44  As I demonstrate below, the novel's pantheistic vision draws on disparate sources. Although I do not perceive it as being informed by the blues, I reject Gerald Early's characterization of it as "a fairly dim-witted pantheistic acknowledgement of the wonders of human potential that begins to sound quite suspiciously like a cross between the New Age movement and Dale Carnegie" ("*The Color Purple*," 42).

45  For an argument that insists on more specific parallels between the blues and African spiritual traditions, see Marvin, " 'Preachin' the Blues.' " Marvin argues, for example, that "both Bessie Smith and Shug Avery can be considered 'children,' or followers of Legba, a West African spirit closely associated with musicians, who opens the door to the spiritual world and provides opportunities for the social and psychological growth of the individual" (411–12).

46  For a discussion of these issues, see Wilentz, *Binding Cultures*, 73–76. Walker responds to these criticisms in her afterword to *Possessing the Secret of Joy*, where she writes: "I do not know from what part of Africa my African ancestors came, and so I claim the continent. I have created Olinka as my village and the Olinkas as one of my ancient, ancestral tribal peoples. Certainly I recognize Tashi [the novel's protagonist] as my sister" (283).

47  Raboteau, *Slave Religion*, 11.

48  I develop the idea of Janie's spiritual journey in *Women of the Harlem Renaissance*, 191–95. Walker's critique of organized religion dates from her earliest writing. See especially the short story "Diary of an African Nun," in which the title character, a missionary in Uganda, perceives her vocation to be a betrayal of her people.

49  Walker notes, for example, that her essay "Everything Is a Human Being" "explores to some extent the Native American view that all of creation is of one substance and therefore deserving of the same respect" ("Universe Responds," 187). Walker's long-standing interest in Native American cosmology and in the history of African American and Native American relations is reflected in her 1976 novel *Meridian*. An earlier poem, "Eagle Rock," represents the Indian mound that is a key setting for *Meridian*, a site of historical memory and spiri-

tual release. See Walker, *Revolutionary Petunias and Other Poems*, 20–21, and *Meridian*, especially "Indians and Ecstasy," 53–59.

50   Allen, *Sacred Hoop*, 56, 5.

51   Thompson, *Flash of the Spirit*, 73.

52   Ibid., chap. 1, especially 12–16. In *Yoruba Ritual*, Drewal expands this definition in ways that seem particularly apposite to *The Color Purple*. "*Ashe* has no moral connotations; it is neither good nor bad. Rather it is a generative force or potential present in all things — rocks, hills, streams, mountains, plants, animals, ancestors, deities — and in utterances — prayers, songs, curses, and even everyday speech. *Ashe* is the power of transformation" (27). (For the sake of consistency, I have retained Thompson's spelling of *àshe*.)

53   Shug's vision is frequently cited in work by feminist theologians as a model of the alternative theology they seek to define. See, for example, Christ, "Rethinking Theology and Nature"; Keller, "Feminism and the Ethic of Inseparability"; and Williams, *Sisters in the Wilderness*.


*Chapter Seven*

 1   Naylor, *Mama Day*, 7. Subsequent references to this work are cited parenthetically.

 2   For analysis of Naylor's allusions to Shakespeare, see Erikson, "'Shakespeare's Black?'"; Kubitschek, "Toward a New Order"; Storhoff, "Only Voice Is Your Own"; and Traub, "Rainbows of Darkness." For analysis of intertextual connections between Naylor's fiction and African American texts, see Awkward, *Inspiriting Influences*; Fowler, *Gloria Naylor*; and Kubitschek, "Toward a New Order."

 3   Gates and Appiah, *Gloria Naylor*, ix.

 4   Kubitschek cites *Sula* as a "point of reference" for *Mama Day* before exploring the novel's "expanded appropriation of *Song of Solomon*" ("Toward a New Order," 78). In "'*Aesthetic and Rapport*' in Toni Morrison's *Sula*," Barbara Johnson observes that Morrison manages to hold out so strong a promise of "home" precisely because she presents it "as always already lost." Jacqueline De Weever analyzes inversion in *Sula* in "The Inverted World of Toni Morrison's *The Bluest Eye* and *Sula*."

 5   hooks, *Yearning, Race, Gender, and Cultural Politics*, 48.

 6   Michael Awkward has argued that Morrison's work is for Naylor an "inspiriting influence," whose "texts are celebrated even as they are revised, praised for their insights even when those insights are deemed inadequate to describe more contemporary manifestations of Afro-American women's peculiar challenges in a racist and sexist society" (*Inspiriting Influences*, 8). Awkward analyzes Naylor's revisions in *The Women of Brewster Place* of Morrison's narrative strategies in *The Bluest Eye* to illustrate his point.

 7   Naylor, "A Conversation," 568.

8    As Kimberly Benston argues, faces in African American literature are "not so much objects of description as living palimpsests, quickening the characters' exegetical powers." He calls for critics "to encounter the texts [of the African American tradition] as faces composing an intricate genealogical matrix" ("Facing Tradition," 107).

9    Mirrors are a recurrent trope in Naylor's fiction. In the epigraph to *Linden Hills*, Grandma Tilson tells her grandson Lester that to experience real hell he has only to "sell that silver mirror God propped up in your soul." Later in the novel he glosses the meaning of the metaphor as "giving up that part of you that lets you know who you are. . . . So you keep that mirror and when it's crazy outside, you look inside and you'll always know exactly where you are and what you are. And you call that peace" (59).

10   Henderson, "Speaking in Tongues," 20.

11   Morretti, *Atlas of the European Novel*, 3.

12   Hélène Christol makes a complementary point when she writes: "[I]n *Mama Day*, especially, topography and genealogy are the two essential elements that determine the stance of the narrative voice and allow Naylor to reconstruct a parallel black history, to reinvent America by subverting its historical and mythical elements" ("Reconstructing American History," 348).

13   Morrison, *Sula*, 4. Subsequent references to this work are cited parenthetically.

14   Lee, *Granny Midwives and Black Women Writers*, 138–39.

15   Spillers, "Hateful Passion, a Lost Love," 112.

16   Hirsch, "Maternal Narratives," 419.

17   Baker, *Workings of the Spirit*, 99.

18   Twining and Baird, *Sea Island Roots*, 1.

19   Jones-Jackson, *When Roots Die*, xii. Joyner contributed the preface. See also his study *Down by the Riverside*.

20   See, for example, Harris, *Power of the Porch*; Lee, *Granny Midwives and Black Women Writers*; and Tucker, "Recovering the Conjure Woman." See also historian McFeeley's *Sapelo's People*.

21   In a 1996 interview, Naylor described a projected novel in which Sapphira would be the "cornerstone." Set in the early nineteenth century, the novel would depict the relationship of a Fulani woman, Sapphira, and the Norwegian Bascombe Wade (Naylor, interview in *Critical Response*, 255–56).

22   Tucker, "Recovering the Conjure Woman," 182.

23   In "A Conversation," Naylor goes on to cite as an example the line from *Sula*, "All along I thought I was missing Jude." "The impact is then tremendous," Naylor observes. "And I believe writing is at its best when it's done that way" (579).


## Chapter Eight

1    Marshall, *Praisesong for the Widow*, 137; emphasis in original. Subsequent references to this work are cited parenthetically.

2 Busia, "What Is Your Nation?," 199.

3 Coined by Vévé Clark, "diaspora literacy" denotes the ability to read and comprehend the discourses of Africa, Afro-America, and the Caribbean from an informed, indigenous perspective. See Clark, "Developing Diaspora Literacy," 303–19.

4 For example, Susan Willis analyzes the novel as an act of cultural recovery, but for her the community begins in the Caribbean, not Africa, and commodity capitalism, rather than slavery, is the root of alienation. "Haunted by the notion that there once existed a whole" that has been sundered by immigration and the pressures of life under commodity capitalism, Marshall as a writer attempts "to recreate the whole." Willis, *Specifying*, 67. In her study entitled *Toward Wholeness in Paule Marshall's Fiction*, Pettis sees *Praisesong* as the culmination of "a particular vision that compelled Marshall's fiction beginning in the mid-1950s," that is, the attainment of "spiritual wholeness" (8).

5 Graulick and Sisco, "Meditations on Language and the Self," 292–93. Christian, "Ritualistic Process and the Structure of Paule Marshall's *Praisesong for the Widow*," 76. Subsequent references to the latter work are cited parenthetically.

6 Davies, *Black Women, Writing and Identity*, 24–25.

7 According to Goodwine in *The Legacy of Ibo Landing*, St. Simon's Island is thought to be the historical site of Ibo Landing.

8 References to "second-sight" are recurrent in the fictions analyzed in this study, as they are in African American folklore. In African American literary tradition the references extend at least to *The Souls of Black Folk*, in which Du Bois imputes it to the experience of the Negro in the New World: "After the Egyptian and Indian, the Greek and Roman, the Teuton and Mongolian, the Negro is a sort of seventh son, born with a veil, and gifted with second-sight in this American world,—a world which yields him no true self-consciousness, but only lets him see himself through the revelation of the other world" (5). For Du Bois, then, second-sight is historically produced. The source of this "gift" in the myth that *Praisesong* builds on is less clear and, as a consequence, more likely to be dismissed as essentialist. For reasons that my further analysis of the novel makes clear, I think this criticism is unfair. Marshall is also very much committed to exploring the intricate connections between history and culture.

9 Olly Wilson, "The Heterogeneous Sound Ideal in African-American Music," quoted in Floyd, *Power of Black Music*, 28.

10 Stuckey, *Slave Culture*, 12, 30.

11 The African Methodist Episcopal (AME) bishop Daniel Alexander Payne recorded his long campaign to stamp out the ring shout in his denomination. He described one shout he observed in Philadelphia in 1878 that he insisted be stopped, judging the ritual "heathenish" and "disgraceful" to the participants, "the race, and the Christian name." He referred to many instances in which his order to end the practice was ignored; ministers explained that their congregants would leave the church before they would give up the shout. Payne

decided that the solution was a better-educated clergy. See Payne, *Recollections of Seventy Years*, 253–56.

12 Lomax, "Afro-American Spirituals, Work Songs, and Ballads." The liner notes explain that, in an effort to attract young people to the church, the ring shout had recently been reintroduced into the Louisiana community where the recording was made. Bernice Johnson Reagon and Lisa Pertilla Brevard also note the changing content of the ring shout in the twentieth century. For another example of the ring shout, "Sign of the Judgement," performed by the McIntosh County Shouters of Bolden, Georgia, a coastal community that is culturally similar to the Sea Islands, see "African American Congregational Singing."

13 Marshall, "To Da-duh," 95. Subsequent references to this work are cited parenthetically.

14 Similarly, in *Praisesong for the Widow*, Lebert Joseph is not impressed that Avey comes from New York; the city serves only to mark her as a "stranger."

15 Hall, "Cultural Identity and Diaspora."

16 Busia, "What Is Your Nation?," 198–99.

17 Hayden, "Runagate, Runagate," 128; emphasis in original.

18 A second epigraph to the section quotes a stanza from Amiri Baraka's poem "leroy": "I want to know my mother when she sat / looking sad across the campus in the late 20's / into the future of the soul, there were black angels / straining above her head, carrying life from the ancestors, / and knowledge, and the strong nigger feeling." This allusion gives Avey's individual situation historical context. But, unlike the maternal figure in Baraka's poem, born too soon to be "saved" by the new racial consciousness of the sixties, the novel's protagonist is able to work out her own "salvation."

19 As LaMotte asserts, "in this image of the flesh as temple of the spirit the material is spirit; it is to this fusion that Avey must return" (*Places of Silence, Journeys of Freedom*, 99). LaMotte's gloss of the passage describing Jay's bequest of "the whole of his transubstantiated body and blood" is also telling. "In life Jerome's sexuality became a kind of property; in death he bequeathed his wife his 'body,' having turned his very flesh and blood into capital. In this image of man transubstantiated into property, late twentieth-century capitalism performs the function of slavery" (96).

20 Fauset, "Sleeper Wakes," 1–25.

21 Talley quoted in Floyd, *Power of Black Music*, 49. Talley's book, *Negro Folk Rhymes, Wise and Otherwise*, was published in 1922. Among the "Negro Dance Rhymes" Talley collected are "Juba," "Frog Went a-Courting," "Did You Feed My Cow?," and "The Old Black Gnats." For the symbolism of the ring, see Floyd, *Power of Black Music*, 22.

22 This androgyny is consistent with Gates's discussion of Esu-Elegbara, who is "figured as paired male and female statues" and whose sexuality is indeterminate (*Signifying Monkey*, 29). As discussed in chapter 2, Lorde believes that Esu-Elegbara was modeled on Afrekete, a female deity.

23 For a discussion of Northrup's narrative, see Floyd, *Power of Black Music*, 53.

24 See, for example, Collier, "Closing of the Circle," 312, and Denniston, *Fiction of Paule Marshall*, 139.

25 Thompson, *Flash of the Spirit*, 18–19. According to a legend recounted by Thompson, "at a crossroads in the history of the Yoruba gods when each desired to find out who, under God, was supreme, all of the deities made their way to heaven, each bearing a rich sacrificial offering on his or her head." Outsmarting the others, Eshu-Elegbara had consulted the deity of divination beforehand and arrived not with a sacrifice but with a single red parrot feather, the "very seal of supernatural force and àshe." As a reward God granted him the substance of àshe, the force to make things happen and multiply. *Flash of the Spirit*, 18.

26 Gates, *Signifying Monkey*, 6. At the end of an extended discussion, Gates offers a definition that clarifies his project and that resonates with Marshall's novel. "Legba is the indeterminacy of the interpretation of writing, and his traditional dwelling place at the crossroads, for the critic, is the crossroads of understanding and truth" (25).

27 The surname is only one of the biblical allusions associated with this character. After snubbing Avey in their initial meeting, Lebert begins to relate "his family history, going on like some Old Testament prophet chronicling the lineage of his tribe" (163).

28 In her essay "A Laying On of Hands," Gabbin defines the term as "an ancient practice of using hands in a symbolical act of blessing." She notes that "some identify the practice with the gifts of the spirit that Paul speaks of in Corinthians, whereas others consider it a reflection of the African concept that the body and spirit are one" (247).

29 Smith, *Kinship and Community in Carriacou*, 130.

### Chapter Nine

1 Walker, *In Search of Our Mothers' Gardens*, collects essays, speeches, and reviews written between 1966 and 1982. This chapter focuses on that volume. Other collections of Walker's essays are *Living by the Word* (1988); *The Same River Twice* (1996); *Anything We Love Can Be Saved: A Writer's Activism* (1997), and *Sent by Earth: A Message from the Grandmother Spirit after the Attack on the World Trade Center* (2001).

2 For interesting perspectives on the formal qualities of the essay, see Hall, "Essay and Discovery."

3 McDowell, "Reading Family Matters." Among many trenchant observations, McDowell remarks: "[T]hough black women writers have made black women the subjects of their own family stories, these [black] male readers/critics are attempting to usurp that place for themselves and place it at the center of critical inquiry" (84).

4 Walker, *Revolutionary Petunias and Other Poems*, 31–32.

5 Writing of her fiction, Gayl Jones reaches conclusions that are suggestive for Walker's essays as well. "In Walker's work the precedents of Wright and Hurston gain a sense of a formed whole. She maintains the intimate focus of

Hurston, the perspective that Hurston restored within the African American community, and cultivates Hurston's interest in psychology, motivation, human complexity and possibility; but hers is a more violent and teratologic South than Hurston's, a South of social and economic terrors that still do not cause us to shift our attention from the black people themselves" (*Liberating Voices*, 154).

6    Walker, *In Search of Our Mothers' Gardens*, 241. Subsequent references to this work are cited parenthetically.

7    Hurston, "Characteristics of Negro Expression," 834. Subsequent references to this work are cited parenthetically.

8    Robert Hemenway, Hurston's biographer, estimates that Hurston wrote this essay in 1930, but it was first published in *Negro: An Anthology*, edited by Nancy Cunard, in 1934.

9    Wright, "Blueprint for Negro Literature," 8. All subsequent references are to this edition and are cited parenthetically.

10   Wright introduced this evocative phrase to refer to "folk utterances, spirituals, blues, work songs, and folklore" in "The Literature of the Negro in the United States," 83.

11   I borrow the term "generative source" from Baker, *Journey Back*.

12   "No one listening to a Southern white man talk could deny this," Hurston wrote (831). She pointed to specific changes, such as the softening of strongly consonanted words like "aren't" to "ain't," and more generally to the adoption by whites of metaphors invented by blacks.

13   Not only was it the birthplace of the blues, which, as she pointed out, were the foundation of jazz, but the jook was the point of origin as well for the dance and theater that had so lately defined popular culture in the United States (841).

14   Baker, "'Utile Dulci' and the Literature of the Black American," 3.

15   The reference to slums is perhaps Walker's sop to the white liberal readership of the journal, which she assumed thought that Negroes in 1967 had grown up in urban communities. As Walker has emphasized throughout her subsequent writings, she grew up in rural Georgia.

16   Walker's short story "Everyday Use" fictionalizes the impact of television on the mother. In both the essay and the story, the mother imagines herself thin, white, and blond until she is shocked back into the reality of her life. Despite the media interference, Walker depicts the heavy-set brown-skinned woman with callused hands as the heroic figure.

17   See the chapter "The Meredith March," in Hampton and Fayer, *Voices of Freedom*.

18   Henderson, *Understanding the New Black Poetry*, 3.

19   Gayle, introduction to *Black Aesthetic*, xxii.

20   Among the notable critiques and assessments of the Black Aesthetic are Gates's "Preface to Blackness" and Baker's *Blues, Ideology, and Afro-American Literature*.

21   An important exception was Larry Neal, who wrote introductions to the reprints of Hurston's first novel, *Jonah's Gourd Vine*, and autobiography, *Dust Tracks on a Road*, in 1971.

22 "Black Writers' Views on Literary Lions and Values," *Black World*, January 1968; extended statements from the writers' questionnaires are reprinted in the article. The group of writers, described as "both famous and unknown," was diverse enough to include poets Robert Hayden and Don L. Lee, critics Addison Gayle and Saunders Redding, novelists John A. Williams and Ernest Gaines, and newcomers Alice Walker and John Edgar Wideman.

23 Wright, "Between Laughter and Tears," 22, 25. Subsequent references to this work are cited parenthetically.

24 In his conclusion, for example, Wright compares Hurston to a black male writer, Walter Turpin, whose novel *These Low Grounds* was also under review: "Turpin's faults as a writer are those of an honest man trying desperately to say something; but Zora Neale Hurston lacks even that excuse" (ibid., 25).

25 I am, of course, not suggesting that the debate between Hurston and Wright is only about gender. The debates between Wright, Baldwin, and Ellison raise many of the same issues of how to represent African American life and culture. But I would maintain that attention to the gendered inflections in the exchanges between Hurston and Wright clarify some of the unspoken assumptions in all these debates.

26 Hurston, "Stories of Conflict," 32. Subsequent references to this work are cited parenthetically.

27 Signifying is the generative source of Gates's theory of Afro-American literary criticism; the definition I refer to here is borrowed from J. L. Dillard and quoted in Gates, *Signifying Monkey*, 70.

28 Walker, "Beyond the Peacock," in *In Search of Our Mothers' Gardens*, 58. Subsequent references to this work are cited parenthetically.

29 In his article "The Essay and Discovery," Hall makes the following observations on the essays of Montaigne, who named and defined the genre. "The many quotations from and allusions to classical authors, along with anecdotes from history and Montaigne's personal experience, are not deployed as proofs or as undisputed authority presented to confirm a single thesis but are assembled as conflicting cases and contradictory evidence" (80). Through her references to modern American authors, contemporary history, and her own experiences, Walker employs a similar technique.

30 Walker, "My Father's Country Is the Poor," in *In Search of Our Mothers' Gardens*, 221. Subsequent references to this work are cited parenthetically.

31 Wright, *Black Boy*, 42.

32 Walker, "Zora Neale Hurston," in *In Search of Our Mothers' Gardens*, 85.

33 Walker, *Revolutionary Petunias and Other Poems*, 29.

34 Walker, "From an Interview," in *In Search of Our Mothers' Gardens*, 266. Subsequent references to this work are cited parenthetically.

35 Walker, "A Talk" and "But Yet and Still the Cotton Gin Kept on Working," in *In Search of Our Mothers' Gardens*. When Walker met her, Mrs. Hudson was writing an autobiography. As an activist, she knew her life was in jeopardy, and she wanted "to leave some kind of record" of that life for her community (24). She

did not seek a wider audience. Walker, who became her typist and editor, gives Mrs. Hudson a wider readership by including an excerpt from her writing in *In Search of Our Mothers' Gardens*.

36 Walker, "Choosing to Stay at Home," in *In Search of Our Mothers' Gardens*, 159. Subsequent references to this work are cited parenthetically.

## Epilogue

1 Morrison, "Site of Memory," 115.

2 Dash, "*Daughters of the Dust*," 141. Subsequent references to this work are cited parenthetically. In addition to the screenplay, the book includes essays by Dash and Toni Cade Bambara, a dialogue with Dash and bell hooks, a "word" from Greg Tate, excerpts from the Gullah translation of the script, traditional "gee-chee" recipes, and lists of awards and suggested readings.

3 Dash and Baker, "Not without Daughters," 57–58. Dash adds that in her dormitory she and her friends performed poems by Sonia Sanchez and acted out Bambara's stories, a practice that might be a reason the latter influenced her film. Her recollection calls to mind the way in which Zora Neale Hurston learned the oral performances of rural black southerners that she not only transcribed but that subsequently shaped her aesthetic. See Wall, *Women of the Harlem Renaissance*, 157–59.

4 Bambara reads the image of the woman in the white dress with a veiled hat as Dash's appropriation "from reactionary cinema for an emancipatory purpose. She intends to heal our imperialized eyes" (xii).

5 Another allusion to *Cane* may be the shot of the pages of the Koran that are seen flapping in the breeze near the beginning of *Daughters of the Dust*. It seems to refer to a repeated image in "Becky," the sketch in *Cane* that relates the story of a white woman "who had two Negro sons." In a comment on the ineffectuality of Christianity in the segregated South, the first and last paragraphs of the story end: "The Bible flaps its leaves with an aimless rustle on her mound" (Toomer, *Cane*, 5). In the film the Koran belongs to Bilal Muhammed, the African who came over on the last slave ship. Like Christianity, Islam has not protected its believers from slavery, but his religion has not alienated Bilal from his neighbors. However, he has developed an interpretation of the myth of Ibo Landing that is different from theirs. He is sure that the Ibos have drowned.

6 *New York Times* reviewer Stephen Holden describes it as "a film of spellbinding visual beauty" ("'Daughters of the Dust'"), and Tate writes, "[O]f course, it is in *Daughters'* representations of black women's beauty, particularly dark-skinned black women, that the film breaks cinematic ground" ("Word from Greg Tate," 70).

7 The most damning critique that I have seen, "*Daughters of the Dust*: The Making of an American 'Classic,'" appeared in the short-lived journal *Reconstruction*. Signed by Klaus de Albuquerque (presumably a pseudonym), it asserts that the "soporific" film is an artistic "flop." But the praise the film received posed seri-

ous dangers, especially if it is assumed to be historically and ethnographically accurate. It is not. The review points out that the Sea Islands were not a major point of disembarkation for Africans in America; Ibos made up a tiny percentage of the slave population; only two of the film's minor characters speak proper Gullah, while the others speak "or try to speak" a range of West Indian dialects; and the identification of the Native American character as Cherokee is a historical impossibility. In my view the last error was avoidable. Inaccurate accents would be a serious problem in an ethnographic documentary but are at most only irksome here: linguistic accuracy is very rare in U.S. films. Whether or not Ibos constituted a significant portion of the slave population is beside the point. Myths about Ibo Landing are long standing; they date at least from the 1930s when researchers collected them for *Drums and Shadows* and presumably well before. The transmission of myths from generation to generation suggests that they perform important cultural work, whatever their literal truth value. I accept Dash's characterization of *Daughters of the Dust* as a "mythopoetic" film; it seems to me to explore the work that myths like Ibo Landing have done and can do.

8   Ironically, one negative criticism of *Daughters of the Dust* is that it is *too* beautiful. Writing in the *Village Voice*, Georgia Brown found Arthur Jafa's "impressive cinematography . . . gorgeous but . . . distracting." In a parenthetical aside, she claimed, "I realize this is supposed to represent the 'new black aesthetic' but it sure looks like *Vogue*, Fellini, even Spielberg to me" ("How We Grew," 52). I urge readers to watch *Daughters of the Dust* after *The Color Purple* to test this observation for themselves. The indoor scenes in the latter look prettier (and ahistorical), but the actors do not. Of course, as the headline of Rich's review reminds us, beauty is "In the Eyes of the Beholder." Rich points out that "people of color are supposed to produce films of victimization." In contrast, films by Charles Burnett, Isaac Julien, and Lourdes Portillo, like *Daughters of the Dust*, "look at the richness of their cultures instead of their poverty. . . . They seek to evoke a different range of emotions in their audiences. . . . They luxuriate in the traditions they seek to inherit and describe a defiant aesthetic continuity into their images. Implicitly, they testify to the poverty of WASP culture and wear their own traditions like a fabulous shawl, shimmering in its colors and textures" (60, 65).

9   See hooks, "In Our Glory," 173.

10  Dash published a novel with the same title as the film in 1997.

# bibliography

"African American Congregational Singing: Nineteenth-Century Roots." Volume 2 of *Wade in the Water*. Smithsonian/Folkways 40073.

Albertson, Chris. *Bessie*. New York: Stein and Day, 1972.

Alexander, Elizabeth. "'Coming Out Blackened and Whole': Fragmentation and Reintegration in Audre Lorde's *Zami* and *The Cancer Journals*." *American Literary History* 6.4 (1994): 694–715.

Allen, Paula Gunn. *The Sacred Hoop: Recovering the Feminine in American Indian Traditions*. Boston: Beacon Press, 1986.

Angelo, Bonnie. "The Pain of Being Black: An Interview with Toni Morrison." 1989. Reprinted in *Conversations with Toni Morrison*, edited by Danille Taylor-Guthrie, 255–61. Jackson: University Press of Mississippi, 1994.

Angelou, Maya. *I Know Why the Caged Bird Sings*. New York: Random House, 1970.

Askeland, Lori. "Remodeling the Model Home in *Uncle Tom's Cabin* and *Beloved*." *American Literature* 64.4 (1992): 785–805.

Awkward, Michael. *Inspiriting Influences: Tradition, Revision, and Afro-American Women's Novels*. New York: Columbia University Press, 1989.

———. "'Unruly and Let Loose': Myth, Ideology, and Gender in *Song of Solomon*." In *Negotiating Difference: Race, Gender, and the Politics of Positionality*, 137–53. Chicago: University of Chicago Press, 1995.

Baker, Houston A. *Blues, Ideology, and Afro-American Literature*. Chicago: University of Chicago Press, 1984.

———. *The Journey Back: Issues in Black Literature and Criticism*. Chicago: University of Chicago Press, 1980.

———. *Modernism and the Harlem Renaissance*. Chicago: University of Chicago Press, 1987.

———. "'Utile Dulci' and the Literature of the Black American." 1972. Reprinted in *Singers of the Daybreak*, 1–6. Washington, D.C.: Howard University Press, 1974.

———. *Workings of the Spirit: The Poetics of Afro-American Women's Writing*. Chicago: University of Chicago Press, 1991.

Baldwin, James. *Another Country*. 1962. Reprint, New York: Vintage Books, 1993.

———. *The Fire Next Time*. 1963. Reprinted in *James Baldwin: Collected Essays*, edited by Toni Morrison, 291–48. New York: Library of America, 1998.

———. *Go Tell It on the Mountain*. 1953. Reprint, New York: Dell, 1970.

———. *James Baldwin: Early Novels and Stories*. Edited by Toni Morrison. New York: Library of America, 1998.

———. *Notes of a Native Son*. 1955. Reprint, with a new introduction, Boston: Beacon Press, 1984.

———. "The Outing." In *James Baldwin: Early Novels and Stories*, edited by Toni Morrison, 771–96. New York: Library of America, 1998.

———. "Revolutionary Hope: A Conversation between James Baldwin and Audre Lorde." *Essence*, December 1984, 72–74, 129–30, 133.

———. "Sonny's Blues." 1957. Reprinted in *James Baldwin: Early Novels and Stories*, edited by Toni Morrison, 831–64. New York: Library of America, 1998.

Bambara, Toni Cade. Preface to *"Daughters of the Dust": The Making of an African American Woman's Film*, by Julie Dash, xi–xvi. New York: New Press, 1992.

———. *The Salt Eaters*. New York: Random House, 1980.

Barksdale, Richard K. "Castration Symbolism in Recent Black American Fiction." *College Language Association Journal* 29.4 (1986): 400–413.

Barlow, William. *"Looking Up at Down": The Emergence of Blues Culture*. Philadelphia: Temple University Press, 1989.

Barthes, Roland. "The Rhetoric of the Image." In *Image Music Text*, translated by Stephen Heath, 32–51. New York: Hill and Wang, 1977.

Bay, Edna. *Wives of the Leopard: Gender, Politics, and Culture in the Kingdom of Dahomey*. Charlottesville: University of Virginia Press, 1998.

Bell, Roseann P. "Judgment: Addison Gayle." In *Sturdy Black Bridges: Visions of Black Women in Literature*, edited by Roseann P. Bell, Bettye J. Parker, and Beverly Guy-Sheftall, 209–16. New York: Anchor Books, 1979.

Benjamin, Walter. "The Work of Art in the Age of Mechanical Reproduction." In *Illuminations*, edited with an introduction by Hannah Arendt, 217–52. New York: Schocken Books, 1969.

Benston, Kimberly. "Facing Tradition: Revisionary Scenes in African American Literature." *PMLA* 105 (January 1990): 98–109.

Billops, Camille, ed. *The Harlem Book of the Dead*. Dobbs Ferry, N.Y.: Morgan and Morgan, 1978.

"Black Writers' Views on Literary Lions and Values." *Black World*, January 1968, 10–48, 81–89.

Blesh, Rudi. *Shining Trumpets: A History of Jazz*. 1946. Reprint, New York: Da Capo Press, 1976.

Blume, E. Sue. *Secret Survivors: Uncovering Incest and Its Aftereffects in Women*. New York: John Wiley and Sons, 1990.

Brooks, Gwendolyn. *Family Pictures*. Detroit: Broadside Press, 1970.

———. *Report from Part One*. Detroit: Broadside Press, 1972.

———. *Selected Poems*. New York: Harper and Row, 1963.

Brown, Georgia. "How We Grew." *Village Voice*, 21 January 1992, 52.

Brown, Sterling A. "The Blues." *Phylon* 13 (Autumn 1952): 286–92.

———. *Collected Poems*. New York: Harper and Row, 1980.

Busia, Abena. "What Is Your Nation? Reconnecting Africa and Her Diaspora through Paule Marshall's *Praisesong for the Widow*." In *Changing Our Own Words: Essays on Criticism, Theory and Writing by Black Women*, edited by Cheryl A. Wall, 196–212. New Brunswick, N.J.: Rutgers University Press, 1989.

Campbell, Barbara. "New Book Bridges Gap in Black History." *New York Times*, 5 March 1974, 26.

Carby, Hazel. "'It Jus Be's That Way Sometimes': The Sexual Politics of Women's Blues." *Radical America* 20.4 (1986): 9–24.

———. "The Politics of Fiction, Anthropology and the Folk: Zora Neale Hurston." In *New Essays on "Their Eyes Were Watching God,"* edited by Michael Awkward, 71–94. New York: Cambridge University Press, 1990.

———. *Reconstructing Womanhood: The Emergence of the Afro-American Woman Novelist*. New York: Oxford University Press, 1987.

Carruthers, Mary. *The Book of Memory: A Study of Memory in Medieval Culture*. Cambridge: Cambridge University Press, 1990.

Charters, Samuel Barclay. *The Country Blues*. 1959. Reprint, New York: Da Capo Press, 1975.

Chinasole. "Audre Lorde and Matrilineal Diaspora." In *Wild Women in the Whirlwind: Afra-American Culture and the Contemporary Literary Renaissance*, edited by Joanne M. Braxton and Andrée N. McLaughlin, 379–94. New Brunswick, N.J.: Rutgers University Press, 1990.

Christ, Carol P. "Rethinking Theology and Nature." In *Weaving the Visions: New Patterns in Feminist Spirituality*, edited by Carol Christ and Judith Plaskow, 314–25. San Francisco: Harper and Row, 1992.

Christian, Barbara. *Black Women Novelists: The Development of a Tradition, 1892–1976*. Westport, Conn.: Greenwood Press, 1980.

———. "But What Do We Think We're Doing Anyway?" In *Changing Our Own Words: Essays on Criticism, Theory, and Writing by Black Women*, edited by Cheryl A. Wall, 58–74. New Brunswick, N.J.: Rutgers University Press, 1989.

———. "Fixing Methodologies: *Beloved*." *Cultural Critique* (Spring 1995): 5–15.

———. "Ritualistic Process and the Structure of Paule Marshall's *Praisesong for the Widow*." *Callaloo* 6.1–2 (1983): 74–84.

Christian, Barbara, Deborah McDowell, and Nellie Y. McKay. "A Conversation on Toni Morrison's *Beloved*." In *Toni Morrison's "Beloved": A Casebook*, edited by William Andrews and Nellie McKay, 203–20. New York: Oxford University Press, 1999.

Christol, Hélène. "Reconstructing American History: Land and Genealogy in Gloria Naylor's *Mama Day*." In *The Black Columbiad: Defining Moments in African American Literature and Culture*, edited by Werner Sollors and Maria Diedrich, 347–56. Cambridge: Harvard University Press, 1994.

Clark, Vévé. "Developing Diaspora Literacy: Allusion in Maryse Condé's *Hérémakho-*

non." In *Out of the Kumbla*, edited by Carol Boyce Davies and Elaine Savory Fido, 303–19. Trenton, N.J.: Africa World Press, 1990.

Clifton, Lucille. *Blessing the Boats: New and Selected Poems, 1988–2000*. Rochester, N.Y.: BOA Editions, 2000.

———. *The Book of Light*. Port Townsend, Wash.: Copper Canyon Press, 1993.

———. *Generations: A Memoir*. New York: Random House, 1976.

———. *Good News about the Earth: New Poems*. New York: Random House, 1972.

———. *Good Times*. New York: Random House, 1969.

———. *Good Woman: Poems and a Memoir*. Brockport, N.Y.: BOA Editions, 1987.

———. *Next: New Poems*. Brockport, N.Y.: BOA Editions, 1987.

———. *An Ordinary Woman*. New York: Random House, 1974.

———. *Quilting: Poems, 1987–1990*. Brockport, N.Y.: BOA Editions, 1991.

———. "A Simple Language." In *Black Women Writers, 1950–1980: A Critical Evaluation*, edited by Mari Evans, 137–38. New York: Anchor Books, 1984.

———. *The Terrible Stories*. Brockport, N.Y.: BOA Editions, 1996.

———. *Two-Headed Woman*. Amherst: University of Massachusetts Press, 1980.

Collier, Eugenia. "The Closing of the Circle: Movement from Division to Wholeness in Paule Marshall's Fiction." In *Black Women Writers, 1950–1980: A Critical Evaluation*, edited by Mari Evans, 295–315. New York: Anchor Books, 1984.

Conrad, Robert Edgar. *Children of God's Fire: A Documentary History of Black Slavery in Brazil*. Princeton: Princeton University Press, 1984.

Dance, Daryl Cumber. "An Interview with Paule Marshall." *Southern Review* 28 (Winter 1992): 1–20.

Darling, Marsha. "In the Realm of Responsibility: A Conversation with Toni Morrison." In *Conversations with Toni Morrison*, edited by Danille Taylor-Guthrie, 245–54. Jackson: University Press of Mississippi, 1994.

Dash, Julie. *Daughters of the Dust*. Directed by Julie Dash. Kino International, 1992.

———. *"Daughters of the Dust": The Making of an African American Woman's Film*. New York: New Press, 1992.

Dash, Julie, with Houston Baker. "Not without Daughters." *Transition* 57 (1992): 150–66.

Davies, Carole Boyce. *Black Women, Writing and Identity: Migrations of the Subject*. New York: Routledge, 1994.

Davis, Angela Y. "Afro Images: Politics, Fashion, and Nostalgia." In *Picturing Us: African American Identity in Photography*, edited by Deborah Willis, 171–80. New York: New Press, 1994.

———. "Black Women and Music: A Historical Legacy of Struggle." In *Wild Women in the Whirlwind: Afra-American Culture and the Contemporary Literary Renaissance*, edited by Joanne M. Braxton and Andrée N. McLaughlin, 3–21. New Brunswick, N.J.: Rutgers University Press, 1990.

———. *Blues Legacies and Black Feminism*. New York: Pantheon Books, 1998.

de Albuquerque, Klaus. "*Daughters of the Dust*: The Making of an American 'Classic.'" *Reconstruction* 2.2 (1993): 122–25.

Denniston, Dorothy H. *The Fiction of Paule Marshall: Reconstructions of History, Culture, and Gender*. Knoxville: University of Tennessee Press, 1995.

De Weever, Jacqueline. "The Inverted World of Toni Morrison's *The Bluest Eye* and *Sula*." *CLA Journal* 22 (1979): 402–14.

Dhairyam, Sagri. "'Artifacts for Survival': Remapping the Contours of Poetry with Audre Lorde." *Feminist Studies* 18 (Summer 1992): 242–43.

Diedrich, Maria, Henry Louis Gates Jr., and Carl Pedersen, eds. *Black Imagination and the Middle Passage*. New York: Oxford University Press, 1999.

Dixon, Melvin. "The Black Writer's Use of Memory." In *History and Memory in African-American Culture*, edited by Geneviève Fabre and Robert O'Meally, 18–27. New York: Oxford University Press, 1994.

———. *Ride Out the Wilderness: Geography and Identity in Afro-American Literature*. Urbana: University of Illinois Press, 1987.

Douglass, Frederick. *Narrative of the Life of Frederick Douglass*. 1845. New York: Signet, 1968.

Dowling, Colette. "The Song of Toni Morrison." *New York Times Magazine*, 20 May 1979, 40–58.

Dreifus, Claudia. "Chloe Wofford Talks about Toni Morrison." *New York Times Magazine*, 11 September 1994, SM 72–76.

Drewal, Margaret. *Yoruba Ritual: Performance, Plays, Agency*. Bloomington: Indiana University Press, 1991.

Dubey, Madhu. *Black Women Novelists and the Nationalist Aesthetic*. Bloomington: Indiana University Press, 1994.

Du Bois, William E. B. *The Souls of Black Folk*. 1903. Reprint, with introduction by Donald Gibson, New York: Penguin, 1989.

———. *W. E. B. Du Bois: A Reader*. Edited by David Levering Lewis. New York: Henry Holt, 1995.

duCille, Ann. *The Coupling Convention: Sex, Text, and Tradition in Black Women's Fiction*. New York: Oxford University Press, 1993.

———. *Skin Trade*. Cambridge: Harvard University Press, 1996.

Dumas, Henry. *Ark of Bones and Other Stories*. Carbondale: Southern Illinois Press, 1970.

Early, Gerald. "*The Color Purple*: Everybody's Protest Art." In *Tuxedo Junction Essays on American Culture*, 33–45. Hopewell, N.J.: Ecco Press, 1989.

Ellison, Ralph. "Blues People." In *Shadow and Act*, 247–60. New York: Signet, 1966.

———. *Invisible Man*. 1952. Reprint, New York: Vintage International, 1995.

———. "Richard Wright's Blues." In *Shadow and Act*, 77–94. New York: Signet, 1966.

Erikson, Peter. "'Shakespeare's Black?' The Role of Shakespeare in Naylor's Novels." 1991. Reprinted in *Gloria Naylor: Critical Perspectives Past and Present*, edited by Henry Louis Gates Jr. and K. A. Appiah, 231–48. New York: Amistad, 1993.

Evans, David. *Big Road Blues: Tradition and Creativity in the Folk Blues*. New York: DaCapo Press, 1982.

Fabre, Geneviève, and Robert O' Meally, eds. *History and Memory in African-American Culture*. New York: Oxford University Press, 1994.

Fauset, Jessie. "The Sleeper Wakes." 1920. Reprinted in *The Sleeper Wakes*, edited by Marcy Knopf, 1–25. New Brunswick, N.J.: Rutgers University Press, 1993.

Floyd, Samuel, Jr. *The Power of Black Music*. New York: Oxford University Press, 1995.

Fowler, Virginia. *Gloria Naylor: In Search of Sanctuary*. Boston: Twayne, 1996.

Freilicher, Lila. "Editor's Personal Commitment Shapes a Scrapbook of Black History." *Publishers Weekly*, 10 December 1973.

Freyre, Gilberto. *The Masters and the Slaves*. 1946. 2nd English-language ed., New York: Alfred A. Knopf, 1956.

Gabbin, Joanne V. "A Laying On of Hands: Black Women Writers Exploring the Roots of Their Folk and Cultural Traditions." 1977. Reprinted in *Wild Women in the Whirlwind: Afra-American Culture and the Contemporary Literary Renaissance*, edited by Joanne M. Braxton and Andrée N. McLaughlin, 246–63. New Brunswick, N.J.: Rutgers University Press, 1990.

Gates, Henry Louis, Jr. "Preface to Blackness: Text and Pretext." In *Afro-American Literature: The Reconstruction of Instruction*, edited by Dexter Fisher and Robert B. Stepto, 44–69. New York: Modern Language Association, 1978.

———. *The Signifying Monkey: A Theory of Afro-American Literary Criticism*. New York: Oxford University Press, 1987.

Gates, Henry Louis, Jr., and K. A. Appiah, eds. *Gloria Naylor: Critical Perspectives Past and Present*. New York: Amistad, 1993.

Gayle, Addison. *The Black Aesthetic*. New York: Anchor Books, 1972.

Gibson, Donald B. "The Good Black Poet and the Good Gray Poet." In *Langston Hughes: Black Genius*, edited by Therman B. O'Daniel, 65–80. New York: William Morrow, 1971.

Gilroy, Paul. "It's a Family Affair." In *Small Acts: Thoughts on the Politics of Black Cultures*, 192–207. London: Serpent's Tail, 1993.

Goodwine, Marquetta. *The Legacy of Ibo Landing: Gullah Roots of African American Culture*. Atlanta: Clarity Press, 1998.

Gordon, Avery. *Ghostly Matters: Haunting and the Sociological Imagination*. Minneapolis: University of Minnesota Press, 1997.

Graulick, Melody, and Lisa Sisco. "Meditations on Language and the Self: A Conversation with Paule Marshall." *National Women's Studies Association (NWSA) Journal* 4.3 (1992): 282–302.

Hall, James. "Towards a Map of Mis(sed) Reading: The Presence of Absence in *The Color Purple*." *African American Review* 26 (Spring 1992): 89–97.

Hall, Michael L. "The Essay and Discovery." In *Essays on the Essay: Redefining the Genre*, edited by Alexander J. Butrym, 73–91. Athens: University of Georgia Press, 1989.

Hall, Stuart. "Cultural Identity and Diaspora." In *Theorizing Diaspora: A Reader*, edited by Jana Evans Braziel and Arita Mannur, 233–46. Malden, Mass.: Blackwell Place Publishing, 2003.

————. "The Dialogics of Identity in the Age of Globalization." Lecture, Rutgers University, 15 April 1993.

————. "Negotiating Caribbean Identities." *New Left Review* 209 (January/February 1995): 3–14.

Hampton, Henry, and Steve Fayer. *Voices of Freedom: An Oral History of the Civil Rights Movement from the 1950s through the 1980s.* New York: Bantam Books, 1990.

————, eds. "The Meredith March." In *Voices of Freedom: An Oral History of the Civil Rights Movement from the 1950s through the 1980s,* 283–96. New York: Bantam Books, 1990.

Harper, Michael. "Gayl Jones: An Interview." In *Chant of Saints,* edited by Michael Harper and Robert Stepto, 352–75. Urbana: University of Illinois Press, 1979.

Harper, Michael, and Robert Stepto, eds. *Chant of Saints.* Urbana: University of Illinois Press, 1979.

Harris, Janice. "Gayl Jones's *Corregidora.*" *Frontiers: A Journal of Women's Studies* 5.3 (1980): 1–5.

Harris, Middleton, with Morris Levitt, Roger Furman, and Ernest Smith. *The Black Book.* New York: Random House, 1974.

Harris, Trudier. "Beloved: Woman, Thy Name Is Demon." 1991. Reprinted in *Toni Morrison's "Beloved": A Casebook,* edited by William Andrews and Nellie McKay, 127–58. New York: Oxford University Press, 1999.

————. *The Power of the Porch: The Storyteller's Craft in Zora Neale Hurston, Randall Kenan, and Gloria Naylor.* Athens: University of Georgia Press, 1996.

Harrison, Daphne Duval. *Black Pearls: Blues Queens of the 1920s.* New Brunswick, N.J.: Rutgers University Press, 1988.

Hayden, Robert. "Middle Passage." In *Angle of Ascent,* 118–23. New York: Liveright, 1975.

————. "Runagate, Runagate." In *Angle of Ascent,* 128–30. New York: Liveright, 1975.

Henderson, Mae Gwendolyn. "*The Color Purple*: Revisions and Redefinitions." *Sage* 2 (Spring 1985): 14–18.

————. "Speaking in Tongues: Dialogics, Dialectics and the Black Woman Writer's Literary Tradition." In *Changing Our Own Words: Essays on Criticism, Theory, and Writing by Black Women,* edited by Cheryl A. Wall, 16–37. New Brunswick, N.J.: Rutgers University Press, 1989.

————. "Toni Morrison's *Beloved*: Re-membering the Body as Historical Text." In *Comparative American Identities: Race, Sex, and Nationality in the Modern Text,* edited by Hortense J. Spillers, 69–86. New York: Routledge, 1991.

Henderson, Stephen. *Understanding the New Black Poetry.* New York: William Morrow, 1972.

Herman, Judith. *Father-Daughter Incest.* Cambridge: Harvard University Press, 1981.

Hirsch, Marianne. "Maternal Narratives." In *Reading Black, Reading Feminist,* edited by Henry Louis Gates Jr., 415–30. New York: Meridian Books, 1990.

Hite, Molly. "Romance, Marginality, Matrilineage: Alice Walker's *The Color Purple* and Zora Neale Hurston's *Their Eyes Were Watching God.*" *Novel* 22 (Spring 1989): 257–73.

Holden, Stephen. "'Daughters of the Dust': The Demise of a Tradition." *New York Times,* 16 January 1992, C19.

Holloway, Karla. *Moorings and Metaphors: Figures of Culture and Gender in Black Women's Literature.* New Brunswick, N.J.: Rutgers University Press, 1992.

hooks, bell. "In Our Glory: Photography and Black Life." In *Picturing Us: African American Identity in Photography,* edited by Deborah Willis, 42–53. New York: New Press, 1994.

———. *Yearning, Race, Gender, and Cultural Politics.* Boston: South End Press, 1990.

Hughes, Langston. *Not without Laughter.* 1930. Reprint, New York: First Collier Books, 1969.

Hull, Gloria (Akasha). "Channeling the Ancestral Muse: Lucille Clifton and Dolores Kendrick." In *Female Subjects in Black and White,* edited by Elizabeth Abel, Barbara Christian, and Helene Moglen, 330–48. Berkeley: University of California Press, 1997.

———. "Living on the Line: Audre Lorde and *Our Dead behind Us.*" In *Changing Our Own Words: Essays on Criticism, Theory, and Writing by Black Women,* edited by Cheryl A. Wall, 150–72. New Brunswick, N.J.: Rutgers University Press, 1989.

Hurston, Zora Neale. "Characteristics of Negro Expression." 1934. Reprinted in *Zora Neale Hurston: Folklore, Memoir and Other Writings,* edited by Cheryl A. Wall, 830–46. New York: Library of America, 1995.

———. *Dust Tracks on a Road: An Autobiography.* 1942. Reprint, with a new introduction by Larry Neal, Philadelphia: Lippincott, 1971.

———. *Jonah's Gourd Vine.* 1934. Reprint, with a new introduction by Larry Neal, Philadelphia: Lippincott, 1971.

———. "Stories of Conflict." 1938. Reprinted in *Zora Neale Hurston: Folklore, Memoir and Other Writings,* edited by Cheryl A. Wall, 912–13. New York: Library of America, 1995.

———. *Their Eyes Were Watching God.* 1937. Reprint, New York: Harper Perennial, 1990.

Jacobs, Harriet. *Incidents in the Life of a Slave Girl.* 1861. Reprint, Cambridge: Harvard University Press, 1987.

Johnson, Barbara. "'Aesthetic and Rapport' in Toni Morrison's *Sula.*" *Textual Practice* 7.1 (1993): 165–72.

Johnson, Charles. *Middle Passage.* New York: Atheneum, 1990.

Jones, Gayl. "About My Work." In *Black Women Writers, 1950–1980: A Critical Evaluation,* edited by Mari Evans, 233–35. New York: Anchor Books, 1984.

———. *Corregidora.* New York: Random House, 1975.

———. *Liberating Voices: Oral Traditions in African American Literature.* Cambridge: Harvard University Press, 1991.

———. *Song for Anninho.* 1981. Reprint, Boston: Beacon Press, 1999.

Jones, LeRoi. *Blues People: Negro Music in White America.* New York: William Morrow, 1963.

Jones-Jackson, Patricia. *When Roots Die: Endangered Traditions in the Sea Islands.* Athens: University of Georgia Press, 1987.

Joyner, Charles. *Down by the Riverside.* Urbana: University of Illinois Press, 1985.

Kaplan, Justin. *Walt Whitman: A Life.* New York: Simon and Schuster, 1980.

Keating, AnnLouise. "Making 'Our Shattered Faces Whole': The Black Goddess and Audre Lorde's Revision of Matriarchal Myth." *Frontiers: A Journal of Women's Studies* 13.1 (1992): 20–33.

Keller, Catherine. "Feminism and the Ethic of Inseparability." In *Weaving the Visions: New Patterns in Feminist Spirituality,* edited by Carol Christ and Judith Plaskow, 256–66. San Francisco: Harper and Row, 1992.

Kent, R. K. "Palmares: An African State in Brazil." In *Maroon Societies: Rebel Slave Communities in the Americas,* edited by Richard Price, 170–90. 3rd ed. Baltimore: Johns Hopkins University Press, 1996.

King, Katie. "Audre Lorde's Lacquered Layerings: The Lesbian Bar as a Site of Literary Production." In *New Lesbian Criticism: Literary and Cultural Readings,* edited by Sally Munt, 51–74. New York: Columbia University Press, 1992.

Knight, Etheridge. "The Idea of Ancestry." In *Poems.* Detroit: Broadside Press, 1968.

Kubitschek, Missy Dehn. *Claiming the Heritage: African-American Women Novelists and History.* Jackson: University Press of Mississippi, 1991.

———. "Toward a New Order: Shakespeare, Morrison, and Gloria Naylor's *Mama Day.*" *Melus* 3 (Fall 1994): 75–90.

LaMotte, Eugenia. *Places of Silence, Journeys of Freedom: The Fiction of Paule Marshall.* Philadelphia: University of Pennsylvania Press, 1998.

Landy, Francis. "The Song of Songs." In *The Literary Guide to the Bible,* edited by Robert Alter and Frank Kermode, 305–19. Cambridge: Harvard University Press, 1987.

Lazer, Hank. "Blackness Blessed: The Writings of Lucille Clifton." *Southern Review* 25 (Summer 1989): 760–70.

LeClair, Thomas. "The Language Must Not Sweat: A Conversation with Toni Morrison." 1981. Reprinted in *Conversations with Toni Morrison,* edited by Danille Taylor-Guthrie, 119–28. Jackson: University Press of Mississippi, 1994.

Lee, Valerie. *Granny Midwives and Black Women Writers: Double-Dutched Readings.* New York: Routledge, 1996.

Leeming, David. *James Baldwin: A Biography.* New York: Henry Holt, 1994.

Levine, Lawrence. *Black Culture and Black Consciousness: Afro-American Folk Thought from Slavery to Freedom.* New York: Oxford University Press, 1977.

Lieb, Sandra R. *Mother of the Blues: A Study of Ma Rainey.* Amherst: University of Massachusetts Press, 1981.

Lomax, Alan, ed. "Afro-American Spirituals, Work Songs, and Ballads." Album 3 of *Folk Music of the United States.* Archive of American Folk Song, Library of Congress.

Lorde, Audre. *The Black Unicorn: Poems.* New York: W. W. Norton, 1978.

———. *The Cancer Journals.* Argyle, N.Y.: Spinsters Ink, 1980.

————. *Chosen Poems, Old and New*. New York: W. W. Norton, 1982.

————. "Grenada Revisited: An Interim Report." In *Sister Outsider: Essays and Speeches*, 176–90. Trumansburg, N.Y.: Crossing Press, 1984.

————. "An Interview with Audre Lorde and Adrienne Rich." In *Sister/Outsider: Essays and Speeches*, 81–109. Trumansburg, N.Y.: Crossing Press, 1984.

————. *Sister/Outsider: Essays and Speeches*. Trumansburg, N.Y.: Crossing Press, 1984.

————. "Uses of the Erotic: The Erotic as Power." In *Sister Outsider: Essays and Speeches*, 53–59. Trumansburg, N.Y.: Crossing Press, 1984.

————. *Zami: A New Spelling of My Name*. Freedom, Calif.: Crossing Press, 1982.

Madhubuti, Haki. "Lucille Clifton: Warm Water, Greased Legs, and Dangerous Poetry." In *Black Women Writers, 1950–1980: A Critical Evaluation*, edited by Mari Evans, 150–60. New York: Anchor Books, 1984.

Marshall, Paule. "From the Poets in the Kitchen." In *Reena and Other Stories*. New York: Feminist Press, 1983.

————. *Praisesong for the Widow*. New York: E. P. Dutton, 1983.

————. *Reena and Other Stories*. New York: Feminist Press, 1983.

————. "To Da-duh: In Memoriam." In *Reena and Other Stories*. New York: Feminist Press, 1983.

Marvin, Thomas F. " 'Preachin' the Blues': Bessie Smith's Secular Religion and Alice Walker's *The Color Purple*." *African American Review* 28 (Fall 1994): 411–21.

Mayer, Sylvia. " 'You Like Huckleberries?' Toni Morrison's *Beloved* and Mark Twain's *Adventures of Huckleberry Finn*." In *The Black Columbiad: Defining Moments in African American Literature and Culture*, edited by Werner Sollers and Maria Diedrich, 337–46. Cambridge: Harvard University Press, 1994.

Mays, Benjamin. *The Negro's God As Reflected in His Literature*. 1938. Reprint, New York: Negro Universities Press, 1969.

McCluskey, Audrey T. "Tell the Good News: A View of the Works of Lucille Clifton." In *Coming to Light: American Women Poets in the Twentieth Century*, edited by Diane Middlebrook and Marilyn Yalom, 214–21. Ann Arbor: University of Michigan Press, 1985.

McDowell, Deborah E. *"The Changing Same": Black Women's Literature, Criticism, and Theory*. Bloomington: Indiana University Press, 1995.

————. "New Directions for Black Feminist Criticism." 1980. Reprinted, with author's commentary, in *"The Changing Same": Black Women's Literature, Criticism, and Theory*. Bloomington: Indiana University Press, 1995.

————. "Reading Family Matters." In *Changing Our Own Words: Essays on Criticism, Theory, and Writing by Black Women*, edited by Cheryl A. Wall, 75–97. New Brunswick, N.J.: Rutgers University Press, 1989.

McFeeley, William. *Sapelo's People: A Long Walk into Freedom*. New York: W. W. Norton, 1994.

McKinley, Catherine E., and Joyce De Laney, eds. *Afrekete: An Anthology of Black Lesbian Writing*. New York: Anchor Books, 1994.

Middleton, Joyce. "From Orality to Literacy: Oral Memory in Toni Morrison's *Song* of Solomon." In *New Essays on Song of Solomon*, edited by Valerie Smith, 19–40. New York: Cambridge University Press, 1995.

Mitchell, W. J. T. *Picture Theory*. Chicago: University of Chicago Press, 1994.

Mobley, Marilyn. "A Different Remembering: Memory, History, and Meaning in *Beloved*." In *Toni Morrison: Modern Critical Views*, edited by Harold Bloom, 189–99. New York: Chelsea House, 1990.

Morretti, Franco. *Atlas of the European Novel, 1800–1900*. London: Verso, 1997.

Morrison, Toni. *Beloved*. New York: Alfred A. Knopf, 1987.

———. *The Bluest Eye*. New York: Holt, Rinehart and Winston, 1970.

———. "Memory, Creation and Writing." *Thought* 59 (December 1984): 388–89.

———. "Rediscovering Black History." *New York Times Magazine*, 11 August 1974, 14–24.

———. "Rootedness: The Ancestor as Foundation." In *Black Women Writers, 1950–1980: A Critical Evaluation*, edited by Mari Evans, 339–45. New York: Anchor Books, 1984.

———. "The Site of Memory." In *Inventing the Truth: The Art and Craft of Memoir*, edited by William Zinsser, 123–24. Boston: Houghton Mifflin, 1987.

———. *Song of Solomon*. New York: New American Library, 1978.

———. *Sula*. New York: Alfred A. Knopf, 1974.

———. "Toni Morrison: The Art of Fiction CXXXIV." *Paris Review* 128: 82–105.

———. "Unspeakable Things Unspoken: The Afro-American Presence in American Literature." *Michigan Quarterly Review* 28.1 (1989): 29.

Morrison, Toni, and Robert Richardson. "A Bench by the Road: *Beloved*." *The World* 3 (January–February 1989): 4, 5, 37–41.

Murray, Albert. *Stomping the Blues*. New York: McGraw Hill, 1976.

Naylor, Gloria. "A Conversation." *Southern Review* 21 (Summer 1985): 567–93.

———. Interview. In *The Critical Response to Gloria Naylor*, edited by Sharon Felton and Michelle C. Loris. Westport, Conn.: Greenwood Press, 1997.

———. *Linden Hills*. New York: Ticknor and Fields, 1985.

———. *Mama Day*. New York: Ticknor and Fields, 1988.

———. *The Women of Brewster Place*. New York: Viking, 1982.

Nora, Pierre. "Between Memory and History: *Les Lieu de Mémoire*." *Representations* 26 (Spring 1989): 9.

Ostriker, Alicia. "A Holy of Holies: The Song of Songs as Counter-Text." Lecture. Rutgers University, February 1997.

———. "Kin and Kin: The Poetry of Lucille Clifton." In *Dancing at the Devil's Party: Essays on Poetry, Politics, and the Erotic*, 78–100. Ann Arbor: University of Michigan Press, 2000.

Painter, Nell. *Sojourner Truth: A Life, a Symbol*. New York: W. W. Norton, 1996.

Palmer, Robert. *Deep Blues*. New York: Penguin Books, 1982.

Payne, Daniel Alexander. *Recollections of Seventy Years*. 1878. Reprint, New York: Arno Press, 1968.

Pettis, Joyce. *Toward Wholeness in Paule Marshall's Fiction*. Charlottesville: University of Virginia Press, 1995.

Raboteau, Albert. *Slave Religion: The "Invisible Institution" in the Antebellum South*. New York: Oxford University Press, 1978.

Rampersad, Arnold. *The Art and Imagination of W. E. B. Du Bois*. Cambridge: Harvard University Press, 1976.

Raynaud, Claudine. "'A Nutmeg Nestled inside Its Covering of Mace': Audre Lorde's Zami." In *Life/Lines: Theorizing Women's Autobiography*, edited by Bella Brodzki and Celeste Schenck, 221–42. Ithaca, N.Y.: Cornell University Press, 1988.

Reynolds, David S. *Walt Whitman's America: A Cultural Biography*. New York: Vintage Books, 1996.

Rich, Adrienne. *Of Woman Born: Motherhood as Experience and Institution*. New York: W. W. Norton, 1976.

———. "When We Dead Awaken: Writing as Re-vision." 1971. Reprinted in *On Lies, Secrets, and Silence: Selected Prose, 1966–78*, 33–50. New York: W. W. Norton, 1979.

Robinson, Sally. *Engendering the Subject: Gender and Self Representation in Contemporary Women's Fiction*. New York: State University of New York Press, 1991.

Rody, Caroline. "Toni Morrison's *Beloved*: History, 'Rememory,' and a 'Clamor for a Kiss.'" *American Literary History* 7 (Spring 1995): 92–119.

Rowell, Charles. "Interview with Gayl Jones." *Callaloo* 5.3 (1982): 39–42.

Rushdy, Ashraf. "Daughters Signifying History: Toni Morrison's *Beloved*." Reprinted in *Beloved: A Casebook*, edited by Williams Andrews and Nellie McKay, 37–56. New York: Oxford University Press, 1999.

———. *Remembering Generations: Race and Family in Contemporary African American Fiction*. Chapel Hill: University of North Carolina Press, 1997.

Rushing, Andrea Benton. "Lucille Clifton: A Changing Voice for Changing Times." In *Coming to Light: American Women Poets in the Twentieth Century*, edited by Diane Middlebrook and Marilyn Yalom, 214–21. Ann Arbor: University of Michigan Press, 1985.

Russell, Michele. "Slave Codes and Liner Notes." In *But Some of Us Are Brave: Black Women's Studies*, 129–40. Old Westbury, N.Y.: Feminist Press, 1982.

Sadoff, Diane F. "Black Matrilineage: The Case of Alice Walker and Zora Neale Hurston." *Signs* 11 (Autumn 1985): 4–26.

Said, Edward. "Secular Criticism." In *The Word, the Text, and the Critic*, 1–30. Cambridge: Harvard University Press, 1983.

Salaam, Kalamu ya. Review of *The Black Book*. *Black Books Bulletin* 3 (Spring 1975): 71–73.

Scruggs, Charles. *Sweet Home: Invisible Cities in the Afro-American Novel*. Baltimore: Johns Hopkins University Press, 1993.

Shange, Ntozake. *A Daughter's Geography*. New York: St. Martin's Press, 1983.

———. *for colored girls who have considered suicide when the rainbow is enuf*. 1977. Reprint, New York: Bantam Books, 1980.

Shapiro, Nat, and Nat Hentoff, eds. *Hear Me Talkin' to Ya: The Story of Jazz by the Men Who Made It*. New York: Grove Press, 1957.

Smith, Barbara. "Toward a Black Feminist Criticism." 1977. Reprinted in *The New Feminist Criticism: Essays on Women, Literature, Theory*, edited by Elaine Showalter, 168–85. New York: Pantheon Books, 1985.

———. "The Truth That Never Hurts: Black Lesbians in Fiction in the 1980s." In *Wild Women in the Whirlwind: Afra-American Culture and the Contemporary Literary Renaissance*, edited by Joanne M. Braxton and Andrée N. McLaughlin, 213–45. New Brunswick, N.J.: Rutgers University Press, 1990.

Smith, Michael G. *Kinship and Community in Carriacou.* New Haven: Yale University Press, 1962.

Smith, Theophus H. *Conjuring Culture: Biblical Formations of Black America.* New York: Oxford University Press, 1994.

Snead, James. "Repetition as a Figure of Black Culture." In *Black Literature and Literary Theory*, edited by Henry Louis Gates Jr., 59–79. New York: Methuen, 1984.

Sontag, Susan. *On Photography.* New York: Farrar, Straus and Giroux, 1977.

Spillers, Hortense J. "Cross Currents, Discontinuities." Afterword to *Conjuring: Black Women, Fiction, and Literary Tradition*, edited by Hortense Spillers and Marjorie Pryse, 249–61. Bloomington: Indiana University Press, 1985.

———. "A Hateful Passion, a Lost Love." 1983. Reprinted in *Black White and in Color: Essays on American Literature and Culture*, 93–118. Chicago: University of Chicago Press, 2003.

———. "Interstices: A Small Drama of Words." 1984. Reprinted in *Black White and in Color: Essays on American Literature and Culture*, 152–75. Chicago: University of Chicago Press, 2003.

———. "Mama's Baby, Papa's Maybe: An American Grammar Book." 1987. Reprinted in *Black White and in Color: Essays on American Literature and Culture*, 203–29. Chicago: University of Chicago Press, 2003.

———. " 'The Permanent Obliquity of an In(pha)llibly Straight': In the Time of the Daughters and the Fathers." In *Changing Our Own Words: Essays on Criticism, Theory, and Writing by Black Women*, edited by Cheryl A. Wall, 127–49. New Brunswick, N.J.: Rutgers University Press, 1989.

Stampp, Kenneth. *The Peculiar Institution: Slavery in the Ante-Bellum South.* 1956. Reprint, New York: Vintage Books, 1989.

Stepto, Robert. *From behind the Veil: A Study of Afro-American Narrative.* 1979. 2nd ed., Urbana: University of Illinois Press, 1991.

———. " 'Intimate Things in Place': An Interview with Toni Morrison." In *Conversations with Toni Morrison*, edited by Danille Taylor-Guthrie, 1–29. Jackson: University Press of Mississippi, 1994.

———. "The Phenomenal Woman and the Severed Daughter." *Parnassus* 8.1 (1979): 312–20.

Storhoff, Gary. "The Only Voice Is Your Own: Gloria Naylor's Revision of *The Tempest*." *African American Review* 29 (Spring 1995): 35–45.

Stuckey, Sterling. *Slave Culture: Nationalist Theory and the Foundations of Black America.* New York: Oxford University Press, 1987.

Sundquist, Eric J. *To Wake the Nations: Race in the Making of American Literature.* Cambridge: Harvard University Press, 1993.

Talley, Thomas. *Negro Folk Rhymes, Wise and Otherwise.* 1922. Reprint, Port Washington, N.Y.: Kennikat Press, 1968.

Tannenbaum, Frank. *Slave and Citizen.* 1946. Reprint, Boston: Beacon Press, 1992.

Tate, Claudia. *Black Women Writers at Work.* New York: Continuum, 1983.

―――. *Domestic Allegories of Political Desire.* New York: Oxford University Press, 1992.

Tate, Greg. "A Word from Greg Tate." In *"Daughters of the Dust": The Making of an African American Woman's Film,* by Julie Dash, 69–72. New York: New Press, 1992.

Thompson, Robert Farris. *Flash of the Spirit: African and Afro-American Art and Philosophy.* New York: Vintage, 1984.

―――. "The Song That Named the Land: The Visionary Presence in African American Art." In *Black Art: Ancestral Legacy.* New York: Harry N. Abrams, 1989.

Toomer, Jean. *Cane.* 1923. Reprint, New York: Liveright, 1975.

Traub, Valerie. "Rainbows of Darkness: Deconstructing Shakespeare in the Work of Gloria Naylor." In *Cross-cultural Performances: Differences in Women's Re-visions of Shakespeare,* edited by Marianne Novy, 35–45. Urbana: University of Illinois Press, 1993.

Tucker, Lindsey. "Recovering the Conjure Woman: Texts and Contexts in Gloria Naylor's *Mama Day*." *African American Review* 28 (Spring 1995): 173–88.

Twining, Mary, and Keith E. Baird, eds. *Sea Island Roots: African Presence in the Carolinas and Georgia.* Trenton, N.J.: Africa World Press, 1991.

Walker, Alice. *The Color Purple.* New York: Harcourt Brace Jovanovich, 1982.

―――. "Coming in from the Cold: Welcoming the Old, Funny-Talking Ancient Ones into the Warm Room of Present Consciousness, or, Natty Dread Rides Again." In *Living by the Word: Selected Writings, 1973–1987,* 54–68. New York: Harcourt Brace Jovanovich, 1988.

―――. "Diary of an African Nun." In *In Love and Trouble: Stories of Black Women,* 113–20. New York: Harcourt, 1973.

―――. "Everything Is a Human Being." In *Living by the Word: Selected Writings, 1973–1987,* 134–38. New York: Harcourt Brace Jovanovich, 1988. Originally published as "When a Tree Falls: Alice Walker on the Future of the Planet," *Ms.,* January 1984.

―――. "Giving the Party." In *Anything We Love Can Be Saved: A Writer's Activism,* 137–43. New York: Random House, 1997.

―――. *Her Blue Body Everything We Know: Earthling Poems, 1965–1990 Complete.* New York: Harcourt Brace, 1991.

―――. *In Search of Our Mothers' Gardens: Womanist Prose.* New York: Harcourt Brace Jovanovich, 1983.

―――. *Meridian.* New York: Pocket Books, 1977.

―――. *Possessing the Secret of Joy.* New York: Harcourt Brace Jovanovich, 1992.

―――. *Revolutionary Petunias and Other Poems.* New York: Harcourt Brace Jovanovich, 1973.

———. *The Third Life of Grange Copeland*. New York: Harcourt Brace Jovanovich, 1970.

———. "The Universe Responds: Or, How I Learned We Can Have Peace on Earth." In *Living by the Word: Selected Writings, 1973–1987*, 187–94. New York: Harcourt Brace Jovanovich, 1988.

Wall, Cheryl A. *Women of the Harlem Renaissance*. Bloomington: Indiana University Press, 1995.

Wallace, Michele. "Blues for Mr. Spielberg." In *Invisibility Blues: From Pop to Theory*, 67–76. London: Verso, 1990.

———. "Multiculturalism and Oppositionality." *Afterimage* (October 1991): 5–9.

———. "Negative Images: Towards a Black Feminist Cultural Criticism." In *Invisibility Blues: From Pop to Theory*, 241–56. London: Verso, 1990.

———. "Variations on Negation and the Heresy of Black Feminist Creativity." In *Invisibility Blues: From Pop to Theory*, 213–40. London: Verso, 1990.

Washington, Mary Helen. "'The Darkened Eye Restored': Notes toward a Literary History of Black Women." In *Invented Lives: Narratives of Black Women, 1860–1960*, xv–xxi. New York: Anchor Books, 1987.

Weinstein, Philip. *What Else but Love? The Ordeal of Race in Faulkner and Morrison*. New York: Columbia University Press, 1997.

Weisenburger, Steven. *Modern Medea: A Family Story of Slavery and Child-Murder from the Old South*. New York: Hill and Wang, 1998.

West, Cornel. *Race Matters*. Boston: Beacon Press, 1993.

Whitman, Walt. *Leaves of Grass*. 1881. Reprint, New York: Barnes and Noble Books, 1993.

Wideman, John. *Damballah*. New York: Avon Books, 1981.

Wilentz, Gay. *Binding Cultures: Black Women Writers in Africa and the Diaspora*. Bloomington: Indiana University Press, 1992.

Williams, Carolyn. "The Revision of Epistolary Address in *The Color Purple*." In *Writing the Female Voice: Essays on Epistolary Literature*, edited by Elizabeth Goldsmith, 273–85. Boston: Northeastern University Press, 1989.

Williams, Delores S. *Sisters in the Wilderness: The Challenge of Womanist God-Talk*. Maryknoll, N.Y.: Orbis Books, 1993.

Williams, Patricia. *The Alchemy of Race and Rights*. Cambridge: Harvard University Press, 1990.

Williams, Sherley Anne. "The Blues Roots of Contemporary Afro-American Poetry." In *Afro-American Literature: The Reconstruction of Instruction*, edited by Dexter Fisher and Robert B. Stepto, 72–87. New York: Modern Language Association, 1978.

———. *Dessa Rose*. New York: William Morrow, 1987.

———. *Some One Sweet Angel Chile*. New York: William Morrow, 1982.

Willis, Susan. *Specifying: Black Women Writing the American Experience*. Madison: University of Wisconsin Press, 1987.

Wilson, Anna. "Audre Lorde and the African-American Tradition: When the Family

Is Not Enough." In *New Lesbian Criticism: Literary and Cultural Readings*, edited by Sally Munt, 75–94. New York: Columbia University Press, 1992.

Wilson, August. *Joe Turner's Come and Gone: A Play in Two Acts*. New York: New American Library, 1988.

———. *Ma Rainey's Black Bottom*. New York: Plume, 1985.

Wright, Richard. "Between Laughter and Tears." *New Masses* 5 (October 1937): 22, 25.

———. *Black Boy*. 1945. Reprint, New York: Harper and Row, 1966.

———. "Blueprint for Negro Literature." 1937. Reprinted in *Amistad* 2, edited by John A. Williams and Charles F. Harris, 3–20. New York: Random House, 1971.

———. "The Literature of the Negro in the United States." In *White Man Listen!*, 69–105. 1957. Reprint, New York: Anchor Books, 1964.

Yarnall, Judith. *Transformations of Circe: The History of an Enchantress*. Urbana: University of Illinois Press, 1994.

Yeats, W. B. "The Second Coming." In *The Norton Introduction to Literature: Poetry*, edited by J. Paul Hunter, 269–70. New York: W. W. Norton, 1973.

and photographs, 235, 237, 239–
42; and *Praisesong for the Widow*, 235;
and images, 236, 237, 239–40; cinematography of, 239, 276 (n. 6); and
slavery, 240, 242, 243; critics of,
276–77 (nn. 7, 8)

Davies, Carole Boyce, 185

Davis, Angela, 124, 225, 226

Dhairyam, Sagri, 252 (n. 39)

Dispossession: and Du Bois, 27–28, 35;
and *Song of Solomon*, 35; and *Zami*, 46;
and *Mama Day*, 168; and *In Search of
Our Mothers' Gardens*, 213, 225

Dixon, Melvin, 66, 131

Domestic tasks: and *Beloved*, 99, 259
(n. 30)

Domino, Fats, 56

Dorsey, Thomas, 154, 267 (n. 29)

Douglass, Frederick: and interracial
conflicts, 6; and family genealogies,
10; and spirituals, 36, 251 (n. 19);
and Lorde, 42–43; and *The Black Book*,
88; and Morrison, 94; and Garner,
97; and *Corregidora*, 137; and *Praisesong
for the Widow*, 205

Dreams: and gaps in history, 9, 20; and
intuited meanings, 20; and *Zami*, 44;
and *Corregidora*, 124, 129; and *Mama
Day*, 177; and *Praisesong for the Widow*,
182–83, 184, 185–86, 190, 195, 199–
200, 201, 203; and *In Search of Our
Mothers' Gardens*, 225, 227, 228

Drewal, Margaret, 269 (n. 52)

Dubey, Madhu, 264–65 (n. 35)

Du Bois, W. E. B.: and color line, 6,
247 (n. 2), 251 (n. 23); *The Souls of
Black Folk*, 11, 26–36, 38–39, 217, 271
(n. 8); and African American literary
tradition, 15; and spirituals, 36–37,
251 (n. 19); as hero, 50; and *The Black
Book*, 88; and *Praisesong for the Widow*,
205; and Wright, 214; and Walker,
217

DuCille, Ann, 131

Dumas, Henry, "Ark of Bones," 249
(n. 33)

Dunbar, Paul Laurence, 182, 196, 197,
263 (n. 18)

Early, Gerald, 268 (n. 44)

Edison, Thomas, 1

Elaw, Zilpha, 261 (n. 48)

Ellison, Ralph: and interracial conflicts, 6; and African American
literary tradition, 15; *Invisible Man*,
26; and Morrison, 91; and blues, 119;
and Smith, 141; and Wright, 221; and
free-floating literacy, 252 (n. 27)

Essays: and preservation of stories, 7;
and Walker, 210–11, 275 (n. 29). See
also *In Search of Our Mothers' Gardens*
(Walker)

Ethnic differences, 11

Evans, David, 151

Family genealogies: and black women's
writing, 5; and *Generations*, 5, 59–
60, 65–66, 68, 78, 82; and *Mama
Day*, 5, 8–9, 165, 176–77, 248 (n. 15),
270 (n. 12); and *Zami*, 5, 23, 42, 58,
161; and gaps in history, 8–9; and
photographs, 62

Family metaphors: and feminist and
queer theorists, 13; and patriarchy,
13, 21; and postcolonial theorists, 13,
249 (n. 25); and *Beloved*, 112–13; and
*The Color Purple*, 160, 161

Faulkner, William: *Absalom, Absalom*, 26;
*Go Down, Moses*, 26; "The Bear," 163;
house of, 224

Fauset, Jessie: and Marshall, 15–16, 23,
194, 198–99, 245; and stasis and
claustrophobia metaphors, 21; "The
Sleeper Wakes," 198; and racism, 247
(n. 3)

Field holler: and blues, 18

Fitzgerald, Ella, 125

Flack, Roberta, 143

and *Zami*, 42, 43–44, 58; and *Generations*, 62, 68, 70, 74, 77, 82; and photographs, 62; and *Beloved*, 84, 87–88, 100–101, 107, 110, 114–15; and *The Black Book*, 87–88, 90, 95–96, 102, 257–58 (nn. 9, 18); and *Corregidora*, 116–17, 119–20, 124, 125, 126, 128, 131, 132–33, 135, 137, 138–39; and *Mama Day*, 162–63, 165, 167, 168, 175–77, 178, 179–80; and Marshall, 194; and blues, 244

Holiday, Billie, 125, 140, 143, 153

Holloway, Karla, 67

Home: and *Zami*, 47, 252 (n. 36); and *Generations*, 75; and *Mama Day*, 164, 180; and Morrison, 164–65, 180

Homer, *The Odyssey*, 26

hooks, bell: and photographs, 62, 239; and homeplace, 164

Hudson, Mrs. Winsom, 231, 275–76 (n. 35)

Hughes, Langston: "I, too, sing America," 15; "The Negro Speaks of Rivers," 21, 182, 196; and Marshall, 23; and Morrison, 91; and music, 144; "Harlem Sweeties," 207; and Walker, 210; "The Backlash Blues," 217; *Not Without Laughter*, 265–66 (n. 8)

Hull, Gloria, 42

Hunter, Alberta, 146, 154

Hurston, Zora Neale: and African American literary tradition, 12, 15, 23; *Their Eyes Were Watching God*, 15, 141, 142, 157, 161, 163, 220, 222, 254 (n. 64), 268 (n. 41); *Dust Tracks on a Road*, 17; "Characteristics of Negro Expression," 19, 99, 213–16, 230–31, 266 (n. 18); and stories as lies, 26; and Morrison, 91; and black female blues singers, 119; and language, 126, 216, 274 (n. 12); and Walker, 140, 141, 143, 149, 180, 210, 211, 221–23, 227, 229–31, 245, 266 (n. 23), 267

(n. 28), 273–74 (n. 5); *Mules and Men*, 142, 143, 267 (n. 28); and *Praisesong for the Widow*, 199, 207; and Black Aesthetics movement, 219; and Wright, 220, 221; and *Daughters of the Dust*, 239; and racism, 247 (n. 3); and journey back, 254–55 (n. 6)

Images: and *The Black Book*, 1–2, 3, 95, 115; and Morrison, 2–3, 95, 96; and family genealogies, 9; and *Generations*, 9, 17, 62, 70, 71, 72, 82; and spirituality, 15; and *Beloved*, 17, 23, 95, 96, 98, 99, 100, 104, 106–7, 108; and memory, 17, 96, 102, 260 (n. 36); and *Corregidora*, 119–20, 121; and *Daughters of the Dust*, 236, 237, 239–40

Individual desire, representation of, 6

Inner cities, 22

*In Search of Our Mothers' Gardens* (Walker): and family genealogies, 5; and reading and writing scenes, 18–19; and authority of literary tradition, 24, 210, 232; and civil rights movement, 210, 217–18, 231, 232; and politics, 210, 211, 212, 213, 225–26, 228, 231; and spirituality, 210, 225, 227–28; and language, 211, 217–18; and poverty, 213, 225, 226, 227, 228; and Hurston, 221–22; and O'Connor, 223–25; and Wright, 225; and womanist principles, 229; and *Daughters of the Dust*, 235

Intertextual connections: and African American literary tradition, 11, 82–83, 163, 248 (n. 19); and family metaphors, 13; and sacred place, 21; and *Praisesong for the Widow and Daughters*, 184, 196, 198, 203, 205, 207, 208, 248 (n. 19)

Intimate relationships: and racism, 6; and *Song of Solomon*, 36, 38; and *Zami*, 48, 50, 56, 57–58; and *Generations*, 73; and *Beloved*, 106; and *Corregidora*, 117,

118, 119, 123–24, 131, 134, 138; and
blues, 118–19, 124; and *Praisesong for
the Widow*, 197, 272 (n. 19)

tradition, 15, 23; *Sula*, 15, 23, 32, 87, 163–74, 176, 177–78, 180, 269 (nn. 4, 6); and language, 19, 38–39, 62, 179, 250 (n. 14), 270 (n. 23); on slavery, 20; *The Bluest Eye*, 32–33, 86–87, 250 (n. 14), 257 (n. 34), 260–61 (n. 42); "Rootedness: The Ancestor as Foundation," 38; *Tar Baby*, 87, 163; "Rediscovering Black History," 90–92, 94, 102, 178; and literary archaeology, 94–95; and *Corregidora*, 128; and Middle Passage, 249 (n. 33). See also *Beloved* (Morrison); *Song of Solomon* (Morrison)

Mother-daughter relationship: and *Zami*, 45–47, 48, 49–50, 51, 52–53, 56, 57–58; and sexual abuse, 77; and *Beloved*, 99–101, 107, 108–9; and *Corregidora*, 132, 134–35, 137–38, 264–65 (n. 35); and *Sula*, 172–73, 180

Murray, Albert, 119, 263 (n. 17)

Music: and gaps in history, 9, 17; and memory, 10, 17; and beat, 16; and cut, 16; as metaphor for unspeakable, 17; and *Song of Solomon*, 35, 37, 199; and Du Bois, 38; and *Zami*, 46, 57; and *Generations*, 63, 73; and Whitman, 63; and Morrison, 91; and *Beloved*, 102, 103, 105, 112, 114; and Walker, 144; and *Praisesong for the Widow*, 181–82, 184, 188, 196, 197, 199–200, 205; and Hurston, 213, 216; and Black Aesthetic movement, 219. *See also* Blues

Naming of self: and *Zami*, 42, 46, 58; and *Generations*, 65

Native Americans: cosmologies of, 15, 141, 157, 268–69 (n. 49); robbed of land, 27–28

Naylor, Gloria: and literary matrilineage, 12; and African American literary tradition, 23; and Morrison,

86, 96, 164, 179, 180; *The Women of Brewster Place*, 203; *Linden Hills*, 270 (n. 9). See also *Mama Day* (Naylor)

Neal, Larry, 219, 274 (n. 21)

Neglected texts, 12, 15

Newton, Huey, 226–27

Noble, Thomas Satterwhite, 98

Nora, Pierre, 27, 28

Northrup, Solomon, 200

O'Brien, John, 144

O'Connor, Flannery, 210, 222, 223–25, 226

Osceola (Indian-Negro chief), 31

Ostriker, Alicia, 35, 59, 80

Palmer, Robert, 118

Patriarchy: and family metaphors, 13, 21; and Lorde, 42; and Baldwin, 52; and *Generations*, 65–66; and slavery, 77; and *The Color Purple*, 156, 159

Patton, Charley, 118

Payne, Daniel Alexander, 271–72 (n. 11)

Petry, Ann, 217, 247 (n. 3)

Pettis, Joyce, 271 (n. 4)

Photographs: as part of printed text, 17, 61; and *Generations*, 60, 61–62, 64, 65, 69–74, 77–80, 82, 257 (n. 38); and Whitman, 64; and *The Black Book*, 88, 90, 92; and *The Color Purple*, 147, 152; and *Daughters of the Dust*, 235, 237, 239–42; and *Corregidora*, 265 (n. 36)

Poetry: and preservation of stories, 7; and *Zami*, 47–48, 49; and Clifton, 59–60, 63; and *Generations*, 60, 66, 80; and *Corregidora*, 122; and *Praisesong for the Widow*, 184, 194, 196, 197, 203

Politics: lesbian, 26, 44, 56; and Whitman, 64; and *Generations*, 71; and *The Black Book*, 89, 258 (n. 18); and *Beloved*, 98; and blues, 124, 263 (n. 17); and *Corregidora*, 127; and *Mama Day*, 174; and Marshall, 191; and *In Search*

Sayles, Samuel, 60, 65, 67, 68, 69, 74–80, 82

Sayles, Thelma Moore, 60, 80–82

Scruggs, Charles, 110, 112

Second-sight, 186, 271 (n. 8)

Sexual abuse: and *Generations*, 76–77, 82, 256–57 (nn. 30, 32); and *Corregidora*, 77, 117, 123, 125, 129, 132, 257 (n. 34); and *The Color Purple*, 152

Sexual exploitation: and *Zami*, 43; and slavery, 94, 105

Sexuality: and Baldwin, 52, 53–54; and *Zami*, 54; and *Corregidora*, 117, 137; and blues, 118, 145, 146; of blacks, 128, 264 (n. 27); and *The Color Purple*, 151, 267 (n. 31)

Sexual preferences: and racial identity, 11; and *Zami*, 46, 47–48, 50, 51–52, 54, 55–57, 58; and Baldwin, 53–54; and *The Color Purple*, 141–42, 151–52, 161, 267 (n. 32)

Shakespeare, William, 163

Shange, Ntozake: *A Daughter's Geography*, 21–23; *for colored girls who have considered suicide when the rainbow is enuf*, 22, 203; and music, 144

Simone, Nina, 143, 262–63 (n. 13)

Slave narratives: and African American literary tradition, 11, 15, 20, 25, 217; and *Zami*, 43; and *Generations*, 72; and Morrison, 94

Slavery: and *Beloved*, 3, 20, 84–85, 86, 97–102, 104–6, 107, 112, 114, 115, 245, 257 (n. 3); and family genealogies, 10, 77; and gaps in history, 17; as disremembered, 20; and family dispersal, 21, 25, 105–6, 194; and black bodies as commodities, 22, 117, 138; and Du Bois, 28, 29, 30; and exploitation of blacks' labor, 28; and *Generations*, 60, 63, 65, 68, 69, 72–73, 82–83; and familial boundaries, 77; and Morrison, 86–87, 257 (n. 3); and *The Black Book*, 88–89, 92;

and marriage, 99, 259 (n. 31); and *Corregidora*, 117, 127, 128, 129, 131–32, 138; in Brazil, 127, 133, 136, 264 (nn. 25, 33); and *Mama Day*, 168, 180; in Barbados, 193; and *Praisesong for the Widow*, 195, 205–6; and *Daughters of the Dust*, 240, 242, 243; and Whitman, 255 (n. 16)

Smith, Barbara, 11–12, 248 (n. 21)

Smith, Bessie: as symbol of female creativity, 7–8, 143; and beat, 16; and human emotion, 118; and Williams, 125; and Walker, 140, 143; and blues, 144–45; background of, 146; and *The Color Purple*, 147, 151; and Jackson, 148; and morality, 149; and selfhood, 150; and sexual preferences, 152; and spirituality, 154

Smith, Middleton, 90

Smith, Valerie, 263 (n. 18)

Snead, James, 16, 249 (n. 28)

Social mobility: and cultural identity, 7; and *Generations*, 71; and *Praisesong for the Widow*, 182, 183, 196, 198. *See also* Class differences

Social positionality, 6

*Song of Solomon* (Morrison): and images, 2–3; and family genealogies, 5, 23; and black female blues singer, 8, 26, 41; and autobiography, 23, 25; and ideal of Western nuclear family, 25; as quest story, 25, 26, 34, 37, 250–51 (n. 15); and African American folklore, 26, 185; and lineage, 26; and *The Souls of Black Folk*, 26–36, 38–39; and singing, 27, 35; and feminism, 33–34; and history, 33, 58, 199, 251 (n. 15); spaces in text, 37, 251 (n. 22); and color line, 38; and preservation of oral traditions, 38; and language, 39; and Till's murder, 39–40; and *Generations*, 59; and slavery, 87; and *Mama Day*, 163

Sontag, Susan, 61, 78, 203

and *The Black Unicorn*, 42; and *The Color Purple*, 157–59, 269 (n. 52); and *Generations*, 254 (n. 4)

## gender and american culture